Right in Michigan's Grassroots

RIGHT IN MICHIGAN'S GRASSROOTS

From the KKK to the Michigan Militia

JoEllen McNergney Vinyard

THE UNIVERSITY OF MICHIGAN PRESS • ANN ARBOR

Copyright © by the University of Michigan 2011

Published in the United States of America by
The University of Michigan Press
Manufactured in the United States of America
⊚ Printed on acid-free paper

2014   2013   2012   2011   4   3   2   1

A CIP catalog record for this book is available from the British Library.

Library of Congress Cataloging-in-Publication Data

Vinyard, JoEllen McNergney.
    Right in Michigan's grassroots : from the KKK to the Michigan
militia / JoEllen McNergney Vinyard.
        p.   cm.
    Includes bibliographical references and index.
    ISBN 978-0-472-07159-3 (cloth : alk. paper) — ISBN 978-0-472-
05159-5 (pbk. : alk. paper) — ISBN 978-0-472-02763-7 (e-book)
    1. Right and left (Political science)—Michigan—History.
I. Title.
JK5835.V56   2011
322.4'209774—dc22   2011003375

To Sidney Gendin

Contents

Acknowledgments

Like thousands of others, I migrated to Michigan following a husband, graduate school, and a job. This was a strange land. In Nebraska we did not make cars so we kept ours at least ten years before trading them in. Polish farm kids were the one ethnic minority in our school. Going "Up North" meant an annual trip to Omaha for new shoes. Our lakes were usually ponds and our pine trees were short. I did not expect to stay long in Michigan. Now, I can not imagine leaving. In graduate school and forever after, the more I studied the history of Michigan the more understandable it became, the more meaningful in so many ways. When I arrived I knew no one. Now, there is not space enough to acknowledge the hundreds of friends, neighbors, students, colleagues, and passing acquaintances who have contributed in one way or another to this book, who have become so important in my life, and who have made Michigan home. Thank you all. I am grateful to be in your midst.

Eastern Michigan University has not only given me the opportunity to teach about Michigan but provided the concentrated time so vital for research by granting a sabbatical and faculty research leave for this project. That time was significantly extended by a two-semester grant from the trustees of the Earhart Foundation, whom I thank not only for their generosity but for the almost singular lack of bureaucratic paperwork associated with that grant.

Michigan's archives are a treasure trove for researchers, made more valuable without exception because of the knowledgeable, helpful people who staff them. The Bentley Historical Library at the University of Michigan has been through two buildings and an addition since I first sat at its polished tables as a graduate student. Bentley archivists, in turn, have unfailingly taken the trouble to unearth documents or some collection I would have missed. The staff at Central Michigan University's Clarke Library hauled out box after box and shared important information about their valuable Ku Klux Klan collection. Primary materials held at the Walter Reuther Library at Wayne State University, the Detroit Public Library's Burton Historical Collection, and the State of Michigan Archives yielded wide-ranging records.

Several of the small, specialized museums and archives in Michigan have been especially valuable. The Archives of the Sisters, Servants of the Immaculate Heart of Mary (IHMs) in Monroe, Michigan, is a remarkable gem with well-cataloged materials reaching far beyond the confines of the congregation and into the history of Michigan Catholics. For the chapters on Charles Coughlin, volunteer archivist Jack Hoolehan was, himself, a storehouse of detailed information in addition to the carefully assembled files, sermons, and miscellanea he has preserved at the Shrine of the Little Flower parish. Roman Godzak, director of the Archives of the Archdiocese of Detroit, was able to find meticulously preserved records—although even his dedication can not seem to resurrect missing Coughlin materials. Certain basic libraries were of great help—Northwestern College in Traverse City, which has a far-reaching collection of regional newspapers, the Grosse Pointe Library with its clipping files and newspaper collection, Marygrove College, which has one of the few available and complete microfilm collections of the *Michigan Catholic.*

The most surprising finds came by accidental good luck—meeting the right people who were willing to share materials or memories stored away. Rick Haynes has been especially important. Mr. Haynes gave me access to minutes, memos, organizational files, letters, and an amazing array of materials dating from the first meetings of the Michigan Militia—in its various forms and names. He answered questions, filled in dates, and did all he could to make my account accurate without trying to bias it. Tom Wayne, Norm Olson, and Joe Pilchak also took the time to share their perspective on the Militia. Birch Society organizers and opponents welcomed me into their homes, and Daniel Rhodes's parents brought down trunks from the attic, materials stored away since their aunt was Father Coughlin's secretary. Summer after summer when my students and I gathered in her yard, Carolyn Bumgardner shared the story of her fight with the National Park Service, giving us a unique perspective on citizens' discontent. These people and the many others who offered personal information or family stories have taught me far more than appears in the notes that refer to them.

A number of students have contributed by their own research papers—Michael Thibault, Jennifer Wolak, Dan Crots, and Timothy Weber among them. To countless others who were in campus classes or trekked around with me to study in Detroit, Traverse City, and other corners of the state, your enthusiasm has kept me going. Two students have been invaluable at critical points: John Maynerik was there at the outset, he helped launch initial interviews with Militia spokesmen, and tirelessly, he gathered tapes, videos, and a substantial amount of printed material. Matthew Penix was there for the final push, tracking down incomplete footnotes, checking certain quotations, and ferreting out others; his insightful comments on points of analysis have been even more helpful. John and Matt, I'll not forget you.

As always, I thank my family—growing by the year with new grandchildren and nephews-by-marriage. May life bring you all the joy you have given me. Know that Dale Vinyard's voice echoes always in my head too; throughout this project I could hear him speaking of Father Coughlin, Joe McCarthy, and the political process in general.

Finally, for one hundred reasons and more, this book is dedicated to Sidney Gendin. Unparalleled as a writer and editor, he read every word, repeatedly sharpened the focus, and incessantly pushed me to think harder. While I obsessed over one chapter or another, he took on the mundane tasks, from fetching reams of paper to grocery shopping; he kept me standing, sometimes literally. Above all, he kept me laughing. I am uncommonly fortunate that this man—with Brooklyn in his heart and in his accent—wandered west to Michigan.

INTRODUCTION

Here is the real political story, the one most politicians won't even
acknowledge: the reality of the anonymous, disquieting daily struggle of
ordinary people, including the most marginalized and vulnerable Americans
but also young workers and elders and parents, families and communities,
searching for dignity and fairness against long odds in a cruel market world.

Everywhere you turn, you'll find people who believe they have been
written out of the story. Everywhere you turn there's a sense of insecurity
grounded in a gnawing fear that freedom in America has come to mean the
freedom of the rich to get richer even as millions of Americans are dumped
from the Dream.

—BILL MOYERS, *Nation*, January 22, 2007

The term *grassroots* was probably coined early in the twentieth century by
Senator Albert J. Beveridge of Indiana. Enthusiastic about the new Progressive Party and a champion of Theodore Roosevelt who was its presidential candidate in 1912, Beveridge proudly declared, "This party has
come from the grass roots. It has grown from the soil of people's hard necessities." That election year, all 15 of Michigan's electoral votes went to
Theodore Roosevelt—the only time the Republican Party lost the state
since 1856 when it first fielded a presidential candidate. Roosevelt, this
maverick Republican running on the third-party ticket, roused Michigan
hearts and votes in part out of "hard necessities," but he also articulated a
vision and version of America that they shared. Roosevelt had rallied his
faithful with a platform of reforms and a crusade he promised to lead. Together they would "stand at Armageddon and battle for the Lord."[1]

Throughout the twentieth century Michigan would be home to nearly
every political movement in America that emerged from the grassroots.
Citizens organized on behalf of concerns on the "left," on the "right," and
in the "middle of the road." These were people not so easily described or
explained, whatever the cause or era. This book is about the people who
supported movements that others, then and later, would denounce as dis-
graceful. It is about the members of the Ku Klux Klan during the 1920s, the
followers of Father Charles Coughlin in the 1930s, anti-Communists and
the John Birch Society in the post–World War II era, the members of the
Michigan Militia who first appeared in the 1990s. And it is about circum-

stances in Michigan that prompted men and women to act on behalf of America as they saw it.

As soon as Michigan Militia members made their way into public view the scramble for explanations was on: "Who *are* these people?" Nightly newscasters looked appropriately shocked while the screen shifted to camouflage-clad men toting guns and gas masks across a Michigan pasture. Then, the inevitable follow-up: "What's going on in Michigan *now*?" Was it a breeding ground for hate? Journalists searched their back-files. Academics provided scholarly perspective. A pattern was not hard to come by, usually starting with Henry Ford who publicized his anti-Semitism alongside his Model T. The Ku Klux Klan nearly elected a mayor of Detroit and burned crosses on the steps of the city hall. Father Coughlin was often labeled the father of "hate radio," and his notoriety as an anti-Semite rivals that of Henry Ford. The small town of Howell became synonymous with a revived, white-supremacist Klan because Robert Miles, a founder and leader, lived in the vicinity. The Michigan Militia seemed, indeed, on a path well trod by "extremists." Michigan, the state that produced automobiles and cherries, appeared to be a longtime producer of right-wing groups, a term conjuring up bigotry in mean and ugly forms.

To cast the state as a cauldron of hate ignores the other side of the coin. Michigan was a focal point for Progressive reforms in the early part of the century and a pioneer in civil rights legislation by the 1950s; it was home to radical labor activists from the Industrial Workers of the World to the Communist faction in the United Auto Workers. Michigan idealists planned a "peace ship" voyage to end World War I, Michigan students went off to join the Spanish Civil War in the 1930s, and Students for a Democratic Society was launched at Port Huron in the 1960s. Ordinary citizens joined Martin Luther King to march through Michigan streets, civil rights advocates headed South as freedom riders, and Michigan's peace activists faced tear gas and riot sticks in their protests over the Vietnam War. Time and again, the "extremist" movements of whatever cause or concern proved to be on the edge of an emerging broad-based public opinion. Michigan was an exaggerated reflection of the hopes, fears, passions, and disappointments common across the nation.

Movements termed *right-wing* are too easily relegated into a heap piled high with people all presumed to harbor hate in their souls or illness in their heads. *Right* and *left* were terms traditional to European parliaments; the conservatives sat on the right and the liberals on the left. These labels became increasingly common to describe the American political scene during the 1950s. *Right-wing* was usually a disparaging characterization—such people were authoritarians and rigid, righteous and paranoid. The *left wing* was at the other end of the spectrum, but scholars and journalists often used kinder words to describe them—romantics and dreamers, idealists and fuzzy thinkers. Extremists all. These labels have made sound bites, newspaper articles, and campaign speeches simpler. Characterizing groups like the Klan or the Militia as right-wing extremists makes it oddly comforting to account for the people who gather there. But when it comes to these mostly nameless American citizens, the labels also make it too easy to draw boxes around them, dismiss their complexity, and thereby relegate them to political insignificance. If they are no more or no less than "right wing extremists," they take on meaning as a "dark aberration" in their time and in a state conveniently labeled a "cauldron" or "petri dish" of hate. On the contrary, these are no curiosities of the past, no strangers in the present. They were the butcher, the baker, the tool and die maker, the doctor, the lawyer, and the chief of police. They are the neighbor next door, the clergyman, the farmer at the Saturday market, your great-aunt or her friend or you.

The men and women who people this book generally shared a few characteristics. They were white and they were Christians, whether churchgoing or not. Michigan had been home to their families, often two or more generations back—but there was a solid representation of second- or third-generation immigrants, even in the anti-immigrant Klan. They were ordinary people, known mostly to family, friends, coworkers, and neighbors, but they were not down-and-outers. Except for the Coughlin followers, they were Republicans, although especially at the local level they backed the person rather than the party. Unlike their popular image, these particular people in Michigan were attracted to grassroots political activism, not to the wanton violence that marked the much smaller groups like the Black Legion and the neo-Nazis. A few had private gain and personal power in mind when they encouraged others to join in the cause; a few were vicious. Most just hoped to keep their lives on track and their dreams intact. Bent on protecting the nation from those endangering it, these citizens aimed to protect themselves and their kind.

Similar concerns surfaced, one movement after another, fed by men and women who believed in common that it was their duty to rescue their country and reclaim their place in it. Children, so often at the heart of their parents' concerns, went along to meetings as a matter of course and helped with the cause however they could be enlisted. The Klan had junior auxiliaries; Father Coughlin began his radio career with the Children's Hour, and his audience sat around the radio as families. The Birch Society sponsored anti-Communist speakers in schools; Militia parents held firearms and field exercises for their youngsters. Patriotic citizens, they were people who feared that their country was straying from its historic moorings as they understood them to be. Maxims memorized in elementary classrooms generation after generation provided an oft-repeated mantra: The founding fathers had created "a more perfect Union" than the world had ever known. But now, in this, their generation—whether it was the twenties, the thirties, the fifties, or the nineties—misguided voters had elected local, state, and national politicians who, left to their own devices, had put Americans in peril. It was an item of faith in each movement that "government of the people, by the people, and for the people" would not perish from the earth on *their* watch.

One decade after another, some of the same fears and panaceas inevitably surfaced among the friends, family, neighbors, and new acquaintances who mobilized. They were all shaped by historical memory, yet the people in each movement belonged within their own place in time with answers suited to their own problems. In each era, these activists took on concerns that were afloat in a larger public. They often represented a grab bag of prejudices and hostility more extreme than most other Americans voiced out loud—against people of other religions or of no religion, Communists, people of another class whether at the bottom of society or at the top, distrust of immigrants, dislike of blacks. Such outspoken prejudice could make these men and women targets for scorn among their contemporaries, but at the same time, they served to provide cover for other people who could distance themselves from "the likes of the Klan" or the "Coughlin Catholics" or the "Red-hunters" or the "kooks in camouflage." It is a measure of how well they dovetailed with public sentiment that so many issues pressed by "extremists" made their way into law—from immigration quotas to gun-owner rights. They claimed to gather, rally, march, or drill on behalf of their nation that was in peril, but their desperation was most often driven by situations close by. The Michigan Klansmen and Klanswomen, Coughlin's faithful audience, the Birchers, and the Militia members all aimed for more influence over American political doings, starting with what concerned them most—their own backyards.

Twentieth-century Michigan was America not only at its best but at its worst. If much was offered and could be attained by dint of individual effort, much could also be lost. Alongside a national culture nourished by hope lurks a well-honed habit of fear. In a state and nation so fine, threats seem to loom on every side. From the Ku Klux Klan to the Michigan Militia, grassroots protesters held fast to the lessons of their grade school classrooms, strengthened along the way by the words of trusted leaders from the pulpit to the presidency. The American Dream danced in their heads. But too often dangers were dangled in front of their eyes. Steeped in messages to "take responsibility"—in one's family, church, neighborhood, workplace, military unit, or local polling place—people stepped forward. Sometimes it was Protestants who joined forces despite denominational differences; sometimes Catholics and Lutherans and Quakers made common cause. People banded together across lines of class, ethnicity, and even race to ward off Communists in their midst; Polish Catholics and third-generation Presbyterians rallied to keep their neighborhoods white. Here were men and women who headed off despite ridicule or condemnation with unsanctioned plans and unorthodox tactics, variously brandishing weapons of intimidation, discrimination, fearmongering, and terror. Sometimes they waved banners of hope and promises of better days. They viewed themselves not as radical departures from American values but as last-ditch efforts to preserve their birthright.

These people in Michigan are not strangers. They are at the heart of a national story. Time and again, too many Americans of every color, creed, and generation fear they have been written out, written off. If democracy is a government of the people, by the people, and for the people, it takes more than high-minded phrases to make it so. Too many Americans have needed better reasons and more resources to believe that "the only thing we have to fear is fear itself." Too many Americans have feared each other.

NINETEENTH-CENTURY LEGACY

It is not by chance that Michigan provided the home base or a center of solid support time and again when ordinary, anonymous Americans rallied to take a stand. Grassroots movements that figured so prominently in the history of Michigan were a mark of the state's abiding complexity. From the 1830s when pioneers flooded in and pushed Michigan from backwoods territory to boom state, people who came and stayed found themselves on a roller coaster. When they were on top of the world there was no place like Michigan—its lumber-rich forests and mines, the family farms and business opportunities, its inventors and inventiveness, the factories with their stunning wages, the praise and amazement won from all corners of the world. When they were at bottom, there was no place quite like Michigan either. No generation escaped the experience.

Present-day Michigan was initially part of the empire the French founded in North America in 1608 just one year after Jamestown. Taken over by the British during the French and Indian War, after the American Revolution a huge area known as the Northwest Territory was ceded to the victorious and new United States. The area remained remote and unknown to the founding fathers when they fashioned plans for its land and laws in the 1780s. At the time, the British still occupied the forts in Michigan, and they found pretexts to stay there until 1796, thirteen years after the treaty that ended the war. Then they were back again during the War of 1812 when they seized the forts at Detroit and Mackinac.

Meanwhile, population growth was slow so long as prospective settlers had better options elsewhere in the Northwest Territory. In 1805 Michigan had become a territory even though it lacked the required 5,000 free white males the Northwest Ordinance required. After the War of 1812, territorial governor Lewis Cass did his best to promote its reputation for good, cheap farmland, land he was gaining from the Native Americans, insistent treaty after treaty. At the same time, Cass was also making agreements with John Jacob Astor whose American Fur Company, headquartered on Mackinac Island until the 1830s, was the economic mainstay of the territory. As Cass well knew, Astor was trying all the while to discourage settlers from migrating to Michigan in order to maintain animals' wooded habitat. It was the beginning of a tangled, symbiotic alliance between politicians and businessmen that would endure in Michigan for the following two centuries, often detected only after the participants had accomplished their aims or moved on.

Detroit, the territorial capital and only settlement of any size, had burned to the ground in 1805. Residents—French-speaking Catholics topped off by an assortment of adventurous traders, merchants, and soldiers at the fort—were still trying to recover when the War of 1812 interrupted any glimmer of development. Finally by the 1820s, as would occur so often in the history of Michigan, outside developments accelerated local change. Steamboats appeared on the Great Lakes, and Congress approved road building; links from Detroit began to stretch west from Lake Erie toward Lake Michigan. Congress also lowered the price of land in the Michigan Territory, making it more affordable than the previously preferred land in Ohio and Indiana. Then in 1825, New York's Erie Canal was completed. Travelers could go by water from the East all the way to Michigan; Michigan goods and farm produce could go the other way to markets in the East.

In 1830, the census counted only 31,639 residents of the territory, but "Michigan fever" began sweeping New York and New England. Stevens T. Mason, the young acting governor of the Michigan Territory, confidently conducted a special census in 1834 that showed the population to be over 92,000, well exceeding the 60,000 required for statehood. Pioneer families who had come from the East were eager for the same rights and privileges they had known back home. In quick succession, in 1835 voters elected delegates to a convention and approved the constitution those delegates wrote, and the Territorial Legislature requested admission to the Union. Michigan was to be a "free state," however, and slave interests demanded that another state be added to balance representation. More troublesome yet, Ohio's governor, members of Congress, and its state legislators demanded that Michigan relinquish claim to a disputed strip of land on their common border. After a farcical show of force by both sides in the mostly bloodless Toledo War, Michigan backed down under pressure from President Andrew Jackson. A quickly assembled convention revised the constitution according to the demands of President Jackson, who had not wanted to anger his Ohio constituents and was furious with Michigan's acting governor for his bold defiance. Michigan voters agreed to give up the "Toledo Strip" and reluctantly accepted in trade the remainder of the Upper Peninsula not already within the territory. In January 1837, Michigan became the twenty-sixth state in the Union, following on the heels of the new slave state of Arkansas. Michigan voters ignored Jackson's disapproval, however, and proudly elected Stevens T. Mason as their first governor.

By the time Michigan gained statehood, forces of nature compounded by politician-fashioned compromises and economic realities had made it a state of two peninsulas with several very distinct regions. The heavily forested Upper Peninsula was too cold for much productive farming, and glaciers had scraped away the fertile topsoil at any rate. But, unexpectedly, this frozen tundra of a land that Michigan residents resented when it was forced on them turned out to be a prize by the early 1840s when vast deposits of iron ore and copper were discovered there. The Upper Peninsula, so distant in miles from most of the state's residents, soon took on a permanent character of its own shaped by mining companies and miners, lumber companies and lumber crews.

The mitten-shaped Lower Peninsula was the center for much of the population, most of the state's economic activity beyond mining, and the lion's share of the political decision making. But every section of the Lower Peninsula was significantly different from the others. The Thumb poked out into Lake Huron, an almost-separate region unto its own. There was the northern quarter of the Lower Peninsula, the central mid-Michigan heartland, the west shoreline region along Lake Michigan, the fertile band of southern counties three-deep that stretched along the Ohio and Indiana borders, and then the region of southeast Michigan anchored by Detroit. Always different in climate, topography, and natural resources, each region contributed in its own way to the overall economy of the state in the nineteenth century, and the exploitation of these resources had made the regions even more different from one another by the beginning of the twentieth century.

For most of the time after the Civil War, Michigan led the nation in production of lumber, copper, and salt. Significant deposits of iron ore, gypsum, and limestone added up to more wealth that trickled down in the form of a variety of jobs. Despite the importance of Michigan mines, it was farms and farmers who consistently accounted for most of the state's wealth and population. A variety of crops and dairy products gave farmers cash for farm equipment and store-bought goods. Family-owned factories and mills processed the products from forests, mines, and farms. Michigan-made cereal, furniture, ships, carriages, chemicals, shoes, and stoves found ready markets well beyond the state's borders.

All of this economic activity generated more in the way of transportation developments. By the mid-1850s, a canal and locks at Sault Ste. Marie made shipping relatively cheap and easy from the mines and forests along Lake Superior to the lower Great Lakes. Detroit became one of the nation's busiest ports. Crushed rock or dirt roads kept passable by farmers along the route connected one town to the next until travelers could get on the plank roads that led to bigger centers. Railroads pushed north, east, and west through Michigan's valuable forests, encouraging settlement as they went. Timber stands along the right-of-way were offered to railroad investors as incentive, and thus these rail lines made fortunes for a few investors in the process of opening new opportunities to ordinary people. Still, if transportation and economic interdependence linked Michigan residents ever closer, they spent their day-to-day lives within their neighborhoods and communities, most preoccupied with local concerns.

After an initial, heady rush of settlers from New England and the East Coast, Michigan had grown at a gradual if steady pace. By 1900, the state could claim 2,420,982 residents; almost a million and a half—60 percent—were farmers or lived in one of the hundreds of communities that had fewer than 2,500 people. The only two cities of any size, diversity, and complexity were Detroit with a population of 285,704 and Grand Rapids with 87,565 residents. The only dramatic, explosive growth in the last forty years of the nineteenth century occurred in the Upper Peninsula mining regions and company-dominated towns, but Escanaba, with just over 13,000 residents, was the largest city there.

Michigan's population at the start of the twentieth century was mostly American-born—over three-fourths of them—and more than 99 percent of the state's residents were white. Many, both white and black, were born in Michigan and frequently in the same particular part of it that their parents or even their grandparents had always called home. Most immigrants to Michigan across the nineteenth century came from the countries of northwestern Europe, the Germans a solid majority among them. From midcentury, the state was marked also by settlements and neighborhoods that were distinctively Irish, Dutch, Norwegian, Swedish, and, in the Upper Peninsula, Finnish. Central and southeastern Europeans, the "new immigration," had just begun making their way to Michigan; only in the mining towns of the Upper Peninsula and enclaves in Detroit were they much of a presence. Overall, the proportion of foreign-born in Michigan was on a decline, bolstered only by the constant, sizable number of emigrants from Canada.

Most towns of any size in the Lower Peninsula had at least some black residents; in a few pockets like Cass County and Covert on the southwest side of the state, black farming communities dated back to the 1840s and 1850s. Always, the largest concentration of Michigan's black residents was in the city of Detroit and the surrounding Wayne County where they had been a presence since well before the American Revolution when first the French and then the British brought them as slaves. Like the immigrants, the black population had been growing in absolute numbers but more slowly than the white. Totaling just under 16,000 in 1900, they were a smaller proportion of the state's residents than in any previous decade. The same pattern held true in Wayne County.

To maintain a sense of order and control, or just to enjoy themselves, men and women organized with people of their same religion, background, sex, color, or class—into churches, clubs, benevolent societies and fraternal associations, into sewing circles, fire brigades, and temperance societies. In part through these encounters, people found they had problems in common and strength in numbers. Movements bubbled up, taking one form or another depending on the concern and the constituency. Some were mostly violent outbursts; others aimed for a political impact.

Farmers turned to the Grange and the Greenbackers and the Populists for relief against a variety of outside forces. Sporadic strikes or labor organizing in the mines led to violence between workers and state troops dispatched by the governor or private guards hired by management. Property owners occasionally took it upon themselves to tear up railroad lines that upset their lives or livestock. In the 1850s when public education was just getting under way, Catholics and Protestants waged political war over which Bible schoolchildren would read. Catholics lost in their effort to gain control over a share of their tax dollars for their own separate schools, and so ever after, where the Catholics could manage it, they built parochial schools alongside their ethnic parishes staffed by nuns who were of their same nationality. One group after another sought control over its own fortunes, one way or another. When Polish immigrants were multiplying in Detroit toward the end of the century, housewives grabbed brooms and rolling pins to do battle with each other—or the bishop if necessary—over financial control of their parishes. In the hard times of the Panic of 1893, day workers fought each other in the streets over who should have the few jobs there were.

Repeatedly, even though they were such a minuscule minority, blacks were a target of whites. Michigan had an active core of abolitionists dating from the early 1830s when black and white residents began working together to move slaves from the South, across the state, and on over the river into Canada. In the 1850s, antislavery speakers made frequent visits. Many more residents were reluctant to interfere with slavery in the South, however. Like so many others in the North, Michigan troops went to war amid cheers to "save the Union" rather than to free the slaves. Tensions surfaced when, in the middle of the Civil War, Detroit had a race riot. Voters refused to give black males the vote until the Fifteenth Amendment to the U.S. Constitution made it necessary, schools were segregated, and blacks were confined to the lowest of jobs unless they served their own people as doctors, lawyers, undertakers, or shopkeepers. As early as the 1830s, black families necessarily started churches and schools and organizations of their own where they gathered on behalf of causes of their own.

Michigan entered the twentieth century with a solid reputation as the most Republican state in the nation. In the summer of 1854, Michigan's antislavery and disaffected Democrats had come together with Whigs "under the elms" in Jackson to organize a new political party. By November of that year, Michigan voters elected the first Republican governor in the nation, and Republicans lost control of the governor's office only twice throughout the rest of the century. A majority of Michigan voters backed John C. Fremont in 1856 when he ran as the first Republican seeking the presidency, and every four years thereafter until 1932, the Republican presidential candidate captured the state with the exception of 1912 when Michigan's electoral votes went to Theodore Roosevelt, the Republican-turned-Progressive.

Republicans dominated the state legislature thanks, in part, to districts drawn according to geography rather than population size. The legislators unfailingly elected Republicans to represent Michigan in the U.S. Senate; in Washington, the senators were in the company of a Michigan congressional delegation filled mostly with Republicans. Long-serving Republican lawmakers gained seniority and used it to advance the interests of their various constituents in Michigan—the tariff positions that protected lumber, mining, and manufacturers' interests; the support for railroads, the land grants, and an agricultural college that pleased farmers. Abolitionists, temperance advocates, and "nativists" all found a home under the Republican umbrella too.

Still, the Michigan voters were not as predictable as the electoral vote suggested. Political contests generated a great deal of activity, especially at the local level where candidates were familiar and issues had the most impact on day-to-day life. In these elections, party affiliation was a peripheral factor. Even in the presidential elections the Republican presidential candidate's success was rarely a sweep. With its Catholic, immigrant, and working-man bloc, Detroit was a Democratic stronghold. The miners in the Upper Peninsula were always a volatile group, and, depending on the candidate and the issues, enough outstate farmers and small-town voters might move to the Democrat ticket to trim the Republican presidential candidate's margin of victory—in 1884 to less than 1 percent statewide. Moreover, the state's Republicans were not all of a mind. By the 1890s, the Progressive reformers were at odds with stand-pat conservatives, and Republicans outside Detroit were more uncomfortable all the time with any immigrant or working-class voters their party attracted from the city.

A giant-sized Michigan-made stove and a massive stained-glass Polish church window were just a few examples of the state's "finest" that went off to Chicago's Columbian Exposition in 1893. Henry Ford and Ransom E. Olds were just two visitors from Michigan who went there too and saw, among the other amazing inventions, the gasoline-powered internal combustion engine. Three years later, a few weeks apart in the spring of 1896, Charles R. King and then Henry Ford appeared on the streets of Detroit, each in his horseless carriage running on a gas engine. When church bells rang and whistles blew to signal the new twentieth century, Michigan residents had a nineteenth-century wind at their backs.

Within a decade after those first autos sputtered out onto Detroit's streets, Michigan was the unrivaled center of the new automobile industry. It was no accident or single individual that led to such an early lead. The state was an established powerhouse based on its natural resources plus the advantages that came from sitting in the middle of four of the five Great Lakes. Capitalist-entrepreneurs who had made fortunes in lumber, railroads, or banking had the daring to risk some of their money on new ventures. Here were skilled and semiskilled workers employed in the mills that made steel, in the big stove factories, and in railroad car or carriage factories. An unskilled pool of immigrant workers was just beginning to arrive from central and southeastern Europe.

The environment encouraged enterprising individualism regardless of one's station in society. Ford, Olds, Durant, and Buick soon became household names that prompted hundreds of other hopeful inventors to try their luck. Sufficient cheap land beckoned new factories and put home ownership within reach of workers' families. Immigrant-owned shops anchored booming ethnic neighborhoods. Farmers bought more land to feed the urban crowds. Michigan offered a package of advantages that soon left other competitors far behind. In the first dozen years of the century, companies organized, reorganized, folded, or prospered, and in the process local automakers and their suppliers grabbed a commanding lead.

By the time World War I began in Europe, Michigan had become famous as the place that put the world on wheels, and its residents were off on a dizzying ride. Men and women hung on to those who were familiar and clung to the customary messages that urged self-reliance. Churchmen intoned, "The Lord helps those who help themselves." So, help themselves they would. Politicians insisted, "True Americans must stand up and be counted." Throughout Michigan's turbulent twentieth century, there were men and women who would refuse to be counted out.

THE KU KLUX KLAN

1 · WEAVING A TANGLED WEB
The Great War and Its Aftermath

Persons supposed to be dangerous radicals [are] but simple, ignorant foreigners, unaware of what was being done to them. . . . The very principles
of Americanism have been undermined by this hysteria and panic.
 —CHARLES D. WILLIAMS, Bishop of the Episcopal Diocese of
  Michigan, on the Red Raids in Michigan

Just before Christmas in 1917 a group of local men in the mid-Michigan
county of Newaygo hauled their neighbor Ben Kunnen from his home.
Rumor had it that he had made unpatriotic statements. Kunnen was
forced into a cottage at Fremont Lake, made to sign an apology to the public for his alleged pro-German attitude, and required to kiss the flag of the
United States. An iron cross was shaved upon his head with barber's clip-
pers and the word *Hun* printed upon his forehead with iodine.[1] It was just
one measure Michigan citizens took to do their part in the "war to end all
wars," the "war to make the world safe for democracy." Five years after the
war ended, patriots in Newaygo County agreed with other patriots across
the state: They must continue doing their part for their country as members in the Ku Klux Klan.

The Great War and its aftermath bore down with special weight on
Michigan because it arrived in tandem with the new automobile industry
that was reshaping all manner of habits. In 1913 immediately prior to the
war, interchangeable parts coupled with the moving assembly line
demonstrated the dramatic advantages of mass production at Henry
Ford's Highland Park factory. Needing a stable, productive workforce—
soon numbering 40,000 in the Highland Park plant alone—Ford announced the fabled "$5 Day" in January 1914.[2] Other manufacturers
emerging from the pack similarly pulled in more work and more workers
to southeast Michigan. General Motors was being created out of the mergers that would soon take it from holding company to corporate structure.

Chrysler Company was not far behind. Inventiveness invigorated auto competitors, suppliers, and assorted industries from shipbuilding to housing construction, from architecture to banking. By 1914 when Austria's Archduke Franz Ferdinand and his wife Sophia were assassinated in far-off Serbia, Michigan factories were ready with production capabilities beyond any nineteenth-century-honed imagination. They were extending the reach of twentieth-century ambitions at home and abroad.

The Great War accelerated the many changes already under way. Michigan farms, mines, and factories were at the forefront of the nation's mobilization because they had the proven capability to produce. In wartime, however, they had to produce more and faster. A simple tally of residents is just one measure of the dramatic developments in the single decade between 1910 and 1920. Detroit in 1910 had 286,000 residents; by 1920 the city's population was nearly 466,000, and seven counties in southeast Michigan accounted for more than a third of the state's total population, which was 2,810,173 in 1910 and 3,668,412 in 1920. These years brought new immigrants, new migrants, new work ways, new uncertainties; all came hand in hand with new calls for loyalty. For the first time in American history, efforts orchestrated to rally the home front helped cast a wide net of suspicion over any and all who might not be "100% Americans"—the socialists and Communists, the immigrants and blacks, the Catholics and the Jews, and anyone else whose loyalty might seem dubious for one reason or another. Michigan, some maintained, had been collecting more than its share of such people. With government encouragement, thousands of citizens dutifully stepped forward to point fingers at neighbors, coworkers, or casual acquaintances who seemed a possible threat to the cause.

It would not be easy to set suspicions aside once the armistice was signed on November 11, 1918. An inconclusive peace treaty coupled with the recent Bolshevik Revolution in Russia ended the grand dream of making the world safe for democracy. Now it seemed more imperative than ever to make sure democracy at home was safe, protected from the likes of those who might not understand, appreciate, or value it. Toward that end, Michiganians would soon find themselves involved in the Red Raids to round up socialists, Communists, and labor agitators. They would take sides in a bitter campaign about requiring all children to attend public schools. And, before suspicions finally eased, a sizable number of people in almost every county of the state would join the ranks of the Ku Klux Klan. Michigan came away from war with new sprawling factories and giant workforces, with larger, more mechanized farms operated by fewer farmers, with polyglot urban populations sorted by race and class for jobs and housing. It came away also with patriotism turned ugly and turned loose.

Influences of the Great War

Michigan residents, like most Americans, were shocked and baffled when European nations declared war on each other in the whirlwind between July 28 and August 5, 1914. Heirs to thrones had been assassinated before. Why a conflagration now? The calculated purposes promoting this war were beyond view of even the American president. Reflecting a national tilt, many in Michigan had greater sympathy for the Allies—Britain, Belgium, France, and Russia—than the Central Powers anchored by Germany, Austria-Hungary, and the Ottoman Empire. Still, there were 80,000 German-born people living in Michigan, and about 300,000 more were of German parentage, making them Michigan's largest immigrant population. In addition, nearly 130,000 residents were Austrian either by immigration or heritage.[3] The Allies' cause was not theirs, and they preferred to keep their new American homeland neutral rather than side with the Allies against their old homeland.

It was a sentiment shared by the significant number of Irish-born and Irish Americans in the state who hoped Ireland might finally wrest its independence from a weakened Britain. Woodrow Wilson had run third behind Theodore Roosevelt and William Howard Taft among Michigan voters in the 1912 election. But now they generally applauded President Wilson's quick, official proclamation of American neutrality even though their longtime hero Roosevelt believed the nation should get into the war at once.

Neutrality connoted the right to trade with all nations, and exporting had special urgency because America was just pulling out of the severe 1913 recession. Michigan farms, mines, and factories, able to supply considerably more than demand required, were in need of customers. Early on, Britain's superior navy was able to blockade trade with her enemies, and even while America remained officially neutral, the nation's exports went to Britain, France, Italy, and Russia. U.S. trade with those countries increased nearly fourfold between 1914 and 1916. This more than offset the drop in trade with the Central Powers. The Michigan economy made a gratifying recovery.

Henry Ford, Michigan's popular if quixotic idol, pronounced that he was not just neutral, he was a pacifist and would burn down his factories before he would produce any war equipment. His expressed willingness to spend his entire fortune on behalf of bringing the peace led him to charter an ocean liner for a pacifist group, and he sailed with them to Oslo in December 1915. Ford soon abandoned the disorganized mission with the conviction that, if nothing else, he had at least tried to bring about peace. By 1916 he supported Woodrow Wilson's candidacy for a second term, and, like Wilson, while hoping for peace he was quietly gearing Ford factories for war production.

Public opinion was nudged along by the sinking of the *Lusitania*, the German submarine attacks on American ships, the well-publicized plight of Britain, the escalating trade with the Allied nations, the measured words of President Wilson. Michigan's governor, Albert Sleeper, sent a message to President Wilson in February 1917 assuring him of support if war came to the United States, and the state legislature established a War Preparedness Board with a $5 million fund to use for various war-related expenditures. By the time Wilson went before a joint session of Congress in April 1917 to ask for a declaration of war, Michigan's thirteen representatives and two senators were ready to vote with the majority. Governor Sleeper favored voluntary enlistment and initially opposed the draft. But, widely criticized and with his loyalty to the country questioned, the governor backed away and helped ready the state's draft registration process. With a few exceptions, German, Austrian, and Hungarian residents muted their dismay about American participation. In concert, people sang the lyrics for which George M. Cohan received a congressional citation: "We'll be over, we're coming over, And we won't come back 'til it's over Over There!" Doubt should not dampen the mood set by high-minded hyperbole: People of the Wolverine state could and would help make this the war to end all wars, the war to make the world safe for democracy.

Contracts cascaded into Michigan thanks only in part to the remarkable production capabilities the auto factories were demonstrating. For several decades Michigan had been among the world's leading lumber, salt, copper, and iron ore producers. Its chemical and pharmaceutical companies pioneered products that brought leadership in the field and worldwide attention. Detroit, followed closely by Bay City, had been one of the nation's major shipbuilding centers since the 1890s. While the war boosted the American economy generally, it gave certain of the suppliers a critical edge. Once the United States embarked on preparedness and then war, government agencies sought out those companies and factories most likely to meet necessary production levels with speed and efficiency. The biggest firms got bigger.

Apart from Ford, Michigan entrepreneurs had been busy with the war from its onset in Europe. Factories already in the business of supplying European customers were major participants in the expanding war-created markets. No corner of the state was left outside the effort. Ann Arbor's newspaper reported "a banner year for business" in 1915 thanks to the war, and in 1916 it rejoiced that practically every manufacturing plant was "enjoying extraordinary prosperity."[4] Copper and iron ore mines in Michigan's Upper Peninsula had been staggered in 1913–14 by lessened demand and a crippling labor strike, but now they were breaking past production records. Government contracts purchased steel ships, transport trucks, ambulances, tanks, food, chemicals, ambulances, steel helmets. New plants and ideas implemented out of emergency produced Packard's Liberty airplane engines, Ford's submarine chasers, Aladdin Company's almost-overnight housing, and Kellogg's packaged food. The 1916 Federal Highways Act pumped money into better roads for better transport. The War Preparedness Board gave seed to Michigan farmers and sold a thousand Ford tractors to them at cost, and food production in the state jumped 25 percent in 1917. Ten million government construction dollars built Camp Custer in Battle Creek as an army training base; more government contracts built Selfridge Field near Mount Clemens as a training ground for fliers and aerial gunners.[5]

The all-out war effort consumed Michigan's people and brought newcomers to join in. Women and children took on new or more work to help replace the 135,485 men Michigan sent to the armed forces and to meet the escalating need for additional hands. With immigration nearly choked off during the war, employers encouraged foreigners already in the United States to relocate to Michigan, recruited American-born migrants from the South, and were more willing to hire blacks than earlier. Polish immigrants now constituted the largest group of foreign born in Detroit, and immigrants together with those of the second generation came to make up a majority of Detroit's population—six out of every ten residents by 1920. Meanwhile, the Great Migration of blacks out of the South gained momentum. In May, June, and July 1917, 1,000 blacks were arriving in Detroit each month. By the summer of 1920, the Urban League estimated the figure at over 1,000 per week. Between 1910 and 1920, the black population of Detroit soared from less than 6,000 to 40,838, an increase of 611 percent.

Native-born whites of native-born parents were only a third of the city's population.[6]

War boosted Americanization efforts to a frenzy. For at least a decade, Michigan's business, civic, and educational leaders had contributed to the snowballing national preoccupation with new immigrants coming in heavy numbers from central and southeastern Europe. Often Catholic or Jewish, these particular tired, poor, and huddled masses were commonly regarded as people not only unfamiliar with the language and the laws but lacking habits of the earlier arrivals from northern Europe. *The Melting Pot*, Israel Zangwill's popular play, had special local appeal soon after it had hit the stage in 1908. Zangwill drew upon imagery from industry where multiple pure metals were melted over hot fires to create the single and stronger steel alloy. His vision held forth the promise that the melting pot of America, sitting atop the burning fires of democracy, would amalgamate the Polish, Lithuanians, Hungarians, Irish, Germans, and other assorted immigrants. A single, stronger "American" population would be the end product. Toward a similar end but with a rational, institutionalized approach, progressive reformers like John Dewey stressed education as the means to ensure a citizenry who appreciated American democracy in common.

Employers imbued with notions about their special opportunity were trying to help the process along. Americanization equaled a proper work ethic. By the $5 Day Henry Ford intended to encourage workers, once trained, to stay in his factories. The year before this wage incentive, Ford's employment office processed between 50,000 and 60,000 workers just to maintain the necessary 13,600 employees.[7] A champion of welfare capitalism, Ford also believed that the better wage accompanied by profit sharing would give factory workers a stake in the company's success plus an incentive to adopt appropriate habits of thrift, reliability, and responsibility. He established a Sociology Department staffed by about 200 investigators whose task it was to monitor workers' home life, charting evidence they had—or had not—sufficiently embraced the "American standard of living" to qualify for the "American pay" of $5 a day.

Several other employers followed Ford's lead and made it mandatory for immigrants who did not speak English to attend classes in their plants after work. Similarly, the Detroit Board of Commerce formed the Detroit Americanization Committee in 1915, a group controlled by the large employers, the assistant superintendent of the city's schools, and various governmental officials. The committee's official purpose was to "promote and inculcate" the principles of American institutions, language, history, laws, and government of the United States, along with the rights and duties of citizenship.[8] Public schools hurried to comply. Catholic bishops, priests, and nuns promoted the patriotic message in local parish schools, organizations, and outreach programs. To add to the overall effort, the Detroit public schools opened certain buildings in the evening to teach English to foreigners, advertising their presence by a red, white, and blue light on top of the school buildings. Workers' families were soon targeted for these programs too with classes for wives and kindergartens for children.

Immigrants were often eager to learn American ways, anxious to create bonds of loyalty to their employer as well as to their new town and country. One Mexican who found an auto factory job in Detroit in 1916 joined the effort to help his countrymen succeed as Detroiters. As he told a *Detroit News* reporter, "The Mexican is in Detroit to become a Detroiter. . . . America to him signifies the same ideals as it does to the man born in Michigan."[9] From the mid-Michigan Belding silk mills to the Upper Peninsula mining towns, paternalistic employers were mandating loyalty to company and country along with sobriety and orderliness. Many people anticipated that they, their communities, and the country would be the better for it.

Not considered for inclusion in the melting pot, black migrants who poured north to work in Michigan were treated separately. In 1915, Detroit became the site of a branch of the National Urban League, formed five years earlier in New York City to examine and help relieve the miserable conditions of so many black residents there. The Detroit Urban League was closely tied to the Detroit Employers Association whose all-white members were anxious for an efficient, thrifty, sober, and calm workforce. The Urban League drew its black members from among the community's educated upper and middle classes, people who were respected in the white community. Aware of what happened to well-established blacks when new arrivals began moving into places like Chicago and New York, these Detroiters wanted to avoid being dragged down by a "Negro stereotype." At the same time, they genuinely hoped to be able to improve conditions for the newcomers.[10] In the process of making the case for more job opportunities, however, black leaders unwittingly leaned toward stereotypes. Forrester B. Washington arrived to head the Detroit Urban League when it was created in 1916. He had been born in Salem, Massachusetts, and educated at Tufts, a white college, and he attended graduate school at Harvard before taking the post in Detroit. Washington told an assembled group of employers in 1918 that black workers were perhaps "superior to the Foreign element that are coming into Detroit." As he explained it, "a Negro's physique is superior to the physique of the South European, and . . . you can get more [muscular labor] for your money than you do of any other nationality." In addition, "the Negro is docile, tractable, teachable, good natured, and fairly intelligent, very frequently highly so. And he is an American."[11]

In haste to find wartime workers, employers hired blacks for a wider range of semiskilled and even skilled positions, but this did not translate into equal facilities in the factories. The norm remained segregated washrooms, lunchrooms, and sometimes, in the case of black women workers, separate workstations, different workrooms, or separate occupations. Workplace segregation did not mollify white coworkers, whether immigrants or longtime Americans. They excluded blacks from their picnics and dances, from their bowling and baseball teams. Black leaders realistically warned black employees to follow all rules, be punctual, work hard. Otherwise, "you may not be able to keep your job after the war is ended and foreign labor is again available."[12] The situation was ready-made for postwar racial trouble.

Myopic federal and local agencies, intent on enforcing patriotism, offered additional opportunities to divide worker against worker and for employers to intimidate employees. Within weeks after the United States declared war Congress enacted the Espionage Act to make it a federal crime to "convey false reports or false statements . . . cause or attempt to cause insubordination, disloyalty, mutiny, refusal of duty . . . or obstruct the recruiting or enlistment service."[13] And more. It left considerable latitude for judicial interpretation. The postmaster general could also deny the use of the mails to any publications that he regarded as advocating treason, insurrection, or resistance to the law. His power over the domestic foreign-language press was further extended by the Trading-with-the-Enemy Act passed in October 1917.[14] The Sedition Act, signed by President Wilson in May 1918, went farther. It empowered zealous government agents to arrest people for whatever they considered to be disloyal, profane, scurrilous, or abusive remarks about the American form of government, flag, or uniform of the United States.

The Espionage and Sedition Acts became a means to censor Socialist publications, stamp out any criticism of the war, and portray labor union sympathizers as disruptive un-Americans. On the whim of judges prison terms were meted out to highly visible, vocal Socialist leaders like Eugene

V. Debs. Debs expressed his revulsion over the war before a convention of Socialists in Ohio in June 1918, and he was speedily sentenced to ten years in federal prison where he stayed until 1921 when released by President Harding. Rose Pastor Stokes, wife of a wealthy Socialist, outraged President Wilson by stating "the government is for capitalists," one line in a letter published in the *Kansas City Star*. She went to prison for a speech she gave to clarify that letter. Such action taken against the prominent sent signals about the government's mood. As a unanimous Supreme Court soon ruled in *Schenck v. United States* (1919), the constitutional guarantee of free speech did not hold in wartime when its exercise might constitute a "clear and present danger."

In the righteous hunt for traitors came the chance for employers to strike out against union agitators. Before the war, Michigan's mines and factories were familiar territory for labor organizers. Daniel DeLeon moved the headquarters of the radical Industrial Workers of the World from Chicago to Detroit in 1909, and the IWW had been actively encouraging various types of sabotage as a response to worker exploitation in the auto plants. The IWW, along with the Carriage, Wagon, and Automobile Workers' Union, had some success, and in 1913, 3,500 workers at the Detroit Studebaker plant walked out.[15] Workers in various trades showed interest in organizing until Ford's $5 Day plus the 1913–14 recession cooled their enthusiasm. Now, in wartime, union leaders and sympathizers could be rounded up for interfering with production. With patriotic impunity, management's labor policies became more restrictive in one Michigan factory after another.

More insidious, the Justice Department enlisted approximately 260,000 citizens nationwide with the creation of the American Protective League (APL) as its semiofficial auxiliary to help unearth possible traitors. As responsible members of the APL, neighbors should watch neighbors, coworkers should watch coworkers. This army of patriotic volunteers bearing Justice Department auxiliary badges quickly elevated nosiness or occasion for gossip into a good citizen's responsibility. Zealously, they took up the task of spying on people around them and anyone within reach whom they heard about. They compiled lists of names accompanied by assorted descriptive accounts of individuals' anti-American activities and turned the "information" over to the Justice Department's Bureau of Investigation. Any Justice Department officials who refused to go along with the hysteria risked their own reputations and jobs.[16]

With area war industries so important to the military effort the Detroit

APL was particularly busy. Under the leadership of a former city police commissioner, its nearly 4,000 members had collectively turned over evidence on more than 30,000 investigations by the end of the war. The APL office conveniently shared the same floor as the Justice Department in Detroit. The special "Plants Protection Department" placed operatives in each major Detroit factory; they recorded findings, suspicions, or fabricated notions and willingly turned over this "documented" evidence not only to the government but to company managers as well. These employer-encouraged spies zealously reported disgruntled fellow workers as un-American, possibly even German agents. Efficiency and high rates of productivity equated with one's patriotic duty; refusing to work overtime, complaining about the speed of the line, or breaking a piece of equipment equated with sabotage or treason. Workers who refused or complained when pressured to buy Liberty Bonds were transferred to harder work. Once the war ended and workers pressed for better working conditions, wages, and hours, employers remained in possession of a war-provided list of "troublemakers" or "potential troublemakers."

Working hand in hand with the APL, the Detroit Americanization Committee departed from its 1915 intent to educate immigrants so they would be prepared for citizenship. As soon as America entered the war, the committee hurried to establish alien information bureaus directed toward making the "foreigner" into an "American and a dependable labor supply." The Americanization Committee intended to counter "German propaganda and misinformation, lies, disloyalty, spying, distrust, and intrigue."[17] Fanatics nationwide renamed hamburger "liberty sausage," sauerkraut "liberty cabbage," German measles "liberty measles," and frankfurters "hot dogs." They splashed yellow paint on homes of people who did not buy Liberty Bonds or support various war drives. Public and parochial schools stopped teaching the German language. American flags appeared on the altars of immigrant churches. The federal government's Committee on Public Information ground out its "red, white, and blue books" to tell Americans why the war came, who the enemies were, and why it was vital to be a 100 percent American instead of a German-American, Polish-American, Irish-American, or some other half-American "hyphenate." In the large Polish community, parents worried over their children's future in America. Men learned some English in the workplace, but mothers who rarely left the neighborhood had little need to learn the language. Families spoke Polish in the frame homes they proudly built near their new factory jobs at places like the Dodge Main Plant. Their neighbors were mostly all Polish, and they attended masses said by Polish-speaking priests at huge churches they had sacrificed to build; their children attended the parish schools taught by Polish-speaking nuns. Now, with some reluctance, parents acknowledged that the nuns must spend more time drilling the children in English and less in Polish. In turn, the nuns hurried off to take classes on weekends and in the summer because many had only a rudimentary knowledge of English themselves.

Those with German names or ancestry, many whose families had been in the state for several generations, were automatically suspect. So it was that Ben Kunnen found himself in the hands of angry Newaygo County neighbors who chose to teach him a lesson for his reported pro-German sentiments and lack of loyalty.[18] In Michigan communities small and large, housewives heard that foreigners were putting ground glass in sugar. German families changed their names, and voters in a little mid-Michigan German farming village decided to change their town's name from Berlin to Marne, the site of a battle in 1914 where the French defeated the Germans. It was rumored that an old German on the west side of the state was using the tower he had built overlooking Lake Michigan to relay wireless messages back and forth between Germany and Mexico.[19] Ann Arbor, home of the respected University of Michigan and home also to long-established respected German families, could not escape the madness. The university regents dismissed a professor in the German department in 1917 for alleged pro-German comments, reported by one of his particularly patriotic colleagues. Four more professors in the department lost their jobs six months later with the official explanation that enrollment had decreased and they were, accordingly, unnecessary. A German woman was dismissed from rolling bandages with the Ann Arbor Red Cross when someone reported she was adding ground glass. A parent complained to the University of Michigan administration: His daughter had a landlady, a high school German teacher, who made critical comments about America and England. The lady's "German Cottage" was removed from the list of suitable student housing. The editor of *Die Washtenaw Post,* the city's German-language newspaper, was accused of sedition, summoned to a hearing in front of the postmaster general in Washington, and denied the right to use the mails for his paper. His son who took over quickly turned it into an English-language paper and declared it was the proper thing to do, for "we are all Americans, and we will be loyal to our country and our home"[20]

In their Americanization efforts before the war, businessmen, educators, and political and civic leaders had pressed images of what it *was* to be a real American. During the war, Americanization efforts were directed at defining actions, ideas, and values that *were not* American, were, indeed, "un-American."[21] Prewar optimism about the magic of the melting pot gave way to a wartime compulsion to legislate or shame or frighten people into conformity. Wartime propaganda and patriotism, promoted by employers they worked for or leaders they respected, made it seem only honorable for ordinary Americans to soldier on with their duty after the war: America itself must be made safe for democracy.

As mistrust metamorphosed into animosity, it was fed by new fears over Communism. The Bolshevik leaders made a separate treaty and withdrew from the war after their revolution in 1917. From their perspective, this was necessary in order to rescue Russia from economic crisis and get their new government on a safe footing. From the perspective of the American president and most Americans, it was a betrayal of the United States and of Russia's other allies. Moreover, the success of the Russian Revolution raised the prospect that Karl Marx and his 1848 *Communist Manifesto* might prove correct; other similar revolutions might threaten capitalism and democracy. The American government was not alone in this worry. A contingent of the Allied forces remained in Archangel, Russia, until the summer of 1919 with the express purpose of helping the tsar's supporters restore the former government and oust the Communists. This Polar Bear Regiment, as the soldiers termed it, was commanded by a British officer, but a majority of the troops were American boys from Michigan. As their difficult stay dragged on, their Michigan relatives along with Michigan newspapers expressed confusion if not outright anger about this nation's involvement in affairs of foreign countries. Some dared wonder aloud about the worth of the Great War that had come to such a perplexing end.[22]

In the Aftermath

Wartime fears about aliens, radicals, socialists, and other un-American types translated into new fears that these people were likely now to sympathize with Bolshevism. Observers blamed race riots in several cities on Communists who had used "educated Negroes, most of them from Harvard," who were "sufficiently discontented and sufficiently unbalanced to make good Communists." And, since "Negroes . . . were easily inflamed to violence," the nucleus of educated black Communists was able to help incite violence.[23] A wave of labor strikes, beginning in Seattle in February 1919, led employers and the press to conclude that Bolsheviks were behind the labor unrest as well as riots. The overarching purpose was to destroy capitalism and basic American institutions. During the war, any wildcat strikes had been disloyal and pro-German; now strikes were pro-Bolshevik. Michigan was one of twenty states that passed "Criminal Syndicalist" laws making it illegal to advocate union activities that violated existing statutes, and, as in twenty-eight states, Michigan's Jensen Law made it illegal to carry a red flag in public.[24] Beleaguered labor groups began fighting among themselves over whether or not to limit their demands to wages and hours so unions would not sound dangerously radical. The American Federation of Labor was so wounded by the antilabor hysteria and the postwar recession that nationally its membership would drop from four million in 1921 to less than three million by 1924.[25]

In the wake of the strikes, two bombs were delivered to well-known political and economic leaders' homes in the spring of 1919; thirty-four more were discovered in the mails around the country. They were addressed to men who were both foes and friends of radicals, but attention centered on the bombs intended for critics of Bolshevism or labor leaders and bombs planned for capitalists John D. Rockefeller and J. P. Morgan. Loyalty crusades once again preoccupied state legislatures and local citizens, usually people recently in the American Protective League.[26] Attorney general A. Mitchell Palmer, whose name was on one of the mail bombs, immediately launched an antiradical campaign. Whether conscientious guardian of the law, as his admirers saw him, or ambitious Democratic contender for president in 1920, as his critics said, Palmer unleashed what came to be known as the "Red Scare." Three decades later it would be renamed the "first Red Scare."

Palmer promoted young J. Edgar Hoover to be the special assistant in charge of the Bureau of Investigation campaign. Hoover came to the task from the Justice Department's wartime Alien Enemy Bureau where he enthusiastically tracked down suspect foreigners. *Aliens,* a term describing people who were not yet citizens, had became a derogatory label often loosely tossed about when referring to anyone of foreign birth. Palmer and Hoover intended to concentrate on radical aliens as a warning to others who lacked the legal protection of naturalized citizens. They aimed to deport as many as 7,000 or 8,000.[27] Spies were planted inside radical political groups, in labor organizations, in coffeehouses and meeting places frequented by certain "suspect" immigrant types. Infiltrators posed as overzealous members anxious to do what they must for the revolution or the cause. Some moved into high-ranking positions where they could promote and coordinate radical activity and then report on it to the Justice Department. The Red Scare and the government-sponsored Red Raids to round up radicals in the nation came to Michigan with a vengeance on January 2, 1920.

At 9:00 in the morning, city, state, and federal agents began a sweep through the state, focusing especially on Detroit. A group of Polish working men were studying an English lesson in a neighborhood Polish social center when Department of Justice agents broke in and took them away. While at work, the editor and assistant editor of a Polish-language newspaper were arrested, and the paper's records were confiscated. Twenty-two men were arrested at the headquarters of the IWW at 514 Gratiot. A key site was the House of the Masses, headquarters of the Socialist Party of Michigan. Located in Detroit's eastside old German neighborhood, the building had long been a German hall under a different name until 1918 when the Socialist Party bought it for their activities, and it remained a community activity center for local residents whether left-leaning or not. When agents smashed through the door of the House of the Masses and rushed in that January day, many of the 200 people there had come for a dance. Some were eating at the short-order restaurant downstairs; others were attending one of the meetings in progress. Without explanation, agents took away all 128 men—including hapless members of the dance orchestra. By nightfall, about 300 were arrested around the city, loaded in vans, and carted to a makeshift prison on the fifth floor of the Federal Building. Two days later the police were back at the Hall of the Masses and filled up vans again with everyone in the building. This brought the total to nearly 1,000 arrests in Detroit, second only to the net in New York.

To avoid any possible embarrassment, the Justice Department quickly released ex-servicemen rounded up in the raids regardless of their political beliefs. Nearly 800 others were detained without being allowed to see any attorneys, crammed in the dark halls of the Federal Building–Post Office where there was one toilet, one sink, and no outside window. The men had just their own overcoats for bedding and little food other than that brought by frantic relatives who managed to locate them. The *Detroit News* chortled, "Reds Get No Food, but Sing Lustily."[28] Over the week, prisoners were released one by one when officials could find no reason to detain them longer or deport them as threatened. It became evident that the focus of the raids was on aliens as much as on suspected Communists because the criterion for release was a "yes" answer to the question, "Are you an American citizen?"

Upon hearing of the raids, Detroit mayor James Couzens immediately protested to the federal government for the manner in which arrests were made and prisoners confined. Couzens forcefully informed the city council that "these conditions are intolerable in a civilized city." The 128 unreleased prisoners who remained on the fifth floor were moved over to the "bullpen" in the basement of the municipal court building. Conditions there were little better. The mayor insisted the Department of Justice remove its prisoners from any city-owned facilities, and he succeeded in getting them transferred to better quarters in the federally operated Fort Wayne where they awaited deportation hearings.[29]

Appalled by such government abuse of power, a number of respected civic leaders came forward to stand with Mayor Couzens, himself a wealthy and a popular progressive reformer. To arrange for bail, attorneys, and funds, Couzens had the help of prominent men including attorney Fred Butzel, chemical company president Frederick Stearns, dime store founder Sebastian S. Kresge, and Bishop Charles D. Williams of the Episcopal Diocese of Eastern Michigan.[30] They were indignant that the Justice Department relied on the aid of local police and forty members of the state constabulary to carry out the raids. Adding to local ire, the Justice Department intruded in a city that, as attorney Butzel explained, "gave the radicals a full and free permission to shoot off their mouths as much as they pleased . . . so long as they interfered with nobody else."[31] Although similar raids and abuses occurred in other cities around the country, Detroit was the only place where leading citizens organized to take action on behalf of the legal rights of the victims.[32]

The Detroit business and civic leaders took it upon themselves to gather information and report their facts to the Labor Department. Some relayed their findings to outside audiences. In a guest sermon at the Cathedral of St. John the Divine in New York City, Bishop Williams explained that he investigated "several of these cases . . . and found persons supposed to be dangerous radicals to be but simple, ignorant foreigners, unaware of what was being done to them. . . . The very principles of Americanism have been undermined by this hysteria and panic."[33] People arrested were "reputable workingmen" with "well-dressed families," not "what we have been led to believe Bolsheviks look like," testified a Detroit newspaper reporter when the Senate Judiciary Committee held hearings on charges of illegal practices in the Department of Justice in the spring of 1921. FBI officials admitted they had planted spies and provocateurs in radical groups. Of the 10,000 plus people arrested nationwide, 6,500 were released without charges being brought, and most were acquitted of all charges and freed.

By the time of their convention in June 1920, Democratic Party leaders had already decided to sidestep A. Mitchell Palmer as their presidential nominee, and both major political parties distanced themselves from the mad excesses of the Red Raids. Still, there were citizens who remained convinced that the threat was real or the attorney general would not have seen fit to order the raids. The Red Scare faded away but its ghosts did not; the vigilant went marching on.

Apprehensive Michigan residents soon felt their concern was particularly justified when internationally prominent Communists were arrested in a wooded rural area near Bridgman on the west side of the state near Lake Michigan. Worse, it turned out not to be the only time they had gathered there. In August 1922, tiny Bridgman, Michigan, provided the persistent J. Edgar Hoover with his first key success in the ongoing crusade against Communism. The squabbling Communist leaders in the United States had decided to bring together nearly fifty high-ranking American Communist Party leaders and three representatives from Moscow for a unity conference, choosing Bridgman because a successful secret Communist convention met there two years earlier and conference planners appreciated the seclusion and beauty of the area. Despite tight security, word of the meeting was leaked from within by a Bureau of Investigation undercover agent who alerted his superiors that the top leaders of the American Communist Party were holding a meeting at a local farm, masquerading as a foreign singing society. On August 22, 1922, the bureau's Red Raid netted William Z. Foster, Earl Browder, and other key party organizers. The Bridgman meeting was not a crime against the United States, but Michigan had enacted its own sedition act during the war, and the bureau vaguely justified overstepping its jurisdiction for "ample reasons under the law" when the American Civil Liberties Union raised questions. Those arrested were charged with violating the Michigan act, and their trials took place in 1923 at St. Joseph near Bridgman, riveting the attention of residents throughout the state. During the trials, Hoover began what would be his career-long practice as director of the FBI: He leaked information to friendly journalists who helped support his cause. Many of the charges were dismissed when juries could not agree, and none of the men arrested in Bridgman ever served time. Regardless, through the alarmist newspaper articles and one journalist's subsequent book, *Reds in America,* the Michigan public stayed abreast of the threat within, and many came away convinced that "where there's smoke, there's fire."[34]

Opportunities to regard some in their midst as potentially dangerous or blatantly objectionable piled one on top of another in postwar Michigan. Trying to keep immigrants out of saloons was a powerful reason a majority of Michigan voters approved a statewide Prohibition law in 1916, and it took effect May 1, 1918, almost two years before the Eighteenth Amendment brought nationwide Prohibition in January 1920. Michigan had a strong temperance movement grounded in the convictions of New Yorkers and New Englanders who began migrating to the state from the 1830s, longtime Americans who were white and Protestant. Most of the breweries were owned and operated by Germans, many started in the nineteenth century. For brewers and for saloon keepers, Prohibition spelled economic disaster. In immigrant communities, the neighborhood saloon regularly served as an important center of communication about politics, jobs, and housing; people were angry that they or their ancestors immigrated for freedom, but drinking was not to be allowed. During the decades of discord over the issue, Catholic, German Lutheran, and Jewish congregations had supported temperance but opposed Prohibition.

The campaign, the vote, and ultimately the whole failed "Prohibition experiment" added to the bulging grab bag of grievances against unregenerate immigrants as well as society's unredeemable "bad element." The vote tally underscored the rural-urban division; 71 of Michigan's 83 counties supported the Prohibition amendment in 1916. Also apparent was the Protestant-Catholic division. In the 12 counties where a majority opposed Prohibition, the population was weighted by a substantial Catholic immigrant presence; 4 were in the iron-mining region of the Upper Peninsula. Outstaters were disgusted but not surprised that voters in 14 out of Detroit's 21 wards went against Prohibition. About half the residents in Detroit were Catholic, but the rest of Wayne County beyond the city limits was home to working-class and middle-class Protestants. Those districts helped account for the county's 48 percent who favored Prohibition. Flint, like Detroit, had grown along with the auto factories; it had 14,000 residents in 1900 and over 90,000 in 1920. But Flint's factory workers were principally Michigan-born white Protestant Americans or migrants from Ohio, Indiana, and neighboring states. Flint, like outlying Genesee County, supported Prohibition.[35] Lansing, which was home to Ransom E.

Olds's reorganized company REO, also had a worker population drawn heavily from the native-born; 65.5 percent of that labor force was from Michigan. Even before state and national Prohibition laws went into effect, Lansing businessmen and civic leaders had already persuaded or coerced workers to go along with a local option to go dry.[36]

Smuggling from Ohio into Michigan along Dixie Highway, the "Avenue de Booze," began within hours after Michigan officially went dry on May 1, 1918. With Ohio itself dry a year later, the techniques of individuals and gangs in the Michigan-Ohio traffic became increasingly sophisticated.[37] As soon as Prohibition went into effect throughout the United States in 1920, Detroit became a nationally known center for bootlegging. Ordinary residents anxious to make many times what they could in their day jobs became smugglers. In boats, in cars, and on foot they traveled back and forth to Canada where the manufacture of alcohol was legal. Detroit's Prohibition-inspired Purple Gang rivaled Al Capone's in Chicago. The Purples were Jewish. Meanwhile, Italian mobs claimed and fought over their own territorial shares of the Detroit-area bootlegging trade. The well-publicized mob activities focused more public attention on unwelcome "foreign" types. In some years, the federal government spent as much as 27 percent of its enforcement budget in Michigan but Prohibition infractions remained brazenly conspicuous all around the state. Workers purchased liquor from cars and trucks parked outside their factories. Blind pigs replaced neighborhood saloons. More people than ever seemed to be drinking in violation of the law, while in the press and popular mind, the lawbreakers were most likely to be foreigners with no respect for the American legal system.

Henry Ford, meanwhile, had his own ideas about the source of rampant immorality as well as the radical trouble and Bolshevism. In 1920, his newspaper, the *Dearborn Independent*, began a seven-year campaign against the "international Jewish conspiracy" and blamed the political and social ills on what its columns detailed as "the Jewish racial problem."[38] Ford dealers around the country were regularly provided with stacks of Ford's anti-Semitic paper for distribution to their customers. Thousands of Michiganders owed their jobs to Henry Ford, directly or indirectly. Farmers wrote him grateful letters, pictures enclosed, about the many benefits the Model T provided them; they could harness its engine to saw trees, hitch the hay wagon to it, pull out a cow trapped in a muddy pond. To people in the Upper Peninsula—where he had built model company towns and comfortable lumber camps, and introduced specialized industries—Henry Ford was the one person in the state who had not abandoned them. Henry Ford's well-reported opinions had widespread currency in Michigan, whether about the virtues of ballroom dancing or anti-Semitism.

Like tumbling dominoes, one problem after another landed on those toward the end of the line. The economy was ready-made for postwar trouble among the most vulnerable, the small proprietors, the self-employed, and the wage workers. For two years following the war, factories contracted, retooled, and speeded their lines. In 1920 and 1921, Michigan was in a severe depression. With more than four-fifths of the industrial labor force out of work, anti-immigrant sentiment spiraled alongside the bad times. Returning World War I veterans charged that immigrants had taken their jobs while they were away. As Detroit's public assistance rolls shot up—by 700 percent in the year 1920—when foreigners who were not citizens applied to Detroit and Wayne County for assistance they were reported to the Immigration Bureau, which routinely issued warrants for their arrest.[39]

This industrial contraction was part of the widespread national recession that also hit Michigan mining communities, farmers, and small-town businessmen. Glutted markets meant drastically lower prices for copper, and in its annual reports after 1920, the venerable Quincy Mining Company relayed the message that it "has been impossible to operate the mine at a profit not withstanding every effort to reduce prices." Like the state's logging businesses, newer and better sources elsewhere diminished the possibilities for the return of prosperity, and new mining techniques and equipment had led to job reductions even before the drop in production. Employment in Keweenaw copper mines fell from around 14,000 in 1918 to about 8,000 in 1922.[40] Upper Peninsula workers and their families left for downstate factory towns where they lined up to compete with other workers and their families for jobs and housing.

Agricultural surpluses led to a sharp drop in prices after World War I, just as farmers were borrowing to buy the laborsaving tractors and other equipment that encouraged them to go more heavily into debt so they could buy additional acreage to cultivate. Michigan crop receipts, already sliding by 1920, would continue a long-term decline. The federally backed Farm Loan Bank that had been so eager to make loans during the war became just as eager to foreclose. Companies that had been flourishing on the base of agricultural produce shared now in the downturn. Michigan sugar companies that initially paid Mexicans' train fare to bring them from Texas to work in sugar beet fields now refused to pay the costs of their return. Left abandoned on rural farms, field hands migrated into towns in search of work or aid only to be met by hostile townspeople. In Saginaw, officials refused relief, and 200 beet workers were ordered out of the county and back to Mexico in February 1921; Catholic charitable groups organized to help 514 Mexicans accept repatriation and get to the Texas border from Detroit.[41]

Resentment smoldered in small communities. Residents in almost every region outside the southeast corner of Michigan jealously guarded their disproportionate representation in the state legislature, but the 1908 constitution mandated reapportionment in 1923, fast approaching, and their relative position in the state had been sliding away. While the state added more than 1,200,000 people between 1900 and 1920 to reach a total of 3,668,412, the proportion of rural and urban residents reversed. The number of residents on farms or in villages dropped to 1,426,852, and by 1920, they were no longer in the majority. The rapid growth of industrial centers had tipped the population ever farther toward the southern one-third of the state at the expense of the northern two-thirds. Recent political reforms such as the direct election of U.S. senators were ominous signs to the "old stock" in rural communities who recognized correctly that they stood to lose state legislature seats and might be outvoted in statewide contests. Indeed, by the 1925 Apportionment Act, Wayne County would gain seven more state legislators at the expense of other regions.[42] Complex changes under way for two decades hit home with people who were always mistrustful of cities and city folk, and who worried anew about immigrants.

Still, the political reforms were part of an overall intention to protect, energize, and empower citizens. The primary election law enacted in 1909 was designed to do just that. It made primaries mandatory for major parties to nominate candidates for governor, lieutenant governor, members of the House of Representatives, the U.S. Senate, the state legislature, and city officials in Grand Rapids and Detroit. With Republicans long dominating in Michigan, the primary was now more important than the general election for many offices. In the early 1920s, for example, every member of the state senate and state house of representatives was a Republican. Michigan was also at the forefront of the twentieth-century movement that brought legislation like the petition, initiative, and referendum. Michigan residents could now circulate petitions that, if signed by enough people, would put a proposal up for a vote. If approved by this referendum, the proposal became law. As the 1916 state amendment for Prohibition proved, organized people with a cause could triumph at the ballot box. In time for the election of 1920, rural and small-town dwellers got together with fellow "old stock" Protestants in Michigan's cities to make common cause. They unleashed their fears on the lightning rod of parochial education.

Wartime antiforeign sentiment revived Protestant anger over the Catholic parochial schools that were preferred over public schools by such a large proportion of Catholic parents across Michigan. In classrooms presumed to be dominated by the dictates of a foreign pope who headed an authoritarian church, how could children learn the lessons and values of American democracy? Even foreign-born Protestants or those still attached to an immigrant heritage—especially the German, Finnish, and Dutch—were often sending their children to denominational schools. Responding to xenophobic fears of their constituents, fears many politicians themselves nurtured, the Michigan state legislature passed a new law in 1919 requiring all schools in Michigan to conduct classes in English except for religious instruction. That was not enough to satisfy the alarmed. Democracy was at stake.

The opportunity to do more was at hand. The Wayne County Civic Association spearheaded by James A. Hamilton had been mobilizing since 1918, circulating petitions on behalf of amending the Michigan constitution to require that "all residents of the State of Michigan between the ages of five and sixteen years shall attend the public schools in their respective districts until they have been graduated from the eighth grade" or as many years as provided in the district school if it did not extend through grade eight.[43] The number who signed made the school amendment petition the largest filed on any moral issue up to that time, including Prohibition. Once the petition was filed in February 1920, the Wayne County Civic Association retitled its movement as the Public School Defense League and reached out for a statewide constituency.

Support for the amendment snowballed into a loose alliance of like-minded people who were receptive to stereotypes, old and new. Speeches, pamphlets, cartoons, and lurid tales warned that the pope controlled the parochial school curriculum, had been in alliance with the Central Powers during the war, and used the schools to perpetuate a foreign language, custom, and creed. Parochial schools had "furnished 65 percent of the criminals of the country" and "foreigners and illiterates 30 percent."[44] It was all of a package; the "wrong women" were having babies, thereby threatening "to exterminate the American Protestant home," and those children were going to parochial schools, multiplying the threat. Parochial schools were said to be hotbeds of Bolshevist ideology since Bolshevist doctrine and Catholic dogma, in common, insisted upon "unthinking obedience."[45]

Hostile exchanges grew more heated. At a weeklong Methodist revival in Monroe County in late June 1920, traveling evangelist Lewis J. King filled his sermons with examples of Catholic villainy—that cowardly Catholic soldiers hid in the trenches during the war, that a girl in Poland had been kept in a convent dungeon for twenty-one years, and more. Every night, King and another visiting preacher dodged eggs and insults from some in the crowd. Certain men took on the task of "standing guard," and by the fourth night, trouble seemed waiting to happen when two carloads of Catholics from a nearby parish arrived. They were there only to heckle King, they later maintained. The Catholics went into the church and were indeed among the hecklers present that night. As they started to leave late in the evening, shots were fired, a melee broke out, and two Catholics in the crowd were fatally wounded.[46] Accounts of the night's events were confused and contradictory from beginning to end. The *New Menace,* an anti-Catholic weekly, editorialized that the motive "for this Roman Catholic savagery is not known, but Rome is furious over the pending school amendment to the Michigan state constitution, which fact may have inspired the lawless brutality."[47] Weeks of investigation and months of delays led to the trial of one Protestant for murder. Protestant feelings ran high about the "papal rioters" who had come to cause trouble. Catholics believed they had been the victims of an unprovoked attack. After 13 ballots, the jury acquitted the accused man. Upon hearing the verdict, there were no outbursts from the crowd that packed the room. People filtered back to their homes, but the whole episode was accompanied by rumors and accusations run wild.

Those who organized to support the "anti–parochial school amendment" to end parochial schooling not only were likeminded on that issue but characteristically shared other views. They stood on common ground as white and Protestant, either longtime Americans or people of northwest European Protestant immigrant origins. The anti–parochial school amendment issue reminded them of their need to stick together and reinforced their mutual allegiance. By contrast, those who fought the amendment more often found themselves in strange company, bedfellows on this single issue. A few opposed the amendment out of principle, but most who mobilized against it had interests of their own to protect.

Passage would effectively close all parochial and private schools, not only the Catholic schools that were the primary target of the amendment drive. Although estimates varied, as many as 120,000 children were attending schools operated by religious denominations in 1920, with Catholic, Lutheran, Seventh-Day Adventist, Greek Orthodox, Russian Orthodox, and Lithuanian schools among the list. Almost 50,000 children in Detroit alone were enrolled in Catholic schools. Statewide, Catholics were only 20 percent of the population, however, and they were divided into ethnic parishes, separated by ethnic animosities, and overloaded with new immigrants. Others' votes were critical, but Catholics needed to mobilize their own to make common cause. Toward that end they formed the Educational Liberty League to direct the Catholic campaign against the amendment.

Missouri Synod Lutherans who operated nearly all of the Lutheran parochial schools planned their strategy independently from the Catholics, set up their separate headquarters, and organized their own "fighting units" to visit individual Lutheran homes. According to figures from the Missouri Synod Lutheran Church, their schools enrolled 10,354 pupils in 185 schools throughout Michigan.[48] The Missouri Synod represented the most conservative wing among Lutherans, and as one member said, "being a Lutheran, I cannot be anything else than anti-Catholic."[49] Still, Lutherans took comfort in seeing that other longtime enemies of the "Romish church" were allying with the Catholics on this particular battle.

Certain Presbyterian, Methodist, Episcopalian, Congregational, and Unitarian ministers denounced the amendment and its backers, referring to them as agnostics and Bolsheviks, generally bad company. Catholic parents, they said, had the right to educate their children along religious lines so long as they also met the requirements of the state. Jewish families traditionally sent their children to public school and provided religious instruction after school hours or on weekends, but Jewish leaders spoke out against this amendment as "conceived in bigotry" and "not a matter where it is fair or wise to exercise coercion."[50] Many of the same civic leaders who spoke out against Palmer's Red Raids stepped forward again. Invoking the Fourteenth Amendment, they lined up behind the position that the amendment would not be constitutional even if it were passed.[51] The *Detroit News* and the *Detroit Free Press* willingly helped school board leaders alert teachers and taxpayers to the budgetary implications if so many children were suddenly moved from the parent- and church-funded parochial schools into public school classrooms.

The bitter, often vicious campaign offered an entire generation of Michigan residents another reason to focus on their differences. Catholics took pride in the praise their schools received from outside supporters during the campaign; nonetheless, they came away seriously damaged by their opponents who successfully hammered on stereotypes, old and new. Catholic leaders importunely fed into the enemy's stereotype by holding a mass in Navin Field in Detroit just before the election. The crowd, between eighty-five and a hundred thousand, included a procession of thousands of orderly children who sang in unison to praise God, America, and their schools. They performed under the watchful eyes of nearly 1,500 sister-teachers garbed in their long black, blue, or brown habits. To their foes, they appeared a solid, unified force with brainwashed children and too many of them, at that. Many people who ultimately voted against the amendment simply did not want to pay more taxes to educate Catholic children in public schools and did not like the idea that their neighborhood schools could be "flooded" with them.

By the time election day arrived in November, this anti–parochial school amendment had indeed energized and mobilized citizens throughout the state. Catholic immigrants had hurried to become citizens so they could vote to save the schools. Women, able to vote for the first time in 1920, needed little urging from their husbands, ministers, priests, and bishops to make their votes count for or against the amendment. In Detroit, as many as 90 percent of the registered voters turned out in what was the largest vote in the city's history. Statewide, the tally was 610,699 against to 353,818 for the proposition.[52] In outstate rural counties where Catholics and their advocates were few, the vote was regularly reversed. In Newaygo County the amendment won by 2,415 to 2,220.[53] The election statistics, to agrarian and small-town Michigan residents, were one more ominous sign that their power at the ballot box was waning.

By all accounts, the amendment proposal generated more interest among Michigan voters than the national slate of candidates. Republican presidential candidate Warren G. Harding won a solid majority in Michigan in 1920. Whether they voted for him or not, most Michigan residents shared Harding's stated preference for a return to "normalcy," and they went about their private lives. For other people, the Great War and its aftermath helped underscore the imperative to make America safe for democracy. Local citizens accustomed to or seeking respectability within their communities or among their peers hunkered down. They put their shoulders to the wheels of county politics, local churches, schools, chambers of commerce, rotary and fraternal organizations. Not coincidentally, a new organization appeared to offer another avenue: The Invisible Empire, Knights of the Ku Klux Klan.

Thousands of citizens opted to suit up and mobilize in peacetime just as they had mobilized for war. Deadly earnest about the enormity of their task, they climbed to the high ground to plant crosses fashioned of pipe lengths wrapped in burlap soaked with gasoline. There, fortified by prayer, the Pledge of Allegiance, and stirring songs of their own, white-robed men in tall peaked hats gathered with torches in hand. They pledged to do their part to save their own communities, thereby the nation. They swore to do whatever necessary to protect America from people whom they judged unable to respect democratic values: Bolsheviks, socialists, and lawbreakers, many of them likely found among the unwelcome Catholics, blacks, and Jews. Separate but equal to the effort, concurring women carved out their own roles alongside the men. These were people proud to be within the circle of the Ku Klux Klan.

2 · AMERICANS WE
People of the KKK

> We shall ever be devoted to the sublime principles of a
> pure Americanism.
> —Women of the Ku Klux Klan Kreed

The Invisible Empire, Knights of the Ku Klux Klan, had little to recommend it to Michigan people when it was first revived on Stone Mountain near Atlanta in 1915 by a small group of sixteen men. Alabama-born William Joseph Simmons, founder and Imperial Wizard, was fulfilling a dream to restore the Southern Klan his father rode with during Reconstruction. As he explained it, the Invisible Empire's mysterious name represented brotherhood: *Ku Klux* came from a division of the Greek word for circle, *kuklos,* and *Klan* from the Scottish word *clan.* From his alliterative imagination, Simmons spun enticing titles for functionaries and new rituals for followers. Like the first Klan, Simmons's brotherhood aimed to assert the rightful place of white Protestant sons of the American-born, these legitimate guardians of bedrock American values. In the bargain Simmons anticipated the Klan fraternity would be a source of clients for his insurance business plus offering untold new business opportunities. As surely as it was anchored in the excesses of American patriotism, the Klan was one more entrepreneurial scheme to emerge in the era.

For the first five years following its revival, the Klan was only a few thousand members strong, just one among a multitude of small fraternal societies in the South. Simmons, with dreams still intact, signed on Edward Young Clarke and Elizabeth Tyler in June 1920 to be recruiters-for-profit. As partners in the Southern Publicity Association the pair had successfully mingled propaganda and advertising while recruiting for the Red Cross, Anti-Saloon League, Salvation Army, and War Work Council. They promptly reshaped the Klan's message to fit the postwar national climate: Patriotic 100 percent Americans should regard the Klan fraternity as a means to check blacks, immigrants, Catholics, Jews, Bolsheviks, and assorted radicals. Recruiting for this multiheaded cause now became a big business based on fee splitting. Clarke and Tyler trained Klan representatives, "kleagles," who began carrying the message north, supplemented along the way by a cadre of sympathetic northern ministers who joined the speakers' circuit. Racism, religion, politics, and economics entwined in this energized Klan. Interested Americans could choose their own emphasis. Once that became clear, northerners became more attentive to the words, robes, hoods, and crosses.

Between 1923 and 1924, the Klan would enroll tens of thousands of members in Michigan. Although the state had only 83 counties, it ultimately had 97 chartered Klans and an unknown number of others that attained provisional status. Almost every county in the Lower Peninsula would have a klavern, and in the more remote Upper Peninsula, at least two-thirds of the counties soon had some sort of Klan presence.[1] Atlanta-based Klan officials recorded more members in Michigan than any state in the South and put it variously in seventh or eighth place nationally.[2] Estimates of actual membership vary between a low of 70,000 up to a high of 265,000.[3] If women and junior Klan members are to be considered, 80,000 understates the number; if fellow travelers and sympathizers are to be taken into account—as is sometimes the case in estimates of Communist and Socialist strength—265,000 might not be unrealistic. The neighboring states of Indiana, Ohio, and Illinois had more Klan members, but these states also had a larger pool of potential members—native-born men born to native-born parents. In Michigan, 10 percent of the total population consisted of American-born white males 21 and older whose parents were also born in America. By contrast, in Indiana nearly 24 percent fell into that category and in Ohio, about 20 percent.[4] Given also that nearly a quarter of Michigan's residents were Roman Catholic, many of them native born to parents born in this country, the Ku Klux Klan won over a significant share of its most likely supporters, probably at least two or three in ten.[5]

Blazing through Michigan

Detroit was the first base in the state for Kleagle C. H. Norton, who arrived in the summer of 1921 to test the waters. His efforts got a boost when a three-week series of articles published in the *New York World* and syndicated newspapers gave the Ku Klux Klan wide publicity. The articles appeared in September 1921, detailing 152 cases of violence that extended from floggings to tar-and-feather warnings to murder. Intended to kindle repugnance for all the Klan represented, the exposé instead caused Congress to summon Imperial Wizard Simmons, who seized the opportunity to hold forth for a two-hour dramatic defense of the Klan. In the hearings, Simmons put the main themes of the Klan's public agenda on center stage: It was a "purely loyal American Protestant fraternal organization."[6] Contradictions went unchallenged by the assembled congressmen, and their responses were generally couched in wait-and-see terms. The hearings gave the Klan more valuable publicity; rather than being repulsed by Simmons's message, there were Americans who welcomed it.

All this attention helped the Wayne County Provisional Klan pick up about three thousand members in and near Detroit that fall, but Kleagle Norton was less effective than some recruiters, and the national Klan headquarters preferred to concentrate on Ohio and Indiana. Steering a cautious course, the Wayne County Klan met behind locked doors and canceled a parade scheduled for Thanksgiving Day after the city council president instructed the police to treat any Klan demonstrators as disturbers of the peace. In the summer of 1922, a *Lansing State Journal* reporter described the initiation ceremony he had been invited to witness—after being transported blindfolded to the site—in which the assembled Klansmen accepted new initiates with the charge, "God give us men, God give us men, God give us men."[7] Such reports or rumors of Klan activities in Michigan were usually greeted at the time with warnings but then discounted.

Throughout the fall of 1922 and into the first five months of 1923, the Klan gathered members nationwide until it claimed to have 3,000,000 by June.[8] Articles in the *Free Press* reported on Klan activities in other states almost daily—revelations of top Klan leaders arrested for sex, alcohol, and prostitution violations; leaders' fraud and graft in Georgia; a mayor flogged by the Klan in Kansas; lynch threats against the Oklahoma governor; thousands of Klansmen gathering for a reunion in Valparaiso, Indiana; and even "Britain Houses Ku Klux Klan." Alleged activities of the Klan in several Michigan cities led James A. Burns, a Catholic-educated Republican state representative from Detroit, to introduce a concurrent resolution in January 1923 providing for a legislative investigation of the Klan presence. Two months later Burns introduced a law making it a minor offense to wear masks or coverings that would conceal the whole or part of the face in any

Ku Klux Klan at the State Fair Grounds in Detroit, 1924. The KKK took hold all throughout Michigan by the spring of 1923, and at its peak in 1924 the state had the seventh- or eighth-largest Klan membership in the nation, members who included well-respected ministers, businessmen, politicians, policemen, farmers, and factory workers. Their popularity was such that many Klansmen were proud to march without masks. In defense of 100 percent Americanism and the Protestant faith, Michigan Klan chapters focused on immigrants and parochial schools, rumrunners, speakeasies, Prohibition violators, and blacks. (Walter P. Reuther Library, Wayne State University.)

assembly, march, or parade on streets, highways, and public places. Violators were to be punished by a fine of not less than $25 or more than $100 or by 30 days in the county jail or both. By a solid vote of 76 to 2 in the House and 27 to 0 in the Senate, the legislature enacted the "mask law," Public Act Number 276, which was to take effect on August 29.[9] Before then, however, the Klan would sweep through Michigan, igniting so much enthusiasm that the law proved to be of little consequence.

On June 14, 1923, a photo and front-page headline in the *Detroit Free Press* announced, "Fiery Cross Glares as Host Join Klan Near City." According to the report, the night before, a "Lurid light" from a blazing 30-foot cross illuminated the farm field where about 1,000 initiates on bended knee swore allegiance to the Ku Klux Klan. It was the first meeting to capture photos and significant publicity, although the organization had held its initial outdoor rally in the same field April 4.[10] The farm, soon to prove a popular gathering spot, was near Royal Oak in Oakland County and just 35 miles from downtown Detroit. This night, a *Free Press* reporter and one other "Philistine" were permitted to stand at a distance to watch. The astounded reporter estimated there were about 8,000 "fantastically robed knights" on hand from surrounding counties who participated in the "weird rites." Hundreds sent their white headpieces hurtling into the air when the Imperial Wizard's emissary shouted that the Klan aimed to bring about "America for Americans." Sharing hot dogs and coffee after the ceremony, many of the knights talked of their aim to get the majority of Americans to use their ballots so the nation might be purged of all who are not "100% Americans."[11] The newspaper account derided the night's "hocus pocus," but it failed to make an important if ironic connection: The meeting of 100 percent Americans took place the night before June 14, the now-annual Flag Day that President Woodrow Wilson had officially proclaimed seven years earlier in his zeal to promote a homogeneous nation. It was just the beginning of what would become a typical response to the Klan by its Michigan press opponents. They mocked what was easiest to mock and overlooked leaders' responsibility for contributing to the climate of intolerance.

Manly L. Caldwell, a new recruiter, had arrived to organize Detroit's Wayne County Klan early in 1923, and his effectiveness helps explain the success of this attention-grabbing gathering. Kleagle Caldwell boosted Wayne County Provisional Klan membership from 3,000 to 22,000 within eighteen months, and he earned $76,000 in membership commissions for his efforts.[12] The *Fiery Cross*, the official Ku Klux Klan newspaper published in Indianapolis, began printing a Michigan edition with local editor-in-chief Milton Elrod and managing editor Ernest W. Reichard based in Detroit.[13] From the spring of 1923 through the summer and fall, crosses blazed across Michigan illuminating people who were persuaded their flag and God needed them in the ranks of the Klan.

Burning crosses were the evidence that the Klan had arrived in a vicinity; several newspaper articles reported them as the sign that 100 members in the area had joined. Usually a week or two before a visiting Klan representative's scheduled address, a "loud report as of a gun being fired" attracted attention to a flaming cross on some nearby hill.[14] These dramatic signals sparked the intended interest, and advance announcements urged people to give Klan speakers "the courtesy of a fair and open-minded hearing."[15] Many who helped swell the crowds were more curious than prepared to join. In Saugatuck, no unusual case, "Pretty nearly everybody in town was on hand and the streets were filled with autos from the surrounding county."[16] Recruiters who fanned out to small-town and rural crowds carried with them the same message so popular among the crowds around Detroit: The Ku Klux Klan was "preaching the gospel of Americanism."[17] Vigilante justice, an established tool of the Klan's gospel in action, went unmentioned at these public meetings.

With tent revival fervor, circuit-riding preachers told and retold the drama of the Klan's rebirth on Memorial Day in 1915 when Simmons and the small group of men from Georgia ascended Stone Mountain near Atlanta, built an altar, spread Old Glory over the stones, and laid an open Bible on the flag. With nightfall approaching, the men put two small sticks of wood across each other on the altar and lighted them against the darkness—the Klan's now-symbolic flaming cross. In its light, the circle of men read the twelfth chapter of Romans in the Bible, took each other's hands, and proclaimed "America for Americans."[18] The Klan's burning cross represented "the sacrifice of Jesus of Nazareth; the flames the light which the Savior shed upon the world."[19] Judged "brilliant speakers," even by most of their critics, the recruiters' styles were different but each could explain the Klan platform in simple terms: The Klan is the friend of the "good Negro," but he should keep his place and not mix with white Americans. The Jews control every industry in America. They are always the middle men. "We must remove Catholic supervision from our public schools."[20] Message bringers thundered that it had become necessary in America to act on the Savior's behalf because of the tremendous influx of foreigners coming here who were "taught and trained in foreign dogmas and creeds." Along the Atlantic coast was a "vast mongrel population" speaking more than 28 different languages; they were "living in filth, breeding crime and anarchy, hoisting the red flag as a proclamation of war against Old Glory."[21] Local audiences often had little personal familiarity with the Atlantic coast but were sure they would not want to live in places like New York City and did not want those kinds of people and problems to take hold here. They were familiar enough with tales about Detroit's Prohibition-violating foreigners and aware that the Red Scare and Bridgman raid netted red flag–wavers in Michigan. Catholic schools continued to multiply in one community after another. Trouble was right here on the doorstep.

Catholics were sometimes part of the audience. Any curiosity a local priest in the Mount Pleasant audience had was soon satisfied. He rose from his seat to declare the speaker's statements were a direct attack on the pope and Catholic faith, and he requested that all Catholics present withdraw from the hall. This prompted "considerable excitement" when others took exception, and even "danger of violence" until someone disconnected the electricity.[22] Aware that their audiences did contain people who would be unwelcome and ineligible members, an occasional pragmatic organizer concluded his general speech with an invitation for native-born, Protestant, white citizens to remain and hear more. Others, clearly, were expected to leave.[23] Klan defenders objected to any complaints about the "exclusiveness" of the Klan in its rejection of black, Catholic, and Jewish members. Pastor Hugh Emmons from the First Christian Church of South Bend, Indiana, explained the Klan's rationale to a Niles, Michigan, audience: Catholics were not eligible because the Klan is a secret order, and the Catholic Church does not permit its members to become affiliated with secret orders. Jews were not eligible because the Klan is based on the teaching of the Bible, and Jews do not believe in the Bible. The "colored race" was not eligible because the Klan stands for white supremacy and opposes intermarriage.[24] The Klan's right to exclude whom it chose was certainly neither unusual nor illegal.

All the while Klan recruiters motored around Michigan, the nobility of direct action was playing out on movie screens in towns large and small. *The Birth of a Nation* played over and over again, bringing the first Klan to life on the screen. Hooded knights riding sure-footed horses galloped to the dramatic rescue of a white woman faced by marauding freed Negroes bent on rape. The Ideal Theater in Fremont was managed by a Klansman who, as a prelude to *The Birth of a Nation,* eagerly booked *The Toll of Justice,* also depicting the work of the KKK. School groups in the Upper Peninsula were taken to Calumet when the movie played there, and Bernard DesRoches, one youngster in the audience, remembered this terrible lesson in bigotry to the end of his long life.[25] More often, capacity crowds across Michigan cheered at the conclusion of the award-winning film. Why not? It won cheers and high praise from people supposedly more worldly than the small-town and farm families sitting on blankets in the grass watching it on the local movie screen, a sheet tacked to the grocery's outside wall. Woodrow Wilson himself pronounced the tale sad but "all too true."

A year before Michigan klaverns were in an organizing frenzy the national Klan leadership was already crumbling under the weight of scandal and internal power struggles. A 1922 coup displaced founder William Simmons in favor of new Imperial Wizard Hiram Wesley Evans; their subsequent bitter wrangling over finances and copyright claims wound up in the courts. Evans remained, and Simmons was banished from the Invisible Empire he had started. He did not go quietly but, rather, continued his public denunciations of the new Klan leadership while trying in vain to develop an alternative base. Meanwhile, chief recruiters Clarke and Tyler were out, toppled by opponents who capitalized on sensational revelations about disorderly, disreputable conduct that included their apprehension in a house of prostitution and his arrest for possessing liquor in Indiana while there for a speech on law enforcement.[26] Evans put an end to the commissions, and, instead, kleagles were put on salary; he also tried to emphasize the basic themes of temperance, Protestantism, Americanism, and morality and downplay or check the lawless, violent activities associated with the Klan.[27] All the while, scandals within the Southern-headquartered Klan damaged the membership cause more in the South than in the North where the Klan was growing.

Members who joined klaverns across Michigan paid $10 in dues and received a free robe in return. Later generations would mock Klan dress, but in the 1920s distinctive outfits were proud acquisitions for members who opted to join organizations from the Boy Scouts to the Women's Christian Temperance Union to the Catholics' Knights of Columbus. The garb, ceremonies, and Klan titles had their own appeal apart from the Klan message. Donning the high-peaked white hat added at least two feet to a short or medium-sized man; the tall stood even taller. Induction into the "mysteries" of the Ku Klux Klan was sufficiently solemn and ceremonious to awe participants. These "naturalizations" took place at night and always in the eerie flickering light from a blazing cross. Whether 15 or 40 feet high, the crosses were situated on a hill if one was available so they would be visible for miles around. One by one, each new Klansman stepped forward, went down on bended knee, and with his right hand raised to high heaven and his left hand placed over his heart, three times he promised loyalty to Klan convictions: America for Americans.[28] Their robes and crosses gave this "second Klan" the appearance of the early Reconstruction Klan, but in almost every other regard, here were members belonging to their own era.

Card Carriers in the Klan

Because identities were guarded, the rank and file easily slipped into the shadows. Names did get out when members took a Klan-related public role or marched unmasked around their own communities, but the profile of people who joined the Klan has long been a matter of debate. Evidence still surfaces. In its bits and pieces, it reveals a Klan that was indeed uniformly white, Anglo-Saxon, and Protestant. But otherwise, there appear an assortment of Klans more reflective of local communities than they were homogeneous in membership or cause. Here and there in Michigan, contrary to the orders from the Imperial Wizard's headquarters, record keepers stored away materials rather than destroying everything when their klaverns disbanded. Correspondence, account books, minutes, and identifying information on more than 1,500 members survive for several klaverns or units that made up Mecosta County Klan No. 28, Newaygo County Klan No. 29, and the Grand Haven Provisional Klan in Ottawa County, all of them in west central Michigan.[29] Newaygo County's Klan No. 29 was by far the largest. It attracted at least 697 members, or 16 percent of the males in the likely pool—those who were native-born, white, and over the age of 21. The Newaygo Klan also included 18 foreign-born men, and the women's Klan enrolled 403 members. In Mecosta County, Klan No. 28 drew only about 255 men, which represented a lower proportion of the potential pool. If there was a women's Klan, the records disappeared. Ottawa County was more than double the size of the other two, and men came even from a neighboring county to join the Grand Haven Klan. Still, membership cards total only 160, and the klavern never moved from provisional to chartered status.[30]

Because records are so elusive, it is tempting to read too much into those that are available; yet taken for what they are, the lists of Klan members in western Michigan provide a glimpse of the members—people so commonly thought to be somehow so aberrant. There were similarities among members of these western Michigan klans, especially Klan No. 28 and Klan No. 29. Those similarities and Grand Haven's variation reflect how much the Invisible Empire belonged within commonplace, everyday ways of the residents.

Once it made its appearance in western Michigan, men and women did not wait and see how the Klan might take hold. Those who were inclined to join signed up right away by the fall of 1923 or in the early months of 1924; latecomers were pulled on board just prior to the fall elections of 1924. Members came to the Klan two by two and more; fathers and sons, brothers, husbands, wives and daughters, extended families, fellow workers, lodge brothers, ministers and friends. The Klan was part of the circle of their lives. In Mecosta, Newaygo, and Ottawa counties the Klan took root because it was planted in the personal relationships of like-minded people and because some part of the Klan's platform reinforced some local concern.

Newaygo County was in the middle of Michigan, one county away from Lake Michigan. Mecosta was the next county to the east. Except for the special distinctions locals used to differentiate their own particular hometown or section of farmland, Newaygo and Mecosta counties had a lot in common. Everyone who lived here in the 1920s was economically dependent upon agriculture or natural resources in one way or another even when it came to local factories. Land in this part of the state was not the best for tilling—hilly, wooded, dotted by small lakes and ponds and affected by the winds coming in from across Lake Michigan throughout long winters. Farms, a sprinkling of tiny villages, and a few bigger towns with light industries fixed the borders of life. The same names had been around the area for generations; many families were descended from native-born Protestant pioneers who began migrating from the northeast or north-central states after midcentury seeking affordable land and new opportunity. Other local residents traced their ancestors back to the northwest European immigrants who had also arrived in the nineteenth century. The majority of those immigrants were Germans or Scandinavians, Protestants with an image as the solid hardworking type of foreigners the state legislature began to encourage when the *Emigrant's Guide to Michigan* appeared in the 1840s. Irish and German Catholics came too, but always they remained in the minority. Ever since 1890, people had been moving away at a faster rate than newcomers or babies were arriving. The percentage of foreign-born declined even more rapidly than the total population once the older generation died and emigration from northwestern Europe slowed. In both Newaygo and Mecosta counties, in 1920 only about 10 percent of the residents had been born in foreign countries. Catholics were a small slice of the area's families.[31] Neither county recorded any Jewish congregations or members.

Apart from Sundays when the churches sorted Catholics from Protestants, Protestants from each other, and the unchurched from everyone else, people shared much the same day-to-day outlook. Few, including Catholics, had any use for the types one early Klan speaker in Mecosta County labeled as the Invisible Empire's arch enemy: "the corrupt politician, the major vices, the bootlegger, the moonshiner, the radical agitator, and the alien."[32] When an organizer first arrived to promote a Mecosta County Klan in the fall of 1923, the *Big Rapids Pioneer* assessed it could make little headway because of the "friendly feeling that exists among the people of different denominations of this city."[33] Black and white residents had a long-established habit of coexisting too. The few black families in the area had arrived in the 1870s and 1880s, staking out small farms, developing pockets of settlements, and looking forward to good lives for their children. Their heirs still worked much the same land in the 1920s, but the younger generation began to leave farming for other jobs, and at the same time, new work in the factory cities diverted any potential migrants. Mecosta County had 213 black residents in 1920 and Newaygo just 31.[34]

Strangers in general were a novelty. This entire region was dominated by a solid majority who were staunch Republicans as well as conservative Protestants, but they were people who also asserted their own independent judgments on occasion. Since Republicans had little to worry about from Democrats, contentious internal disputes customarily marked Republican party politics, especially personal and bitter once primary elections became a factor. On occasion, the Republican voters deserted a candidate who had been carried to primary victory by downstate Republican votes, and instead, they cast their ballots in the general election for a Democrat whose position seemed more acceptable on such issues as strict enforcement of Prohibition. People who joined the Klan were uniformly Republican, but they too divided among themselves over candidates in local and statewide elections. Similarly, congregants in the various Protestant churches made class as well as doctrinal distinctions among themselves. Men, women, and their ministers were likely to be conscious of the religious compatibility among their separate denominations only when it came to contrasting Protestantism with Catholicism or Judaism.

Individual Catholics and Protestants likely did express a "friendly feeling" for each other when they had some personal connection. And hundreds of Protestants in the area turned out to vote against the "anti–parochial school" amendment in 1920 whether out of friendship, tolerance, self-interest, or unwillingness to expand government control. Missouri Synod Lutherans had mounted a statewide campaign against the amendment, reluctantly joining the Catholics in this cause because their own schools would have been closed had the amendment passed. Mecosta County had a substantial German Lutheran population, and there, the vote was 2,117 for the amendment and 2,433 against it. Newaygo voters did support the amendment but by a narrow margin, with 2,415 in favor and 2,220 against.[35] Still, in this part of western Michigan, anti-Catholic stereotypes were alive and well.

Those men and women who opposed parochial schooling remained unyielding after the amendment failed. The vehement joined the Klan out of their abiding hatred for Catholics, near or far. A few joined to strike out at Catholics with whom they were in direct economic competition. Others joined more out of an enduring mistrust of Catholic dogma, institutions, and the papacy. All of them welcomed the notion that the Klan's program "calls for your filling your mission in life as an American . . . as a Protestant American."[36] Conviction born of the Reformation was the common denominator among these Protestants of different denominations and separate motives who joined the Klan. Recast as a defense of American democracy, their fidelity became religious jingoism.

The Mecosta Klan was first promoted by an outside organizer who set up an office in Big Rapids. It found a foothold in Remus where the Catholics and their parochial school St. Michaels, just about a mile west of town, made the Klan's agenda immediate and meaningful. Remus and the small mostly rural school districts around it had voted in 1921 to consolidate and build a central public school in this village of about 600 people. Catholics remained opposed because they would be taxed to help support it. The school issue easily translated into a battle for local control. Each side had taken up economic boycotts of the other. Certain businesses closed, and families moved to get away from people they so disliked. In 1923 when fiery crosses beckoned, people around Remus were anxiously girding for another fight at the ballot box the next year.

Remus and its neighboring town, Mecosta, had most of the county's black population, but for decades, black and white farmers neighbored and their children played, attended school, and grew up together. Other than opposing the idea of racial intermarriage whenever the topic came up, people on this side of the state didn't spend much time talking about a "Negro problem." Blame was sometimes attributed to Catholics if there were rumors of trouble in the black community. A February 1924 Michigan edition of the *Fiery Cross* warned that Catholics in the Muskegon area along Lake Michigan were trying to incite a race riot between the Negro and the Klan, then "sit idly back themselves." For three months, the paper reported, many revolvers had been coming in and out of the post office, and "negroes are arming" because these "foreign trained propagandists" are misleading the "colored population" to believe the Klan is about to attack them. "In fact" Muskegon area Negroes should know the "class of men who are their best friends are the Knights of the Ku Klux Klan."[37]

Between 1923 and 1924, three major centers of Klan strength emerged in Mecosta County: Remus, Morley, and Big Rapids. They were the only communities with a visible Catholic presence. Remus had St. Michaels, Big Rapids had St. Mary's, and Morley had a mission church served by a visiting priest.[38] Those who chose to join the Klan were determinedly vigilant Protestants, but more than pious purpose encouraged membership. People came forward to sign cards out of various personal incentives. Friendships, kinships, ambitions, and overlapping allegiances brought them and held them for a time in the 1920s when they hoped their participation might make a statement, perhaps a difference.

On Home Ground

In this region weighted by families whose various connections stretched back for decades, about three-fourths of the Klansmen whose birthplace can be established were born in Michigan, and usually they had lived in the same county all their lives. Most of the rest had been born in New York, Pennsylvania, or one of the North Central states. Over three-fourths of the Mecosta Klansmen's parents were American-born, and a third of those were born in Michigan.[39] The Klansmen were most often married, seven out of ten in the Newaygo County group. Men who signed the Klan cards were people asserting their stake in society, a conviction easily shared with others in the brotherhood because they were often among friends known since childhood. Sometimes, their parents and even their grandparents had known each other too. Klan activities in this rural, rather self-contained area were one more expression of a lifelong habit of socializing with friends, neighbors, and extended family. That their relatives or in-laws were joining the Klan could offer ample justification or subtle pressure to do the same.[40] Twenty-two-year-old Ted Branch, a barber in White Cloud, paid his dues in February 1924, and over the next three months, eleven other men in his family joined, four with his recommendation. They were all businessmen or professionals in White Cloud, one a 72-year-old doctor and another a 74-year-old Baptist clergyman.[41] In part because of intergenerational ties like the Branch family represented, Klan members were of all ages; the median age varied from 33 in Grand Haven's Klan to 37 in Newaygo's.

Like the national Klan, Michigan leaders made a deliberate effort to recruit those in highly visible, respected positions. State leader Carr sent a typical request to chapters: "Will each Klan, if possible, obtain a mailing list of ministers, protestant lawyers, Doctors, school teachers and bankers in their territory . . . so we can mail the *Kourier Magazine* to these professional men."[42] In both Mecosta and Newaygo counties, the first to sign their membership cards were the professionals, the business proprietors, and the men who held middle-level or clerical jobs. For its duration, the Klan overrepresented their ranks. These were the men who regularly took part in several organizations and activities and who also made it a habit to patronize the various tradesmen and stores in town; it was "good business" to spread yourself around. The Mecosta Klan attracted forty-one businessmen, a county newspaper editor, at least one dentist, two bank cashiers, nine public school teachers, and two college professors. The Newaygo Klan included a state senator, probate judge, justice of the peace, the county agricultural agent, the sheriff, chief of police, and the principal of the Newaygo high school. The town of Fremont contributed its mayor, the superintendent of public schools, a dentist, physician, bank president, and a newspaper editor.[43]

Ministers were especially sought after. Organizers were well aware that it was worthwhile to encourage ministers to become members because religious credibility and congregants came along with them. The Mecosta Klan enrolled four—a Methodist, one United Brethren, and two from the Church of Christ. At least two ministers belonged to the Klan in Newaygo County. Free memberships for clergymen were intended as an incentive, although the Klan was not alone in this courtesy since it was a widespread custom to provide men of the cloth with all sorts of financial privileges in recognition of their meager church salaries and in return for their contributions to the community.

Minister-members performed appropriately. Reverend James Leitch from Newaygo's Methodist Episcopal Church, who was born in Glasgow, Scotland, applauded the Klan for its defense of his adopted homeland as well as for its religious positions. Reverend Jay N. Booth of Church of Christ in Fremont spoke from his pulpit about the good works of his fellow Klansmen who distributed food and clothing at Christmas to the poor. Such charitable efforts were in fact common among many klaverns, not only to win public approval but as a matter of course among these seasoned church and club members. Pastor Booth regarded such help for the needy as an example of the finest thing about the Klan, further evidence that "the Bible is the basis for their constitution."[44] Men like Pastors Leitch and Booth not only held forth in their own churches but were regular fixtures on the stage at high school graduation ceremonies and almost every other gathering from Memorial Day commemorations in the "Protestant" cemetery to Fourth of July speeches in the park where patriotism and religion were routinely intertwined.

Farmers, a significant portion of the area's population, were also well represented in the Klan. In the Mecosta and Newaygo klans, about four out of ten members were farmers. Usually they owned the more prosperous farms or, certainly, not the poorest land around. Often these men farmed adjacent land or were within easy walking distance of each other. The Klan usually gathered in their fields and barns. It would seem likely that many of the businessmen, professionals, and comfortable farmers who were such a presence in the Mecosta and Newaygo klans joined because they regarded themselves as guardians of their communities' best interests. They knew their duty to church and state and shouldered it, often securing their reputations with each other in the bargain.

Lewis Delos Capen was a typical stalwart member of his community, a sensible choice to take on responsible positions in the Mecosta Klan as soon as he proved willing. Born in the village of Millbrook and graduated from the local high school, he went away to the School of Applied Arts at Battle Creek, came back to be the teller in charge of collections and commercial deposits at the Big Rapids Citizens State Bank, and then joined the Great War. After a training stint at the University of Michigan, he served in France with the army's 311th Engineers of the 86th Division. Back home again, by 1922 he settled into a 40-year career as postmaster. Customarily, in every community the postmaster's appointment went to someone who had sufficient ties to make it through the patronage system. Capen had more than enough. He was a Republican in a reliably Republican district, and not only was he a veteran, but when the Veterans of Foreign Wars post organized at Mecosta, he was its first commander. His family heritage brought him membership in the Society of Mayflower Descendants, and he also followed in the footsteps of his grandfather who was a charter member of Level Lodge No. 219 at Millbrook. Lewis Capen was initiated when he was 21. For the rest of his life he would follow this path, belonging to a number of lodges and organizations and holding important positions in one after another.[45]

Capen threw his considerable organizational energy and prestige into promoting the Klan, which he regarded as a necessary bulwark against papist influence. At the time he was single and in his early thirties. Record keeper and organizer at the Klan's outset, postmaster Capen advanced to become Exalted Cyclops from 1926 to 1929 when the Klan was struggling to maintain its footing. His efforts quickly made him well known to Klan leadership in the state and beyond. The *Fellowship Forum,* a weekly newspaper that shared and promoted the Klan's agenda, contacted him about becoming a member of the permanent advisory board for a "powerful" radio station they intended to headquarter in Washington, D.C., "for the dissemination of Protestant Americanism over the air."[46] If not for Capen's commitment to recruitment, letter writing, and record keeping, the Mecosta Klan would have had even more challenges given what he termed the "lack of cooperation" demonstrated by "most of the county's Protestant residents."[47]

Like Capen, men who joined the Klan were often members of other organizations. Americans were structuring themselves around all types of associations and for all manner of purposes in the first decades of the twentieth century. On top of the long-established church societies, ethnic associations, fraternal lodges, and temperance organizations, now came chambers of commerce, rotaries, literary clubs, Young Men's and Young Women's Christian Associations, Boy Scouts, Girl Scouts, athletic clubs, dance clubs, and white-only "neighborhood improvement associations." Two weeks before the Klan's appearance in Michigan began to grab headlines, 4,000 members of one typical lodge, the Knights Templar, held their annual state conclave. Host city Flint decided to welcome them appropriately with a huge "Old Glory" strung over the street alongside the "sacred" black, white, and gold flag of this fraternal order.[48] The Invisible Empire, Knights of the Ku Klux Klan, was not a lodge, its leaders insisted. It was a mass movement of Protestant Americans. Still, it presented a new opportunity for brotherhood among those already accustomed to fraternal orders or those who wanted to be.

In smaller communities where social pressure, economic advantage, or easy access to meetings made it worth the time, people were especially prone to join more than one organization. In Newaygo County, for example, 6 out of 10 Klansmen belonged to some other fraternal organization.

Some came to the Klan with the encouragement of a fellow member; one Odd Fellow recommended 9 men from his lodge, and another brought 7 more. Altogether, 158 members in Klan No. 29 were Odd Fellows. Still, there were three times as many Odd Fellows in the county who did not join. The Masons, with 1,350 members, were the largest of the fraternal organizations, but only 173 became Klansmen. Lodge membership was not synonymous with Klan sympathy or with Klan membership. Men in these various fraternal organizations were making their own separate decisions for their own reasons.[49]

While Klansmen most commonly were from the ranks of the propertied and the professionals—the "better off"—certain members with less status were accepted as equally respectable. The usual employment classifications that are applied to work in America become less meaningful in such places as central Michigan in the 1920s. Small-town residents and farmers knew each other well enough to pass judgment based on more than a neighbor's job or the size of his farm. A barber, an upholsterer, or a local plumber who worked hard, attended church, kept up his house, and helped out neighbors might in fact have more standing in the community than an alcoholic businessman or a large farmer who inherited his land only to let the buildings run down and weeds choke the crops. Familiarity among the members also meant talents could be tapped without much delay. Ledford Anderson worked for the Fremont Auto Company as a bookkeeper in 1923 when he signed up with the Newaygo Klan. Although he was unmarried and only 23 years old, he moved into the responsible position as *klabee* or treasurer, probably because of his ability with figures. The secretary or *kligrapp* was Leonard Somers, a single 39-year-old painter.

The butcher, the baker, the local watchmaker, and a collection of men with skilled and semiskilled jobs helped fill out the ranks in Klans No. 28 and No. 29.[50] These men frequently recruited each other from their workplaces. When Kleagle Cyril Waters moved from Chicago to Newaygo to organize the local Klan, he found a job at the Newaygo Portland Cement Company. The largest manufacturing employer in town, it provided him with a living plus a base for proselytizing. He soon recommended 9 fellow workers, and several, in turn, nominated others until 40 employees at the cement company were in the klavern. Klansmen at the Fremont Canning Company likewise brought along their coworkers, and so the pattern went. One independent contractor recommended a total of 14 men, eight of whom were his employees. The men who were not well represented

among the Klan in either Mecosta or Newaygo counties were the men oc-
cupying bottom rungs on the pay and status ladder. Although unskilled
and common laborers made up a substantial portion of the local workforce, fewer than one in ten belonged to Newaygo's Klan No. 29. Laborers
who did join usually worked at Portland Cement or Fremont Canning, or
they were farmhands. Mecosta's Klan included only 15 laborers. Perhaps
men of marginal means had less interest and less time to be joiners; perhaps they were more transient. Probably their absence also reflected the
others' hesitation to seek out men from that "element" of the community.

The "Right Kind" of Foreigners

In keeping with its "100% American" fervor, national Klan policy allowed
certain types of acceptable immigrants to join as associates but not as full
members. Officially, they were to be shunted into an adjunct organization
called the American Krusaders. Regardless of the dictate, the western
Michigan Klans felt perfectly capable of making their own decisions on
foreign-born members. In both Mecosta and Newaygo Klan chapters,
foreign-born Protestants or their children could participate on equal
footing so long as they provided all the required information: "Church
Affiliation"—of self, mother, father, wife? "Can You Read and Write English?" "Have You Made Application for Citizenship to the United States?"
"In What Court?" "Were 1st Papers Granted?" "Were 2d Papers Granted?"
"If Denied Citizenship, Upon What Ground?"[51] Apart from culling out
acceptable from unacceptable foreigners with these questions, there was
undoubtedly some selective recruitment involved when it came to the
foreigners.

Mecosta County's Klan welcomed at least four foreign-born members,
and, in addition, several Klansmen had foreign-born wives. Almost a third
had at least one foreign-born parent, in all cases either from Canada or
northwestern Europe. Newaygo Klan No. 29 included eighteen foreign-
born Klansmen, and, as in the Mecosta Klan, they came either from
Canada or northwestern Europe.[52] The median age in the Newaygo Klan
was 37, but most of the foreign-born men were older; at least nine were 50
or older, and five were in their forties. They were more often established
merchants or professionals from White Cloud or Fremont, two important
centers of Klan strength. Several were area farmers. All but one—a 64-
year-old English-born bank cashier—were American citizens or in the

process.[53] All the foreign-born Klansmen in Newaygo were added to the rolls between October 1924 and May 1925; membership cards for ten of them were dated within the two or three weeks immediately prior to the important November 1924 election. Whether the klavern made the decision at about that time to let foreign-born join or whether they were swept in along with others in this period of heavy recruitment, the timing is probably no coincidence.

Foreign-born or native-born, these Klansmen were locals who knew each other and could agree that the "alien" threat came from the others of foreign background—the radicals, anarchists, or papists. Distant policymakers in Atlanta who opposed regular membership for the foreign-born could just be disregarded. Mecosta and Newaygo men would sort out their own neighbors. That is what they had been doing all their lives and just as deliberately. It was near Fremont where residents had seized Ben Kunnen, shaved the iron cross in his hair, and branded his forehead with iodine as a "Hun" during World War I.

The Klan in the "Dutch Belt"

As the Klan moved along the Lake Michigan shore to places like Muskegon and Grand Haven, Detroit newspapers reported the Dutch were "flocking to the Klan." This was just one more mistaken assessment in a time marred by misunderstandings. Many residents in that region were the descendants of immigrants from the Netherlands who began coming in the 1840s to settle communities along the lake, beginning with the town of Holland. Dutch culture still held sway in the region, although many German immigrants and other nationalities had also moved in over the decades. To outsiders, however, the variety that existed went unnoticed; whether they were third-generation Dutch, German, Swedish, or descendents of American pioneers, they were all labeled "the Dutch." What most people in this Dutch belt did share in the 1920s was a staunchly Republican, religiously conservative outlook.

Schisms had, in fact, fractured the Dutch immigrant community within a few years after its settlement. Internal disputes over issues of assimilation, church practices, and membership in secret societies led the immigrants to divide into the Dutch Reformed and Christian Reformed churches. Although they maintained distinctions reflecting their separate views on religion, church-related schools were a habit among many fami-

lies. The younger generation was more open to the option of public education, but when the amendment that would require all children to attend
public schools was on the ballot in 1920, Dutch congregations helped defeat the effort by solid majorities in Allegan, Ottawa, Muskegon, and Kent
counties. Ottawa County voters had rejected the 1920 anti–parochial
school amendment by a margin of more than two to one.[54] The Klan's
mobilization against parochial schools was hardly a rallying cry to them.
That the Klan was a secret society was another flaw. Moreover, since
speakers and kleagles generally came from elsewhere, they were suspect;
Dutch residents regarded even longtime residents who were not from
Dutch families as outsiders in their midst. The *Grand Haven Tribune* and
the *Holland News* were antagonistic toward the Klan as it moved up the
shoreline and organized in Grand Haven in September 1923.

Grand Haven, for which one Klan list survives, was a port town on
Lake Michigan, midway in the Dutch belt that stretched from Allegan
County to Muskegon and inland to Kent County. Grand Haven, a small
factory city of 7,200, was the county seat of Ottawa County, which included the still predominantly Dutch-populated towns of Holland and
Zeeland.[55] A substantial proportion of Ottawa County residents declared
themselves to be church members, more than two-thirds of whom belonged to either the Dutch Reformed or Christian Reformed congregations.[56] Itinerant Klan organizers anticipated the second- and third-generation Dutch residents who were conservative, Protestant, and vested in
the land would identify with their platform rather than any longer regard
themselves as among the Klan's targeted "foreigners." They were soon disappointed.

Within the first two months, the local Grand Haven unit enrolled
about 141 members from the town and from Holland to the south. Over
the next months, however, only about 20 more signed membership
cards.[57] Given the settlement patterns of this area, it is not surprising that
over half these members were the children of immigrants from the
Netherlands or Germany. It is likely that many of the Grand Haven Klansmen whose parents were American born were the grandchildren of immigrants from the Netherlands or Germany.[58] The Grand Haven Klan
reflected local circumstances in several additional ways. At that time the
men who came to Grand Haven Klan meetings were younger as a group
than those in the Mecosta and Newaygo klans, and they were drawn heavily from the factories that provided much of Grand Haven's work. Unlike
the Mecosta and Newaygo klans, membership was weighted by workers at

the lower end of the economic ladder.[59] The chapter included some businessmen and merchants, but there were no ministers, doctors, lawyers, or teachers among the group. Few members of long-established families belonged, a factor that may have contributed to the general lack of interest. Men who did join were those generally regarded as outsiders. The Grand Haven Klan never managed to move beyond provisional status. This area was just not such fertile ground as nearby Mecosta and Newaygo counties. There was no sufficient audience that concerned itself with any of the planks in the Klan's platform. The professionals and the "better classes" ignored the Klan and so did almost everyone else.

The Tie That Binds: Women and Children of the Klan

Twenty-nine-year-old Lynda Stone was a housewife in Fremont in March 1924 when she became the first woman to join the Newaygo County Klan. Over 400 women in the county would soon fill out membership cards and carry home their own white robes. From birth to death, the Klan became a family affair. Upcoming Klan marriages were sometimes announced in the local paper or circulated among correspondents.[60] Children frolicked with each other at Klan family camps. Funerals for members were marked by specific Klan rites. Whether they signed cards or not, women were a vital presence in the movement.

Although the national Klan platform decried the "modernism" that encouraged women out of their traditional roles, Klan leaders were well aware that women were a significant body of potential supporters. Some women had begun holding their own meetings as an offshoot of activities they attended sponsored by the men. After Simmons was displaced by Hiram Wesley Evans as Imperial Wizard in November 1922, he had turned his attention to creating the Kamelia, with himself as its highest official, El Magnus.[61] Evans also had been planning a women's auxiliary and was furious at Simmons's usurpation of power—plus the women's dues. Imperial Wizard Evans quickly announced that the Kamelia had no connection with the Klan and established a counterorganization, Women of the Ku Klux Klan, which he intended as an arm of his Empire.

The national headquarter of the WKKK was set up in Little Rock, received an official charter on June 10, 1923, and immediately installed the first head, Lulu Markwell.[62] According to the Little Rock leadership and the "Constitution and Laws of the Women of the Ku Klux Klan," members had to be gentile, native-born women at least 16 years old who believed in values and ideals of the Knights of the KKK. Abiding by their own Ku Klux Klan Kreed, the women promised to "reverentially acknowledge the majesty supremacy of Almighty God" and to recognize also the supremacy of the Constitution and its laws. That said, the women pledged, "we shall ever be devoted to the sublime principles of a pure Americanism." They avowed "the distinction between the races of mankind as decreed by the creator" and promised to be true to the "maintenance of White Supremacy." They pledged appreciation of the "value of practical, fraternal relationship among people of kindred thought, purpose, and ideals and the benefits accruing therefrom."[63] Patriotic politics coupled with vigilant Protestantism undergirded the Klanswomen's agenda, but they intended to focus on activities appropriate to the women's sphere of influence—child welfare, education, civics, public amusements, disarmament, peace. Borrowing the men's idea of commissioned kleagles and open public meetings, the WKKK set about expanding its base with lightning success.

No female kleagle counterparts were needed to recruit Lynda Stone and the other women who joined in Newaygo. Even before some paid out-of-state recruiter arrived, women in several counties took the initiative to organize themselves. Initial members were women familiar with the Klan through their menfolk, immediately comfortable in a WKKK structure that introduced a similar litany of manufactured titles and the same welcome requirements for admission. Far away from the struggles between Simmons and Evans over which women's organization was legitimate, Michigan women had been standing alongside men at public Klan meetings and sharing Klan work with fathers, brothers, husbands. Klanswomen knew the route to effective action without much prompting. Many were seasoned by the successful petition drive to bring Prohibition to Michigan even before the Eighteenth Amendment brought it to the nation; they were foot soldiers in the petition campaigns that put the anti–parochial school amendment on the ballot in 1920 and would bring it back again in 1924.

Patriotism, religion, and theatrics learned from the men's Klan meetings entwined with the practical business of enlisting allies in their cause. Church meetings were a favorite forum because here they were among women they knew, women who shared many of the same values and worries. At one probably typical gathering, Lansing women tended to their usual church-centered activities, turned to patriotic songs including "America," and then were treated to a suddenly darkened room illuminated by a large electric fiery cross. From a room off the main auditorium came voices singing "The Old Rugged Cross."[64] It was the prelude to a presentation on the Klan.

The upcoming primary elections added urgency to the drive when the WKKK began intensive recruiting by the early winter of 1924. Successes mounted. In Allegan County, 60 women were naturalized before a large crowd in the light of a fiery cross. On the other side of the state, Adrian Klan supporters also reported a large group in the women's order.[65] And in the state capital of Lansing, 200 women signed membership application cards at the end of an organizational meeting. Jackson County women had begun to sign up in the early months of the Klan's sweep through the state. Between 60 and 75 had joined the women's order in November 1923, and another 61 were inducted in December. The Jackson women's order was growing so fast that it had to find a new meeting place to accommodate their numbers.[66] Soon the number of women's chapters in Michigan made it one of the leading states along with Pennsylvania, Ohio, Indiana, and New York.[67]

An occasional enterprising woman recognized the economic advantage of all this enthusiasm. Klanswoman F. C. Dunn who joined the Lansing chapter made a fortune by going to local meetings of the WKKK to introduce her invention, a new antiseptic powder.[68] As clubwomen and churchwomen, such pitches were familiar to the Klanswomen who could take it or leave it. Klanswoman Dunn was more uncharacteristic among her female peers than Klansmen who regularly hustled business from the fraternity. Rank-and-file women were there for the Klan's platform of concerns; they gave more than they received—their time at meetings, their baked goods for fundraisers, their shoe leather for petition campaigns, and $10 in dues. They were there because sharing the values and ideals of the Knights of the Ku Klux Klan was part and parcel of their family life.

Within a year after Lynda Stone became the first to join the Newaygo Klan, a total of 403 women in this county had signed up. Stone came from Fremont, which, with farms nearby, soon accounted for almost half the members in the Newaygo County women's Klan. Fremont, of course, was also a stronghold of the men's Klan.[69] It is not surprising that seven out of ten women in this county's Klan were married to Klansmen. Marriage was the habit of small-town and rural communities, and, like Mrs. Stone, almost nine in ten Klanswomen in Newaygo County were married or widowed, and three-fourths were housewives. The women often had a life-time attachment to the area; a majority had been born in the Midwest or in Michigan.[70] Whether by birth or by settling in, they "belonged" here. Klan speakers and literature harmonized with their own resolve to protect the communities they regarded as rightfully theirs.

The women's Klan constitution required that any potential member be recommended by at least two others, but in Newaygo County, the application card required only one, and often Klanswomen came nominated by a relative or a friend from a fraternal organization. Thirteen women who married into the Branch family of White Cloud joined the Klan, and so did one of their daughters, a 21-year-old student; they were better represented even than their menfolk; 92-year-old Anna Branch was likely the matriarch of them all.[71] Occasionally a man provided the recommendation even though he himself was not in the Klan. Lynda Stone recommended many in Fremont, often those who were her sisters in the Order of Eastern Star, which was the women's auxiliary of the Masons. Almost half who joined the Klan belonged to at least one other fraternal organization or club—the Order of Eastern Star, Maccabees, Royal Neighbors, Rebeccas, Grange, the Gleaners, the Mystic Workers of the World, or a "literary" group.[72]

A quarter of the Newaygo Klanswomen worked outside the home. The largest group were the 18 public school teachers. From the White Cloud schools alone came 7 teachers. These women no doubt solidly supported the Klan's opposition to parochial schooling and likely shared the WKKK's concern about protecting youth from a variety of evils. The other working women, whether single or married, held a range of jobs—as clerks, bookkeepers, dressmakers, a milliner, a postmistress, nurses, telephone operators, employees in the Fremont Canning Company, domestics, waitresses, and women in "businesses." A few perceptive farmers' wives reported "farming" was their work, and 2 women married to ministers regarded their occupation to be "minister's wife."

Parents brought their children into the cause informally and, when they could, by providing formal structures such as the Junior Order of the Klan, which began appearing around Michigan by late fall in 1923.[73] By 1925, Michigan's Junior Klan ranked as one of the largest in the country along with those in Indiana, Ohio, West Virginia, and New Jersey.[74] The Junior Order, restricted to boys, sometimes served as a sort of social club for the members as well as a center for potential recruits whose parents might not be members. The word was spread to the wider community of children by Klan speakers who occasionally were welcomed in area schools. The high school children in Fostoria, Michigan, were said to have "listened attentively to a speaker from the Ku Klux Klan, who outlined the principles of the organization in a clear way." Moreover, these youngsters were "very enthusiastic," and after the address many asked how to make application for the Junior Order. "The girls were just as interested in the movement as were the boys."[75] Girls found their chance to participate in their own Tri-K Klub. At local chapter Tri-K Klub meetings, girls often focused on training for their future roles as mothers. Dues for the youngsters were $3.

Community facilities, bricks and mortar, preoccupied Klan families much as other fraternal, religious, and social organizations whose members were anxious to establish a physical presence in their communities. By late 1923, the Detroit Klan secured 40,000 square feet for meeting space on two floors at 206 Hancock Avenue East. They promptly hung the fiery cross symbol over the door.[76] The *Fiery Cross* newspaper announced each accomplishment. Saginaw's Klan purchased a "solid brick two story building" for its home.[77] In Jackson, the Junior Order had "wonderful growth" and nearly completed a headquarters of its own by January 1924. These new rooms, a report effused, "are filled daily with Klan Kids who are as busy as bees with paint and brush, mop and water, and hammer and nails." It was a "real club" with rooms for regular business meetings but also had a club room where games could be played "in comfort and warmth" and a "well-stocked library" with works of "an educational character" and a "fascinating line of fiction especially fitted for boys and young men."[78]

Another proud investment that fostered family activities was the Klan Kamp owned and operated by Michigan's Knights and Women of the Ku Klux Klan. Located on Woodward Lake, seven miles north of Ionia just off Route M-43, the Kamp offered Michigan Klan families the chance to mingle. Klan families from other states were invited without charge to share all the camp offered—a bathing beach, eight boats, a large Klavern center set in concrete with first-floor bathing booths and meeting space on the second floor, a beautiful cottage and grove, good fishing.[79]

No Anomaly

Their embarrassed contemporaries preferred to regard the Klan's appearance in Michigan as an irregularity of peculiar times, a shameful blot on a solid record of progressive, democratic accomplishments; to optimists,

Klan members were an unrepresentative, temporarily misguided lot. Harsher critics then and later would regard them as fear-driven bigots, hate-filled and vicious. The men and women of the Klan were, however, the same people who were praised when they answered calls to wave the flag, to raise the factory or the farm production, and to do the Lord's work. Western Michigan records plus the varied references to Klan members in communities around the state describe a grassroots movement that flourished, not so much inimical to democracy and American life in the 1920s as firmly rooted within it.

These were strange and fast-paced times—with a rush of black and white migrants plus new types of immigrants; with overcrowded city centers bulging out toward neat worker-owned neighborhoods; with mechanized farm equipment adding to escalating farm debts; with unheard-of hourly wages but unpredictable layoffs; with Prohibition, more drinking, and worse crime than ever before. Countless people who joined the Ku Klux Klan for a time were respectably zealous, people of purpose with an enthusiasm for friends and family, for coworkers and fellow church members. They believed the messages from teachers and ministers, presidents and heroes: that they and theirs *should* prevail. Whether from Fremont or Grand Haven, Detroit or Flint, men and women in the Klan had local issues of their own to settle and a common cause to share. The Klan held out the possibility of strength in numbers.

3 · THE KLAN IN ACTION

I believe that we will have enough Klansmen who are deputy sheriffs on hand to cope with any situation that may arrive, therefore, I would suggest that nothing be done in the way of getting State Police on the ground.

—MICHIGAN GRAND DRAGON, on planning for a Klan parade in Big Rapids

"Do you have an automobile?" membership cards asked. "How many will it hold?" The automobile that had brought such change and population readjustment to Michigan literally powered the 1920s Knights of the Invisible Empire. This second Klan could move faster, farther, and more comfortably than its predecessors on horseback. And they had many places to go—initiations, demonstrations, speakeasy raids, political rallies. Piling into cars, they headed out to protect God and country.

Klan members believed in common that too many people in positions of leadership were indifferent to their obligations, that some had been duped, while still others were cynically opportunistic. As a result, the situation had now become so dire that the true Americans must take action. Without needing any other battle plan, people who joined a Klan chapter in Michigan chose familiar and proven tactics: They became self-appointed enforcers of the law, they had the help of sympathetic public officials and Protestant ministers, and they worked through the Republican Party. Now and then, some men opted also for intimidation and violence. And always, the Klan invoked beneficial laws and the constitutional rights guaranteeing them freedom of press, speech, and assembly.

In the Name of the Law

It required no stretch of the imagination for people in the Klan to regard themselves as an unofficial arm of the law, operating much as the American Protective Association had during the war. Now, rather than tracking down a traitorous element, these law-and-order champions advocated direct action to rout the criminal element, especially Prohibition violators. As part of its "constructive patriotic program," the Klan under both Simmons and Evans consistently pledged to take action against bootleggers. Klaverns in Michigan drew heavily from those who had helped win Prohibition at the ballot box only to see its enforcement quickly fail. Rural Michigan residents had been the backbone of the Prohibition drive, and now their local papers were filled with such headlines as "LIQUOR FLOOD IN NATION'S CAPITAL."[1] More worrisome, signs of the times were close to home. Newspapers eagerly spread the word to let residents know of such local events as "Synthetic Gin Seized" while "Jazz is reported to reign unconfined at Benton Harbor Riverside road resort."[2]

When Klan members took on the self-appointed task of law enforcement, agents and institutions of the justice system often appreciated their assistance or were themselves in the brotherhood. Newaygo County Sheriff Noble McKinley, a staunch Klan member, took the lead in the Klan crusade to halt rumrunners and bootleggers who blatantly violated Prohibition. In 1921 he had earned attention for rounding up scofflaws at the "Moonshiners' Convention." Anyone arrested in Newaygo County could expect to face city, village, and county officials who, like Sheriff McKinley, were in the Klan and had the law on their side.[3] The chief of police and several officers in Pontiac were also alleged to be Klan members active in local politics. The chief was relieved of his duty, not for his complicity in renting the Detroit armory under false pretenses for a massive Klan meeting, but upon an unrelated charge that he was involved in framing a holdup.[4] Connections between law officials and the Klan differed from place to place, however, and sometimes the Klan regarded the police and sheriff's office as part of the problem. Macomb County northeast of Detroit was the target of one more Klan cleanup campaign, but there, Klansmen suspected certain local public officials of tipping off liquor dealers before raids. To thwart these inside leaks, the Macomb Klan imported men who were unknown in the area to hang out in roadhouses, win the confidence of the roadhouse proprietors, and make liquor buys.

In Detroit, as in many other communities, law officers were divided about the Klan. The police force in Detroit was uniformly white, but a significant number were Catholics with immigrant backgrounds who were opposed to the Klan. On at least one occasion, the Klan turned to the legal system for protection against Detroit policemen. Certain police officers detained men circulating the *Fiery Cross* on the streets of Detroit, and they went to the city's corporation counsel to ask if legal steps could be taken to stop the paper's circulation so these street vendors could be charged. A few days later, the superintendent of police asked the prosecuting attorney the same question. In October, the corporation counsel approved continued sales of the *Fiery Cross*. When determined police officers continued to arrest the paper's newsboys, the Klan successfully obtained an injunction from the Circuit Court.[5]

On the other hand, however, the Detroit and Wayne County police forces earned a reputation for racism and bigotry that would endure for decades. Shortages in the booming twenties led officials to recruit from among whites who were eager to migrate north. Many black residents were convinced that this was a deliberate effort to attract Ku Klux Klan adherents. In the Wayne County jail, the chaplain and staffers routinely expressed Klan sympathies, on one occasion prompting disgusted prisoners to erupt in a jail riot in the middle of chapel. One rioter confined to bread and water after the melee said prisoners would not lie down with any "religious outfit that is fostered by the Klan." Indeed, since "we have to fight the Klan outside. . . . I do not see why we should have to carry our battles inside the county jail." In the ensuing investigation, Wayne County deputy sheriff Floyd Thierry was alleged to be under salary from Klan headquarters in Atlanta as one of two chief organizers of the Michigan Klan. Thierry defended himself on the grounds that "if I have anything to do with the klan, it has no connection with my duties as a deputy sheriff."[6]

Overlap between Klansmen and law officers was no more out of the ordinary than their overlap with so many other occupations. As deputy sheriff Thierry plainly said, they believed their Klan activities during off-duty hours had nothing to do with their jobs. After work, law officers claimed the same right as other citizens to a private life so long as they did nothing illegal. It was obvious in one situation after another, however, that personal opinions carried over into on-the-job performance. This mattered in some cases more than in others. Congregants could pick a pew in another church if they did not like the tone of their minister's sermons; customers could shop at another store if they did not like the proprietor's attitude. Citizens did not have that ready option, however, when it came to encounters with their law officials.

Who Is That Masked Man?

When the Burns Law was first passed in the spring of 1923, optimists anticipated that Klansmen would hesitate to make their identities public, and without the mask the Klan would be "as dead as a doornail."[7] Masks continued to be worn at will, however. Soon after midnight on the first day the law went into effect, Wayne County deputy sheriffs came upon an assembly of three thousand hooded Klansmen celebrating a raid by one hundred of their members on two roadhouses that served liquor. Without a warrant in hand, the ten officers present decided to leave, and within a few hours, they reported to the prosecutor's office that there was "no need of making an investigation." Not only had the meeting started before midnight, the sheriff pointed out, but this rally was on private property and therefore not in violation of the Burns Law.[8] No doubt there were officers on the force who privately welcomed the Klan's help with enforcing Prohibition laws and keeping the "undesirable element" in check.

There were problems enforcing the law from the outset, in part because of its loopholes. The act excepted costumed children on Halloween, those going to and from masquerade parties, those in the parades of minstrel troops, circuses, or other amusements. In addition, it also excepted participants in any public parade of an educational, religious, or historical character. This was the provision resourceful Klan leaders seized upon.

When four thousand KKK members gathered at the County Building in Detroit on Christmas Eve 1923, many were dressed as Santa Claus and sported Santa masks, whether out of their jolly feeling for the season's jolly old fellow—or as a way to wear a mask within the law. An astonished crowd of onlookers gathered, some angrily belligerent over the Klan demonstration. A fiery cross was lighted on the topmost step and hurled down into the street. One of the Klan Santas who identified himself as a "minister of the gospel" righteously questioned the Americanism of a policeman who tried to bring a stop to the rally.[9] Elsewhere, Michigan Grand Dragon Carr advised local planners to say they were holding a historical pageant when they applied for a parade permit; someone should paint a banner reading "In Memory of the Old Ku Klux Klan," and Klansmen could proceed to march with their visors down "within the limits of the law entirely."[10] Guessing identities was sport for locals who watched the feet parading by and tried to name neighbors based on farm shoes and overalls peeking out from under white robes. Or, if it was a mounted parade, people along the route identified the robed and masked riders by their familiar horses.

At least one Klan speaker had explained to an audience that the purpose of the robes and masks was to conceal the identity of members so they could be protected against retribution and persecution in the process of bringing about moral and political reforms. Just as likely, in fact, men used the masks to hide behind when attacking their friends and neighbors. In the small town of Corunna where everyone knew everyone else, Italian immigrant Tony Spaniola was open for business in his ice cream and candy shop when a robed and masked KKK member burst in the door and began smashing the store fixtures. Anger gave Spaniola strength. He grabbed the intruder, ripped off the sheet, found his best friend under it, and threw him through the plate glass window of the shop. The friend returned a few days later to explain. He had to prove to the guys in the Klan—who "liked Tony too"—that the KKK meant more than their friendship.[11]

The decision to wear masks or not differed from one occasion to another and from place to place. Whether aiming to comply with the law or to disarm local detractors, in advance of gatherings Klan leaders often spread the word through newspaper announcements: "Masks and robes will not be worn by the klansmen."[12] None of the five thousand Klansmen wore a mask at a demonstration of an electric cross erected at the Seven Mile Road farm near Detroit in October 1923.[13] With pride in their cause as well as support from among their acquaintances, some Klansmen believed that hiding under masks was unnecessary and even cowardly.

Taking Sides

Newspaper editors, like almost everyone else, either supported, opposed, or equivocated when it came to the Klan. Sometimes town newspapers tried to ward off Klan enthusiasts. One Upper Peninsula newspaper reminded readers, "We have a few Jews in the Upper Peninsula, and our observation and knowledge of them is that they measure up most credibly as American citizens. They are good friends and good neighbors. . . . We also have a few Negroes in this peninsula and . . . they average up well as citizens. . . . As for the Catholic, approximately one-third of the population of the peninsula are adherents of that faith." In the paper's opinion, Kluxers were getting a poor reception in the area and should.[14] The *Newberry*

News opined, "No doubt part of the organizers were sincere men" but predicted the wrong sort would gain control in certain communities and use the power of the order for "personal and evil ends." As for this county, said the editor, "We have enough troubles around these parts without the Ku Klux Klan 'butting in.'"[15]

Other editors were either outright members of the Klan, sympathetic to the Klan aims, or unwilling to alienate powerful local Klan supporters. Michigan Klan members, like the majority of Michigan voters, were solidly Republican. So were a majority of county newspapers—all four, for example, in Newaygo County. The *Newaygo Republican* described a visiting Klan speaker approvingly: "Nothing was said of a nature that would offend. . . . It was just a plain talk on one hundred per cent Americanism."[16] A reporter in Saugatuck assessed that the Klan speaker he heard "was not anti anything, but was advocating a constructive patriotic program." Nonetheless, he hedged, "the Jews, the Catholics, and some others might reasonably construe some of his remarks as being somewhat 'anti.'"[17] In Adrian, an infiltrator from the *Daily Telegram* was threatened if he published members' names, and the paper was accused of being run by Catholics. When the newspaper's editor criticized a wave of local cross burnings, he was careful to append the comment that the paper supported Klan aims.[18] He was no doubt mindful that local Klan leaders included the former pastor of the Methodist Church and his successor. Both were respected residents with close ties to community organizations and to Adrian College.

In some towns, citizens found that their objections to Klan meetings could make little difference. The Mount Pleasant board of directors of the chamber of commerce pronounced: "That there being no race, color, or religious problems in this city or county that need correcting, and that we wish no interference from any outside organization, [we] wish to urge all loyal members and peace loving citizens to use their utmost influence to stop all efforts of the Ku Klux Klan . . . from gaining a following here." The chamber refused to let the KKK hold a meeting in the town park, so a local dance-hall-for-hire accommodated the many who showed up. In Traverse City when the city commission refused permission for an open-air meeting on public land, the Klan found a resident willing to let them use his vacant lot.[19]

If the Klan's *Fiery Cross* accounts were correct, direct action against the Klan could backfire. In Sandusky near Saginaw, some people broke into the Klan headquarters and wrecked the place, prying open the file case, tearing up cards and letters, and turning over chairs. Klan leaders seized the opportunity to charge that the vandals left the impression "by these acts of violence" that they had been "foreign trained." According to the Klan newspaper, this act of violence resulted in "an immediate flow of applications for membership in the order."[20] In Cheboygan, however, efforts to organize a Klan were abandoned on the heels of a small riot. There, when a burning cross alerted area residents that the Klan had arrived, a crowd of more than 100 massed around a hall and prevented a planned meeting. They then moved on to storm the home of a woman where the visiting Klan organizer was staying. Amid their threats to tar and feather him, Klan sympathizers showed up, and fistfights broke out in the street. With difficulty, police stopped the riot and Klan opponents dispersed with their end accomplished at least for the time being.[21]

Children got into the fray too. The *Fiery Cross* was "disgusted" over "disrespect" displayed by students of the Catholic schools in Saginaw who showed up at an "American meeting" held by the Klan; they "formed a circle around the speaker's stand and hissed, cat called, and indulged in boisterous laughter while our national anthem 'America' was being sung."[22] Catholic parents in River Rouge outside Detroit charged Ku Klux Klan influences were involved in the assignment of lockers in the public school gym and in blocking their children's accustomed use of the high school for a St. Patrick's evening.[23]

In the crusade against liquor, the Klan could often count on ministers for significant support; it dovetailed with their long-standing, hard-core convictions about Catholics. After one major raid in Macomb County, Klansmen rendezvoused at a Presbyterian church whose pastor, Thomas P. Sykes, had the local nickname "Trooper Tom" because of his leading part in the war on liquor. When questioned by reporters, Pastor Sykes denied any role and explained the presence of a thousand men in his church at two o'clock in the morning as a purely "accidental gathering" of men who "just dropped in." In fact, as well as celebrating the night's successful raid, they were laying plans to raise more money for more "buys" in Hamtramck, a nearly all-Polish working-class enclave entirely surrounded by Detroit. The community was regarded as a fine target since it represented the "class" of Catholic people who drank away their paychecks, refused to surrender their language, and gave obedience to the pope.[24]

Approving ministers saw the Klan as an avenue to proselytize. Occasional Klan visits could add drama to routine religious services. The Methodist Protestant Church in Lansing had an unannounced visit from a Klan contingent one March evening in 1924. About 1,000 people were in their pews at the church on East Main Street about to start evening services when "the doors opened and a band of about 40 white robed, unmasked men filed down the aisle."[25] In a ceremony typical at sympathetic congregations, they paraded to the front of the church where their spokesman addressed the pastor, praised him for his patriotic principles, and then presented him with a Bible, a bouquet of white lilies, plus a silk American flag for the church. A Klan fife-and-drum corps played several selections before it filed out along with the robed visitors. Enthusiastic ministers credited the Klan with increasing their membership. A Jackson minister reported a 200 percent increase in church attendance and a 4 percent increase in membership in the first few months of Klan growth. Another said attendance was up 60 percent and membership up 21 percent in the space of three months.[26]

Frederick A. Perry, former pastor at a Lansing Methodist Church and then pastor at the Plymouth Methodist Church in Adrian, lent considerable personal prestige by his leadership of the Klan. He was a one-man symbol of connections that reinforced the Klan's local legitimacy. Pastor Perry had been instrumental in organizing the home front in World War I, had founded the Adrian chapter of the Red Cross, and organized a patriotic organization of businessmen. He briefly served as a YMCA chaplain in England and France, and he often donned his campaign hat and khakis to lead a patriotic group of followers who drilled on the streets of Adrian. He left the pastorate in August 1920 to enter some unspecified work that would aim at "the Americanization of the Foreign Element."[27] By 1924, Perry would be one of the Klan's two candidates for governor of Michigan.

Many churchmen temporized when they made public statements. While they uniformly supported sobriety and living within the law, ministers were likely to be cautious when it came to supporting the Klan on behalf of that goal. When the president of Albion College expressed opposition to the Ku Klux Klan, he was contradicted by the president emeritus of that respected Methodist school. "Many of the objectives of the klan are right, in my opinion," he assured a local luncheon group, even if their methods of waking people at midnight or whipping "on the strength of a rumor" are "wholly wrong."[28] The pastor of St. Mark's Episcopal seized the opportunity to point the finger of blame at Detroit public officials for the rise of the organization when one desperate woman wrote a letter to the *Free Press* appealing to the Klan for help. She needed help, she pled, because the Detroit police refused to arrest a bootlegger in her neighborhood. In her defense, the pastor preached a Sunday sermon charging that the police commissioner, the mayor, and other civic leaders were driving people to the Ku Klux Klan by their failure to act against bootleggers.[29]

When the Conference of Methodist Episcopal Churches took up the Klan issue, the body passed a high-minded resolution affirming "unfaltering loyalty" of members who would use constitutional and legal methods to deal with national problems and urged "all our people to abstain from membership in any organizations which would substitute lawless methods for appeal to the court and the ballot."[30] The Detroit Council of Churches, a Protestant umbrella organization, voted 26 to 20 to table a motion condemning the KKK and any organization advocating violence to establish its aims. Those in the majority took a route familiar to leaders who were juggling divided constituencies. They favored the resolution but believed it should be "more thoroughly investigated" before the council took any action.[31] Instead, the council preferred the unanimity won by a single-minded campaign against wine, beer, bootleggers, and Prohibition violators.[32]

For the most part, the Klan's racism and bigotry passed unnoticed in Protestant circles. The respected Reinhold Niebuhr of Detroit's Bethel Evangelical Church was a voice in the religious wilderness when he pronounced the Klan was "one of the worst specific social phenomena which the religious pride of peoples has ever developed."[33]

The Tactic of Violence

In the opinion of ordinary, law-abiding citizens, it was one thing when Klansmen took the law into their own hands to stop bootleggers. Lawless vigilante action was another, however. Violence or murders that were significant features of Klan efforts in the South would have drawn widespread reproof in Michigan communities.

Local Klansmen tried to hold renegades in check or help apprehend members who were accused of violent acts. Bombs set off in Traverse City offered one opportunity for the Klan to demonstrate disapproval of such tactics. Klan recruiters had first come to Traverse City in the fall of 1923, capitalizing on prejudice against Mexican migrants who swelled the summer labor force in local cherry orchards and came into town on Saturday nights to shop. Kleagle Basil B. Carleton worked the area for several

months, speaking to assembled crowds about the organization's commitment to "law and order." Then suddenly as shoppers and tourists crowded
the Traverse City streets on a Saturday evening in August 1924, three
bombs exploded in the downtown area. Simultaneously, nearly 25 crosses
were lit at street intersections throughout the city, one large cross flared up
nearby across the river, and a car passed through downtown emitting red
flares as it went. Several robed and hooded men riding in the car held a
lighted sign lettered K.K.K. The bombs caused slight damage, but people
in the downtown Lyric Theater and shops rushed for the doors in a panic.
Children screamed, women fainted, and a few persons were slightly hurt
in the crush. Along the main business street, the explosion broke several
store windows.

A Klan spokesman gave the usual Klan response the next day: This was
the work of the organization's enemies trying to discredit them. When
Klan organizer Carleton disappeared after he was charged as a suspect in
the bombing, a group identifying itself as a "Klan Committee" issued a letter to local officials offering help in the case. Apprehended in Indiana, Carleton was put on trial in Traverse City, but ultimately he was acquitted of
the charge that he had possessed explosives, and the jury could not agree
about whether he had violated a city ordinance. The case was dismissed.[34]

Ku Klux Klan violence in Traverse City became news just when the
Traverse City Record Eagle was reporting on sensational murder trials involving immigrants. Front-page coverage of local Klan activities shared
space with the wire reports from Chicago where a doctor identified as an
"alienist" was testifying on behalf of Nathan Leopold Jr. and Richard Loeb,
two young Jewish men on trial for murdering young Robert Franks. Readers had also just been alerted to troublemaking foreigners in Detroit.
There, Sicilians on trial as counterfeiters were receiving behind-the-scenes
help from their "pals" who were making death threats and setting off
bomb explosions to intimidate witnesses. And in another courtroom
nearby, a trial was under way of a "Mohammedan" accused of murdering
a rival leader.[35] It was rather confusing to thoughtful residents in Traverse
City. Did the Klan belong among such lawbreakers or against them as the
organization insisted?

Incidents of threats or violence against individuals did make the news
occasionally. The Michigan Commander of the Veterans of Foreign Wars
reported receiving a crudely written letter warning him to get out of town
or be tarred and feathered "or worse" after he denounced any group whose
members hid behind masks. A prominent Muskegon surgeon found one

pencil-written note in his automobile and another shoved under his office door, both signed "K.K.K." and warning him to "Beware."[36] Why and of what remained unsaid. For several weeks during the summer of 1924, the case of a Berkley minister captured widespread attention. Reverend Oren Van Loon, pastor of the Berkley Community Church in suburban Detroit, disappeared. Twelve days later, he was found nearly 80 miles away wandering semidelirious in the streets of Battle Creek. He could remember nothing. When he was taken to the hospital, a nurse discovered two-inch letters recently branded on his right shoulder: KKK. Loon was put under guard in the hospital under the assumption that he had been the target of a Klan attack. His wife said he had sometimes attacked secret organizations from the pulpit but never the Klan directly, and the Klan had even held meetings in his church. The mystery deepened without resolution, soon displaced by other sensations of the day.[37]

Working the Political System

In a farm field outside Royal Oak, a powerful spotlight illuminated the flag all night, and a huge asbestos cross saturated with oil lit the sky. Every time Henry Ford's name was mentioned for president, a roar went up in his support.[38] Ford shared their values—this antimodernist Protestant who was straightforward in his anti-Semitism, in his opposition to alcohol, dance halls, and radicals. Ford, whose auto factories helped propel so many twentieth-century changes Klansmen resented, was their icon and favorite son. Incongruities did not preoccupy Klansmen. They had no wish to return to the days of horses. They hoped, instead, to have the advantages of technology but rein in its social and political costs. No one understood better than the Klan members themselves that the ballot box was a ready means to their end; they constituted a powerful political bloc.

By habit and philosophy, Michigan Klan members were Republicans, and they took advantage of their familiarity with Michigan politics to press forward with their chosen candidates and issues. Primary elections were the first line of attack because Michigan law made it mandatory for the major parties to use the primary system to nominate candidates for governor, lieutenant governor, U.S. senator, House of Representatives, state legislature, and city offices in Grand Rapids and Detroit.[39] The significance of primary elections was obvious by the 1920s to anyone who was paying any attention. Because Republicans dominated, the primary mattered more than the general election. Most counties in Michigan were solidly Republican, which often led established Republican organizations at the county and local levels to become complacent. This, in turn, gave the Klan an opportunity to exert influence and made Republican campaigns especially rancorous across the state from the spring of 1924 to the September primary election for state offices.

The Klan made a major show of their potential strength on the Fourth of July in 1924 with a two-day state Klonvocation held on 750 acres of farmland rented outside the city of Jackson, the town where the Republican Party was born in 1854. An estimated 100,000 people showed up, and special traffic officers were enlisted to handle the congestion. Six or seven thousand people paraded through the town where the crowd gathered to hear Imperial Wizard Dr. Hiram Wesley Evans discuss the public schools, the church, and issues of patriotism dear to the Klan. A similar and huge Klonvocation was held in Lansing on Labor Day with many of the speakers devoting attention to the upcoming November elections.[40] The Benzie Americanization Committee's Monday Study Club placed a special boxed notice in the county newspaper before the 1924 September primary urging voters to remember the primary was the place to turn out. "Don't forget the undesirable elements in government machines, etc. always vote full strength. . . . Don't forget that every man and his wife represents two votes."[41] And, when the Pontiac Klan met at the First Christian Church before the local primary, all 400 in attendance received marked copies of a sample ballot endorsing five candidates.[42]

Politically astute Michigan residents were also aware of the power of the initiative and referendum, a now-familiar route for taking issues to the voters. With Klan backing this time, the "anti–parochial school" amendment returned to the ballot, and for the motivated, mobilized Klan, this was the key issue in the election. Much like the earlier ballot amendment, if approved the proposed amendment to Article XI of the state constitution would require children between the ages of seven and sixteen to attend public school until they had graduated from the eighth grade. Had the Klan emerged four years earlier, it would have had a significant part in the hostilities over public versus parochial schools during the election in 1920. As it was, the Klan benefited from the failed campaign because those who lost that time around found no comfort in the democratic precept that "the majority had ruled." The majority had erred. Opposition to parochial schools made many members Klan bedfellows in the first place. They remained steadfast.

A candidate's support for the amendment became a requirement for Klan support whether at the state or local level, and the primary was the time to sift among Republican candidates since Republicans would be almost certain to win in the general election. Klan meetings devoted hours to assembling information on office seekers, arguing the relative merits of men who courted their votes, devising strategies to get out the word, and mobilizing the voters who favored their slate. "Acceptability" required that a candidate stand firm for Prohibition, support the principle that all children must attend public rather than parochial schools, be resolute in the demand for state control of parochial schools, and insist that teachers themselves must come from a public school education.

At the time, the Republican Party was heavily influenced by the liberal and reform wing, men including Governor Alex Groesbeck and Senator James Couzens who were popular among Democratic voters too. Incumbent Alex Groesbeck was running in a seven-man field for the Republican gubernatorial nomination in the 1924 primary. Like the socialists, Communists, and other true believers who entered American politics, the Klan had its own internal factions. In the September primary Klan supporters divided between two candidates, James Hamilton and Reverend Frederick Perry. Hamilton, who had initiated the anti–parochial school amendment, got 129,244 votes from Klan members and other voters opposed to parochial schools; this made him second in the seven-way race. Third-place Perry received 79,225, giving him more votes than two other well-known state politicians—W. W. Potter, chairman of the State Public Utilities Commission, and Thomas Read, incumbent lieutenant governor. Combined, the total for Hamilton and Perry was substantially less than Groesbeck's 348,955, but it was a measure of the numbers who supported at least some portion of the Klan's political agenda. The *Michigan Catholic* ran urgent headlines warning that the enemy was strong and that "DEFEAT THREATENS UNLESS CATHOLICS RALLY TO SCHOOLS."[43]

Aspirants for office, especially some previously marginal candidates, decided to ride the Klan wave into office. Others hastily repudiated unsolicited Klan endorsements that threatened to hurt their chances. In common with the national leaders of both parties, most state and county politicians straddled, sidestepped, and dodged the Klan issue. When the Wayne County Republican convention met that fall, some delegates successfully blocked an attempt to condemn the Ku Klux Klan by name and at the same time repudiated the Klan's political help.[44] It was apparent that

Klan chapters had sufficient strength to score victory or near-victory in several campaigns at the local level in November.

Seizing Control in Flint

Flint was one city where the Klan set its sights on winning local political control. Located in Genesee County 60 miles northwest of Detroit, Flint metamorphosed once it became the center for General Motors operations before World War I. The town had 13,000 residents at the turn of the century and 125,000 by 1920; ten years later it would have over 156,000 with another 24,000 living in the surrounding suburbs. More than half the residents in Genesee County worked for GM.[45]

Flint had become a patchwork of separate neighborhoods. Before and soon after the war, this "GM town" experienced the simultaneous arrival—in almost equal numbers—of English-speaking immigrants from western Europe, non-English-speaking immigrants from southern and eastern Europe, and a quick flood of black and white migrants from the upper South. These newcomers topped off a population of longtime white Americans from Michigan or the surrounding states. Apart from the blacks who were generally relegated to low-paying jobs outside the auto industry, the people who settled in Flint had factory wages that enabled a better standard of living than they had ever known. All of the groups, including the blacks, opened new churches and organizations for people who were their own kind. Flint's public schools were dominated by the Protestant majority, and in response, by the mid-1920s Flint Catholics were operating four parochial schools. Despite all the ethnic-based energy, Flint remained a town whose residents were predominantly native-born Americans who had migrated from rural areas. By 1930, two-thirds of the people in Flint had two American-born parents; more than half of the immigrants were of Canadian and British stock.[46]

Flint's factory force learned to savor advantages of the corporate business-class culture during the twenties. Many Flint autoworkers, even newcomers, were home owners. Houses were readily available in Flint for under $3,000, within the reach of families whose earnings put them ahead of national averages. According to the income standards for a family of five first set down in 1925, although 21 percent of American families lived below the poverty line, none of Flint's auto workforce were in that category.

When they could, men migrating toward the auto boom deliberately chose Flint. Female workers found jobs in auxiliary plants like AC Sparkplug. They were poorly paid compared to the men, but four-fifths were young and single, and their new earnings likely gave them a sense they were women of independent means. Most had not finished high school, yet now they could afford to eat in restaurants, buy the latest fashions on installment plans, and go with friends to the huge new dance hall or to one of the city's 15 movie theaters.[47] Transients always came and went, but most of those who came and stayed found reason to share a citywide faith in capitalism, Protestant morality, and the flag. Middecade enthusiasm for the Ku Klux Klan flourished among people persuaded they needed to preserve those core values in their hometown and protect their own opportunities that might be in jeopardy.

Good times in Flint during the twenties bought workers a rough equality of lifestyle, regardless of where they had come from, and the children of the early-arriving immigrants were now making their own moves into the Flint mainstream. On one hand, this contributed evidence of the American Dream to residents who dreamed of a move up the ladder for their children. On the other hand, people understood that there might be only a limited number of opportunities up that ladder. The children of immigrants might get better jobs than the children of "true" Americans. In addition, Catholics were emerging in various appointed political offices in Flint where, according to their opponents, they were contributing to a general breakdown of civic morality. Little wonder, Klan proponents pointed out; after all, Flint Catholics were educating their children separately in their own parochial schools.

As a trump card in the Klan's hand, Flint was said to be a subsidiary for the Wayne County bootlegging industry and wetter than any other town outside Detroit. Obliging dealers delivered to homes and offices, or walk-in customers could find a drink at drugstores, cigar stores, poolrooms, and even a women's store. Intoxication figures climbed steadily alongside arrests of those charged with selling liquor. The blame, according to the *Detroit News* account of the situation, belonged with the thousands of immigrants who worked at the auto factories and who lived in "squalid frame houses filled with women and children who speak little or no English." Such people and their neighborhoods were reminiscent of Hamtramck, said the newspaper. These people "get their liquor and drink it." Some had come directly from Europe, others from Detroit, but regardless, they arrived in Flint "accustomed to getting as much liquor as they could pay for."[48]

In July 1924, Genesee County Kleagle Maurice "Bob" Steenbarger gathered the local Ku Klux Klan behind a petition drive to recall Mayor David R. Cuthbertson, a Democrat elected to a two-year term the year before. Cuthbertson had succeeded in enforcing Prohibition better than any other place in the state during his first term in office but had not managed to halt it. The Klan petition charged he had failed to control the liquor traffic and vice. His hiring of a Catholic police chief and several married women for City Hall jobs made him unacceptable. The Kleagle hired a plane to drop anti-Cuthbertson propaganda, and Klansmen's work to get out the vote on election day succeeded. Cuthbertson was recalled. He ran a month later in a special July election against Judson L. Transue, a schoolteacher turned banker. Transue based his campaign on promises to clean up the city, attacking both ends of society—the foreign born, who he said were a large percentage of the bootleggers in Flint, and the local rich, who he said were controlling the city for their own advantage. Transue's targets were the Klan's targets too, and they gave him wholehearted backing. Cuthbertson had the support of both major newspapers as well as prominent businessmen. Those Republicans who could not abide Transue crossed over to Democrat Cuthbertson, but thousands of voters who had not gone to the polls before compensated for Republican defections. Transue won the mayor's office with 53 percent of the vote.[49]

Feeling the power of their numbers, the Flint Klan rolled on. Prior to the Republican Party convention, the local Klan delegates managed to get control of the Genesee County convention. The Flint daily newspaper pointed out that party leaders and "wheel horses" who had been attending the county conventions "since time immemorial" were missing from the lists except for the few the Klan backed.[50] By dominating the convention votes at that level, Klan activists were able to select their own men to represent Flint wards and townships as delegates to the state party convention. When the state Republican primary took place in September, a majority of Flint delegates supported Klan candidate James Hamilton for governor rather than incumbent Alex Groesbeck. Candidates the Klan endorsed for other state offices received at least a plurality of Flint votes.[51] As the November election of 1924 drew closer, it was evident that state and local contests more than compensated for the lackluster national presidential race going on between Coolidge, Davis, and LaFollette.

Elections in Detroit

Detroiters girded for a bitter fall. The year before, on election day in November 1923, a fiery cross was set up and ignited at the east entrance of the city hall just as the polls were closing and the Democrat, Frank E. Doremus, was about to be elected mayor. The fire department put the fire out and destroyed the cross, and police dispersed the crowd.[52] At election time in 1924, Detroit police anticipated worse violence and bloodshed. Emotions were running high over the parochial school issue and the mayor's contest; the Klan, now much bigger than the year before, had more practice organizing demonstrations. The September mayoralty primary was the first demonstration of Klan strength. Illness of the incumbent mayor made it necessary to fill the nonpartisan post for one year, and in the primary, John Smith and Joseph A. Martin won places on the general ballot in November since they were the top two vote-getters. Smith, former postmaster, polled about 13,000 more votes than Joseph A. Martin, who had been acting mayor. Charles Bowles came in third, only about 2,500 votes behind Martin.[53] Third-place candidate Bowles thereupon decided on the unprecedented move to run as a write-in candidate. The Klan threw their efforts into getting him elected and showed up to promote his candidacy at every opportunity. Election issues became tangled with the advocacy or denunciation of Klan issues.

All three candidates were Republicans. Bowles, who grew up in a small Michigan town, was educated as a lawyer at the University of Michigan, was a high-ranking Mason, and held office in several fraternal lodges. His campaign emphasized fiscal efficiency and strict law enforcement, which impressed residents who were worried over increased governmental costs and rising crime of all sorts. Martin, a graduate of the University of Detroit at a time when most graduates were Catholic, made no mention of his religion, nor did his opponents. He was acting mayor in 1924 and had held a variety of city posts before becoming an auditor and accountant in private business. Martin was favored by established business and civic leaders and, according to rumors, was preferred also by the Detroit Catholic bishop. Smith grew up Catholic, one of seven children in a poor German Polish family in Detroit. With a widowed mother needing help, he dropped out after elementary school to work as a plumber and steamfitter until he gained a series of patronage jobs. Smith publicized the Ku Klux Klan support for Bowles, and Smith's base developed among Catholic, Jewish, black, and recent immigrant voters.[54]

In mid-October Klan opponents brought in a speaker from Oklahoma who was well known for his lectures about Klan outrages. Hours before the appointed event, 5,000 people descended on the blocks around Arena Gardens to protest his appearance. Observers described bumper-to-bumper traffic in the area with as many as 2,000 automobiles bearing "Charles Bowles for Mayor" bumper stickers. A "riot call" went out for every available police officer. To ward off trouble, baton- and gun-wielding Detroit police hurled teargas bombs and red pepper at the crowd. One person in the crowd was knocked unconscious when he was struck on the head with a teargas bomb; he was the only casualty of the "riot" that was confined to police action. The crowd continued to mill around throughout the speech going on inside the arena, periodically chanting "Bowles for Mayor."[55]

Election day in November brought 308,415 out to vote. It was the heaviest turnout in Detroit's history, thanks as much to the high level of interest as to the recent increase in population. John Smith won victory with 116,807 votes to Bowles's 106,679 and Martin's 84,929. Bowles would have become mayor, however, had it not been for a large number of ballots that were spoiled when voters misspelled his name. Stunned election-watchers around the country regarded his near-success as a statement of Klan strength. In fact, however, none of the three men running for mayor had impressive credentials; they reflected the mediocrity and infighting that had come to characterize city politics once the Republicans of established substance and reputation moved on to the state or national political arena.[56]

End of a Campaign

Republicans once again swept Michigan. Calvin Coolidge received 75 percent of the popular vote cast for president. Groesbeck was elected governor, and Couzens was elected U.S. senator. Both from the reform wing of the party, their success was a blow to the Klan. Beyond any candidate, many Michigan voters regarded the amendment about parochial schools to be the critical reason for going to the polls in November 1924, and they turned out in record numbers all around the state. Even in areas where the population had remained steady or dropped, many counties recorded their biggest vote ever. When the results were in, the amendment that would have required all children to attend public schools went down to defeat. Statewide, the vote was 760,571 against it and 421,471 in favor. This was a bigger margin than four years before. Majorities in 63 of Michigan's 83 counties voted against the amendment. Marquette County, with its multiethnic mining families, recorded the most lopsided vote against it—10,390 to 3,614. The amendment was defeated in Wayne County with 263,786 opposing it and 100,690 favoring it. In some areas, residents remained adamant, and in places like Newaygo County where the Klan had made the amendment their priority for months, support for the amendment had grown since the 1920 election. At that time, a majority of Newaygo County voters had supported the "anti–parochial school amendment," but the margin of victory was slim, just 215 votes. Now, nearly 900 more Newaygo citizens turned out to vote than four years before, and the vote in favor of the "anti–parochial school" amendment netted 746 more votes than previously.[57] Quite apart from Michigan voters' decision about the amendment, the U.S. Supreme Court ultimately settled the issue after deliberating an Oregon law that would require public education for all children. In *Pierce v. the Society of Sisters,* the court ruled in 1925 that parents had the right to send their children to nonpublic schools.

Losing Steam

In this decade when political and moral concerns often entwined with economic interests, 1924 marked a high point for political agitation. The fortunes of the Klan stalled and then went into a tailspin precisely because the organization was in almost every way such an exaggeration of the time—an era when rumors about President Harding's mistresses raced through proper people's parlors, when advocates of Prohibition imbibed at their private clubs or even in the White House, when Teapot Dome became synonymous with bribery in high places, when the attorney general went to prison. The Klan reflected the wheeling and dealing over stakes large and small that preoccupied so much of the nation.

From its initial growth in the hands of recruiters who split membership fees to the various Klan leaders who promised votes for political payoffs, money was the fuel behind the moral crusades. Just when the several scandals associated with the Harding administration were becoming public, Klan members found they had been duped by leaders of their own, men they knew personally. Members had given donations for special projects such as a Klan record company, a Klan temple, and an airplane. Many of these projects disappeared in Klan accounts, and the projects never materialized. By 1924 and 1925, charlatans and scandals cropped up at every level. Klan promoters sued each other. Morale plummeted along with dreamed-of profits.

Similarly, the Klan's crusade against sexual immorality became a public, humiliating mockery when David C. Stevenson, the leader of the powerful Indiana Klan, was found guilty of raping a Klan secretary on a train, drugging her to cover it up, and ultimately causing her death when she took a fatal dose of poison. He was sentenced to life in prison on November 11, 1925. Since the politicians he had put in office in Indiana did not come to his assistance as he anticipated, Stevenson took his former allies down with him by directing his aides to release signed documents showing the extensive corruption that marked Indiana politics. The governor of Indiana, the mayor of Indianapolis, and several others were sentenced to prison for bribery; hundreds of Republican politicians had their careers ruined. The Indiana Klan quickly shriveled from its height of at least 350,000 members. Michigan had been the beneficiary of Klan speakers, organizers, and members who had traveled up from Indiana for a variety of events. Now the Michigan Klan shared the impact of this disappointing embarrassment.

Meanwhile, the Michigan Klan's favorite son, Henry Ford, could no longer be considered viable as a candidate for any political office. Ford's anti-Semitism was paraded in front of wide audiences for months after a libel suit was filed in 1925 against the *Dearborn Independent* for its series of articles on "Jewish Exploitation of Farmer Organizations." The suit finally went to trial in March 1927. Despite editor William Cameron's effort to absolve Ford for the *Independent*'s habitual attacks on Jews, few believed the paper was really independent of him. After days of testimony, a mistrial was declared, but the damage was done. Ford himself apologized to the Jewish community, promised to stop publication of anti-Semitic articles, and closed the *Independent* on December 30, 1927. Anti-Semitism was not put to rest, but Henry Ford's public capitulation was sobering for his true believers in the cause. Marginal zealots pulled back.

The *New York Times* remarked on the waning of the Klan's political strength, a trend it observed in several cities and states north and south by November 1925.[58] Hope for maintaining momentum faded quickly in Flint and Detroit where, just a year before, the Klan had aimed to build political machines. Even men it endorsed or helped put in office turned around and helped render the Klan ineffective. The situation in Flint was an object lesson to the Klan that backing a winner was not always enough.

Once Mayor Transue won a full two-year term in the regularly scheduled 1925 spring election, he moved away from the Klan and courted the mainstream businessmen and property holders by fiscal conservatism. It was the Flint Klan's last feeble hurrah when the last big Klororo or statewide convention met in the city in August 1927. Only 500 Klansmen from all over Michigan showed up to march in the torchlight parade that capped festivities.[59]

Wayne County's Klan was in trouble too. To prepare for the 1925 election season, the Klan headquarters sent in Kleagle Ira Stout who was one of their most effective in political campaigns.[60] Sophisticated by now, the Detroit group brought in organizers from North Carolina, New York, Wisconsin, and Indiana to help plan a block-by-block campaign to get out the vote for the November 1925 election.[61] As in 1924, the Klan supported Bowles who was running for mayor against John W. Smith, the incumbent. Smith and seven of the nine members of the Detroit Common Council had been openly attacked by the Ku Klux Klan, which endorsed five candidates for the city council including one incumbent, Philip A. Callahan, who was a Klansman and a former president of the Detroit Klan.[62] Bowles had disclaimed any connection with the Klan, and according to some assessments, the Klan was anxious to win in the Detroit race no longer out of enthusiasm for Bowles but more for the general effect such proven strength could have on the Klan organization nationally. On election day, Klan automobiles conveying sympathizers to the polls outnumbered the Smith cavalcades, leading the *New York Times* to liken the organization to the Tammany machine. Overall, however, voter turnout in the city was half what it had been the year before in some precincts, and Smith ran well ahead of Bowles, showing strength even in areas where Bowles had run well the year before.[63] Callahan was reelected to the council, but councilman Robert Ewald, whom the Klan endorsed, had rejected their support and endorsement before the election.[64]

Ironically, the Detroit Klan had just received chartered status from the national headquarters in 1925. At their height of power in 1924, the Detroit Klan leaders recognized their significance as an urban base and decided to use their own financial power when the national headquarters kept prolonging the Wayne County chapter's provisional status rather than granting it a charter. Provisional chapters were to the Atlanta headquarters' advantage because those klaverns had to remit all initiation fees they collected. As the situation dragged on into 1924 the Detroit klavern retaliated. They formed a self-designed auxiliary called the Symwa Club—an acronym for Spend Your Money With Americans—and forwarded only five of each ten initiation fee dollars. It was a financial maneuver and a ploy; the Symwa Club maintained the same officers, hall, dues, and goals as the Wayne County Provisional Klan. The same kleagle continued to officially represent the Klan, and Symwa members considered themselves Knights of the Invisible Empire. When the national office capitulated and belatedly conferred the Detroit group chartered status as Klan No. 68, their numbers were on the decline.[65] Soon after the embarrassing 1925 election defeat, the Klan in Detroit ousted Kleagle Ira Stout amid charges of financial incompetence and embezzlement, and when Stout fought back, the scandal hit hard among already disheartened Klan members.

Meanwhile, just days after the election, the trial of Ossian Sweet ended in a hung jury. For a time during the summer and fall of 1925, hopeful Klan supporters had banked on the celebrated Detroit case to stem the waning of enthusiasm for the Klan because it centered on the right of black residents to move into a white neighborhood.[66] Sweet, a black medical doctor, bought a home in a white neighborhood on Detroit's near east side, prompting his neighbors to organize. As soon as the Sweets moved in, a mob gathered outside his home and pushed toward the house, throwing rocks and shouting "Get them!" Shots were fired from inside, and two white men in the crowd were injured, one of whom subsequently died. Sweet, his wife Gladys, and nine friends and family who were in the house were put on trial for murder. The case gained national attention when the National Association for the Advancement of Colored People and the Detroit Urban League brought in Clarence Darrow to defend them. The judge was Frank Murphy who was just beginning what would be a long distinguished career as a liberal reformer. After the first trial ended in a hung jury, the state went forward with a second trial in April 1926, again with Darrow as the attorney and Murphy as the judge. After just four hours of deliberation, the twelve white men on the jury found the Sweets not guilty.[67]

Regardless of Darrow's eloquence, Mrs. Sweet's elegance, or the articulate intelligence of witnesses for the defense, the trial did not change many attitudes. It was a signal to those on every side and in the middle: In a place where fierce, intense attitudes led thousands of men and women to the Klan, a black man with the right lawyer, judge, and an all-white jury could get a fair trial. Detroit was not the South, one more reason for black migrants to keep coming. The case did not open up neighborhoods as some hoped, nor did it help fan Klan fires as advocates anticipated. Rather, opponents of integration moved on—literally to new neighborhoods or on to new strategies. Wayne County Klan No. 68 had lost half its peak strength by 1926 and, two years later, numbered only a few hundred. Grasping about for respectability through family activities, the Klan put on a circus at Danceland in 1929. Financially exhausted, it could not even pay the circus performers.[68]

Conditions in Newaygo and Mecosta counties were indications that outstate support for the Klan also slid away as quickly as it had taken form. By the time of the 1924 election, the Newaygo Klan had gained enough members to advance from provisional to charter status, but when the Klan headquarters finally got around to conferring the charter in the spring of 1925, the local base was beginning to erode. A form letter of inquiry began going out to members who no longer came to meetings or were delinquent with their dues. Recipients should fill in the blanks: "Have you changed your mind in regards to joining this Order?" "If not when will you be in a position to complete your work?" "Do you wish our records of your intentions destroyed?" "Are you satisfied that you have donated (if so) and that your donation be used for the benefit of this movement?"[69]

The women's Klan chapters were struggling too. Lucy Beardslee of Sheridan had been trying in the fall of 1926 to piece together money requested by her superiors on behalf of a Klan cause in Florida. No, she could not take it out of the chapter's treasury "unless it were by the vote of the organization," she was told by Realm Commander of Michigan, La Vola M. Rice from Grand Rapids. And, Rice added, "I am of the opinion that you do not have a sufficient amount in your treasury to take anything from it." This, scolded Commander Rice, was the situation because "you have kept your dues so low." For encouragement, Rice enclosed a few copies of the Women of the Ku Klux Klan Kreed, expressed her "kind personal wishes," and closed sincerely, "In the Sacred Unfailing Bond."[70] Despite the best of intentions, practicalities like finances strained the bond.

Mecosta County was one of the places visited when the national office dispatched kleagles to shore up faltering local klaverns. Kleagle Powers came to recruit and build Mecosta's organization so they, like their Newaygo neighbors, could move from a provisional to chartered Klan.[71] The group still did not manage to achieve the number of members that had been required for full status when the leaders of the national Klan had been feeling more powerful, but now the Mecosta Klavern was approved. The charter was presented in person by a representative who traveled from Atlanta for the event in September 1925. Inducements were coming too late.

Imperial Wizard Hiram Evans stubbornly tried to build group strength on behalf of business endeavors he had in the fire, dreams that required financial support. All the while klavern memberships were fading he pestered local leaders with one scheme after another. Eager to drum up business for the national organization's insurance company, he urged the "Faithful and Esteemed Klansman" to get behind the Empire Mutual Life Insurance Company. Typical was one letter dated March 21, 1927: "I believe that the time has come for the Klansman's insurance dollar to buy the utmost in insurance value that can be given and for these Klan resources to be invested so they will be of service to Klan people and the Cause."[72] A planned radio station, too, needed contributions. And there was the *Fellowship Forum*, an anti-Catholic publication connected with Klan communications and headquartered in Washington, D.C.

Mecosta County's Lewis Capen loyally and diligently organized his followers to help where they could. They put effort into a box supper to raise the $15 they sent off to benefit the *Fellowship Forum*, but the lack of gratitude in return was disappointing. Disgusted, Capen sent a letter complaining that the *Forum* did not print the write-up he sent about their box supper and donation. Moreover, he pointed out, "This was the second article of news I have sent the paper in the past year which failed to reach the printed page."[73]

Klavern leaders became all too familiar with requests for money on one hand and lack of assistance raising it on the other. Capen asked Reverend Seagraves from neighboring Osceola County to speak at the 1927 George Washington Birthday Box Social in Big Rapids because finances "are such that we do not feel like getting a speaker from a distance." He anticipated the pastor would understand since "personally I know that our counties are neither in the best of shape." Pastor Seagraves replied that he could come and speak, but "as you know their will be about ten dollars railroad fair besides the intertainment while their. Could you see your way clear to arange for this?" (spelling reproduced as in original). That same spring, Capen wrote to Michigan Grand Dragon G. E. Carr lamenting, "Somehow it seems impossible to keep up the interest that we feel should be manifest. There are a few of the so-called 'faithful' who like myself have the wellfare of the great order at heart." But it seemed like most of the county's Protestant residents were demonstrating "lack of cooperation." The Mecosta County Klan was unable to meet its quarterly dues. Capen assured the Grand Dragon that he still was one who "hasn't given up" and asked if the state leader could personally come to Mecosta's April 12 meeting because it would bring out a crowd. Or, could he send "some other real 'he' man who would wake them up." Carr could not come then but would "as soon as possible."[74]

Dedicated klavern leaders like Capen who struggled to balance accounts and retain members were driven into deeper difficulty when dues for potential members went up from $10. Effective July 1, 1927, announced Grand Dragon Carr, the donation that must accompany each application for citizenship in the Klan could not be less than $15 nor more than $25. In return, as usual, the applicant would be furnished "one robe and helmet for his free use so long as he remains a member in good standing."[75] Robes and helmets went begging. The Mecosta Klavern, which had had at least 255 members in 1924, was, as of the spring of 1927, "still hoping" to reach 100 by July 1.[76] Already on the ropes, finances and ambitions of the Mecosta Klan dimmed when a local leader ran off with funds. By the early 1930s, the Klan organization was gone.[77] All Capen's efforts and the few remaining men couldn't put the Mecosta Klan back together again.

Lessons Learned, Victories Earned

It had taken political, religious, and moral righteousness to keep Klan members motivated. Now, the righteous found some of their own wanting. People, too, were becoming more preoccupied with their own economic troubles. Farm foreclosures and tax-delinquent land sales were a familiar feature in Michigan's rural areas by the mid-1920s; central Michigan counties like Mecosta and Newaygo were hardest hit.[78] Few recognized the warning signs about systemwide weakness in the industrial structure, but factory layoffs were prompted by more than the usual model changes or down time. Home construction and real estate sales were down in factory and working-class neighborhoods from at least 1926 onward. A ripple effect was well under way before the final crash in the fall of 1929. From rural to urban areas, residents faced with financial difficulty had less energy for the Klan and, perhaps, less heart as well.

Men and women who had been Klan activists could tell themselves there was less need for continuing at a fever pitch. Many of their concerns had indeed been addressed by new legislation or policy changes—because, all along of course, the Klan concerns were not theirs alone. As things turned out, the school amendment campaign helped prompt changes that mollified many who had fought to end parochial education.

Although the amendment died in defeat at the polls and in the courts, public school champions could point to a significant accomplishment: The Dacey bill, passed by the state legislature in 1921, became effective in 1925 and provided state supervision of private, denominational, and parochial schools, including the qualifications of teachers.[79] When Catholics agreed and set about complying, it cut ground out from under their diehard opponents. Given the funding implications revealed in the course of the 1924 campaign, Protestants understood now that Catholics not only paid for their children's parochial education but also subsidized public schools without using them; until that campaign, most people did not realize that local public schools received the per-pupil allotment for each child who was attending parochial schools. This arrangement was obviously to the financial advantage of taxpayers and public schools; those who had worked to pass the amendment could take some comfort in that knowledge. Local hostilities ebbed. Mecosta County's Remus— where Catholics' opposition to more school taxes had encouraged locals into the Klan—got its new consolidated public school in 1929.[80] Jackson Klan members, joined by others, had brought Bible reading back into the public schools, which had been discontinued years before.

Klansmen had been on the winning side also when it came to reducing the flood of immigrants. They had played a role in pressuring and electing sympathetic congressmen who passed a 1924 immigrant quota law that would successfully reduce the flood of immigrants from such countries as Russia, Poland, Czechoslovakia, Yugoslavia, the Balkans, Lithuania, and Latvia by 1927. President Coolidge promptly signed the legislation, and the *Detroit Free Press* approvingly editorialized that tilting the quota to favor northern and western Europe, the Nordic race, would keep America "what it ought to be" because they require "practically no assimilation."[81] Fear of a continuing "immigrant flood" abated.

When it came to hostility toward Communists, socialists, and radicals of every stripe, again the Michigan Klan had been comfortably positioned alongside the mainstream. High-handed vigilance like the Red Scare and the Bridgman raid was politically possible because so many other Americans shared the Klan's attitudes. These movements appeared to be in check now, thanks not only to citizen and government action but because of internal dissension among radical leaders themselves. In 1924, the first year that a Communist candidate ran for national office in the United States, nearly 1 in 200 Michigan voters compared to 1 in 800 nationwide cast a vote for the Workers Party ticket of William Z. Foster and Benjamin

Gitlow. Those who worried about the Communist "threat" were not incorrect in believing there were significant pockets of sympathizers present in Michigan, especially among factory workers in the Detroit-Flint corridor and in the Upper Peninsula's mining region where the 74,000 first- and second-generation Finnish population were, like their countrymen, more radical than most immigrant groups in the nation. Yet, although Michigan represented the second largest percentage of votes cast in the nation for the Workers Party ticket, this totaled only 5,330 votes.[82] The Socialist Party, with its supporters drawn from among schoolteachers, lawyers, and intellectuals, fared no better. By 1928, Communist candidates Foster and Gitlow lost a significant number of voters in Michigan, slipping down to a total of 2,881. Only in the chronically depressed Upper Peninsula did the Communist vote share increase.[83] By any measure, the Michigan Klan had overpowering superiority in numbers compared with the left wing when it came to wielding political power.

Stark lessons of reality played a part in the way people thought about their power as voters. Even diehards were coming to believe the cure intended by Prohibition had worse side effects than the disease. The problems enforcing Prohibition and the failure of the school amendment did not necessarily make people turn away from politics. Rather, they became convinced they must wield more power more effectively and also find alternative routes to accomplish their aims. The restrictive covenant became a common feature of property deeds. White residents who could go into new neighborhoods moved into homes with a statement in the deed that mandated, "said premises shall be owned and occupied only by persons of the Christian persuasion and the Caucasian race."[84] By 1938, a Detroit Housing Commission inventory would find that 85 percent of all housing in the city was closed to blacks, and 50 percent of all housing inhabited by blacks was substandard compared with only 14 percent of housing occupied by whites.[85] The Sweet case was not a sign that segregated neighborhoods would become integrated or that law and the courts were a safe refuge. Sentiments that had invigorated the Klan movement did not disappear but, rather, took on new expressions.

Lewis Delos Capen gave up on seeking new members for the Mecosta Klan and turned to other pursuits. In the 1930s when he was over 40 years old, he married Hilda Marie Hill whose family, like his, was from Millbrook. The two were lifelong members of the local Methodist church. When he died an elderly man, Capen was eulogized for his eleven years of service as state president of the Michigan Branch of the National League of Postmasters, and his listing in *Who's Who in the Midwest* was noted; he was remembered as former Grand Herald and then Grand Master of the Grand Lodge, as holder of the Grand Decoration of Chivalry, which was the highest honor in the Odd Fellow fraternity, and he was a member of the Society of Mayflower Descendants. His part in the Ku Klux Klan was not mentioned. The Mecosta Klan records he so carefully maintained eventually wound up in the archives of Central Michigan University, open for all to see. Here was no apparent vigilante, no hate-monger asserting anonymity or seeking importance. None who knew him in person or through his files could deny Capen's dedication to democracy as he construed it and religion as he practiced it in Mecosta County.[86] There resided the real threat, in the hearts and minds of Americans like him.

From origin to withering, the Ku Klux Klan was a movement peopled mostly by unexceptional Americans, albeit sometimes "solid citizens." They were white, Protestant, and commonly American-born of American-born parents. Apart from that, there was no typical Klan supporter in Michigan. They came from all types of communities, all manner of occupations, and all levels of education. Here were the Americans aiming to restore a past era imperfectly understood, employing twentieth-century ways to boost their own advantage, seeking a place among friends and associates by sharing a cause. They believed what they heard at church, at school, and from government leaders they trusted. Some had selfishness in their souls and hatred in their hearts. More held in their hearts a nurtured perception: Their land of the free and home of the brave was in danger.

The Klan had staked out an extreme position on issues like Prohibition, Catholic schools, and the need to safeguard America for "Americans." Members in their robes with their burning crosses were willing to take extreme measures to make their points. Their platform had not prompted more responsible Americans to confront the problems inherent in unfettered capitalism or the dangers of unexamined shibboleths about democracy. Rather, by their very zealous presence, the Klan had made less extreme protectionists, religious bigots, and racists appear in the "middle" of the political continuum.

FATHER CHARLES E. COUGHLIN AND THE UNION FOR SOCIAL JUSTICE

4 · HARD, HARDER, HARDEST OF TIMES

Let those who do not understand why the State should be responsible
for the social and economic welfare of the citizens go to the encyclicals
of Pope Leo XIII and Pope Pius XI.
—DETROIT MAYOR FRANK MURPHY, March 24, 1932

When the Ku Klux Klan was still burning crosses on behalf of "the
sacrifice of Jesus of Nazareth; the flames the light which the Savior shed
upon the world," one was reported in June 1926 near the newly established
Shrine of the Little Flower Catholic Church in southern Oakland County.
Within two months, the young priest at the Shrine told the few dozen
families in his parish congregation that he would soon be broadcasting
from their modest church altar every Sunday afternoon, and he gave the
Klan's presence as his motivation for taking to the airwaves. Catholics
could not always brave the trek to church when they might be threatened
by these white-robed and hooded enemies in their path, explained Father
Charles E. Coughlin.[1] Within five years, Father Coughlin would be broadcasting from a tall marble "Crucifixion Tower" erected at the front of the
site where more construction was about to begin on a splendid new
church to replace the original small wood-frame building. His sermons
would be carried over an independent network of 27 stations around the
country to an audience that numbered several million. If the local Klan
gave Charles Coughlin a convenient rationale for his initial venture on the
radio, the bold entrepreneurship and money around Detroit gave him the
opportunity, and, ultimately, the times gave him the audience.

New city buildings were climbing ever higher, scraping a Michigan sky
that seemed without end to people standing in the right place in the 1920s
and looking up. Farmers outstate, small-town merchants, and onetime
miners in the Upper Peninsula were more accustomed to looking straight

ahead under a familiar cloud cover. As the decade of the twenties neared an end too many Michigan residents were on the edge, whether of betterment or despair. Then came the Great Depression, earlier and with more devastating consequences in Michigan than in most places. Less than two months into the Great Depression Father Coughlin would transform what had started as a religious hour into a program demanding economic reform. When the Depression grew worse rather than better, and people tried to make sense of it all, this Roman Catholic priest would muster one of the most remarkable grassroots movements to emerge during one of the nation's most troubled decades. Although some found his influence astounding and others thought it dangerous, neither Coughlin nor his followers were all that remarkable in their place and time.

Carpe Diem

Coughlin was a newcomer to Michigan and the Detroit diocese in the twenties, one of those residents in the right place at the right time. The priest of Irish ancestry was part immigrant and part American. His father was an Irish-American Catholic who had followed work north to Canada, married a Canadian Irish Catholic, and there in Hamilton, Ontario, the couple brought up their only child Charles who was born in 1891. After attending the University of Toronto, Charles Coughlin joined the Basilian Order of priests in 1916 and taught history, Greek, literature, and drama at Assumption College, a boys' high school in Windsor, until the Basilians were required by Canon Law to reorganize. He had already been assisting at various parishes in Detroit so now Coughlin chose to leave the Basilians and his classroom podium for the pulpit of a parish priest in Michigan. Perhaps he wanted to avoid the vow of poverty that Basilians would be adding to their vows of obedience and chastity. Without any doubt, the Detroit diocese represented a multitude of challenges and opportunities like few other places when the 31-year-old priest arrived to stay in 1923.

Like so many other immigrants and migrants, once the priest made his choice he came to Michigan with the zeal of a convert. He quickly made a place for himself thanks to the expansive entrepreneurial climate where personal connections mattered and where risk takers were willing to try almost magical innovations. He caught the attention of Bishop Michael Gallagher during his first pastoral assignments. In the spring of 1925, Bishop Gallagher tapped him to establish a parish in suburban Detroit.[2]

Father Charles Coughlin and Governor Frank Murphy, June 14, 1931.
When Coughlin and Murphy first met, their Irish heritage and Catholic
religion provided a common bond, but each man also recognized there
was a political advantage to be had from their friendship. For Coughlin,
Murphy was an avenue into Democratic policy-making circles; for the
aspiring politician, the priest's huge radio audience translated into
potential voters. (Walter P. Reuther Library, Wayne State University.)

Gallagher selected The Shrine of the Little Flower as the name for the new
parish in honor of Therese, the Little Flower of Lisieux, recently canon-
ized in Rome. Coughlin selected the site in Royal Oak on Woodward Avenue at Twelve Mile. Saint Therese had longed to be a missionary. Coughlin welcomed the opportunity to fulfill her ambition and to have charge of
building his own parish.

This crossroads was fertile ground for a missionary. Four miles north
of the Detroit city limits and the Wayne County boundary, the Shrine
parish site was on the frontier of the new suburban corridor that middle-
class white families were traveling on their way out of former neighborhoods. Until recently, it had been a region of farms and small towns populated by longtime residents, most of them native born. Oakland County

voters approved the Prohibition amendment in 1916 by a comfortable margin, and countywide, Protestants outnumbered Catholics by more than three to one in the mid-twenties, but Catholics were filtering in to the areas like Royal Oak.[3] South Oakland County was frequented by huge Klan rallies in 1923 and 1924. Crosses were burned in the summer of 1923 in front of the Catholic mission church, St. Mary's, at 11 1/2 Mile in Berkley. And there was the cross reported at 12 Mile and Woodward in June 1926 just two weeks after the Shrine's first church building was completed.[4] In mid-November, the Klan mustered about 150 members in uniform and masks for a parade through nearby Berkley. Ten years later, the Foreword of the souvenir book celebrating the Shrine's dedication memorialized what, by then, was Coughlin's authorized recollection: The Klan cross flaming within twenty yards of his new church that spring of 1926 led the young priest to resolve: "I shall build a Cross which they shall not be able to burn!"[5]

Coughlin recognized that the newest advantage for rallying supporters was not the automobile that powered the Klansmen but the radio. Klan leaders had only unfulfilled ambitions for a Klan broadcasting station before the movement shriveled, but for Coughlin, the up-and-coming radio was an opportunity within reach. The Catholic press was calling attention to the "great possibilities of good" that could come from Catholic "radio-casting of a high order." The few privately owned Catholic stations in existence around the country were applauded for helping missionaries and bishops to reach out to a host of people—from those "who would be ashamed to be seen in church" to Eskimos in the Arctic.[6] Coughlin's chances for a radio venture were improved because Detroit was one of the first cities in the nation with a radio station, and the local broadcasting industry was typical of a general local business climate marked by media rivalries, politics, mergers, buyouts, name changes, and marketplace competition. Coughlin probably had the idea of a religious radio program for some time, but the chance to explore the opportunity came when he had been in his new parish only a few months.

In September 1926, a mutual friend introduced him to Leo Fitzpatrick, a new Catholic in town who was the station manager at WJR. Fitzpatrick had been hired to promote the station, and he was in a search of novel programming ideas to boost the station's audience. Fitzpatrick and Coughlin were a good fit. Coughlin had the advantage of his bishop's goodwill plus clerical legitimacy and the contacts that came with being a priest in a large, well-established Catholic population. The diocese had over a half-million Catholics in 1926. Their financial power was apparent in their neat working-class homes, their new middle- and upper-class neighborhoods, and in their presence from the factory shop foremen to the business and professional worlds. In 1926 alone, Catholics in the diocese had dedicated two churches, and four were under construction. They had opened twelve parochial schools and had begun work on five more plus De LaSalle Collegiate High School. Under way were three Catholic hospitals, a new campus for the University of Detroit for men, and the new Marygrove College for women. Such Catholics were a market of obvious interest to potential advertisers.[7] Coughlin saw the radio audience as adding potential members for his congregation, too small and heavily in debt for their little church building. Fitzpatrick and Coughlin quickly became friends as well as collaborators.[8]

Fortified by the vindication of Catholic schools and heartened by the Klan's decline, Coughlin, his bishop, and Catholics statewide were busily staking their claim as part of the American mainstream. Just shaking free of their fiercest foes, Catholics were indeed ready for a priest in their midst who could win the approval—or at least the cautious attention—of a wider audience. Bishop Gallagher was supportive from the outset, and, unlike the treatment Coughlin would have received from most other American bishops, the young priest enjoyed a great deal of latitude with his venture.

When Coughlin announced his radio plan to the Shrine parishioners in the fall of 1926, he explained that the bishop was extending a $5,000 loan to pay for broadcast time. Fitzpatrick, Coughlin soon explained, had wisely advised him to "pay full time" to avoid the "blue pencil of the patron." Initially Fitzpatrick may have arranged for free airtime, but from the outset Coughlin paid $58 a week for the cost of telephone lines that connected him to the station and enabled him to broadcast from his own parish "radio studio." On October 17, 1926, at three o'clock in the afternoon, from the altar of his wood frame church and dressed in his priest's vestments, Father Charles E. Coughlin went on the air live with a "children's hour" and catechism lesson.[9] Seven letters arrived the day after his first broadcast in response to announcer Fitzpatrick's invitation for comments. It was a beginning. About to turn 35, the pastor had been at the Shrine parish for less than six months and in the United States for only three years; he and the atmosphere were energized by possibilities.

Fitzpatrick soon became a part owner of WJR with his friend George "Dick" Richards who purchased the radio station in December 1926.

Richards, president of Pontiac Automobiles for Southern Michigan, was a flamboyant sales promoter who offered free concerts, contests, and galas at his General Motors Building showroom. As new owner, one of his first decisions was to locate WJR studios behind the window of his street-level showroom in full public view. In keeping with Richards's typically grand plans, he also soon purchased a professional Ohio football club, brought it to Detroit, and his Detroit Lions became the championship team in 1935.[10] Richards was an Episcopalian but, like Fitzpatrick, was quickly captivated by the priest and developed a friendship with him. Coughlin's Sunday afternoon broadcasts became one of the new assets on a revamped WJR, "The Goodwill Station." A spate of creative programs boosted listener interest—the 1927 broadcast of Charles A. Lindbergh's triumphant return from his flight across the Atlantic, a radio program from the Michigan Theatre's stage, a broadcast from a Ford Tri-Motor plane at Ford Airport in Dearborn.

In the hands of these new owners, WJR was on its way to becoming the beacon of Detroit's New Center where it was housed. Three miles north of downtown, the New Center was created in the late 1920s when the huge General Motors office building and the spectacular Fisher Building opened for business on opposite sides of West Grand Boulevard. Here high-powered executives and cream-of-the-white-collar Detroiters wielded far-flung influence. For a time, WJR was in the General Motors Building. Then, in 1928, it became the most high-powered station in Michigan when it moved to the Golden Tower, the illuminated top floors of the just-completed Fisher Building. Ever-larger transmitters reached more distant regions where people hurried to buy radios. While WJR was still in the General Motors Building, Detroiters and tourists could stand outside a large street-level window and watch their favorite programs being broadcast live. When the station relocated, the curious had the added treat of the Fisher Building's elaborate, impressive elevators that whisked visitors up to the top where WJR studios were one of the newest attractions in town. To see Father Coughlin in person, however, the faithful and the curious had to travel to the Royal Oak parish that he made familiar to listeners.

Just as he managed financial distance, Coughlin maintained physical distance from company studios, whether deliberately or not. From his first to his last broadcast, the priest stood on his own ground in front of his own microphone—first at his church altar and then, by 1931, in the massive marble tower built in the shape of a crucifix lit by a spotlight on the corner of Woodward and Twelve Mile in front of the Shrine parish. This tower was his "Cross . . . which they shall not be able to burn!" It quickly became a tourist attraction; listeners felt a personal connection with the tower and the priest's work. After just a few months on the air, Coughlin had established the League of the Little Flower that developed into the Radio League of the Little Flower. Members were asked to promote the financial and spiritual interest of the Shrine of the Little Flower by contributing money so the Little Flower would be better known. Contribute they did, if no more than a dollar bill or a few coins taped to the paper when they wrote "the Father." Once he began to build a new church beside the tower, Coughlin's stone carvers put the name of every state around the top of the building to acknowledge the far-flung donations sent to help pay for the construction. Mass-going tourists knew there was always the possibility of seeing important visitors at the Shrine, and Coughlin capitalized on their interest. On one Sunday in the late twenties, word spread that Babe Ruth would be there. Coughlin, through a friend who was a scout for the Detroit Tigers, had extended an invitation for the Tiger players to attend Sunday mass. The timing was good; Babe Ruth and a few of his New York Yankee team members were in town for a series of games and agreed to go along. That Sunday, visitors eager to see The Babe added $10,000 to the usual collection.[11]

In the years when Coughlin first captured people's imaginations and built a following, he placed a heavy emphasis on the Christian heritage and the Ten Commandments. He reached out over the airwaves with a message deliberately familiar to Protestants as well as Catholics. Letters poured in with comments and questions. In contrast to the 150 letters a week WJR was accustomed to receiving, 3,000 arrived after one of the priest's broadcasts in 1927.[12] Here was evidence that the broadcasts could be a forum. His sermons celebrated belief in God, prayer, family life, patriotism, and the nation; they denounced Communists, socialists, and atheists. It was common ground for Catholics and Protestants, and, seizing every opportunity, Coughlin explained Catholic ways to Protestants. A typical letter writer, this one from Adrian, inquired if it was true that Catholics were not permitted to read the Bible on their own. This was one more "common misconception," the priest replied. To be sure, Catholics were not "free to interpret the Bible but are encouraged to read it," and he offered a ready analogy: Americans can read the Constitution, but the Supreme Court has the right to interpret it.[13]

Gradually Coughlin's sermons edged into matters of politics. Initially cautious, during the election of 1928 he did not mention Al Smith even though this first Catholic to run for the presidency shared Coughlin's heritage, religion, and opposition to Prohibition. He did attack Norman Thomas, Socialist Party candidate for president, because "in our scheme of things we cannot get along without capitalists." When he segued into his favorite topic, attacks on Prohibition, he represented other opponents of Prohibition but also gave voice to former supporters of the Eighteenth Amendment who had become disgusted by this "grand experiment."

Hit Hard In Michigan

As the decade of the twenties neared an end, dangerous contradictions within the economy were apparent to some observers. In 1928, Michigan's reform-minded Senator James Couzens led a Senate committee investigation of unemployment and poverty and warned that neither national nor state governments were prepared to help the jobless in case of an economic crisis. With a different notion about reform, Albert Weisbord arrived in downtown Detroit to open an office of the Communist Party because he was convinced that the auto-based economy had fatal weaknesses. And the Black Legion began to organize. This brotherhood of vigilantes took advantage of economic uncertainties to recruit remnants from the Ku Klux Klan or other white men interested in terrorizing assorted victims for fun and workplace control.[14]

Despite all the warning signs, the Wall Street crash on October 29, 1929, took most people by surprise, and they were more surprised still when it became apparent that recovery was not just around the corner. The rich, the poor, and the in-between cast about for new answers or took refuge in old ones. Every Sunday now, Father Coughlin provided explanations about the troubling inequalities within America. By November 1929 and onward, as economic conditions steadily deteriorated Father Charles Coughlin's *Golden Hour of the Little Flower* was most often spent telling his mushrooming audience how to respond in their daily and religious lives, how to make sense of it all, who was to blame, and finally, how to make their influence felt.

Michigan was hit earlier and harder than many other states; its dependency on the auto industry and allied manufacturing had a quick ripple effect. Men and women here might be accustomed to periodic auto layoffs and farm and mining peaks with lengthening valleys, but they now found

Communist parade on May Day, 1932. From the time of World War I, Michigan residents were repeatedly warned that Communists were likely to take hold in the state, especially in its industrialized centers where immigrants and blue-collar workers were thought to be particularly susceptible. Employers were able to blackball troublesome workers and union organizers by branding them as Communist-inspired, but on the other hand, reformers were able to make gains by proposing programs aimed at countering the appeal of Communism. (Walter P. Reuther Library, Wayne State University.)

it hard to believe such a colossal collapse could happen by accident. Old maxims and heroes lost their luster. More than most, Michigan folks became increasingly bitter when men like Henry Ford said the hard times should just be charged off to "experience," that the Depression was "a wholesome thing in general."[15] Ford sales dropped, but payroll cuts were far more dramatic. The company reduced wages and fired workers, trimming the payroll from $145 million in 1929 to $32 million in 1933. By such economies, the Ford family itself managed to continue life as usual. Henry had given his son Edsel a million dollars in gold for his twenty-first birthday at the time when a man making the fabled $5 a day, if he had a job and worked regularly, could look forward to accumulating $1,000,000 in about

700 years.[16] For Edsel's children, Ford had a miniature railroad built on his estate so they could ride it when they visited. Michigan had captured the country's imagination with its automobiles, wages, and opportunities; now it provided the most visceral examples of the nation's miseries.

People in the Upper Peninsula's once-amazing copper country had known hard times but none like this. The big move south from the Upper Peninsula mines to Flint and Detroit factories had already left the people who stayed behind reeling through the twenties on a roller-coaster ride powered more by hope than reality. Persistent rumors had it that explorations would soon discover new deposits—of copper, or of silver, or of something. The Michigan Department of Agriculture touted this region with its poor soil and short growing season as an area of milk and honey that was "boundless in its agricultural opportunities." Meanwhile, Michigan State College initiated an ineffective five-year plan to make sheep raising the centerpiece of the Keweenaw Peninsula's life after copper, while the Upper Peninsula Development Bureau sought tourists as the new economic mainstay.[17] By the early thirties two-thirds of all families in Keweenaw County were on relief. Local governments and employers like the Calumet and Hecla mining company had been aiding laid-off employees, but now they could no longer afford to help. Locals joked that *tariff* was the one word all children knew in spelling bees in the Upper Peninsula since the whole population clamored for protection from foreign copper and iron ore. Now, people began to hope the federal government would get more involved and actively provide them with relief programs.[18]

On the southwest side of the state, Kalamazoo had been a testament to the region's comfortable habits, a prospering midsize community weighted by native-born whites with Yankee or Michigan roots. The town had two colleges, and in the first decades of the century its diversified and stable economy centered around the paper industry, Upjohn's pharmaceutical industry, stove companies, and factories making auto and truck parts. Then the Depression came to Kalamazoo, and the town's experiences were, again, typical for that part of the state. Residents were worried when the city had to spend $50,000 on poor relief in 1930, stunned when a year later the relief fund expenditures amounted to $187,914, and horrified in 1932 when one out of five in Kalamazoo received aid and relief payments took 32 percent of the city budget as compared with 4 percent in 1928. All able-bodied men on relief were required to work for the city, but the roads, parks, bridges, and riverbanks these men improved did not help with the immediate economic problems. The previously staid Republican scene was disrupted by electoral upsets, taxpayers demanding reduction in expenditures, and candidates elected on a tax relief platform yet unable to deliver it.[19]

Ann Arbor was usually buffered from others' hard times because the University of Michigan was its economic anchor. Satisfied and complacent about the state of their town and lives, only about 30 percent of the voters turned out for elections in the twenties; of those who did, four of five voted for Republicans. Like Kalamazoo, soon into the Depression decade Ann Arbor was hit by a drastic drop in construction and retail sales. The semiskilled, unskilled, and black workers were first to go on the welfare rolls, and neither private nor city relief funds had resources left by 1931. Ten percent of the population were registered as unemployed, enough to bring socialist candidates to the local ballot and voters back to the polls. Even Ann Arbor's Republican mayor was quoting Friedrich Engels when he explained that the Depression was "largely due to the indifference of great industrialists to the personal welfare of their employees . . . and to the effect of mass production."[20] Shocking as their unemployment rate was to the Ann Arbor community, other people traveled there from the Detroit area because the chances for finding work in Ann Arbor seemed so much better by comparison.

Flint was staggered early-on in the Depression decade. Disillusionment hit Flint's factory force hard because General Motors had powered an economy that enabled many families to be home owners and a culture that gave young single people reason to believe the good life was just around the corner for them. It took only a few months after the October 1929 crash for them to realize there would be no recall anytime soon. Buick sales, already slipping, had declined by 56 percent in 1930 compared to the 1926 peak. Since it was the town's anchor, Buick pulled along other Flint GM divisions and allied factories. Construction quickly ground to a standstill, and just a year after the crash, unemployment in that industry hit over 25 percent.[21] Work in Flint collapsed like a row of dominoes. By 1932 Flint's auto production and the rest of the business operations were down by one-third and people were desperate. Even those who were saved from layoffs labored in factories and businesses that sped up the pace of work while also cutting hours and wages. The longtime, most experienced workers who were not considered "too old" might manage to keep their jobs at least a few hours a week, but they also earned half or less what they had made in 1929.[22]

Detroit's city government and economy were in shambles. The Detroit

Common Council increased the city's bonded debt by $228,749,695 during the halcyon days of the twenties to provide additional facilities and services for a population that grew by over a half million residents. This meant that when hard times arrived, the city was already hobbled by a huge municipal debt. In 1929, about 20 percent of the city budget went to debt service, and by 1932, 40 percent was required for paying on the debt.[23] Businesses and residents defaulted on mortgages and taxes could not be collected. All the while, welfare demands spiraled until, by the 1932 peak, 192,000 people were on the rolls. Thousands more in need were not even counted. Almost one-third of the labor force was without work in the first months of 1933.[24]

Politically, Detroit seemed equally bankrupt. In 1918 voters had approved a new charter with a package of reforms promoted by experts and citizen advocates of "good government." As a result of the charter provisions, Detroit became the only large city in the country to adopt nonpartisan elections for all officials including judges, and to end representation by wards. The Common Council went from 42 members to 9, all elected at large. During the twenties many of the benefits anticipated from reforms were quickly derailed. Candidates' party identification remained obvious despite the absence of ballot labels, and political issues were blurred by personal attacks. Booming development side by side with organized crime helped contribute to influence-peddling, corruption, and excessive spending. Hopes for electing the best men faded as the most able moved up or out from city government, and turnout at the polls dropped off.

In November 1929, voters elected Charles Bowles mayor. It was his third try for the office, and again he ran against John W. Smith. This time, after incumbent John C. Lodge lost in the three-way nonpartisan primary race, Bowles managed to defeat Smith. Again, as in 1924 and 1926 when Bowles ran, there were allegations that he was supported by the Ku Klux Klan, and again he disavowed any such support, more intent on building a power base in the Republican Party. Bowles campaigned on a platform that he would clean up and shake up the police department. He did indeed appoint a well-regarded lawyer as police commissioner, only to fire him when the commissioner launched raids on gamblers and the underworld while Bowles was out of town attending the Kentucky Derby with his commissioner of public works. Bowles's own reputation was quickly linked with the commissioner of public works who busied himself with taking bribes and dispensing patronage. By July 1930, less than seven months after he took office, Bowles was recalled at a special election. The same night the election results were in, prominent local radio commentator Jerry Buckley was gunned down in the lobby of his downtown hotel. Buckley had spoken out strongly against the Klan, gangsters, and Mayor Bowles. Bizarre charges and countercharges flew around in the failed effort to find Buckley's murderers. An article in the *New Republic,* marveling over the mess, concluded, "Detroit seeks today a big man to take up the burden."[25] To meet the challenge, Detroit voters replaced Bowles with Frank Murphy in a special election. Murphy won easily when he ran for a regular term in 1931.

People in ever-worsening economic straits could neither understand nor excuse the continued excess and indifference of certain rich Americans. Assurances coming from floundering politicians rang hollow. Radio was one convenient and affordable distraction. By 1930 according to the census takers, there were 13,478,600 receiving sets in the nation, a dramatic increase over a short time; eight years earlier stations nationwide had reached an estimated million and a half listeners. Michigan alone had 627,000 radios, one for every five residents in 1930.[26] The radio was a new and important lifeline in this troubling decade when so much seemed uncertain. Hope in finding right answers somewhere hovered side by side with fear that there *were* no answers.

On Earth as It Is in Heaven

In the autumn of 1929 before the stock market crashed, Father Coughlin had two radio programs. Each Sunday from October to April his afternoon Children's Catechism Hour aired on Detroit's WJR, and, in the late afternoon or evening, he aimed specifically for an adult audience with the *Golden Hour of the Little Flower* carried on three stations—WJR, WMAQ in Chicago, and WLW in Cincinnati.[27] Now Coughlin's audience multiplied; beginning in the fall of 1930 his program was carried by CBS on its national radio network broadcasts. Listeners from Newark and New Haven and Hartford and Bangor to Davenport, Des Moines, St. Louis, and St. Paul had these Sunday programs as one common denominator.[28]

His was a familiar enough message: Democracy, capitalism, and Christianity were interdependent. Much like Theodore Roosevelt, Woodrow Wilson, and the Progressive reformers a generation before, Coughlin argued that it was imperative for capitalists to behave responsibly or the whole nation would suffer the consequences of their greed; should they prove unwilling, the government must step in. Coughlin regarded it as his moral duty to popularize the enduring worth of social justice principles set forth by Pope Leo XIII's 1891 encyclical *Rerum Novarum* (On the Condition of Labor) that advocated state intervention on behalf of the laboring classes. People in the Catholic Worker movement soon gratefully noticed that Coughlin was making an impressive effort to educate his audience about the message of justice for the poor that had received little notice outside seminary classrooms. To Coughlin, the pope's encyclical was never more timely, and he soon ventured to link Protestant-Catholic values with matters of church and state.

Historically, Protestant ministers in America had insisted that their religious values were integral to a properly constituted nation, so Coughlin's determination to openly mix religion and politics was a practice common enough. But here was a newcomer, a Catholic priest, addressing an unseen audience. By the last quarter of the nineteenth century, "Americanists" among the Catholic bishops had urged their parochial schools to attend to the important role a Catholic education should play in transmitting democratic values, but most in the Catholic hierarchy were either uncomfortable with the role Coughlin had assumed or outspoken in their opposition to it. As he tapped into Americans' growing disillusionment with the worrisome state of things, however, Sunday audiences found reason to nod in unison. It was not long before he was preaching to a very large choir.

Coughlin's sermons became more insistent. Over the first months of the Depression he repeatedly decried two "radical" extremes: the "ultracapitalist class" on one side and the disciples of Lenin on the other. The audience could almost see him shake his head in amazement that the ultracapitalists would have people believe these periods of depression are unavoidable "normal happenings in the history of civilization." This class, he elaborated, believed that human rights must not take precedence over individual or financial rights, that the government must be conducted "by and for the wealthy," not the people. The other or "second radicals" would tear down capitalism, communize the mines and transportation factories; they would tear down flags of all nations in favor of "one coinage, one government, one equality, one common religion."[29] Capitalism was failing the faithful, and he felt he must provide "plain facts for plain people, couched in plain logic." In true populist style, the priest took after "those gentlemen who hold political sway," the representatives and senators who have "strained at a gnat and swallowed a camel."[30] Prohibition, always his

Meat strike in Hamtramck, 1935. Occasionally, protests were spontaneous and short-lived. In the midst of the Great Depression, Polish and black housewives came together to demand that Hamtramck butcher shops cut their prices. (Walter P. Reuther Library, Wayne State University.)

target, was part of the whole economic problem as he saw it. With only one-tenth the apportionment set aside for enforcing the Eighteenth Amendment the politicians could have put the thirty-five or forty thousand unemployed men in Detroit to work; they could have spent their time devising a plan for old age compensation and addressing the problems of society that were putting too many in prison. But, he chided, Americans could not just "saddle our short-comings on the shoulders of our leaders." The American people as a whole were responsible too—for dabbling in stocks and gambling on the market to get rich quick rather than working for it. Too many thought they could build their homes and lives without Christ. They had been too selfish: "You Catholics who have been Mass-missers and Sacrament dodgers. . . . You Protestants whose only religion has been a dust covered Bible."[31] In these times, there was guilt to shoulder, blame enough to go around, and, in Coughlin's view, a clear and present danger: Communism.

Whatever their religion, the threat of Communism was familiar, and the priest dramatized the choice for listeners: "Christ or the Red Fog." He objected to any dealings with Russia on the part of American firms, was adamantly opposed to any move toward recognizing Russia, and warned that too many Americans were already drifting into the ways of the Communists, turning to divorce and away from traditional values. Coughlin's antagonism toward Communism continued to drive his analysis. The nature of Communism was "both immoral and unpatriotic."[32] To counter what he regarded as its antireligious, anticapitalist, antidemocratic doctrines, Coughlin was unwavering in his own philosophy: Christians, out of their common faith in God, must rally to demand a more just distribution of the nation's wealth in order to stave off a revolt against democracy. The dangers of Bolshevism were hardly news, but throughout the decade of the twenties businessmen were generally praised for their contributions, even likened to Christ in Bruce Barton's best seller *The Man Nobody Knows*. Coughlin called for the capitalist class to put aside greed and to promote Christianity in its own best interest. Otherwise, instead of just turning away "3,000 wretches of humanity" who waited futilely outside their gates for a promised "$5.00 a day job," capitalists would be confronted by an uprising of workers who would break down the "growing system of plutocracy and un-Christliness."[33]

This was his same message a few months later when, in the spring of 1930, a congressional subcommittee headed by Hamilton Fish from New York began holding hearings in major cities around the country to investigate the extent and reach of Communism in America. Father Coughlin was one of eleven witnesses when the committee visited Detroit. It was his testimony that made the headline in the *New York Times* account: "PRIEST SAYS FORD AIDS COMMUNISM."[34] Coughlin asserted that "the greatest force in the movement to internationalize labor throughout the world is Henry Ford." The priest pointed to Ford's statement a year before on the eve of the auto show that he required 30,000 more workers at his factory in Detroit, and then, Coughlin reminded listeners, when 40,000 showed up to stand outside in freezing weather, they were greeted with fire hoses to drive them away. This was not done on purpose, but "through ignorance," just as Ford financed the peace ship to end the war in Europe "through ignorance." And now, the priest pointed out, Ford's money was helping the Soviet government by signing a $13,000,000 contract. Coughlin's picture was one of a naive, unfettered capitalist causing untold damage.

Of those who testified, only Coughlin predicted a revolution was near. Others minimized the presence of Communists in Michigan; estimates of the number in Detroit varied from 1,500 to 5,000 if "sympathizers" were included. It was generally agreed that at least 90 percent of them were foreigners, but no one hinted that foreigners might be potential Communists, not even testimony of the Department of Justice agent who directed the rounding up of 827 suspects during the Detroit Red Raids in 1920. The commissioner of public safety from Hamtramck pointed out that he employed persons of 57 nationalities, and the suburb had "huge numbers of foreigners," but he knew only one bona fide Communist, a candidate running for the legislature. Indeed, he pointed out, more people in Hamtramck were homeowners than in any other city its size in the country, and the "whole spirit of the community is against communism."[35]

It was because of their anti-Communist spirit that so many in Hamtramck and other communities were worried. When the congressional committee moved on to Chicago, a police lieutenant testified that 51,685 persons in the United States were in organizations "definitely affiliated with communism," and 79,325 others in groups sympathetic with Communistic aims—70 percent aliens, 20 percent Negroes, and 10 percent native born. But the situation was "well in hand" because opposed to these were 1,089,107 in organizations that he classed as "active enemies" of the Soviet system—the American Legion and the American Federation of Labor, for example. But Communists were "making headway with the Negro race," and they "had taken special advantage of the unemployment situation, the market depression and dissatisfaction with the prohibition law." Wherever it went, the Fish committee heard of few Communists and legions of anti-Communists. Nonetheless, at the Fish hearings one common sentiment surfaced: "Unemployment tends to increase the interest in such movements."[36] Economic conditions were worsening by the month. Was not an increase in the appeal of Communism to be expected, people wondered?

Coughlin issued no call to arms against the Soviets, however. He used the occasion of Armistice Day in 1930 to assert that the recent "war to make the world safe for democracy" had failed miserably, had left people to "ponder upon the futility and the barren results" of war. Those who lived through it were left to witness the rise of Bolshevism, a society where federal prisons had become overcrowded, where unlicensed saloons triply multiplied, and where more murders happened in Detroit alone in one year than in all the British Isles. Listeners heard not a call to war but a call to target economic injustice and inequalities in order to ward off the appeal of the Communists.[37] His words made sense to people who agreed there was no sense in Hoover's position that relief is a local matter when, as Coughlin pointed out, right there in his own Oakland County they could not raise enough funds to provide milk for preschoolers.[38] Speaking with his familiar passion, certitude, and instructive detail, he was addressing people faced with a shortage of leaders who offered passion, certitude, or explanations for the Depression.

CBS became increasingly wary of the voice turned loose over their network. His "Versailles Talk," on January 11, 1931, charged that international financiers had caused the 1929 crash. Much of it, word for word, came from a speech by the chairman of the Congressional Committee on Banking and Currency, Louis T. McFadden, a maverick Republican from Pennsylvania. The theme linked up the Depression with the Versailles Treaty's harsh terms, bankers, and England and France, which, he charged, were pushing to get the United States into the World Court of the League in order to profit from the billions invested by international financiers in the Treaty.[39] Coughlin believed that the Hoover administration began pressuring the network after this speech, and also that it monitored him now through spies and wiretaps on his phone. CBS started demanding to see his scripts in advance since he was straying so far from theology, and William Paley, chairman of the board of CBS, was increasingly pressured.[40] Coughlin left CBS by the fall of 1931, and, with Leo Fitzpatrick's help, organized his own independent network that soon included 27 stations which were affiliates of either the NBC or CBS networks. He had more listeners than ever.[41] Now his attacks on Hoover escalated, while other prominent Michigan figures such as Senator Arthur Vandenberg continued to agree with Hoover that prosperity could be restored through cooperation of business and government.[42]

His fan mail became a flood. An average of 60,000 people wrote the priest each week in 1931. It was an all-time high for any of their broadcasts, CBS acknowledged.[43] He received more than a million letters after a February 12, 1932, salvo. There was also a "brisk" demand for his sermons in book form, printed at the end of each broadcasting season. The priest assembled a staff of nearly one hundred who sorted the letters, tallied the contributions, and mailed copies of his books or sermons off to listeners. Contributions tucked in letters helped complete the tower that was his new beacon; planning for a new, magnificent church beside it was under way.

Friends in the Cause

Among Coughlin's circle of close friends at the time was Detroit mayor Frank Murphy. The two met soon after the priest arrived in Detroit, and they had a great deal in common. Both were in their early thirties, Murphy just one year older than Coughlin; both were single, Irish, Catholic, and from close-knit families; both were religiously patriotic foes of Communism, champions of justice for the underdog, and ambitious in their flowering careers. They also had a great deal to offer each other. Murphy, from a small town in the Thumb of Michigan, had been brought up as a "catechism Catholic" with all its mechanical answers, rituals, and respect for priests but with little attention to the philosophical underpinnings of Catholicism. He had attended public schools, capped off by the University of Michigan law school. Murphy had already served in World War I, had been the assistant U.S. attorney for the Eastern District of Michigan, and, when he first met Coughlin, had just been elected a Detroit Recorder's Court judge. Staying carefully aloof from the political maneuvering and mudslinging within the Democratic Party, he was a respected attorney who won widespread praise as presiding judge in the Ossian Sweet trial in 1925.

If Murphy's faith remained ritualistic, his grasp of politics had become sophisticated. Coughlin, who was just getting a grasp on the lessons of politics, had lessons of religion and Catholic philosophy for Murphy's benefit. The two men were on equal footing when it came to their assessment of Communists. Before he met Murphy and ventured into partisan politics, Coughlin had a fine-tuned position about the threat Communism posed to the nation. Before he met Coughlin, U.S. District Attorney Murphy cooperated with Attorney General Palmer's raids in 1920 to seize and jail "Reds." Coughlin was sensitive to the possibility that he might be labeled a Communist himself because he attacked the government and capitalists. As he saw it, all who question or contradict or criticize the present system run the risk that they will become "intellectual lepers," people "seriously tainted with the red scourge of bolshevism."[44] Murphy, crusading for a new deal some years before Roosevelt popularized his New Deal, ran the same risk. Both men were nonetheless eager to forge ahead.

Coughlin's broadcasts and Murphy's after-dinner speeches sounded similar refrains in the early years of the Great Depression when both were gaining new attention. Before he became Detroit's mayor, Judge Frank Murphy had often promoted programs of the type championed by progressive Democrats and Republicans. After he and Coughlin became close friends, Murphy began using Pope Leo XIII's 1891 encyclical *Rerum Novarum* to support his own welfare state reform ideas. When, in 1931, Pope Pius XI commemorated Leo's principles by expanding on them in his *Quadragessimo Anno* (Forty Years After), Murphy was already mayor of Detroit, and those arguments became his just as they were prominent in Father Coughlin's sermons on and off the radio.[45] Both men peppered their presentations with facts, figures, and names. The "radio priest" and "reform mayor" spread the popes' messages about the importance of justice for the working class. Murphy told one audience after another, "There should be no poorly paid workers nor extremely wealthy employers." In a just society employees give their best efforts, and the employer pays his employees a reasonable and living wage. And: "Let those who do not understand why the State should be responsible for the social and economic welfare of the citizens go to the encyclicals of Pope Leo XIII and Pope Pius XI."[46] Coughlin and Murphy were in a different camp of Catholics than those like the Rev. John A. McClorey, a Jesuit who also had a series of radio programs and spoke of God's stern compassion. According to Father McClorey, "God, Who wishes to save men from sin," understands that few men can be rich without falling into a variety of sins. Accordingly, God permits "sickness, poverty, failure, worriment," knowing these and other forms of pain rather than a "felicitous environment" will save them from "spiritual ruin."[47] The nature of God and His mercy was a long-standing theological conflict among Christians. In the dark days of the 1930s, social justice encyclicals and Coughlin's benevolent God won more appreciative listeners. The activist stance taken by Mayor Murphy won more champions than the laissez-faire refrain so many businessmen and politicians clung to.

What Is to Be Done?

The "normalcy" that Americans voted for in the years after World War I had become a forgotten possibility in these grim years. More people were showing signs of more militancy with jobless rates ever higher, economic times worse, and per capita income in Michigan sliding to half what it had been in 1929. As policemen and firemen joined the ranks of those laid off to ease city budget crises, worries grew about keeping order under such conditions. Launching a bold yet middle-of-the-road program for relief,

Mayor Murphy soon attracted national attention for his efforts in Detroit. Although an anonymous Citizens' Fact Finding Committee circulated a pamphlet trying to show Catholics had assumed control of the city government, Murphy easily won a regular term in the 1931 November election.[48] It was a victory built more on his ongoing efforts than on accomplished successes. Relief rolls reached a peak that year with 192,000 on welfare and as many as 50,000 more who were out of work. In August the mayor had alerted Senator Couzens that the city lacked the $10,000,000 necessary, at a minimum, to help those on relief get through the winter.[49] When Senator Couzens offered to contribute $1,000,000 toward relief needs in Detroit if other wealthy men in the city would together contribute $9,000,000, he not only was met by their refusal but was criticized for making that "embarrassing offer."[50] Couzens was disappointed, and state Republicans continued to distance themselves from him and from the needy.

Meanwhile, at William Z. Foster's instigation, beginning in 1929 the Communist Party established over 100 Unemployed Councils in industrial centers around the nation. Foster was chair of the recently formed Trade Union Unity League (TUUL). It was the Communist Party's union arm. The most experienced party organizers and trade union activists were intentionally stationed in Detroit.[51] Michigan had 26 Unemployed Councils with 12 or 15 in the Detroit area, usually united around a neighborhood or an ethnic base. The councils mobilized the unemployed to march and demonstrate for more relief measures, for services for the unemployed, and on behalf of reforms such as unemployment insurance. Campus Martius and Cadillac Square in the center of Detroit became rallying spots for speakers and meetings. One protest against unemployment in 1930 drew at least 5,000 demonstrators and 2,500 city police who charged the crowd on horseback. Once Frank Murphy was in the mayor's office, he was determined to support free speech for the Communists and Unemployment Councils. Feelings sometimes escalated as both city merchants near Grand Circus Park and militant Communists faced off; on those occasions, police with tear gas and clubs ruled the day. Generally, however, Detroit police, demonstrators, and other residents managed a relationship of civility and tolerance. As the Depression grew worse, a significant part of the Unemployed Council members' activity was helping evicted families move back into their homes in dogged defiance of landlords and tax collectors. For this, the councils won support from people who had little enthusiasm for Communists otherwise.[52]

Stories made the rounds—about people with little reaching out to help others with less, about families joining forces across generations, about neighbors crossing fences with soup bones to share. Generosity survived, sometimes even revived. So, too, did selfishness and fear. Sometimes those in direct competition for work, space, and hope fought it out in the streets or at factory gates. Oftentimes, racial, ethnic, and religious prejudices were at the ready in the struggle. Unemployed workers looked around and saw foreign aliens, transitory immigrants, and African-Americans. These "outsiders" might be working in the lowest-paying least-desirable jobs, but if they were working they were targets. The Detroit City Council ruled that no foreign-born workers would be hired for city jobs, even if they were in the process of becoming naturalized. This hit especially hard on Mexicans who had taken laboring jobs on city projects like laying sewer pipes or collecting garbage. Out of work, they were also denied welfare because they were not citizens. Many others were not able to prove they had immigrated legally or that they did have citizenship. The U.S. government officially deported 82,000 Mexicans between 1929 and 1935, but almost half a million repatriated to Mexico, either voluntarily or thinking they had no other choices. Caseworkers in Detroit tried to clear Mexicans from relief rolls by pressuring them to leave and by vigilant screening to see who among the nearly 15,000 Mexicans in the city failed to meet the one-year residency requirement necessary to get aid. By 1936, the Mexican population in Detroit would drop to 1,200. Gone too were most of the Mexicans who had been lured in the boom days to industrial towns like Dearborn, Highland Park, Melvindale, Hamtramck, and Pontiac, to the sugar beet fields of Saginaw, or to the cherry orchards outside Traverse City.[53]

Governor Wilbur M. Brucker issued a press release in the late winter of 1932 warning people not to come to Michigan "under the mistaken impression that work is plentiful." He saw "no way" newcomers could get work, nor could they be provided with food and shelter "without adding to the suffering of those who are already dependent upon public and private charity."[54] Detroit district director of U.S. Immigration John L. Zubrick eagerly cooperated with Brucker. He envisioned a more sweeping repatriation that would send not only Mexicans back to their homeland but also other "alien laborers and mechanics," and "by their removals the openings in industry will be left for residents and citizens of the United States."[55] Governor Brucker anticipated that such measures would help the system right itself again. When President Hoover offered help to the states as a last best hope remedy, Brucker loftily rejected it, convinced that the people of Michigan were able to take care of themselves. Take care of themselves they might, but how?

People from top to bottom were mindful—and reminded often—that 1932 meant it was now a presidential election year. In late February, with the presidential primaries about to start, Henry Ford gave an exclusive interview to the United Press to urge the reelection of President Hoover. Michigan newspapers reported Ford's convictions. The country would return to "old fashioned" banking; Prohibition "is a necessity of the industrial age"; Hoover had done a "first class job," and the country could capitalize on the experiences of his first four years. Ford exhorted, "We need a lot of self-starters in this Country, men who will do what needs doing whether anyone hires them to do it or not."[56] That same month, Detroit's Bishop Gallagher called upon the wealthy to stop withdrawing large sums from circulation and for the state and federal governments to guarantee bank deposits. Michigan senator Couzens opposed such a plan as impractical because the whole banking system would have to be revised.[57] Such debates dragged on. The country, the world itself, seemed to continue unraveling. Meanwhile, Father Coughlin transformed what had started as a religious hour into a program demanding economic reform, and he forged his radio listeners into a pressure group with national political significance.

5 · "BALLOTS—NOT BULLETS!"

As a matter of fact Christ was a demagogue in the real,
original meaning of the word.
　　—FATHER CHARLES COUGHLIN, Radio broadcast on
　　　October 16, 1932

In the long year of 1932, events in Michigan continued to demonstrate the
need for urgency and provided grist for Father Coughlin's radio sermons.
He needed only to look around him for examples to show what was wrong
with the nation, examples that tapped into a reservoir of sentiment about
the nation's elite, the rich and powerful, international financiers, and the
Communists. Sunday after Sunday he confidently offered political and
economic counsel, intermingling religious justifications for this advice. In
the doing of it, Coughlin gave shape to his listeners' ideas, firmed up their
suspicions with facts, and fleshed out the enemies of God and justice. Perhaps about 40 percent of his audience shared Coughlin's religion, many of
them his Irish background. Others just shared his dismay over a nation so
special gone somehow awry.

Democrats thought they could not ignore Coughlin and his broad-
based audience as they looked toward the election of 1932. With the plight
of so many growing steadily worse, candidate Franklin D. Roosevelt
quoted the papal encyclicals on wealth and rights of the working man
when he was on the campaign trail in Detroit. But those precepts and the
priest who popularized them called for more radical changes than President Franklin D. Roosevelt intended once he was elected. Coughlin anticipated that his influence could extend to politicians' programs, not just
their successful elections. He urged his audience that "justice demands"
more than the working people and the poor were receiving. From the

gates of the Ford factory to the capitol steps to the ballot box, many people in Michigan decided to demand justice.

Lessons of the "Ford Hunger March"

Politicians, civic leaders, and the state's wealthiest men kept disappointing and even shocking the public. Some of Henry Ford's former employees still found it hard to believe, two years into the Depression, that he would not help if he understood their need. Despite the near-zero temperature and icy wind, between 3,000 and 5,000 men and women joined forces on March 7, 1932, to march from Detroit to the Ford Rouge Plant in Dearborn to ask for jobs. Conviction, desperation, and anger propelled people along the route of this soon-infamous Ford Hunger March. Union leaders hoped to rally workers to their ranks. Local Communist organizers wanted to make their own point about the self-serving, indifferent men of wealth. Others who fell in line that day wanted to plead their case with "Mr. Ford," the man they had respected as their employer. Marchers carried signs proclaiming their purpose: "Now Is the Time to Act!" "Down with the Men Who Destroy Milk!" "Come on Workers, Don't Be Afraid!" And "We Want Jobs!"

The event was planned by the Unemployed Councils who had asked and gained permission from the city of Detroit to process through the city to neighboring Dearborn. They intended, one marcher explained, to halt at the employment gate and send a chosen few in who would talk with Mr. Ford and ask for part-time jobs. Before they got to that step, Ford's security guard led by Harry Bennett and reinforced by the Dearborn police met them, ordered them to disperse, and opened fire with teargas bombs, ice cold water sprayed from fire hoses, and then bullets. Four marchers were killed, and another twenty-nine were shot or stoned.

Huge headlines in the immediate aftermath told readers it was a "RED MOB," a "Prearranged Outbreak." Versions about the sequence of events differed from one eye witness to another. It was a described as a "heterogeneous" group. "All were not Communists" although "faces of familiar agitators were in the ranks." One marcher said the crowd was peaceful and good-natured, and about 50 Detroit policemen were marching with them across into Dearborn when the Dearborn police began throwing teargas bombs; then the crowd retaliated with stones, and the police shot in return. Dearborn police said it started when a Communist agitator hiding behind a parked car fired six shots. An eyewitness said he saw a man come toward Harry Bennett with a gun and fire, then saw Bennett return the fire and shoot his assailant dead. Another said Bennett drove up in a car and threw a teargas bomb out the window. Yet another reported that Bennett was hit by a rock while riding out of the plant in his car. Some said the police "must have fired 200 or 300 times on the mob" and had "no idea" how often the mob returned the fire. Sorting out a reliable single account became impossible. It was certain only that marchers hurled stones and wielded clubs as they fought police who were armed with tear gas and guns. By the time state troopers, Detroit police, and sheriff's office reinforcements arrived with their tear gas, machine guns, and shotguns, the mob had dispersed. Within hours, a Ford official said it was "up to Detroit" to explain the riot, and he blamed the Detroit police for letting the march get as far as the factory.[1] In short order, over 60 men and women were arrested, either at the scene or in a police sweep that followed, and their names were turned over to immigration authorities to see if they were in the country legally.[2]

The dead were immediate martyrs of this Ford Hunger March.[3] Five days after the march to the Rouge Plant, another procession set off from the Art Institute down Woodward Avenue to Cadillac Square for a group funeral. The four coffins were draped in red. Red flags, armbands, banners, and scarves were everywhere in the crowd, which estimates placed between 10,000 and 15,000. Signs peppered the gathering: "Smash Ford-Murphy Police Terror!" "Hunger, Slavery, Bullets Are Ford's High Wages!" Those who assembled sang the "Communist Internationale," and they sang the national anthem. Probably most in the crowd wanted more than anything for the system of capitalism to work. Henry Ford thought it was working. The Ford Motor Company issued a statement that expressed bewilderment over the march "since this company pays higher wages and employs more men than any industrial organization in Detroit."[4] Shocked by the violence, people accounted for the melee according to different notions—a sign of Ford's callousness; a sign of a growing sentiment for revolution; a Communist uprising.

Just the week before the Hunger March, Americans were horrified to learn that Charles Lindbergh's son had been kidnapped. That Sunday, Coughlin's listeners tuned in to hear his broadcast appeal for the kidnappers to take the boy to a Catholic orphanage or rectory where no questions would be asked and the child would be safe. At his urging, they knelt beside their radios to recite the Lord's Prayer with him, asking that "He will soften the hearts of those who have been responsible for this terrible crime."[5] The little boy remained missing. Now, millions tuned in to hear if Coughlin might have something to say about the events at the Rouge Plant gates. They were not disappointed.

This Sunday, his assessment was summed up by the title of the sermon: "Ballots—Not Bullets!" Coughlin said the march "undoubtedly" had Communists as "the chief agitators and organizers." Yet, not Communists but economic and political injustice presented the reason for fear, he explained. The marchers were "jobless, hungry, dispossessed workmen" who were led into the hail of bullets by poverty, not Communists. People should fear the great imbalance of wealth in the country, they should blame the "supine legislators" who had come up with not one single piece of legislation to benefit the laborers but, rather, had offered the laborers only rash optimism while extending "vicious favoritism" to the wealthy. Coughlin gave listeners precise figures, reporting that an American Federation of Labor survey found 9,500,000 families or more than 33,000,000 persons in America below minimum food requirements or with barely enough for a decent life. He totaled the millions more who owned no automobile, no efficient radio, whose homes were without a bathtub or electricity. All of them would buy American products if only their incomes permitted it. Here was a "stupendous, undeveloped empire within our very midst!" Meanwhile, he thundered, our government, our international bankers and international industrialists were concentrating on foreign markets. Foreign countries had received "approximately $31,000,000,000" in foreign loans either directly or indirectly. He offered a fable: The dog crossing the bridge had a bone in his mouth; he glanced into the water and imagined he saw a large bone, plunged into the water to capture the larger one, and as a result lost everything he had.[6]

True to form, Coughlin not only had facts and figures and fables, he had recommendations. First, a political prescription: If Communists were now promising what both Republicans and Democrats formerly promised and failed to accomplish, it was time for Republicans and Democrats to change their elitist ways. The political parties of tomorrow must "become of the people and for the people and not for the chosen few." And voters had a responsibility to remember that Christ "gave us the privilege of our democratic ballots." Second, the entwined religious prescription: People and the nation must come back to Christian charity as outlined in the Epistle of St. Paul to the Corinthians and that Coughlin read to conclude this broadcast.[7]

Critics escalated the cry that Coughlin was setting class against class. William Cardinal O'Connell, head of the Catholic hierarchy in America, said Coughlin was fanning the fire of unrest and had stepped out of his place as a priest. Bishop Gallagher was quick to instruct Catholic readers of the *Michigan Catholic* that Coughlin had said nothing so strong about the abuse of wealth and power as the utterances of popes Leo XIII, Pius XI, or Christ.[8] Gallagher, since his seminary days in Austria, had been nearly obsessed with what he called the "morals of money," and social and economic justice. He was willing to support Coughlin regardless of the price it cost him within the hierarchy.[9] Radio listeners, perhaps as many as 30,000,000 strong and as many as 60 percent of them not Catholics, were willing to give Coughlin's ideas an audience. For many, he was their compass in the maze.

Less than four months after the Ford Hunger March, a Wayne County jury vindicated the Dearborn police for their actions and for the deaths of the men. The grand jury decided that Communist agitators instigated the march and that police were justified in using gunfire to protect "life and property" endangered by the marchers. But the grand jury refused to return an indictment sought by Republican county prosecutor Harry Toy who hoped to use Michigan's Criminal Syndicalist Act of 1931 to prosecute the leaders he deemed "revolutionaries." Henry Ford had turned from the investigations of Communists at his plant gates to tend to business; while the grand jury hearings were under way, he was hosting a large delegation of Soviet scientists and technicians. They were touring the Rouge Plant to study Ford production methods as part of his $30 million financial deal with Communist Russia to school Soviet engineers.[10]

Lessons of the "Bonus Army"

While Ford was negotiating business deals with the Soviet Communists, in June the government resorted to arms against World War I veterans in the Bonus Army, convinced they included Communists marching on the gates of Washington. At issue was the Patman "bonus bill." In the halls of Congress an often bitter debate was raging as members considered the bill that, if passed, would immediately pay veterans the cash bonuses they were scheduled to receive in 1945.

Watchful Americans were divided over this issue. Some regarded the veterans' cause as just, while others saw it as too expensive or worse—as one more sign of dangerous, Communist-inspired civil disorder. Local Michigan papers were filled with letters. Men who had been in World War I, many of them now among the unemployed, were focusing on the issue that carried financial and emotional significance, and they were also divided among themselves. Some Michigan veterans agreed with the argument that it would cost the government too much—about $2,400,000,000—to give the bonuses early. On the other side, one veteran responded, "Did you express your indignation when our Federal Government canceled over $10,000,000,000 in foreign war debts that the taxpayers of this Country have had to pay in taxes?" And, another who "tramped the streets in winter, hungry and cold" asked readers, "How would you like to work hard for a year and not draw a cent of your wages for 15 or 20 years? . . . We [soldiers] were young, gullible fools believing anything."[11]

Unemployed veterans, 15,000 strong, headed for Washington from all over the country to lobby while Congress was locked in debate in the spring of 1932. The members of this "Bonus Army" or "Bonus Expeditionary Force" arrived by the truckload or in old cars carrying along wives and children. They set up a shantytown camp at Anacostia just across the river from the Capitol and trekked in every day to walk around the building carrying signs that urged passage of the bonus bill. Many had already taken out loans against their bonus certificates and, unable to repay the 4 1/2 percent interest the government charged them, the principal of their bonuses was being eaten away. Hoover opposed the bill out of concern for the federal budget. On June 17 the Senate voted it down by a 62 to 18 vote. Michigan's senators Couzens and Vandenberg joined those who voted against it. Senator Vandenberg was responsible for the earlier bill that, since 1931, had enabled veterans to borrow against their bonuses, and Couzens, too, had supported that help for the veterans. But finally both men voted against the Patman bill because they agreed with Hoover that the government could not afford the cost.[12] Most of the marchers drifted away toward home but some stayed on. Reinforcements came to keep the cause alive.

Three hundred Michigan veterans signed up for what the newspapers were calling the "Second Bonus Army," and they were prepared to leave

Detroit for Washington on June 27. Merchants, wholesale dealers, store-keepers, and bakers donated hams, cans of milk, bags of onions, rutabagas, carrots, noodles, salt, and bread. The provisions would feed them better along the way than many had been eating at home. A dump truck accompanied the caravan to carry food, 150 gallons of gasoline, and 50 gallons of oil donated by a couple who operated a service station in the Detroit suburb of Rosedale Park. Each veteran was responsible for finding his own tin cup, eating tools, toothbrush, towel, soap, razor, and a complete change of underwear. A Red Cross worker from the world war helped with bandages, iodine, and minor medical needs. Two trombonists played "Fall In" as 35 automobiles, 7 trucks, and 13 trailers left Detroit for Washington.[13] The mayor of Washington became concerned; so did the police chief. Just when Michigan's contingent was arriving, the situation turned ugly.

President Hoover was persuaded to send in the U.S. Army on July 28 to force the veterans to depart. Douglas MacArthur led the army of four infantry companies, four troops of cavalry, a machine gun squadron, and six tanks. They rolled over the camp populated by people Hoover labeled "insurrectionists"; they tear-gassed women and children along with the men and burned their shacks, and all the while the cavalry chased men and women on foot. Hoover regarded the army's role as a wise action: "Thank God we still have a government that knows how to deal with a mob." This "mob" and countless veterans back home mentally filed away the government's treatment of them, one more unfeeling response to remember.

From the time the Patman bonus bill was first introduced, audiences heard Coughlin insist charity and justice were due the veterans who needed their bonuses immediately rather than in 1945. After all, he instructed, "thirty billion dollars worth of our national and private gold poured out of the country for one purpose or another," but yet the nation had "begrudgingly bestowed" only a "few pitiful million dollars" upon the veterans who returned.[14] Those in the government who hesitated to give bonuses might practice "excellent finance" but they also practiced "poor democracy and poorer Christianity."[15] He ridiculed secretary of the treasury Mellon for saying it would bankrupt the nation to pay the $2,000,000,000 debt owed the men who fought in the last war yet did not seem to think it would bankrupt the United States to create a $1,000,000,000 Reconstruction Finance Corporation to pour money into the banking industries of the nation. Nor, he noted, did the Congress worry over bankruptcy when it canceled debts foreign nations owed us.

Coughlin presented a list of amounts the bonus would come to in the cities where his "Golden Hour" broadcast reached. New York City veterans would total the largest sum, $132,271,518; Detroit was second with $27,370,104.[16]

Coughlin had gone before a congressional committee to advocate for the bonus bill in April 1932 when it was still under consideration. Already angry with the Hoover administration over so many actions and inactions, their treatment of the Bonus Army was one more reason for Coughlin to remind his listeners that another day, another election was coming.

Catholics: "5,000,000 Voters"

The 1932 presidential conventions and campaigns swung into gear accompanied by vivid, mind's-eye memories and daily reminders—of Hunger Marchers and troops turned on former troops, of abandoned mines, farms, and stores, of unemployed men in soup kitchen lines. When Hoover came to Detroit to kick off his campaign, people with nowhere else to go lined up to boo or stand silent along his parade route. Vandenberg offered the president his loyal support and did his best to help the Republicans hold Michigan. Couzens could no longer abide Hoover's economic ideas and remained silent. Michigan Democratic factions buried the hatchet in the interest of winning, and newspapers reported that Father Charles Coughlin went to the convention in Chicago with Mayor Frank Murphy to support the nomination of Franklin D. Roosevelt.

Murphy had been working with the Roosevelt campaign and was sometimes considered a possible vice presidential candidate. Coughlin was drawn into the Roosevelt circle, perhaps through Murphy or G. Hall Roosevelt, FDR's brother-in-law, who was controller of Detroit and who passed along the word that Coughlin had 26 secretaries handling 200,000 letters a week in the spring of 1932.[17] Certainly, by 1932 the priest had a far-flung collection of politically prominent Democratic friends including Joseph P. Kennedy. More significant was his attentive and huge audience.[18] Democratic Party strategists had been maneuvering to turn out and capture the Catholic vote. Some political analysts would later maintain this was the reason for the nomination of Al Smith in 1928 even though he was a sure loser.[19] Smith lost indeed but thousands of Catholic immigrants registered and went to the polls for the first time. In 1932, Al Smith was again contending for the nomination, and although he entered late and campaigned little in advance of the party convention, he had the almost-automatic loyalty of many Catholics.

Coughlin's backing for Roosevelt was especially valuable, and the politically astute priest knew it. In a letter to FDR, he pointedly referred to the 20-odd million Catholics in the United States, "among whom are 5,000,000 voters."[20] Catholics were also watching Governor Roosevelt's treatment of the Catholic mayor of New York, Jimmy Walker, whose administration was under investigation for corruption at the time. Roosevelt asked Coughlin to give "a little bit of help" in explaining why the popular but colorful mayor had to leave office. While the priest did not go on the air about the Walker case, he did agree to attend a hearing Roosevelt conducted in Albany where his presence was interpreted as a show of support for the New York governor.

At the convention in Chicago, Coughlin gave an orchestrated "impromptu" speech just before the nominations for Roosevelt began. Michigan's 38 delegates voted unanimously for Roosevelt from the first ballot to the fourth when he won the party's nomination.[21] Later in life, Coughlin remained convinced that his speech swung a lot of convention votes to the Roosevelt candidacy and recalled Roosevelt's grateful response: "Padre, you can have any damned thing you want after this election."[22] The patrician Protestant presidential candidate and the priest complemented each other. Both charming men, they charmed each other. Each had an agenda.

In the weeks before the November election, some Catholic spokesmen and publications revisited the bones of 1928 when, they argued, Al Smith had been defeated by Protestant Democrats who despised his Catholicism. Charges floated about that Roosevelt had the Ku Klux Klan as an ally in the South where they were mobilizing on his behalf.[23] Father John McClorey, the Jesuit priest at the University of Detroit who frequently spoke on national radio, remained an outspoken critic of Coughlin's theology and his political position. Now he led the ranks of those who believed Al Smith had been denied the nomination this time around because of his religion. They angrily asserted that "Not Wanted" was written over the convention stadium for Smith and all other Catholics to read. Convention delegates would have chosen "the devil himself" in preference to Smith, and now, thundered McClorey, having chosen the weakest man in the party to run for president they wanted everyone to "work together" to elect him. McClorey pelted the *Michigan Catholic* with letters defining his opposition to Roosevelt and to the Democrats with whom he was parting company because they were bigots. He would not vote for Hoover; Smith should be elected, had been rejected, and so the Democratic Party deserved to fall in November.[24] Others wrote to agree, some of them suggesting Smith should run as an independent. Al Smith took to the campaign trail to help Roosevelt. Smith charged that those who said he was barred from the nomination by bigotry were not friends of Catholics but political tricksters trying to siphon votes from Roosevelt.[25] Despite the dire economic times, long-standing religious differences dogged the 1932 election season without end.

There were those who were defecting to the Socialists' candidate for president, Norman Thomas, because they believed the Democratic and Republican parties were both useless when it came to bringing about a just reform of the economic system. Catholics were warned off the Thomas alternative. Like *Commonweal* and *America* which were the two leading Catholic weekly reviews, the *Michigan Catholic* hastened to remind readers that Socialism was international, was inspired by materialism, and was opposed to private property. The Catholic press said Socialism represented principles condemned by the Catholic Church as incompatible with human liberty. The *Michigan Catholic* recognized the differences between European and American Socialists and acknowledged that Thomas did stand for certain reforms that were in harmony with the encyclicals of Popes Leo XIII and Pius XI. Still, the editor warned, there was no guarantee that Norman Thomas could continue to control an independent American Socialist movement, nor that the Socialists would understand votes cast for him were a protest against existing conditions rather than an endorsement of the Socialist platform. If political philosophy was not enough to deter them from the Socialists, *Michigan Catholic* readers were alerted that a leading Methodist politician and Prohibition leader had deserted Hoover and planned to support Thomas! Given this "grotesque" situation, the state's official Catholic paper suggested that Catholics threatening to vote for Mr. Thomas might not want to be in such company.[26]

Happy Days Are Here Again?

The Roosevelt camp had paid attention. Words of the papal encyclicals echoed through their candidate's speech when Roosevelt came to Detroit in early October to campaign. From the podium in the huge Naval Armory, he cited the papal encyclical Coughlin's radio broadcasts had popularized—Pius XI's statement on the concentration of wealth and power. The Democratic candidate for president proclaimed the pope's statement about social justice "one of the greatest documents of modern times" and "just as radical as I am—a declaration from one of the greatest forces of conservatism in the world, the Catholic Church." At length, he quoted the encyclical's words that "immense power and despotic economic domination are concentrated in the hands of a few . . . who administer [invested funds] at their good pleasure." Covering all bases, he also quoted pronouncements by the Protestant Federal Council of the Churches of Christ in America and by Rabbi Edward L. Israel, chair of the Social Justice Commission of the Central Conference of American Rabbis. Prominent representatives from the various religions were all on hand. When Detroit's Rabbi Leon Fram was unable to get through the crowd around the armory to reach the stage on time, Rev. Charles E. Coughlin came forward to give the invocation in his place.[27]

Coughlin's new radio season resumed in mid-October once the baseball season ended. His expanded network now reached listeners in every section of the country east of the Rocky Mountains. His social gospel alternatives were never more significant than in the fall of 1932 when people were weighing their choices. Roosevelt's platform was vague and cautious, even when it came to applauding the pope's principles of social justice; his campaign strategy was to get elected as the "invigorating tonic of change." Coughlin did not hesitate to identify what ingredients the tonic should include. It was not just good enough to restore the "so-called prosperity of 1929" because, he pointed out, layoffs had been accelerating for ten years before the Crash as a result of speedups and technology. He had facts and figures; more goods were produced with fewer men in 1929 than 1919. And as unyielding as William Jennings Bryan 40 years before, he continued to single out the gold standard as a fundamental cause of economic troubles. Thousands of people making an effort to stay informed tried to follow the often technical economic arguments, even the complex matter of reevaluating gold. They wrote to their local newspapers, and they wrote to Coughlin, who called on politicians, bankers, and businessmen to "take note" that the American people "are very wise in their generation."[28] Criticism over Coughlin "the demagogue" mounted from within the Michigan business and industrial sector, but Bishop Gallagher refused to interfere. Coughlin attacked his critics head-on in one radio sermon before the election, pointing out that the original word *demagogue,* according to the dictionary, meant the leader of the people. His audience was left with the reminder, "As a matter of fact Christ was a demagogue in the real, original meaning of the word."[29] They were also left with his pronouncement: "Roosevelt or ruin!"

Michigan residents were caught up in some of the most bitter local campaigns in the state's history. In many districts, Republicans and Democrats were in the first real race they had experienced. Divisiveness among regions and among pockets within regions was heightened because four of the ballot issues were likely to be decided by the metropolitan Detroit vote. These proposals dealt with Prohibition repeal, tax limitation, a $3,000 homestead exemption, and reapportionment. When the votes were in, Michigan drew national headlines: A majority of the state's voters had rejected the Republican candidate for president for the first time since 1856, apart from their support for Theodore Roosevelt in 1912 who was really a Republican running on the Progressive ticket that time. Statewide, Democrats won a landslide victory, electing the governor and gaining control of the Michigan state senate and the house. Repeal won by a comfortable margin.[30] People were in the mood for a change.

It was also the best year the Communist Party had—or would have—in the state. A total of 9,318 voters, one out of every 200, supported William Z. Foster, the Communist Party candidate for president. This meant he had 0.56 percent of the total vote, placing Michigan in fourth place nationally in terms of percentage of votes cast for the Communist ticket. Only Montana, Minnesota, and New York did better.[31] Communist candidates won their strongest support in the mining district of the western Upper Peninsula where Finnish radicals gained more compatriots over the years from 1929 to 1932 when employment in the iron ore and copper mines dropped by two-thirds.

What "Justice Demands"

Despite Coughlin's support for Roosevelt's candidacy, he was obviously wary. Between the November election and the new president's inauguration in March, the *Golden Hour* radio audience heard the familiar voice warn them that politicians often "purposefully" forget what Leo XIII knew: As their first duty the rulers of the state must make sure the laws and institutions produce public well-being and private prosperity; "justice demands" the interest of the poor and working population must be watched over.[32] People not only tuned in on Sunday afternoons, they could read and pore over the details during the week. The season before, the Shrine office had processed requests for 2,500,000 copies of his sermons published in pamphlet form and 613,000 complete books of sermon topics.[33] Books were mailed out with personalized form letters thanking the "dear Friend" who requested the book, assuring the person he and his loved ones would be remembered in Father's prayers, and asking for a "little prayer" for the priest. Letters were often signed in Coughlin's own handwriting.[34] Meanwhile, at Catholic college events, Catholic associations, various religious celebrations, and rallies against recognition of the Soviet government, thousands showed up to hear Coughlin in person as he hammered on his positions. Children attending grade school at the Shrine had a class on Communism added to their weekly lessons, and other parish schools hastened to do the same.

Early in the winter of 1933 Michigan Catholics began organizing a campaign when concern mounted over reports that Roosevelt was under great pressure to open diplomatic relations with the Soviets as soon as he took office. Louis B. Ward, who was Coughlin's parishioner, friend, and a prominent local businessman, helped plan mass meetings in parishes throughout Michigan to oppose recognition of the Soviet Union. The meetings were sponsored by the Holy Name Society, a national association of Catholic men that had several hundred chapters in the state. Their opposition was grounded not only in the Soviet government's denial of God. They also insisted the United States could not and should not be forced into economic competition in a world market with a government that had a collectivized economy and paid low wages to its forced-labor workers. They maintained that the pressure to recognize the Soviet government was coming from business interests anxious to sell goods and machinery in Russia.[35] As many as 2,000 people attended some parish meetings to hear speakers, and thousands signed petitions to be forwarded to the president-elect. On the eve of the inauguration, the 1,000,000 Catholic men in the Holy Name Society were urged by their national officers to offer their Holy Communion so "God may enlighten our new President, cabinet, and Congress." Anti-Communists and isolationists thought a warning flag was already up with the selection of Cordell Hull as secretary of state. The *Michigan Catholic* reported that, according to the *Chicago Tribune,* Hull's appointment might be interpreted as a success on the part of those advocating American recognition of Russia.[36] Michigan Communist leaders marked Roosevelt's inauguration by organizing about 4,000 people for an Inaugural Day demonstration in Detroit's Grand Circus Park. After making their presence visible with a parade of marching children, bands, and speeches, the crowd peacefully departed.[37] What could this "show" really mean? the fearful wondered.

Roosevelt's New Deal came to Michigan within days after he took the oath of office on March 4. One of his first actions was to declare a bank holiday, but Michigan was already in a bank holiday proclaimed by Governor William Comstock 16 days earlier. Checks had not been in use since mid-February in Detroit, and bankers, merchants, and manufacturers came together to devise a method of issuing scrip. Over the preceding months, one after another, 178 banks had closed, and people in many areas had been without money for some time. During the 1920s, two holding companies had emerged out of complicated consolidations to capture most banking in the state. One was the Guardian Detroit Union Group connected with Ford Motor Company and its credit corporation; the other was the First National-Detroit group made up of most of the old-line bankers of Detroit with *Free Press* publisher E. D. Stair as the nominal head. In the last year of the Hoover administration, the Reconstruction Finance Corporation struggled to save the situation, but, despite Senator Couzens's efforts, neither of the two banking companies could gather sufficient capital to operate, and the banks were closed two weeks before Roosevelt took office. When Roosevelt declared a national bank holiday, the federal examiners who came to Detroit insisted on reorganization. The Guardian National Bank of Commerce and the First National Bank were merged into the new National Bank of Detroit. It was an action repeated with banks all around the country.

On Sunday evening March 12 at 10:00 p.m. eastern time, President Roosevelt went on the radio to explain what had been done about the banks in the previous few days. He was seated behind his desk in the White House and spoke as if he were sharing an evening of talk and friendship with the American people who felt he was indeed with them in spirit as they sat around their radios. He offered a simplified explanation about the "readjustment" of the financial system, gave optimistic reassurances, and called for people to have confidence and courage. This was the first of Roosevelt's famous "fireside chats," a term soon coined by a CBS reporter and happily embraced by the president. During his initial four years in office, he would have eight such visits with Americans in their living rooms; over time, there would be a total of thirty-one.[38] Hundreds of thousands who listened throughout the Roosevelt years would have sworn

these fireside chats were a common Sunday night occurrence, an exaggerated memory that would endure into the next generation. His persuasive
powers seemed to be working when the banks opened and depositors
lined up to put their money back.[39] Nonetheless, blame for the local
Michigan banking mess and finger-pointing over the government's solution had just begun. The bank reorganization plan also foreshadowed the
beginning of the end for the Roosevelt-Coughlin alliance.

Coughlin's assessments, first of the Depression and now of the New
Deal, rested significantly on examples from his local Detroit base. He was
initially encouraged that the government took on Detroit bankers "whose
god was gold and whose creed was greed," but he thought it a very bad
omen when many of those same men were put back in charge of the newly
organized bank. In his next Sunday nationwide broadcast, he exulted that
the money changers had been driven from the temples, but he warned it
was only the first battle; the war had just begun. As he explained the banking crisis, Detroit's major bankers had used the holding company to evade
liability, and with government investigations on their doorstep, they
profited by inside information, withdrew millions of their money before
the bank closings, and now were back in business as members of the board
of the new National Bank of Detroit.[40] He specifically attacked *Free Press*
publisher E. D. Stair who was president of the Detroit Bankers Company
and was a party, Coughlin charged, to the bankers' practice of loaning
money to themselves and speculating for their own profit with other
people's money. Coughlin was not alone in this insight. Senator Couzens
offered the same analysis of the "manipulation, greed, and dishonesty"
among the bankers.[41] He demanded access to confidential reports and
testified as federal examiners dug into the banker's manipulative schemes.
Michigan's Senator Vandenberg supported Couzens and agreed that evidence of bank fraud was clear.

Although the *Free Press* bitterly blamed Couzens for failing to support
a loan to the banking trusts earlier when Hoover created the RFC, it retaliated most against Coughlin who was denouncing publisher Stair and the
banking schemes to his audience of millions. The newspaper not only
listed "falsehoods" in Coughlin's charges against the bankers but went on
the attack with documents it managed to get from a clerk at Coughlin's
bank showing he'd bought Kelsey-Hayes Wheel Corporation stock
through the bank on February 27, 1929, and to do it, transferred money
from the Radio League of the Little Flower account to supplement his own
personal funds. Bishop Gallagher found Coughlin's charges against the

bankers "unthinkable" and "ill-advised," but he also saw nothing wrong with the priest's effort to invest donations to support his radio activities.[42] The *Free Press* invoked religion with heated passion, emphasizing a history of religious peace and tranquility in the community from the days when Reverend Monteith and Gabriel Richard worked together in the early nineteenth century. Coughlin, the paper charged, was sewing the seeds of religious dissension, fanning the flames of bigotry. The *Detroit News* waded in and so did the *Detroit Times,* a Hearst paper that consistently applauded Coughlin's economic ideas and political positions. The rector of Detroit's St. Joseph's Episcopal Church took to his pulpit to read a letter he had sent Roosevelt, charging that his advisers had been "bamboozled by a radio priest" who had been making unsubstantiated charges against Detroit bankers. Letters, telegrams, and phone calls flew back and forth on each side. Separation of religion and politics was, as always, an idealistic illusion when economic interests came into play.

Coughlin answered, especially through a just-published biography written by his friend and parishioner Louis Ward. Ward portrayed the priest as a frugal investor who, on behalf of his parish, had purchased this stock rather than following bankers' advice to invest it in banks. Coughlin's core of supporters had little trouble believing the priest's version because for years, various congressional committees had been reporting on corrupt practices of financiers. And it looked to them like an underhanded trick when the local office of the Internal Revenue quickly began an investigation into Coughlin's tax returns. In the midst of the controversy, a bomb exploded in the basement of Father Coughlin's home next to the church. Windows were blown out, pipes were damaged, and goods stored there were affected. Mayor Murphy arrived at his friend's home almost as quickly as the police, but investigators were not able to find whoever planted the bomb. Among the possibilities were the members of the Black Legion, successor to the Ku Klux Klan. There were those who agreed with Boston cardinal O'Connell's unsympathetic assessment that "a priest has his place. If he remains in his place he is highly honored."[43] WJR received threats that the station would be bombed if it did not cancel his broadcasts, and, for a time, police were assigned to guard it day and night.[44] A few days later on Good Friday when many Detroit churches held three-hour midday services, Coughlin preached at the Fisher Theater on the main floor below the WJR headquarters, one of the finest and most visible sites in the city.

More than ever, Coughlin was front-page news as well as a voice heard by millions. The charges and countercharges over banking and finance permanently poisoned relationships between the *Free Press* and Coughlin. Here also was a red flag to the Roosevelt administration, an alert that Coughlin could be unpredictable, independent, and a possible liability in their camp now that the election was won. Coughlin was not a politician with a constituency to consider or an office he planned to seek. So far as the new Roosevelt administration was concerned, the priest was a wild card in the deck. So far as Coughlin was concerned, he was the voice and champion of the little man.

In the first year of Roosevelt's administration, with programs flying through Congress, the president was defining himself as the guardian of the people's interests. One government alphabet agency after another went into action—to set prices and wages through the National Industrial Recovery Act, to help raise farm prices by creating scarcity with the AAA, to promote conservation and put young men to work with the CCC, to reorganize banks, to provide mortgage relief. Beer and wine with a 3.2 percent alcoholic content became legal while the amendment repealing Prohibition altogether made its way through the states. Michigan's two Republican senators, Vandenberg and Couzens, supported a number of these, whether out of agreement with Roosevelt's efforts to revitalize capitalism, or because local industrialists and businessmen assured them that certain of the bills would have small consequences, or because they knew Michigan voters wanted the bills. As seasoned politicians, they knew which bills were sure to pass the Senate anyway.[45] Coughlin's friend Frank Murphy was named governor-general of the Philippines soon after Roosevelt took office, an appointment for which the priest claimed some credit. It was a lesser post than that of attorney general, however, a position both Coughlin and Murphy had hoped for. Murphy continued building his political career but with Coughlin more on the margins.

Between March 1933 and September 1934, Roosevelt had six fireside chats to explain programs he was initiating and to assure Americans that he was looking for every way possible to promote their well-being. Meanwhile, from the reorganization of the banks onward, Coughlin assumed the role of pressing the New Deal president and Congress to be more bold. He urged his audience to support the remonetization of silver and promised to support Vandenberg's reelection in 1934 if he would back a bill for unlimited coinage of silver that the president opposed. Both Michigan senators voted against it, however, and Vandenberg claimed they had saved the president's program because this silver bill lost by two votes.[46]

If Coughlin had any notions about his influence within the administration, the currency debate demonstrated otherwise. Coughlin became a target when secretary of the treasury Morgenthau published lists of people and firms holding silver on January 31, 1934, just when FDR was opposing any mandatory silver-purchase programs being brought before the Senate. One name on the list was Miss Amy Collins, who had five million ounces of silver futures and was treasurer of Coughlin's Radio League of the Little Flower. Coughlin explained the purchase, but he was now a permanent foe of Morgenthau, whom he blamed for this smear campaign. Although Roosevelt was not above using the power of his administration to discredit opponents or those with opposing views, Coughlin would always maintain that the president did not know in advance that Morgenthau planned to release this list. Still, Coughlin was increasingly disappointed in what he regarded as Roosevelt's business-as-usual capitalism.

The administration's treatment of veterans came in for furious attacks in Coughlin's sermons and broadcasts. Roosevelt had never indicated he would support a bonus bill before he was elected, nor was he persuaded once in office; moreover, among the early cost-cutting measures he sent to Congress was a plan to reduce war veterans' benefits. The president would continue to oppose the Patman bonus bill until it was finally doomed by his veto in 1936. In his opinion the New Deal had provided sufficient relief, and veterans did not need or deserve special treatment.

Conservatives, with Herbert Hoover helping give them voice, thought the government was doing too much, that Roosevelt and the federal government were growing too powerful. They organized the American Liberty League in August 1934 to champion free enterprise, the American way, and individual freedoms. Coughlin went on the attack against the league at once, but he had come to think that Roosevelt was closer to Liberty League positions than to principles of social justice. The priest was in the company of a growing chorus on the left who opposed the New Deal for doing too little, for leaving too many people still destitute. In Michigan, the state convention of the Farmer Labor Party adopted a resolution on July 4, 1934, stating its reason for existence: "We believe that both old political parties are dominated and controlled by the 'money interests' and therefore a real New Deal in government is impossible [because of] the very system which puts control beyond the reach of the individual."[47]

Hard times were not over or, indeed, much improved when off-year elections came around in 1934. Michigan families remained in the grip of unemployment or underemployment. One letter in the *Michigan Catholic*

Readers' Forum argued that Father Coughlin's plan rather than the New Deal's Federal Reserve banks could rescue homes and jobs. Another writer raised a potential option: "Mr. Roosevelt is on trial. If HE fails, Huey Long is preferable to the gentlemen of the past-decade."[48]

The November 1934 elections showed the mood of many Americans when additional reform-minded congressmen were chosen to head for Washington, among them a number of mavericks interested in pushing reform farther than their president had proposed. In Michigan, however, Democratic Party infighting and factionalism resulted in a loss of seats, and a Republican governor was elected as a result, even though people were in a mood for continued reform. Many still-suffering voters wanted a less timid New Deal that would act more effectively on their behalf. When Coughlin began his new broadcast season in the fall of 1934 he asked his audience to write and let him know if they wanted him to continue criticizing the New Deal.[49] Continue he did.

6 · THE CENTER RESTORED

When all is said and done, those programs to redistribute income
and help the little man would have been better in the long run. But,
people live in the short run.

   —ABE ROSENKRANZ, an elderly Michigan voter
   looking back on the 1930s

In the late fall of 1934, Coughlin's audience was ready to give the president
and the newly elected congressmen a push. The priest who had forged his
radio listeners into an amorphous pressure group was ready to give his listeners a structure and a name announcing their purposeful cause. He
called on them to become members of the National Union for Social Justice. More than the 5,000,000 Coughlin aimed for did indeed join. Some
went on to support the Union Party he put together by 1936. Most
"Coughlinites" would never really embrace an organization or a political
party despite his various efforts, however. Most of them would not attend
any meetings or conventions, even at the state or local level. Many million
strong, they were men and women gathered around their individual radios who responded collectively as a force of letter writers, senders of
telegrams, and voters. For a while, they were a legion of citizens prepared
to answer his call to demand a more just society, more than the New Deal
was doing in the way of thoroughgoing reforms. They shared Father
Coughlin's determination to keep America out of European conflicts and
to stand steadfast against Communism. For a while, until he turned too
combative and too angry, the priest and his followers gave shape and force
to public policy.

   Like other "reforms" demanded of politicians in other eras, Coughlin's
recommendations for far-reaching change and his substantial support in
the grassroots nudged the New Deal farther than it might have gone. Once
idealism and restive radicalism began to be tempered, however, familiar

American habits would reemerge, replacing wariness toward elected leaders, overcoming suspicion about accustomed allies like Britain, and lessening interest in causes of economic and social justice. Father Charles Coughlin would be out of step with his audience before he knew or could tolerate it.

Mobilizing: The National Union for Social Justice

Father Coughlin first announced his plans for a new organization on the Sunday in November following the 1934 off-year election. Bishop Gallagher lent his weight to the cause by his unusual appearance at the beginning of the broadcast to ask listeners to give Coughlin their closest attention for "today he undertakes the application of Christian social teaching to our problems." With that, Coughlin announced the formation of the National Union for Social Justice. It would combat "the greedy system of an outworn capitalism" on one hand and the "slave whip of Communism" on the other.[1] It was, in effect, to be a lobby of citizens who organized in their own communities where they might command attention from locally elected politicians on behalf of more thoroughgoing reforms than the New Deal had so far delivered. It would remain nonpartisan but would fight for social and economic reform in the name of social justice—"the justice that one human being or one group of human beings should have toward another group of human beings, who make contributions to the well-being of total society."[2] He envisioned the NUSJ would have units in every city, county, and town and, he hoped, would obtain 5,000,000 members.

The 16-point program Coughlin listed called for a just and living annual wage for workers and for liberty of conscience, but these were modest demands by comparison with his monetary recommendations.[3] Included as the most radical point among the 16 was the demand for the nationalization of banking, credit, currency, power, light oil, natural gas, "and our God-given natural resources." By nationalizing natural resources, he soon explained, the government could scrutinize and rationalize rates and profits. And, too, he saw nothing to prevent the government—federal, state, or local—from building power plants to compete with privately owned utilities.[4] While he supported private ownership of property, Coughlin advocated its control "for the public good." He would abolish the Federal Reserve System with its board of private bankers and would establish a government-owned central bank; he would recall nonproductive bonds and abolish tax-exempt bonds. In time of war, he would conscript wealth as well as men.

The National Union for Social Justice platform had wide appeal. Among others who approved its thrust, Michigan's generally Protestant farmers could find much to like; the Farm Labor Party platform in the summer of 1934 had called for several of the same demands including public ownership and democratic operation of public utilities and banking.[5] Laid-off autoworkers applauded Coughlin's attack on the chamber of commerce and those inside government who called for "share the work" programs. They nodded when the priest thundered that it was "half-baked" to advocate a 30-hour or 24-hour week that did not provide a salary sufficient to provide a just wage; they agreed that it amounted not to "share the work" but to "share the poverty." Industrial strikes were futile in Coughlin's opinion, but there must be a just distribution of wealth to change the current situation in which, according to his statistics, one and a half percent of the families in America received one-fourth of the total income. Coughlin's message was emphatic: "Capitalism and communism both destroy private ownership."[6] People in his audience agreed that capitalism needed to work properly.

Telegrams and hundreds of thousands of letters poured into his office; 200,000 had joined within two weeks of formation of the NUSJ. To squelch critics who said memberships were padded with names from phone books, people were instructed to sign the form before mailing it in. Dues, at 10 cents a month, were within reach. Within three months, Coughlin claimed the NUSJ had 6,000,000 members.[7] In those first three months, they had already contributed $97,269.71 and provided the base of financial support for the *Golden Hour* broadcasts. Much of the total came as the result of small amounts, $1 and $5 bills enclosed in hand-addressed envelopes. He was grateful, Coughlin told listeners, yet another $41,000 would be needed to meet expenses without taking out a loan. Coughlin reminded his audience that the newly formed American Liberty League, a conservative group of businessmen and politicians who advocated free enterprise without government regulations, had spent less but had collected more on behalf of their rival cause.[8] Listeners responded within days, and the debt was erased.

Coughlin was one of many, including Michigan's Senator Couzens, who were calling for public works programs more far-reaching than those the New Deal introduced. The priest went on the air before Christmas of 1934 to propose a permanent plan to build roads, plant trees, harness the St.

Lawrence, reclaim 60 million acres of agricultural land, and build homes for the poor in the slums. The Cincinnati chapter of the Daughters of the American Revolution charged he was an "inciter of revolution."[9] Critics agreed. Support, however, came from other corners. Rabbi Leon Fram, the respected leader of Temple Beth El in Detroit, praised Coughlin for becoming well informed on economic questions and defended the priest's right to speak especially since he was raising human questions, moral questions. The voice of the church needed to be heard, said the rabbi. In a sermon to his own congregation, Fram said Coughlin's 16 points were not radical at all. Indeed, various Protestant and Jewish organizations, along with the National Catholic Welfare Conference, had published even more thoroughgoing programs of social justice. Rabbi Fram emphasized, however, that Coughlin's ideas were too centered on the monetary system and lacked the international aspect significant to recovery and security. At the time, millions of Americans were more interested in economic recovery and regarded isolationism as their best form of security.

A sentiment to stay out of European affairs helped power the newly created NUSJ. President Roosevelt had prompted Congress to recognize the government of the Soviet Union in order to stimulate the economy, but many Americans remained unconvinced that the economic advantages were a sufficient justification. When Coughlin addressed issues of internationalism, it was part and parcel of his economic perspective. He insisted that the collusion between munitions makers and power brokers helped certain men profit by war at the expense of American lives. This tapped a common concern, and a well-publicized Senate committee was investigating the munitions industry at the time. People were disposed to agree with Coughlin's call for the "truth" about collusion, bribery, and corruption in government that enabled "merchandisers of murder" like DuPont to make huge profits by selling explosives to Japan.[10]

Public opinion had also been opposed to the World Court ever since it was established after World War I. Despite presidential efforts to persuade Congress, the United States was not a member. Another vote to join the Court was scheduled at the end of January 1935. Two days before the Senate was to vote, Coughlin went on the air, denounced the measure, and told his army of listeners to contact their representatives in Washington. In his view, the Court represented an internationalism that was more dangerous to American prosperity than the Soviet Third International. He especially disliked the Court because he regarded it as run by the British, for whom he harbored permanent animosity. Many Americans disliked the idea that the Court might get us into another war and were angry too that European nations had defaulted on their war debts to the United States. Within hours before the vote, senators were deluged with a flood of over 40,000 telegrams opposing the World Court.[11] The Court went down to defeat. The Court had also been opposed by Will Rogers, Huey Long, and the Hearst newspapers, but the Roosevelt administration and many others attributed its defeat to Coughlin's listeners. Their strength as a lobby could not be discounted.

The Roosevelt camp was increasingly worried about the possibility that Coughlin could mount a third-party challenge by the election of 1936. Immediately after the priest's show of influence over the World Court, FDR requested that Frank Murphy visit Michigan so he might serve as an "unofficial liaison to placate" Coughlin.[12] Murphy had begun floating the possibility of a run for governor of Michigan, but he remained especially eager to be appointed as attorney general of the United States. When the president beckoned, he quickly returned from the Philippines, tried to persuade the priest that Roosevelt's heart was with the people, and enlisted Joe Kennedy to help. After talking with Coughlin, Murphy reported to the White House that the priest would support FDR if his case were given the "intimate and persistent attention it deserves." Roosevelt apparently decided at that point to bring Murphy home permanently as soon as possible so he could help neutralize the "Coughlin situation."[13] Coughlin, meanwhile, continued to press his issues and mobilize his base.

The Michigan chapter of the NUSJ, the first to take organizational form, held its initial state meeting in April 1935. Over 15,000 people jammed into Detroit's Olympia Stadium, and for over three hours, the crowd heard prominent U.S. senators and representatives speak—North Dakota's Lemke on the Frazier-Lemke bill to refinance farm mortgages and Nye on the bill against war profiteering, O'Malley from Wisconsin for the soldiers' bonus bill, Sweeney from Ohio for the central bank bill, Thomas of Oklahoma for inflation. The twelve speakers represented causes familiar to NUSJ members. The crowd cheered every time Coughlin's name was mentioned, and it booed at every mention of programs or people he had denounced—the Du Pont family, the New Dealer Hugh Johnson, international bankers, the League of Nations, the World Court. When he rose to give the last speech, Coughlin thundered that the "first objective of the organization" would be to solidify autoworkers of Michigan into a unit that could successfully bargain for its rights.[14] Unmentioned was his ambition to undercut the UAW and CIO, which he believed to be influenced by Communists.

One purpose of the meeting in Detroit was to explain the organizational structure the NUSJ would take. Coughlin outlined his plan for a board of nine national trustees who would, in turn, appoint nine trustees for each state chapter who would represent agriculture, labor, small business, small industry, the professions, the civil service and soldiers, school teachers and housewives and feminine organizations. Addressing any fears that the NUSJ was trying to usurp other organizations, he emphasized that it would not be a federation of other organizations already in place among laborers, farmers, or business organizations, nor would it interfere with them. Rather, the NUSJ would join the effort to support their causes. The NUSJ was not to be a tool of either party for, after all, "The Democratic Bourbons and the Republican reactionaries are not the same breed of cats. They are the same cat." He challenged the crowd to remember that the president "is only our hired man, and if he doesn't make good, we'll fire him. . . ."[15] The *Free Press* editorialized the next day that the most sensible and practical speaker was Rabbi Isserman from St. Louis, a widely known liberal, who declared that the first platform for any social justice group must be "rededication to and redeclaration of faith in democracy and liberty."[16] Though the editor clearly regarded the mass meeting as a frenzied expression of discontent, thousands in this "extremely heterogeneous" crowd came precisely because they had faith in democracy and liberty.

A few days after that meeting, President Roosevelt gave his first fireside chat in seven months. "My friends," he said to the American radio audience, legislation necessary to the country's welfare "is making distinct progress." He attempted to represent the New Deal as a coherent, well-considered plan that, just then in 1935, was adding more programs. Unlike Coughlin's Sunday broadcasts that were peppered with facts, figures, and details, this and other fireside chats had just enough information to make the president's reassurances credible without becoming cluttered by details that could confound the audience or come back to haunt him. This Sunday evening the president projected confidence: "We have survived all of the arduous burdens and threatening dangers of a great economic calamity." Fear was vanishing and confidence was growing on every side, he enthused. Faith in the democratic form of government was receiving its just reward, and "for that we can be thankful to the God who watches over America."[17] By this point, the editors of the *New Republic* were denouncing Coughlin as a dangerous demagogue, not because he promised too much but because he was incapable of carrying out his promises. It was not a label they would have applied to Roosevelt, however—or to presidents before or after who fell short of their promises.

Both Coughlin and the circle around Roosevelt understood the cautious dance they were performing. With the New Deal into its third year and the economy still staggered, discontented Americans were looking about for alternatives. Huey Long's Share-the-Wealth followers wanted to redistribute income, Milo Reno's Farm Holiday Association wanted more help for farmers than the Agricultural Adjustment Act envisioned, and Dr. Francis E. Townsend's "Townsend Clubs" were a widespread network of the elderly who advocated a pension plan. Although there were overlapping members, the NUSJ generally attracted its own constituency, and its guiding "16 Points" were more sweeping. Following the Michigan NUSJ state meeting, Long announced he would welcome the support of Coughlin in a third-party movement because the priest's ideas were "right down my alley," but Coughlin distanced his group and denied rumors that he would join Long or any third-party movement. Critics charged that the priest wanted to be in charge of his own show, probably a correct assessment.[18] It was probable too that Coughlin still believed he could influence Roosevelt, especially if he could separate the president from certain men around him.

Coughlin spent the summer on a speaking tour, addressing crowds who paid between 25 cents and $2 to hear him—25,000 came in Cleveland, 18,000 in Madison Square Garden—and on to Chicago, to St. Louis, and to Massachusetts where he addressed the state's House of Representatives.[19] Often, Coughlin's barnstorming took him into territory where the Catholic hierarchy was openly hostile. Boston's Cardinal O'Connell denounced Coughlin for his "demagogic talk," "hysterical harangues," "humbugging," and "pure sham." Father Coughlin promptly responded that "for 40 years the Cardinal had been notorious for his silence on social justice."[20] Detroit's Bishop Gallagher left no doubt about his ongoing support and again went on Coughlin's *Golden Hour* program to tell anyone who cared, "It so happens that I do not only find in Father Coughlin's addresses nothing against the faith and morals but I do most heartily approve their content. It is a content based on truths which I have directed him to preach." Furthermore, "until a lawful superior rules otherwise," said Gallagher, he intended to "stand steadfastly behind this priest . . . encouraging him to do the will of God as he sees it and I see it."[21]

Although a Gallup Poll in late June 1935 showed that a Coughlin endorsement was far more likely to hurt than help a candidate, FDR and pollsters still saw Coughlin as the "most dangerous indication of Catholic dissatisfaction with the administration."[22] Democratic Party leaders were worried about the extent of Catholic dissent. Al Smith was outspoken in his opposition to FDR and the New Deal; charges that Communists had infiltrated the administration flew about, and the Catholic press and clerics were vocal in their complaints that the administration had not done enough about anticlericalism in Mexico. Roosevelt insiders pinned their hopes on Frank Murphy and Joe Kennedy as conduits to neutralize if not placate Coughlin. In the company of Kennedy, Coughlin periodically visited the president at Hyde Park. Sometimes they stayed overnight. Perhaps each Irishman aimed to persuade the other about the course of Roosevelt's program, and between themselves, the two familiarly referred to the president as "the boss." Roosevelt always addressed Coughlin as "Padre."

Toward the end of his life Coughlin told one interviewer about what may have been the last gathering of the threesome. For a time, at Bishop Gallagher's request, Coughlin had been avoiding Roosevelt because Gallagher had received a photostatic copy of a check from the Bishop of Guadalajara that showed a high-level Treasury Department official had given millions to the Communists in Mexico. In the light of this disturbing disclosure, Coughlin consented to stay away from Washington. Then, Coughlin recalled, Roosevelt asked him to pay a "long overdue" visit. So Gallagher agreed but sent him off armed with the documentation proving that certain officials in the administration were promoting Communist causes.[23] Kennedy and Coughlin went to Hyde Park for an overnight stay in September 1935 and Coughlin talked with the president alone to show him the information. The president, he said, reacted with disbelief. Coughlin left assuming FDR would look into the matter but this discussion was never mentioned between them again. Decades later, a reminiscing Coughlin liked to think the check had been slipped to Mexico without Roosevelt's knowledge.[24] At the time, neither man could charm the other any longer. NUSJ members and Roosevelt voters, often the same people, watched the frayed alliance completely unravel.

Less than two months after their Hyde Park meeting—and one year before the next presidential election—Coughlin went on the air to tell his Sunday afternoon audience that he was breaking with Roosevelt because he could no longer support the present policies of the New Deal. He had been "thrilled by the ringing words" of Roosevelt's inaugural speech on

March 4, 1933, which promised to drive the money changers from the temple. But, according to his way of thinking, policies of the New Deal had degenerated into practices hostile to the principles of social justice. That included social security, which was just "poorhouse security." The administration was Communistic in its disregard of private property; it was leading to Nazism or Fascism in the growing number of bureaucratic employees; it was engaged in "sinful and unnecessary" crop reduction while people were going hungry; it was paying slave wages to laborers through the WPA although manufacturers and bankers who supplied the WPA projects were getting full payment. And the "plutocratic" administration had deliberately supported labor legislation like the NIRA knowing the Supreme Court would declare it unconstitutional. He was "simply disillusioned." The Republican Party was no alternative either, he said. Listeners should support only those congressmen who support "our principles." NUSJ members were asked to repudiate the New Deal or leave his organization; listeners who agreed with him but had not joined were asked to do so now.[25] If his claims were right, the NUSJ then had 9,000,000 members. Even if this figure was inflated, members represented a formidable bloc of active voters, and their contributions had been a significant source of revenue for his projects. Although familiar with Coughlin's criticism of FDR, radio listeners were almost surely stunned to hear him go so far that Sunday. People sorted out their choices.

Election Year, 1936

By spring of 1936, jockeying for votes and influence was well under way on every side. On March 13, Coughlin brought out the first issue of *Social Justice,* an oversize weekly newspaper that had 16 pages, no advertisements, and a masthead statement that read "Produce for Use At a Fair Profit." The paper was published by the Social Justice Publishing Company, and thereby, as an independent rather than "Catholic" publication, it was kept deliberately separate from potential complaints or control by the church hierarchy. The paper would overlap, he said, with the NUSJ organization, which he also equated with his radio audience. He "conservatively" estimated the radio audience to number 12 to 15 million listeners and told readers that this edition would probably go into homes of more than 500,000. Local units of the NUSJ could get bundles of 100 copies to sell on street corners outside churches or theaters; half of the 5 cent charge for each paper would go to cover production costs and the other half the locals could keep for their own work.[26] Readers, by his depiction, mirrored his position. They were "a group of citizens not only dissatisfied with the sham politics and sham policies existing in America, but anxious for a cleansing of both political parties." They wanted the enactment of "just and equitable laws in harmony with social justice." He intended that the newspaper would contribute "some assistance" to the millions "who were attempting to rid this nation of want in the midst of plenty."[27] In each week's paper until the November election, readers found political direction and organizational strategy layered with the principles of *Rerum Novarum* and *Quadragessimo Anno. Social Justice* was the priest's voice in print.

All the while his audience and national prominence had been growing, Coughlin remained pastor of his Royal Oak parish. A new and splendid Shrine of the Little Flower was completed by 1936 with seating for 2,500 at a time. On weekends as many as 20,000 people came to marvel at the octagon-shaped church with the altar in the center where they could see and hear Father Coughlin in person. Tour buses brought visitors who walked around outside the domed edifice, looking up to see carved in stone the names of the various states from which contributions had come for the Shrine building fund. Like other pastors, Father Coughlin took care of his flock; he, however, had more money to do it than most. With the help of contributions from his radio audience and tourist-visitors, he carried out his own version of social justice at the level of his neighborhood. As many as 50,000 children came to a Christmas party at his invitation in December 1931, and he was pleased that they "ate all the ice cream in Detroit."[28] He funded God's Poor Society, a center where people from Royal Oak could come for food and clothing, and he put the unemployed to work where he could. Parishioner Edgar Rhoades, laid off from his auto factory job, learned how to become a stone mason when he went to work on the Shrine's construction; others became carpenters, painters, and groundskeepers. Rhoades's two daughters became Coughlin's personal secretaries, and a bevy of other women sorted and answered the mail pouring in.[29] Father Coughlin's reach was far and wide, but this parish neighborhood remained his most devoted and permanently loyal base when others started to drift or run away. Only later generations would be ashamed that Father Charles Coughlin was so significant a part of their parish legacy. Yet even they would resent outsiders' criticism because they had grown up hearing stories of "Father," the kindly man who walked children home after school and knew the names of their dogs.

Coughlin had often pressed demands in the name of Michigan's autoworkers and farmers, emphasizing the economic problems the system created for them. Still, he began to alienate both when he called upon them to support each other. In the spring of 1936, the Frazier-Lemke Farm Refinance Mortgage Bill pending in Congress was of great interest to farmers because it proposed a federal agency that would supply them with cash to pay off mortgages or buy back their farms lost since 1928. Coughlin's newspaper and broadcasts urged its passage and called on labor to side with the farmers. Sixteen of the 17 Congressmen from Michigan supported bringing the bill to the floor for debate and a vote, Democrats and Republicans alike. Roosevelt had thrown his weight against the bill on the grounds it would unbalance the economy. New Dealers were also keenly aware of American Federation of Labor opposition to Frazier-Lemke; AFL president William Green said it would bring inflation by printing and circulating more currency, which meant commodity prices would rise but wages would stand still and labor would suffer. When the vote came, the Frazier-Lemke bill lost by a margin of 235 to 142. Michigan representatives split, guided not only by party considerations but also by their constituents' sentiment. Republicans and Democrats from agricultural districts generally voted for the bill while those from industrialized districts voted against it.[30] Coughlin blamed the farm bill defeat not so much on the opposition of organized labor but on the Roosevelt administration for catering to AFL leader Green in a bid for votes at the cost of economic and social justice. "Labor Is Used to Beat Relief for Farmers" read the headline in *Social Justice*.[31]

Coughlin was already hostile toward both the AFL and CIO. He especially opposed the United Auto Workers with its ties to the CIO, which he considered to be led by many who were Communists. In 1935 he had helped promote the Automotive Industrial Workers Association (AIWA), first established in Chrysler Corporation plants. The secretary of the AIWA, Richard Frankensteen, was a Coughlin supporter, and Coughlin promised NUSJ help with the AIWA's recruiting efforts.[32] Union leaders and local union officials had taken pleasure in attacking Coughlin for using nonunion workers to build his new church. Coughlin countered that large union organizations were as dangerous to political and economic justice as business or banking trusts. He regarded union leaders' opposition to the Frazier-Lemke bill as self-serving, shortsighted, and an attack on him personally.

The priest became ever more strident in reminding audiences of Pope

Leo XIII's conviction: Enduring reform can come only from the cooperation of the three great social powers—Church, State, and the organized
workers themselves. Agriculture and labor, small business and small industry, and every other minority in American life must understand: "It is
one for all and all for one."[33] By that adage, he had voting blocs in mind.
In *Social Justice* articles, speeches, and radio broadcasts, Coughlin made
the case of one interest group to another and another. Farmers learned
they should support the pending bill that would set minimum wages and
hours for businesses and industries who were suppliers to the government; they should patronize business owners like Nunn-Bush Shoe Company and Richman Brothers Clothing who were treating workers fairly by
profit sharing, pregnancy leaves for mothers, guaranteed annual wage,
and more.[34] Urban laborers should understand that the Agricultural Adjustment Act was not helping the small farmers. All consumers should buy
from independent merchants rather than at those chain stores that temporarily charge lower prices to drive local shopkeepers out of business.
Money changers, the Federal Reserve Bank, war profiteers, and the "male-
factors of wealth" remained as one predictable collection of enemies
Coughlin named. Communists were the other. He could not relent.

The Union Party

When radio listeners tuned in one Sunday in June 1936, they learned that
Father Coughlin had formed the Union Party to change course from
"Roosevelt and ruin." Within a month, the Union Party held a national
convention in Cleveland and nominated William Lemke of North Dakota.
Huey Long, the most charismatic of the men who might have challenged
Roosevelt, had been assassinated the fall of 1935 by a man avenging a family grievance. Probably Coughlin would not have championed a Long candidacy. Even though Long had tried to woo him when the NUSJ formed,
the two crowd-pleasing orators always maintained their distance. Coughlin was not interested in promoting Gerald L. K. Smith, who had taken
over the helm of the Share-Our-Wealth movement, nor did he regard
Francis Townsend as any more than a spokesman for the elderly's cause
and a drab figure at that.

From Coughlin's perspective, Representative William Lemke had the
right ideas about finance and farming. He also shared Coughlin's disappointment over Roosevelt, and he was a veteran at challenging the two

major parties through nonpartisan or third-party efforts. Lemke had led various third-party and agrarian radical movements upon going home to North Dakota soon after graduating from Yale law school. In 1925 he helped launch North Dakota's Farmer-Labor Party modeled on the one he had helped establish in Minnesota. Lemke, sometimes a Democrat, had run for Congress in 1932 as a Republican, but he also worked tirelessly for Roosevelt that year and helped carry the North Dakota Democratic primary for him. When Roosevelt met with Lemke at Hyde Park in the course of the 1932 campaign, he gave the North Dakotan reason to think that he would support his farm program once they were both in Washington. It soon became apparent, however, that the Roosevelt advisers shoved Lemke and his ideas aside. By 1936, after the administration had rallied William Green and labor to help oppose the Lemke-Frazier farm bill, Lemke was more than disappointed in Roosevelt. He was the president's enemy.[35] The Lemke-Coughlin alliance was cemented out of their separate despair over any alternatives and their mutual dislike of Roosevelt.

Coughlin had incorporated many of the Farmer-Labor planks when he drew up his "16 Points" guiding the NUSJ. The 15 points in the platform of the new Union Party mapped familiar territory. Some of them were simply announcements of ideals such as talk of national defense against aggression without foreign entanglements, that "human rights of the masses take precedence over the financial rights of the classes," and reasonable and decent security for the aged. Most were prescriptions with content—a central bank, an annual living wage, adequate mortgage refinancing for farmers and legislation to assure their production at a profit, inheritance taxes, permanent federal works for conservation of natural resources, legislation prohibiting imports produced abroad at less than a living wage, civil service instead of patronage to fill all federal positions.[36] Notably missing was any mention or support for collective bargaining, although Lemke had been a friend of organized labor until the AFL's opposition to his farm bill. Like many third parties before and after, the Union Party saw itself as a principled choice not a political echo.

Fired by moral righteousness and idealistic enthusiasms, the Union Party convention crowd cheered when Townsend and Smith spoke. People burst into even wilder cheers once Coughlin took the platform, tore off his coat and clerical collar in the 100 degree heat, and attacked "Franklin Double-crossing Roosevelt."[37] Applause united the Union Party convention audience for the moment, but the alliance between the Townsend, Smith, Lemke, and Coughlin supporters was untested. This Union Party coalition was no more unnatural than those factions that gathered under the Republican or Democratic umbrellas. But the third party lacked the permanence of organization, the habit of symbolic party allegiance, and the grudging appreciation for logrolling that comes through experience. William Lemke was a bright, decent, hardworking representative dedicated to the interests of his farm constituency; he did not inspire enthusiasm or confidence among those not familiar with him.

Lemke's real potential lay in the chance that he might get enough votes to throw the election to the House of Representatives. Coughlin's NUSJ alone represented several million votes if they followed his lead. The Townsend Club membership was difficult to measure, but based on testimony before the House of Representatives in 1936, estimates were at around two million.[38] Campaign workers for Roosevelt reported there was considerable Union Party support in the key states of Massachusetts, Ohio, and Michigan. Frank Murphy alerted the president that his private poll revealed Lemke had almost 10 percent of the presidential vote, and thus he could hold the balance of power.[39] Even once Coughlin stopped claiming that victory for Lemke would or could happen, he reminded his followers that Lemke needed just 6 percent of the vote to throw the election to the House of Representatives. Democratic strategists, including the president, took steps to stop a vote hemorrhage.

Michigan presented a potentially serious wound. Roosevelt, in 1932, was the only Democratic presidential candidate to win the state's electoral vote since 1856. Auto production had returned to the highest level since the beginning of the Depression, but it had not been at its peak then; unemployment persisted. By 1936, the still weak economy might mean votes would flow back to the Republicans. Too, there was the possibility that Democratic votes would drain off to radical alternatives such as the Union Party. A Democratic poll in the spring indicated Roosevelt could be more confident if the popular Frank Murphy were on the ticket for governor and if James Couzens could be persuaded to change parties and run for senator as a Democrat. Such a ticket would be especially successful in Detroit, said pollsters. Couzens declined Democrats' overtures and ran as a Republican, but Murphy was eager to leave the Philippines as governor-general for the chance to advance his political fortunes. When Roosevelt beckoned, Murphy agreed to "do his duty" in Michigan. As an enticement, Roosevelt even outlined a possible scenario that would give a federal judgeship in Michigan to a Protestant who would agree in advance that once the election was over he would resign so he could be replaced by a

Women handling mail sent to Father Coughlin, 1935. At the height of Coughlin's influence, as many as two hundred women worked sorting and answering the mail that poured into his office in the Shrine of the Little Flower. (Library of Congress, Prints & Photographs Division, NYWT&S Collection [LC-USZ62-111003].)

Catholic. Whether Murphy was surprised or offended by the crass suggestion, he needed no such bargain. It would be "no sacrifice" to make any effort that might be helpful, he assured the president.[40] He was more than willing to help Roosevelt ride his governor coattails to victory. Coughlin regarded Murphy's decision to back FDR as opportunistic, an insult to their long friendship, and totally unacceptable. He supported the Republican candidate for governor of Michigan instead. The battle was joined.

Listeners and *Social Justice* readers were put on the alert. Principle was at stake! A just society and liberty hinged on the election! From June to November letters and telegrams flooded in to the Shrine office. After he broadcast support for Lemke, Coughlin immediately answered one telegram in the pages of *Social Justice*. The sender praised Coughlin's "splendid address" and agreed "enthusiastically" about the need for a progressive party to fight for social justice. But, the reader asked, would it be better not to risk defeating Roosevelt by a vote for Lemke? A vote for Lemke could be a vote for Landon and the Republicans. This might have been a bogus telegram that Coughlin planted. Certainly it was a topic he wanted to address since it was the concern uppermost in the minds of many in his audience. From then until election day he repeated the same refrain: We must "eradicate from our minds the philosophy of defeatism." Voting for Lemke and the Union Party platform was fighting "to the last drop of our political blood and with the last ounce of strength" on behalf of liberty. And "a decent citizen will vote for principle rather than for a winner." And Republicans and Democrats hold power because too many voters believe "this heresy" that a vote for a third party will elect a Landon rather than a Roosevelt.[41] But that fear, held even by Coughlin's admirers, dogged the Union Party campaign from beginning to end.

When the NUSJ was first organized, Coughlin had directed chapters they were not to participate in elections except as individual voters; members should support candidates in their state and local elections who were committed to the principles of social justice regardless of party label. By 1936, however, state chapters endorsed slates of candidates. The Michigan NUSJ recognized that the primary was an important battle ground and so poured considerable effort into backing Coughlin's friend and Washington lobbyist Louis Ward for the U.S. Senate. Ward ran as a Democrat against the well-established Prentiss M. Brown. The race, closely watched as a barometer of Coughlin's strength, was a tight one, and Ward lost by less than 5,000 votes. The Michigan NUSJ also endorsed eleven Democrats and six Republicans in the September primary, and Coughlin claimed credit for helping the six on the "endorsed" list who won. Some of the losing candidates, including Ward, now shifted to the Union Party ticket for the November general election.

One of the few high points for national Union Party enthusiasts was the rally in Cleveland on August 16, 1936. The 42,000 who jammed the Municipal Stadium cheered wildly when Coughlin linked his future with Lemke. He would quit the radio, he roared, if Lemke did not receive 9,000,000 votes in November.[42] Lemke nearly faded into the background as Coughlin took the lead to whip up opposition against Roosevelt. In the pages of Social Justice and when the new radio season began in September, Coughlin's attacks on Roosevelt's performance in office were all-consuming. As always, he mixed statistics with exhortations. There were more jobless, 20 million still on relief, taxes were up on the "little fellow," and government expenses were up from five million in 1932 to nearly nine million in 1936.[43] He increasingly linked FDR and Communists. Social Justice had two full pages in October with photos of Coughlin's long-standing targets who were associated with the administration—Rex Tugwell, Felix Frankfurter, Barnard Baruch, Henry Wallace. Under the title "A Vote for Roosevelt Is A Vote For These," their photos were displayed side by side with several he identified as Communists and or Socialists— "red labor leaders" like David Dubinski and John L. Lewis plus Harry Hopkins, a "red sympathizer and architect of the most stupendous failures of the New Deal administration."[44]

Michigan was one of the states where filing laws prevented the Union Party nominees from appearing under that designation on the November ballot. Therefore, all Union Party candidates would be listed as "Third Party." By whatever name, it was clear that the party was Coughlin's party. In Pennsylvania where the Union Party ran 11 candidates for Congress, they and Lemke were designated on the ballot as the "Royal Oak Party." Ohio, Illinois, and Massachusetts had strong NUSJ chapters and fielded several candidates. Illinois had almost a full Union Party slate including the disreputable former mayor of Chicago, William Hale "Big Bill" Thompson, who was running for governor.[45] The Union Party had difficulty getting on the ballot or was plagued by name confusion in several states, and Lemke finally appeared only in 36. Notably, he was omitted from the ballot in New York, Louisiana, and California, states where he might have anticipated strength. Gerald L. K. Smith announced in October that Roosevelt and those around him had become Communists, and he organized his own fascistic Nationalist Front Against Communism (soon renamed "The Committee of One Million") to strengthen capitalism as a defense. With that, Coughlin and Townsend expelled him from the Union Party. Then, once the Union Party was unable to get on the ballot in Townsend's own California, he bowed to his followers who preferred Landon to Lemke and shifted his support to the Republican.[46] The various architects who initiated the Union Party whether out of idealism or pragmatism could not gather their supporters together under one umbrella after all.

As late as September, Michigan representative John Lesinski warned the Democratic National Committee chairman Jim Farley that Coughlin had a major following in the state; some on the scene were predicting that the Union Party would defeat Roosevelt in the state. Such alarms were more the stuff of insider hyperbole; it was increasingly apparent that the Democrats need not worry about the Michigan vote. Coughlin had muted his claims that the vote for Lemke would be enough to throw the election to the House of Representatives. Despite his unrelenting attacks on Roosevelt's failure to help the little man and the jobless, the priest could not fail to recognize that support for Roosevelt ranged from prominent voices in the Church to rank-and-file factory workers.

As the election of 1936 approached, Coughlin's followers began to resent his assertion that he spoke for them. NUSJ members were often drawn from the ranks of people who felt that Catholics, as targets of bigots, were regarded as mindless sheep who did not think for themselves. They were insulted, therefore, when their own well-placed coreligionists presumed to speak for all Catholics. Roosevelt insider J. P. Tumulty was not well received when he blasted Coughlin's attack against the New Deal and congratulated program director General H. S. Johnson "in the name of Catholic citizens of the nation." There was no need, wrote one NUSJ member, for the prominent to fall all over themselves to speak "for us less prominent Catholics."[47] Now, more Catholics began to regard Coughlin as among a class of clerics who presumed to know what was good for the faithful in every regard. Some NUSJ local groups even disbanded because they objected to Coughlin's endorsement of Lemke. "You have not had your farm saved nor your son put to work by New Deal programs," one writer admonished Coughlin. Nor had the priest any need for the right to collective bargaining, which auto factory workers had just won with the Wagner Act. If progress was too limited, too slow, the government was at least doing more than anytime in their memory. "This generation of Americans has a rendezvous with destiny," Roosevelt intoned at the Democratic convention in the summer of 1936 when he accepted the nomination. His rhetoric alone made them feel important, full of promise. One "member of the Catholic faith" shrewdly assessed Coughlin's impact on other Catholics in her letter to the *New York Times:* "The vicious and uncalled-for attack on the President of the United States by the Rev. Charles Coughlin . . . is one that will be resented by them [Catholics]. By his attitude . . . he has won for the Roosevelt administration thousands of votes."[48] Bishop Gallagher stayed loyal to Coughlin, whom he described as "a national institution, invaluable to the safeguarding of genuine Americanism and true Christianity." But he also told the press that he considered Roosevelt the best candidate. For his unwillingness to silence Coughlin, the Detroit bishop was by now isolated, shunned within the church hierarchy from America to Rome. Leading Catholic publications, cardinals, archbishops, and bishops spoke out vigorously against Coughlin and in favor of Roosevelt. Cardinal Pacelli, secretary of state to Pius XI, traveled from the Vatican in early October to meet with Roosevelt and discuss Coughlin. At a mandatory gathering of the bishops in Cleveland, Pacelli refused even to speak to Gallagher and would not receive him when the Detroit bishop traveled to Cincinnati seeking an audience.[49] Coughlin later revealed that Gallagher came home from these failed encounters with the flat announcement: "Boy, have I got news for you. You're finished."[50]

The Union Party alliance was also coming apart in Coughlin's home base. The Michigan Farmer-Labor Party, Lemke's natural stronghold, was in disarray. Farmers in the F-L Party were agrarian radicals, but there were Protestants among them who had also been members of county Ku Klux Klan chapters or somewhat sympathetic to Klan concerns. To throw in their lot with Father Coughlin was unpalatable. Well before the Farmer-Labor Party's state convention, district committees were voicing a variety of separate positions. One F-L District Committee pointed out when it met in Grand Rapids that Coughlin had alleged there were Communists within the Farmer-Labor ranks. It was an accusation that stung these patriotic farmers. Some in the F-L Party took exception to Coughlin's accusations against Roosevelt. A district committee chair reminded the others that if Roosevelt's programs be "communist-IC" or "socialist-IC" or even "revolutonast-IC," they had aimed to seek security and justice for the mass against the "heartlessness and greed" of the few. So, let's get down to "basic, truly Christian principles."[51] Then there was the labor faction in the Farmer-Labor Party that was determined to bar Lemke's name from the Farmer-Labor ticket because they disliked certain of his associates— Coughlin, William Randolph Hearst, and Big Bill Thompson of Chicago among them—who were regarded as opposing the union movement and as advocating "principles and procedures of a decidedly Fascist nature." Wayne County's chapter voted to make no nomination for president and vice president in the interest of maintaining unity between the farmers and workers in Michigan because, as the chapter recognized, "there is some sentiment among the farmers" to support Lemke and "among the city workers" to support FDR and "there is some sentiment among both farmers and workers in the State of Michigan in opposition to both of these candidates."[52]

When the Farmer-Labor Party met for its state convention in September, any chance for unity disintegrated almost immediately. The farmer faction walked off the convention floor in the Owosso armory and reassembled at the high school, accompanied by a large representation of Townsendites and what the minutes described as an "even larger representation of NUSJ units." Once at the high school, that group also split. The NUSJ walked out and held their own convention that nominated Lemke

and O'Brien to run on the Union Party/Third Party ticket. The farmer faction that remained at the high school nominated Lemke on the Farmer-Labor ticket, but soon, in another twist, since he could run only on one party
ticket on the Michigan ballot, Lemke opted for the Union Party/Third
Party slate. Accordingly, like the national trend at other Farmer-Labor conventions, Michigan's F-L Party went without a presidential candidate on
the ballot and ran a slate with only state, congressional, and county candidates. Farm-Laborites were encouraged to show interest in their friend,
William Lemke, but not in the Union Party/Third Party.

Michigan's NUSJ endorsed congressional candidates in November
based either on their record in public office or their pledge of allegiance to
the principles of social justice. NUSJ approval went to four Democrats,
five Republicans, and the four candidates who ran on the Third Party
ticket along with Lemke as the presidential candidate. There was no overlap between Farm-Labor and Third Party endorsements.

A national poll in October 1936, one of the first election polls ever
taken, found that 33 percent of respondents believed Roosevelt's reelection
was essential for the good of the country. Another 26 percent thought he
may have made mistakes but no one else could do as much good. Most indicated they had no expectation that he would change his policies over the
next term. Whether they thought his reelection essential or just better
than the options, people who supported him thought it was time to settle
down and get the existing programs into operation.[53] The interesting segment of the public, possibly the group that included most Coughlin followers, was the 14 percent who said he did many useful things that needed
doing but thought most of his usefulness was now over, and a majority
thought he would either remain the same or become more conservative.
Only a small fraction anticipated that Roosevelt would become more liberal or more radical. In general, there was substantial sentiment that it was
time to settle down and get the existing programs into operation without
new initiatives.

Michigan and the Election

As the election of 1936 neared, New Deal programs were making their
mark throughout Michigan, a prime target for funding during the previous three years. Thousands of young men were employed in the CCC
camps dotting the state. They fought fires on Isle Royal and in the Thumb;

built a ski tow lift, bridges, and dams; they planted millions of trees in neat rows on land that had been covered with stubble and brush since the lumber crews passed through decades earlier. Of their CCC wages of $1 a day, the boys were allowed to keep $5 a month and $25 went back home, making it possible for mothers to feed younger siblings or even to open bank accounts for the first time. The Federal Writers Project paid unemployed teachers, journalists, and librarians to compile a tourist guide to Michigan. This relief program was intended to provide employment, record local histories, and encourage day or weekend travel around the state. Other WPA workers taught art class or painted murals in public buildings; they built schools, post offices, and community halls. The Social Security Act wooed Townsendites and those who welcomed the government's initiative to provide pensions for the elderly and insurance for those suddenly laid off. The National Labor Relations Act gave collective bargaining the force of law and energized the UAW in its efforts to unionize auto plants. Isolationist sentiment prevailed, but Michigan's Senator Vandenberg was its dependable champion, and neutrality legislation seemed safe in the hands of Democrats and Republicans in Congress who backed it. Roosevelt's recognition of the Soviet Union could be grudgingly accepted since he justified it to promote trade.

Hysterical fear was in retreat; Communism remained an ideological threat but not a clear and present danger in the streets. Locally, the worry about Communist-inspired uprisings faded. Neither Hunger Marchers nor Bonus Army veterans were followed by other such demonstrations as people had feared, and Communist organizers made little headway in Detroit. The noted Mexican muralist Diego Rivera was brought in 1932 to paint a series of panels in the Detroit Institute of Arts and quickly learned that he could not rally his countrymen in Detroit to share his appreciation for the advantages of the Soviet system. He arrived just after the Ford Hunger March, and during the year he was in the city, Rivera organized and lectured the mostly jobless Mexicans in an effort to help them envision a classless society where they would never go hungry. The devoutly Catholic Mexicans had left their home country in part to flee the religious persecution of the anti-Church Cristero Revolution, however. Their lives were hardened by a reality Rivera knew only from books and travel. Fortified by the city's clergy, a group of zealous Mexicans organized in opposition to Rivera. They preferred the freedom in America with all its economic hardships to the "godless worker cooperatives" back home.[54]

Autoworkers were disinterested in debating either the merits or dangers of Communism. In October when Coughlin issued a now-familiar attack on John L. Lewis for jumping from the "frying pan of the AFL" into the CIO's "red fire" of a Communist labor movement, the state's autoworkers were inattentive.[55] They were readying to test their new collective bargaining rights in an effort to help their union win a voice within the American capitalist system. The United Auto Workers formally endorsed Franklin Roosevelt, and on every leaflet passed out at every factory gate was FDR's remark, "If I were a factory worker, I would join a union."[56] When Roosevelt campaigned in Flint—where the UAW had only 136 paying members at the time—over 100,000 people lined the streets. Half a million lined the streets from Hamtramck to Detroit, and 250,000 gathered at in the square at city hall to hear him attack the auto industrialists.[57]

When the votes were in on November 3, Roosevelt had swept up 523 electoral votes, winning in all but Maine and Vermont, which accounted for the 8 electoral votes in Landon's column. The popular vote tally in Michigan was 1,016,794 for Roosevelt, 699,733 for Landon, 75,795 for Lemke, and 8,208 for Thomas. The Communist Party won a smaller percentage of the vote for all their candidates on the Michigan ballot than in any previous election, down to less than a quarter of the levels in 1930 and 1932. Earl Browder, the Communist Party candidate for president, received just 0.19 percent of the vote, and the other Communist Party candidates running for state offices registered even smaller percentages. Of Browder's votes, two-thirds came from Wayne County and most of the rest from the Upper Peninsula.[58]

Roosevelt won every industrial city in Michigan and 52 of the 83 counties. Although Frank Murphy won the governor's race, it was on Roosevelt's coattails, not the reverse as Murphy and Roosevelt insiders had anticipated. In Detroit, 65 percent voted for Roosevelt; in Flint, 72 percent. These percentages were especially impressive when compared with the vote in 1928, when 37 percent of Detroiters and 19 percent of voters in Flint cast their ballots for Al Smith.[59] Polish voters, organized into an all-Polish UAW local, had been a focus of the union's effort to get autoworkers to the polls for Roosevelt, and they proved to be the single most important bloc within the Detroit Democratic Party. In some Polish precincts Roosevelt took more than 90 percent of the vote. Coughlin claimed NUSJ endorsements helped seven Democratic and Republican candidates win; none on the Third Party ticket won, however. Ward, Coughlin's candidate for the Senate, won 50,000 votes out of the 1,000,000 cast.[60] Coughlin had supported the Republican candidate for governor over his old friend Frank

Murphy—described now as a "deserter"—but Murphy was part of the Democratic Party sweep of the state.

On the Sunday following the election, an angry, disgusted Coughlin told his audience he was leaving the radio. It was "high time for the National Union to retire, to sleep." It would cease to be active and adopt a "policy of silence" toward the New Deal administration, he said. When the Union Party first organized in the spring, Coughlin had promised Lemke would win 9,000,000 votes or he would leave the air. Fewer than 900,000 materialized nationwide in November. Over the "ten long years" he had been carrying on the battle "of Christianity against communism, of Christ against chaos," he had anticipated that attacks would come from "the concentrators of wealth, from the industrialist, from the banker and from the press." But, he said plaintively, the killing blows had come from within, fellow clergymen and laity of his own church. It was especially hard that the "vast majority of the members of the National Union took advantage of their prerogative to desert." Of the millions of members who had pledged support to the candidates and his 16 Principles, he regretted to announce that "less than 10%" lived up to their promises.[61]

Coughlin, like some others, did not always grasp a key point: Catholics were Americans just as they had long insisted, part of the nation's ways and habits. They were as diverse as their ethnic heritages, their occupations, the places they lived, their educations. Priests and bishops were not always in agreement about secular matters either. Pro–New Dealers and many scholars would continually characterize the Lemke/Coughlin voters as all of a piece: "fiercely angry, dangerously credulous, and pathetically eager men and women who trooped blindly after the messiahs of the Union Party."[62] Such generalizations were easy, like generalizations about the Ku Klux Klan members of the 1920s. The nearly 80,000 Michigan voters who supported Lemke did so out of reasons as various as the 1,000,000 who voted for Roosevelt's programs or personality, or the 700,000 who voted for Landon out of a preference for his version of reforms or isolationism, or because he suited their traditional Republican habit. Some of the 80,000 Lemke votes came indeed from among people who "fiercely" feared Communism, or who did "troop blindly." But their ranks included also those with eyes wide open who wanted a more inclusive, expansive capitalism than was yet on the horizon with the half-measures of the New Deal. Some Lemke supporters were Protestant farmers and farm town businessmen. No less than other voters, they brought their own personal experiences to the ballot box. One loyal Coughlin supporter challenged his critic Msgr. John Ryan: "Don't it stand to reason that you, nor I, nor anybody else" can pay for rent, gas, lights, insurance, clothes, food, and doctor bills on the "few measly dollars" from Social Security. Let Roosevelt try it out first for about three years, living on "what us poor devils would have" and see "how quick he would change his mind."[63] Analysts and scholars would emphasize the illiteracy and the abject poverty expressed in letters sent by Coughlin champions. The same type of penciled mistakes on lined tablet paper poured into Roosevelt's White House, however. The number of these ill-clothed, ill-housed, and ill-fed thousands totaled higher in the Roosevelt column on election day.

One Michigan voter was a 26-year-old who had hitchhiked from New York early in the Depression, bringing along hope for work and loyalty to Norman Thomas. But in 1936 he voted for Roosevelt and became a Democrat for the rest of his life. Still, nearly 70 years later, he understood well what happened with so many like him that election year of 1936: "When all is said and done, those programs to redistribute income and help the little man would have been better in the long run. But, people live in the short run."[64]

Toward Infamy

Circulation figures for *Social Justice* "melted by one-third" after the election according to Coughlin's own report. He was now printing just 600,000 copies—although this was still more than *Time* magazine. He began running contests about the principles of social justice in each issue with prizes including automobiles and cash up to $2,500. To enter the contest, readers must send ten cents in coin to purchase his book *Money: Questions and Answers* that had been available for some time. He said he would return to the radio when and only if the paper's circulation increased to one and a quarter million.[65] It never approached that.

But by late January 1937, only two months after he announced his departure from the airwaves, Coughlin was back on the Sunday afternoon radio. He did this, he stated, out of duty to Bishop Gallagher who had died four days earlier and had asked, as his last wish, that Coughlin return to broadcasting immediately to "expound the doctrines of Christianity and to expose the fallacies of Communism."[66] He was initially cautious, but soon from the airwaves and the columns in *Social Justice,* Coughlin continued familiar warnings: Roosevelt was exercising the power of a dictator, the president's effort to pack the Supreme Court by adding more justices was an example of one in a series of efforts to take over the states' powers, and unions did not understand the best interests of workers.[67] In January, the UAW had initiated its first test of collective bargaining in the GM plant in Flint where for weeks, they persevered to success with the industry's first sit-down strike. Coughlin warned it would not be good enough if they won the 80-cent-an-hour wage they were striking for because the cost of living would increase and the cost of government would continue to mount; only a change in the Federal Reserve System and the bankers "who brought the depression of 1929" would help the laboring classes in a lasting way. The UAW and CIO were paying their union leaders pluto- cratic salaries, thundered the priest; they were using illegal force to coerce men to join the union.[68]

He restructured the National Union for Social Justice into decentral- ized local "Social Justice Clubs" that were directed not to incorporate; thus members would not become liable for any legal action. By ending the cor- porate structure he ended also his role as president of the NUSJ so that any suits lodged against units could not be lodged against him. He ex- plained he could no longer clear up debts incurred by units or settle such suits as one brought when a pop bottle blew up in the hands of a dispenser at a NUSJ picnic in New York. Michigan remained one possible base that could sustain Social Justice Clubs, and some chapters faithfully met to study the 16 Principles; Bay City's group was at least one that sent proceeds from social activities to support Coughlin's radio broadcasts. Still dis- gusted with NUSJ members over their failure to support Lemke's candi- dacy, Coughlin now insisted only the "sincere" should be admitted to the Social Justice Clubs, not "every Tom, Dick and Harry," not the "intellectu- ally lazy" who refused to gain the necessary knowledge to "break the chains of ignorance."[69] To stay behind the scenes himself, Coughlin ap- pointed Walter Baertschi, a Presbyterian from Toledo, to become the na- tional coordinator of the Social Justice Councils or clubs. The restruc- tured effort failed to attract many followers. Here and there the valiant struggled hopelessly to organize local groups around the charge to hold their legislatures accountable in the battle against Communism, Fascism, and anti-Christianity until Baertschi announced the councils were being dissolved in February 1938.

Gallagher's replacement was Archbishop Edward Mooney. He was brought to Detroit in part to keep Coughlin under control. He appointed selected priests to go over Coughlin's radio scripts, which were now to be submitted on Wednesday before each Sunday broadcast. Coughlin would not retreat from controversial topics, but he had less control as well as less influence over the radio listeners. He decided to cancel the 1937–38 season rather than submit to censorship, and he left the air but, again, briefly. Listeners mounted a campaign of protest against his silencing, and petitions flooded in. One effort from Cleveland aimed for 100,000 signatures on a petition to the pope. Pro-Coughlin rallies drew huge crowds in Detroit and Chicago. A worried Archbishop Mooney told Rome that "undiscerning Catholics" and the "exploitations of ignorance and prejudice among Protestants" who reacted against the priest's ban might gain momentum that would be harmful to the Church.[70] Coughlin was back on the air by January 1938, and his broadcast was carried over 63 stations.[71]

He could still rouse people to action. When he charged that FDR planned to seize Catholic schools in a reorganization bill, thousands sent telegrams to Washington; 10,000 wires went from Detroit alone.[72] Coughlin relied on the freedom he had in the columns of his newspaper, which was privately incorporated and therefore outside the purview of Mooney or the Church. His columns in *Social Justice* dealt more and more with the need for American neutrality; always he regarded Britain as the party responsible for trouble in Europe, and always, even after the United States entered the war, he would insist that Germany and Russia should have been left to fight each other to the death. Persistently, he warned of Communist and Jewish influences in high places. *Social Justice* ran a pink-tinted picture of Eleanor Roosevelt with the caption "The First Lady Likes Pink."[73]

"Bad Jews" and Communists

By 1938, Coughlin's vituperative rhetoric escalated; his zealous anti-Communism became zealous anti-Semitism. For most of his radio career, Coughlin had decried "bad Jews"—international bankers and Communist Jews—and said he knew "good Jews." All the while he resented charges that he was anti-Semitic. He had found it hard to understand why he was damned even for his praise of Lewis Brandeis, a "Harvard man who married into a blue-blooded Christian Massachusetts family." Brandeis was a "high-type Jew" unlike "the Frankfurters."[74] He claimed, "If a Hitler ever raises his ugly head in this nation, real Christians and the members of Social Justice Councils will be the first to protect the Jews." And he insisted that although membership in Social Justice Councils was limited to Catholics or Protestants who believe in the divinity of Christ, the policy was not anti-Semitic because the thousands of Jews who are Christians could also join. When "Jews, Brahmin, Mohammedan religionists, and others" openly profess the divinity of Christ and recognize that "if we cheat our fellow man we cheat Christ," membership in Social Justice Councils would be extended to all of them. To be evenhanded, he noted that politicians could not join either, nor could people who worked for them.[75]

In 1938, he had begun correspondence with Father Denis Fahey, an Irish priest whose anti-Jewish theological position fed Coughlin's own.[76] The more he experienced defections from among former listeners and readers, the more he gravitated toward the American Nazi groups parading under flags of anti-Communism and anti-Semitism, many of them in New York. In the spring of 1938 the first chapter of the Christian Front organized in Brooklyn, open only to Catholics and Protestants and purporting to be anti-Communist in intent. Coughlin supported it for a time; according to his explanation in *Social Justice,* this united front was our last-ditch defense against Communism. The group attracted some bishops and ministers and had the support of the *Brooklyn Tablet,* which was the official archdiocesan newspaper edited by a Coughlin friend. But most of its members were little other than thugs interested in attacking Jews on the streets and in the subways. Irish, Italian, and German Catholics resented being linked with such types through Coughlin. Several prominent Catholics—Bing Crosby and Alfred E. Smith visible among the clerics from Catholic University, Fordham, and Notre Dame—organized the Committee of Catholics for Human Rights to counter the Christian Front.

Coughlin had also become friendly with his old target Henry Ford as unions gained strength. The two agreed about labor-management relationships, and their mutual dislike of bankers similarly provided solid common ground. So, too, did their anti-Semitism. In July 1938, *Social Justice* published the already discredited "Protocols of the Elders of Zion" that Ford had distributed in the 1920s. When the editor of the *Detroit Jewish Chronicle* submitted a detailed article explaining why they were a fraud, *Social Justice* printed it but with a staffer's response that it wasn't important whether or not they were genuine but only that Zionists should disavow them.[77]

Coughlin was far from alone in his anti-Semitism; he was, however, a highly visible "embarrassment" for others, Catholics and Protestants, to denounce and thereby cloak themselves in rectitude. They could pretend not to share similar prejudices. Anti-Semitic discrimination and proscriptions were common from top government levels to boardrooms, to the armed services, and on down to schools and neighborhoods. Housing deeds in and around Detroit commonly had provisions that restricted their sale or occupancy to "persons of the Caucasian race and Christian persuasion."[78] In 1938 Congress rejected a bill to admit twenty thousand Jewish children under the age of 14, and in mid-1939 a ship from Hamburg carrying 930 desperate Jewish refugees had to return to Europe when it was prevented from docking at Miami because the passengers did not have proper immigration papers. More than 80 percent of the American public opposed suspending quotas to accept Jewish refugees until all Americans had jobs. Frank Murphy was just one of the many who opposed taking political risks to rescue Jews. In Coughlin's case, however, his strident and unrelenting anti-Semitism gave his foes leverage to silence him.

Coughlin finally stepped beyond acceptable bounds with his broadcast immediately following the November 10, 1938, Kristallnacht rampage against Jewish businesses, synagogues, and homes in Germany. He devoted his broadcast to making a connection between Communism and the Jews who, he asserted, dominated Soviet Russia after 1917. He excused Kristallnacht as a response of Germans to those Jews too closely linked with Communism; it was directed against the "bad Jews," not the "good Jews."[79] Horrified Catholics joined Jews who wrote to Coughlin, wrote to Archbishop Mooney, wrote to anyone who might act. A few months later, when he claimed that Jewish businessmen were going to discharge Christians to hire Jewish refugees, Jewish leaders stepped up their pressure on the Catholic hierarchy to get him silenced.[80] The Church needed no prodding, and onetime admirers did not rally to save him. They had moved on at the time of the election of 1936, and now, buoyed by a recovering economy, they could champion isolationism and anti-Communism on their own.

Back in the Mainstream

Most Americans remained in no mood to abandon isolationism. Republicans were in the majority among Michigan's 17 representatives in the House of Representatives, and they consistently opposed Roosevelt's efforts at preparedness. In early 1938, 10 of them supported formal consideration of the Ludlow Resolution that would require a nationwide referendum before war was declared. Also in the same year, a majority of Michigan's congressional delegation voted against the Naval Expansion Bill; FDR's strong support for it helped hold the votes of the Democratic congressmen. Similarly, in 1939 the Michigan Republicans voted against FDR's appeal to rescind the arms embargo provision in the Neutrality Act. Even the Democrats refused to give the president approval for initiating a peacetime draft. Michigan's senators, Democrat Prentiss M. Brown and Republican Arthur H. Vandenberg, voted against the conscription bill brought forth in the summer of 1940, and all 17 Michigan members in the House voted against the Burke-Wadsworth conscription bill when it was brought before them. The Michigan delegation in the House also rejected the compromise bill, which passed.[81]

Meanwhile, the hunt for Communist traitors in the United States was reinvigorated when Stalin and Hitler signed their short-lived nonaggression pact in 1939, freeing Hitler to invade Poland that September. Once war engulfed Europe, Michigan factories and mines were integral to the Allies' defense, and loyalty oaths became a regular practice among companies involved in defense production. Workers had to swear they were not members of any group advocating overthrow of the government, specifically not a Communist, Fascist, or Nazi Bund organization.[82] By the summer of 1940 the governor authorized a special "Fifth Column" squad within the Michigan State Police. Soon their role and number expanded to better investigate "subversion, communistic activities, and un-Americanism."[83] Now, a high-ranking state police official was emboldened to reveal he'd had a 300-member Michigan Protective League conducting investigations and keeping files on Michigan radicals as a "hobby" since 1933.[84] Detroit CIO president August Scholle sharply attacked this practice and criticized the close ties between the police commissioner and Gerald L. K. Smith. Patriotism drowned out complaints. Within a few months, the state police proudly proclaimed they had 10,000 Fifth Columnists on file.[85] Their spokesman insisted Michigan had more subversive aliens than any state but New York. It was the same ranking put forward in the 1920s, although Communists and socialists on the list were now joined by Nazis and Fascists.

The bandwagon rolled on. A law to deny the Communist Party candidates a place on the Michigan ballot passed in the House but was narrowly defeated by the Senate. Labor unions were once again accused of Communist leanings, and all across the country, antilabor bills came before state legislatures. Michigan's George Dondero from the Seventeenth District took to the floor of Congress to accuse Walter Reuther of unpatriotic behavior for threatening a strike against GM. When an unauthorized strike did occur, Reuther implied that those responsible were Communists.[86]

Over these months, Coughlin's radio approval plummeted, stations dropped his program, and in October 1939, the National Association of Broadcasters adopted a new code aimed primarily against him that prohibited the sale of airtime to "controversial" speakers. Less controversial, apparently, was the less politically significant Reverend Gerald L. K. Smith who moved the headquarters of his ambitiously named Committee of 1,000,000 to Detroit in 1939 and launched a series of broadcasts over WJR. Here, for a brief time, his isolationist, anti-Communist, antiunion, anti–New Deal crusade found a receptive audience along with some of its most important financial backers.

To Coughlin, it must have been a grand irony and an injustice that his two longtime causes—opposition to war and to Communists—were championed by others while he was silenced. He appeared adamantly oblivious to the damage he had done to himself. WJR, Coughlin's flagship station, had opposed the National Association of Broadcasters Code that denied his right to airtime, but to no avail. The 1939–40 season was his last. Most stations had already canceled his program, and he bluntly announced in the September 23, 1939, issue of *Social Justice,* "I have been retired, temporarily, by those who control circumstances beyond my reach."[87] This time the retirement would be permanent.

Coughlin continued on his course in the pages of the *Social Justice* newspaper, although he severed his official ties to the paper in the spring of 1940 at the insistence of Mooney, who threatened, otherwise, to take over the paper. Control was assumed by a group of his Shrine parishioners who made no claim that it was a Catholic paper.[88] Coughlin contributed no more signed articles although he remained as the major influence. His days there, too, were numbered. He now faced a disenchanted former audience, an angry government, a hostile archbishop, and a new pope who was already a foe of Coughlin when he took that office in 1939. Pope Pius XII was the former Cardinal Pacelli who traveled from Rome to meet with Roosevelt and muzzle Coughlin before the election of 1936. From Detroit's chancery to Washington to the Vatican there was more agreement than ever: Coughlin was a liability.

Once Father Charles Coughlin was viewed as an asset—a voice for democratic government, for a more just form of capitalism, and for the Democratic Party in 1932; he had been the most remarkable and inspiring of modern-day missionaries for the Church. For a while, in the heart of the Great Depression, Father Coughlin gave voice to an uncommon vision of what capitalism might mean to the least of Americans, of what religion should mean in a just society. He was idealistic, optimistic, and full of facts, figures, and recommendations when too many leaders were pessimistic, defeated, or full of old platitudes. Yet he also had much in common with many who sought to be leaders of Americans. He was self-righteous, egotistic, driven by a "with us or against us" mentality, confident in his prejudices, bent on exercising power. Autocratic in his patriotism and holiness, he expected men and women to follow wherever he led. Finally, they chose otherwise.

Bernard DesRoches was a Catholic family man who had moved to Detroit in the 1920s to find a better life than the Upper Peninsula offered a young man. He went to the University of Detroit and then to law school; he married an Irish-Catholic nurse and bought a modest home; he joined the local parish and the Democratic Party. DesRoches worked as a Detroit city employee until he retired, and throughout his long life, he would remain dedicated to the church and to causes of social justice. But he had not hesitated one Saturday in the late 1930s when his then-seven-year-old daughter came home from catechism class with an assignment: "Sister" said they were to listen to Father Coughlin's Sunday broadcast. "Absolutely not!" responded DesRoches.[89] Father Coughlin had strayed too far from what was right.

ANTI-COMMUNISM AND
THE JOHN BIRCH SOCIETY

7 · BETTER DEAD THAN RED

Prosperity makes you free!
   —Marshall Plan poster slogan

When the Japanese bombed Pearl Harbor on December 7, 1941, any voices still opposed to war were drowned out. The entire Michigan congressional delegation supported the war vote against Japan on December 8. The following day, Germany declared war against the United States, and people prepared as best they could for all that war would mean. Almost at once, Americans accepted the new reality that defeating the Japanese and Nazis required making common cause with the Allies who included the Soviet Union. Anti-Communist proselytizing was deliberately set aside by politicians, military leaders, and the media. Soviet leaders similarly understood that they must fight alongside the "capitalist" West out of necessity. Extraordinary times called for uncommon adjustments.

Yet, even before war's end, the clash between the "free world" and the "Communist world" resurfaced. The atomic bomb that ended the war introduced new options and horrible possibilities to both sides. In an all-consuming effort to hold the upper hand but avert nuclear disaster, old hostilities took shape as a new era—the Cold War. This, a war of words, prompted new doctrines from Truman and Eisenhower and new phrases—the Iron Curtain, containment, the domino theory, brinkmanship. It also restored the familiar—Christianity versus atheism, capitalism versus collectivism, democracy versus Communism.

Michigan's defense industries played a crucial role throughout World War II. Immediately after the war, the need to stand united and to arm to "keep the peace" helped maintain the momentum. As the focus of so much attention during war, Michigan's people were well aware of their duty when it became necessary to deal with the looming Communist threat in the postwar era. Just as they stepped up to take the lead in providing planes, tanks, and trucks for war, Michigan residents would shoulder their continuing obligation to protect the democratic way of life at home and abroad in the late forties and fifties.

Wartime in Michigan: "We Can Do It!" [1]

War boosted the economy in a way the New Deal had not managed, and Michigan's industries became the "arsenal of democracy" that Roosevelt, Churchill, and most other commentators in turn proclaimed them. The wartime spotlight illuminated remarkable accomplishments—new and mammoth factories like Ford's Willow Run B-24 bomber plant, the Chrysler Tank Arsenal in Warren, the General Motors Tank Plant in Grand Blanc, and the dozens of others around the state that quickly opened or retooled for war. To fill the new jobs and take the places of the 600,000 who left Michigan for the armed services came the "poster girl" defense workers like Rosie the Riveter and the several hundred thousand workers newly arrived from the South. Retirees were welcomed back, and Mexican migrants were readmitted for the first time since the Depression. Even dwarfs and midgets from Hollywood back lots and sideshows answered the need for people small enough to work in tight places assembling bombers.

The sweep of the spotlight sometimes revealed the cracks and fear-filled dark corners—the shop floors where men resented women, the neighborhood streets where blacks and whites congregated apart and emphasized their differences, the factories that would hire neither women nor blacks, the wildcat factory strikes that violated labor's no-strike pledge, the factionalism that damaged unions. Housing shortages and persistent discrimination helped spark a Detroit race riot in June 1943 that left 34 dead. Apprehensive outstate voters watched the population tilt even more dramatically toward the southeast corner of the state. Almost everyone preferred to deal with these problems later and focus instead on winning the war, their one common cause.

It was a cause shared now with the American Communist Party, whose members gained a measure of respectability for behaving according to their patriotic slogan, "Everything for Victory." [2] Michigan Communists were consistent with the protectionist position put forward by the Communist Party of the United States. The day after Pearl Harbor its leaders had suspended all party members of Japanese ancestry and their non-Japanese spouses for the duration of the conflict.[3]

Vigilance against internal subversives was a wartime routine familiar enough to people who remembered World War I and its aftermath. This time, however, Communists were not officially among the suspects. The House Un-American Activities Committee put away its files on Communist subversives for the duration of war, and, in the same spirit, the city of Detroit deactivated its Subversive Detail or "Red Squad" that had been organized in 1932.[4] Now, the Detroit police joined with the state police, the FBI, and manufacturers' security forces to prevent any interference with war production. Even traffic disruptions could be regarded as threats to production. The state legislature helped by passing a variety of acts to make all manner of interference with the war effort a felony, and people were encouraged to report suspicious types, activities, or talk. Hundreds of allegations were found to be groundless, usually the result of personal or labor disputes. Yet, fear was fanned by arrests of a few Nazi agents and members of a Nazi spy ring in Detroit.[5]

The war made it possible, finally, for the Roosevelt administration to silence Father Coughlin, an achievement welcomed by the Catholic Church. Even after Pearl Harbor, the priest remained unrelenting in his criticism of the president, the purposes behind the war, and the regimentation and end of individual liberties that came with it. Just five months after Pearl Harbor, under orders from the attorney general the post office suspended the second-class mailing privilege of *Social Justice*, effectively ending its distribution. Army trucks pulled up to the shrine to take away Coughlin's mailing list, correspondence, and papers. Several of his secretaries were taken to Washington for questioning. The government considered this longtime foe of Communism to be a Nazi sympathizer and even weighed sedition charges. Coughlin's political activities were effectively finished; he was left with his pulpit and role as a parish priest at his Shrine of the Little Flower where he began. Archbishop Mooney dispatched personal thanks to Roosevelt for his "magnanimous" decision not to prosecute.[6] Objections on the priest's behalf were few and feeble. People who had once tuned in every Sunday to hear the Coughlin voice would still make special trips to his church when they were anywhere near Royal Oak. Visitors from afar walked around the outside looking for the name of their state carved in the stone, recognition for contributions sent to help build the church. Several thousand each week still went to the Shrine of the Little Flower to catch a glimpse of "Father," to pray, to light a candle for the boys overseas. Except to his parishioners, Charles Coughlin was already part of the past. Few paused to recognize the weight of that past.

Henry Ford's day was over too. By now he was discredited for his anti-Semitism and for his openly expressed admiration for Hitler. Still a pacifist, he opposed entering the war, and he also opposed working with "meddling" government agencies when first asked to get involved in war production.[7] He came around only when the Japanese bombed Pearl Harbor, but he was often a difficult presence when the plant at Willow Run was under way. The urgency of war production provided the opportunity to push him to the sidelines of Ford Motor Company, an ambition long held by his assorted foes ranging from the Communists to the UAW to the Roosevelt administration. The War Department's need for equipment and materials brought huge contracts to companies; in return, the government was able to make demands. When Ford's only child Edsel died in 1943, his widow joined with the government to insist that effective control be transferred to Edsel's son, Henry Ford II, who was then brought back from the navy to assume the vice presidency that same year. "Old Henry" was marginalized and forced into retirement in 1945. "Young Henry" fired Harry Bennett, the head of the company's private security force who had manipulated and dominated Ford for years.

Gerald L. K. Smith, still angling for power in his own right, remained hopeful that Michigan would be the place he might win political office. In April 1942 with his brief WJR radio career over, the Disciples of Christ minister published the first issue of *The Cross and the Flag*, a broadside devoted to his anti-Communist, antiwar positions. Instead of the anticipated groundswell, he watched his local sympathizers disappear. That fall, Smith ran unsuccessfully for the Senate in the Republican Party primary. He then made a bid as an independent and was badly defeated. Next, Smith established the America First Party to provide an outlet for voters who were dissatisfied with the war, hoping to influence the two major party conventions in 1944. When that failed, he ran for president on the American First ticket as an alternative to Republican Thomas E. Dewey and Democrat Franklin Roosevelt. He appeared on the ballot only in Michigan and Texas, and out of the nearly 2,200,000 ballots cast in his home base of Michigan, Smith received 1,530 votes; in Texas he got 281 votes.[8] Soon after the war ended, Smith would move on, ultimately taking his organization to California and giving his party a new name, the Christian Nationalist Crusade.

At last, in May 1945 the Germans acknowledged defeat; in August the Japanese surrendered. World War II was over. It had brought economic vitality and full employment to Michigan for the first time since the 1920s; it had given Michigan residents one common cause. War's end put all that in doubt. Almost as soon as the fascist enemy was defeated, however, the familiar Communist foe of old was back.

Anti-Communism Revived

Despite the wartime alliance with the Soviet Union, mistrust and hostility toward Communism never really faded away. Tense, often adversarial negotiations among Roosevelt, Churchill, and Stalin marked their wartime conferences. Of the three, Roosevelt usually played the role of jocular conciliator, but he died in April 1945, before the final conference at Potsdam or the peace negotiations. President Harry Truman and his advisers were in no mood to placate Stalin or compromise with Communists; as the United States demonstrated at Hiroshima and Nagasaki, it possessed the atom bomb. In the postwar world, the former Allies jockeyed to secure their positions in one trouble spot after another, and the once-expedient wartime alliance quickly unraveled. By 1946, in a speech at a small Missouri college where he stood side by side with Truman, Churchill warned Americans of an "iron curtain descending across Europe." Already viewing the world in black and white terms, the American president was soon committed to a policy of "containment" to prevent the Soviet Union from expanding farther. By 1947, a new type of conflict was a reality along with the newly coined name, Cold War. An anti-Communist consensus was broad-based, bipartisan, and ready.

The Cold War—interrupted and reinforced by the conflict in Korea—would help propel the peacetime economy, promote a refocused patriotism, and offer up "Communist agitators" as the explanation for any racial dissension in the streets, factories, and neighborhoods. People were determined neither to be fooled into appeasement nor to be caught off guard again as they had been at Pearl Harbor. With every confrontation between the Soviet Union and the West, it appeared that the USSR was stronger than ever and that Stalin was more dangerous than ever. Michigan industrialists had quickly returned to making autos after the war. But they also eagerly stayed in the business of defense production as partners in the Truman administration's determination to contain Communism and to "strive for victory" in the arms race. A variety of Michigan firms were busied with orders paid for by the Marshall Plan credits. Initiated by Secretary of State Marshall in 1947, this multipurpose program funded European governments so they could buy goods from the United States including food, clothing, farm machinery, and heavy equipment; thereby, they could rebuild their economies and, in the process, weaken the appeal of the Communist Party among their people.

UAW leader Walter Reuther was a strong advocate for the Marshall Plan. He spoke of its importance to combat the strength of the Communist Party in Europe, especially in France and Italy. He backed away from his commitment to a 30-hour workweek at 40 hours' pay and pronounced that autoworkers would be willing to work a 44-hour week on behalf of Marshall Plan production needs. Employers, he pointed out, would get 20 percent more in production at a cost of only 4.4 percent more in hourly wages.[9] By 1953, thirteen billion dollars in foreign aid cycled from the American treasury to European governments to American suppliers and back to Europe in the form of goods. Undergirding the Marshall Plan was the slogan "Prosperity Makes You Free."

Father Coughlin used his pulpit to rail against any new foreign entanglements and especially the United Nations, but a much larger audience agreed with Senator Arthur Vandenberg's position. Once a leading isolationist in the Republican Party and in the Senate, Vandenberg had shifted during World War II to champion bipartisan involvement in international affairs as the best deterrent to any future threats. Appreciative of this very significant turnaround, Roosevelt appointed the Michigan senator to the American delegation that helped draft the United Nations charter. Vandenberg best symbolized others who made a calculated decision to support the United Nations so that, under the guidance of the United States, it could hold the Communists accountable for any acts of aggression. An influential member of the Foreign Relations Committee, Vandenberg was instrumental in helping persuade Congress to pass the Foreign Assistance Act that funded the Marshall Plan, and he encouraged President Truman's strong Cold War rhetoric. Congress and the public would back such an unprecedented expenditure in peacetime, Vandenberg warned, only if the president "scared the hell" out of them.[10]

Polls taken within two years after the war ended found that 75 percent

Ford Rouge Plant workers, members of Union Local 600. Members of
Local 600 were targets of HUAC and a challenge to Walter Reuther. One
of the men pictured here was Vito Leone, probably typical of the others
in the plant who were labeled "left wing" or "Communist agitators."
Leone was in the CCC during the Depression and then worked at the
Rouge from 1940 to 1942 until he joined the war effort. He returned
home to "downriver" and resumed work at the plant in 1946, where he
remained until retiring in 1974. Theirs was a family of Democrats, he told
his grandson, because Democrats were more sympathetic to the unions.
(Courtesy of Michael Gervasi and family.)

of all Americans agreed that the Communist Party in America should be
outlawed.[11] Politicians recognized they had a timely issue, and Michigan's
two major political parties moved to the forefront among states when it
came to demonstrating their opposition to Communism. It was a position
harmonizing conviction and necessity since neither party had a certain
majority. Republicans acknowledged that the long dominance they had
enjoyed from the 1850s was no longer automatic. Democrats recognized
that their electoral sweeps during the New Deal belonged to circumstances of the times and did not signal permanent ascendancy. Michigan

voters had given a narrow 7,000-vote majority to Republican Wendell Willkie over Roosevelt in 1940, but in 1944, by a slightly larger majority, they chose Roosevelt over Thomas E. Dewey. They elected a Democratic governor in 1940 but then in 1942 and 1944 picked the Republican candidate. In state and local elections, ticket-splitting remained a time-honored habit with many contests decided by voters who chose the man rather than the party.

Republicans regained strong postwar majorities in the state legislature because district boundaries were defined according to geography rather than population size, giving rural outstate voters disproportionate representation. Since the population tilt had accelerated during wartime, however, critics of that old system were stepping up their claims on behalf of densely settled southeast Michigan. Outstate residents were on the defensive more than ever. Meanwhile, Republicans fought among themselves and guarded their power even when the governor was from their own party. Democrats did the same. Strategists in both parties understood victory at the polls would hinge on coalitions and issues that tapped into broader concerns. Once politicians and the press began emphasizing the threat of Cold War, few issues had such near-unanimous appeal as anti-Communism.

Republican governor Kim Sigler took up the cause of anti-Communism as soon as he was elected in 1946. In his zeal, the flamboyant former prosecuting attorney mistakenly named the Detroit Council for Youth Service as a Communist front group on the basis of state police files containing incorrect information. Under pressure, he abolished the Subversive Investigation Squad in 1947, but this did not signal a change of direction. Efforts of the state police during the war years had legitimated and institutionalized their role in the crusade against un-Americans.[12] Even though it was learned soon after the war that troopers had taken bribes to protect organized gambling in Wayne and Macomb counties for several years, the revelations did not dim the public's confidence in the state police as a whole. The commissioner retired, the guilty men were dismissed, and people were satisfied. Letters to the local newspapers represented the sentiment that these officers were among the bad apples who could be found everywhere. People remained mindful of the troopers who had trained medical personnel, firemen, air raid wardens, and plant guards; troopers, they believed, had been a first line of defense against any possible sabotage. Their good work should proceed.

The anti-Communist campaign continued to widen in Michigan. In 1947, the state legislature enacted a version of the Alien Registration Act or

Smith Act that Congress passed in 1940, which made it a crime to teach, advocate, or encourage overthrow of the government and required all aliens to register with the government. Modeled on the same lines as the state police, the city of Detroit's Red Squad was reinstated in February 1948.[13] At the federal level, bills passed in 1948 and 1949 required registration of the Communist Party and Communist front organizations. Communist Party members could not be employed in the federal government or defense industries, and Communist organizations' use of the mails was tightly controlled.[14] By such legislation, it was hoped that recalcitrant alien Communists would be jailed or deported, others would leave the party, and many would be dissuaded from joining it. Michigan was in the spotlight of investigations stemming from anti-Communist legislation since, from the outset with the Smith Act, labor unions were prime targets for scrutiny. Ironically, the Communist Party in Michigan was losing members on its own.

Communism and the Unions

The Ford Rouge Plant's UAW Local 600 had a number of longtime Communists in leadership positions, and it was the strongest base the Communist Party had in the auto industry. Yet, even here, it had only a feeble toehold. Ever since the 1939 Soviet-German nonaggression pact, one layer of supporters after another peeled off from the Communist Party in America. Militants were angered when the party supported the war effort, defense production, the no-strike pledge, and internment of the Japanese. Blacks in the party believed its white leadership had not been sufficiently aggressive about civil rights and fair employment, asserting that those causes had been subordinated to winning the war. Women in the party welcomed the support they received from certain Communist Party members in the UAW and other industries, but then there were those within the party who opposed equal pay for women. By the end of war, the Communist Party abroad and at home had disappointed too many segments of its constituency. Party leaders also blundered when assessing the American electorate. Communist Party leaders fearfully anticipated that a fascist government was about to win power after the war when Americans began to approve peacetime restrictions and a continued defense buildup in reaction to Cold War and "iron curtain" warnings. Acting on that mistaken assumption, they tried to thwart the possibility by entering politics on the side of the Progressive Party in 1948 and backed its candidate Henry Wallace for president. In Michigan, this angered left-leaning liberals within the Democratic Party who, for years, had been sympathetic to many Communist Party concerns. Doctrinaire Communists who hailed Wallace as an alternative to "oppressive capitalists" also miscalculated the influence that a healthy postwar economy had on an appreciative working class. The net effect was to marginalize the Communists, diminish their influence, and thin out their numbers.

Within the ranks of organized labor, Walter Reuther contributed significantly to anti-Communism in the course of the complicated, factious struggle over union control dating from the 1930s. When war production first took hold, union members were very new to the ways of labor negotiations, and they did not always share a common vision. Activists who held socialist or Communist views demanded more worker control as well as equal hiring and equal pay for black workers. Others, especially those among Jimmy Hoffa's Teamsters, were comfortable with mob ties, influence peddling, and deals. Denouncing both camps, Walter Reuther and August Scholle of the CIO promoted centrist economic and social issues. At a UAW convention in August 1941 before the United States was yet in the war on the side of the USSR, Reuther attacked Communists running for office in the union. No one whose loyalty is "first to a foreign government" could be trusted "to serve the best interest of our union," he asserted.[15] During the war, Reuther expanded his base of support in the UAW by forcefully defending workers' interests, by opposing piecework and incentive pay, and by his opposition to the no-strike pledge when it became obvious that employers used it to their own advantage. To the left wing and Communists within the UAW, he had not gone far enough with his demands on behalf of workers, black and white. The rift widened.

Reuther's shift to a strong anti-Communist stance was of significant importance to Catholics, especially the many factory workers who belonged to the Association of Catholic Trade Unionists. The ACTU was formed in 1937 to mobilize Catholic workers in order to counter Communist influence within unions, especially the CIO and the UAW. The Catholic trade union echoed Coughlin's call to promote social justice in the workplace as an antidote to the appeal of Communism and socialism. But Coughlin advocated company unions, avoidance of class conflict, and opposition to the CIO and UAW. The ACTU believed, instead, that industrial unions independent of employers could be vital in the effort to promote the social justice doctrines expressed in the papal encyclicals *Rerum*

Novarum and *Quadragessimo Anno*. Detroit's Archbishop Mooney threw his support to the ACTU, and the archdiocese helped set up area chapters and Catholic labor schools. The ACTU published a newspaper, the *Wage Earner*, which circulated in UAW shops to counter the Communists' *Daily Worker*. From its founding, the Michigan ACTU was the second largest chapter in the country, surpassed only by the New York City chapter. Co-operation between the ACTU and the UAW became a pattern; the ACTU executive secretary was also the UAW education director in 1940 and 1941. Irish, German, and Polish Catholics in the Rouge Plant became solid Reuther supporters. To help Reuther counter Communist challengers for UAW leadership posts, ACTU members agreed to run joint slates with the UAW. Critics argued that the alliance with the ACTU smacked of unprincipled opportunism on both sides. Reuther, after all, had helped raise money for the loyalists in Spain in the 1930s, a cause the Catholic hierarchy denounced. Still, the wartime alliance between the two unions served both groups on the shop floors. The Cold War cemented the coalition.[16]

In March 1946 Reuther won the union presidency, but his margin was slight, and anti-Communism became more significant as a means to forge an effective alliance between Association of Catholic Trade Unionists and UAW members.[17] It also become more important for the union to parade its anti-Communism when, in the fall of 1946, Republicans gained control of Congress for the first time since 1930. Once in session, the new majority began to cut back on New Deal programs, pass restrictive antilabor legislation, and reinvigorate the House Un-American Activities Committee, which began anew to search for Communists in the labor movement. Such a turn of the political tide made it expedient for Michigan union members to demonstrate their loyalty as patriotic Americans and, at the same time, mobilize their votes for the Democratic Party.

Political Sense

Organized labor had long maintained it would not automatically be in the pocket of either major political party but would promote the party and those candidates who supported New Deal policies. The AFL and CIO abandoned their position of calculated nonpartisanship, however, when Congress passed the Taft-Hartley Act in 1947. The act enabled states to forbid union shops, and the Michigan Republican legislature promptly weakened the state's labor law. Reuther, an active Norman Thomas supporter in the 1930s, had become disappointed in the heart of the Depression when only 2 percent of Michigan voters supported the Socialist Party candidate. He arrived at the conclusion that the two major parties were the only hope for achieving economic and social reform and now threw his political energies into rebuilding the Democratic Party in Michigan.

In 1948, Reuther and August Scholle, who was head of the Michigan CIO-Political Action Committee, joined the core group determined to seize the Democratic Party from the old-guard conservatives and stop the Teamsters' Jimmy Hoffa in his bid for party control. The now determinedly partisan UAW and CIO joined with a young generation of ardent New Dealers, Democratic Party liberals, and blacks to form a strong coalition backing G. Mennen Williams for governor. The result was a victory for Williams over incumbent Kim Sigler, and Democrats also made gains in the state legislature.[18]

The influence they could have as members of this new coalition was not lost on rank-and-file workers who were hoping for a political climate that would promote their interests. A major UAW strike at the Ford Rouge Plant in 1949 demonstrated the unlikelihood that local Communists could any longer hope to strengthen their base in the factories. For six months before workers went out on strike, the Michigan District of the Communist Party tried to recruit by staying on the edges of planned union actions. Saul Wellman, the National Auto Coordinator of the Communist Party, was based in Detroit, and a significant part of his work consisted of staying alert to issues in the various factories and within the community. To keep the Michigan Communists' position visible, Wellman organized volunteers who carried on a leafleting campaign and sold the Michigan edition of the *Daily Worker* at the Ford Rouge Plant gates. Factory workers bought the paper before and during the strike because the major Detroit newspapers remained quiet about the issues. Unfortunately for the movement, sales did not translate into members, and the Communist Party continued to decline.

Even though the Communist faction in the UAW was successfully defeated by 1949, Reuther continued to use its presence as a straw man. When he backed away from demanding a 30-hour workweek for 40 hours' pay, he justified himself by explaining the shorter workweek as a Communist Party ploy to limit production and thus weaken the nation's capability in the Cold War. A shorter workweek would be a "sham gain" for union members because the real benefit would go to the Communists, said Reuther.[19] Governor Williams and the new Democratic coalition were

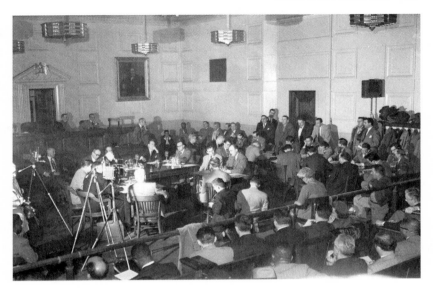

House Un-American Activities Committee courtroom scene, February 26, 1952. When HUAC held inquiries into the extent of Communist influences in Michigan, the focus was on the UAW and civil rights organizations. Witnesses offered sensational revelations; a vast conspiracy was said to reach into factories and schools. No one was ever brought to trial, but in the aftermath, dozens of alleged subversives were fired, beaten, or forced to move. (Walter P. Reuther Library, Wayne State University.)

generally sympathetic with Truman's Cold War programs to stem Communist influence in Europe—especially the Marshall Plan, which intended to help European countries rebuild from war. It fit the time-honored American credo that people would be less vulnerable to socialist and Communist systems if they had a stake in society and hope for the future. It also cycled huge appropriations from the federal budget back to Michigan companies that were filling European requisitions for goods. Combating Communism was a worthwhile cause all the way around.

Radicalism among the Upper Peninsula miners too was tempered as the copper country recovered from immediate postwar slump when the Korean War brought government contracts and subsidies back to the mines. Fights among miners' factions introduced charges and countercharges about people who were Communist sympathizers, and the label "Communist" played into purges. One of the leaders of the International Union of Mine, Mill, and Smelter Workers (IUMMSW) was kicked out of his position in 1949 for "sabotaging" the union's effort to fight wage decreases and for his authoritarianism. He reacted by accusing the union of being a front for Communism. Other union leaders angrily denounced the accusation. The IUMMSW joined the CIO in 1950, but that same year, it was expelled for its "communism." Trying to signal its respectable politics, the IUMMSW supported G. Mennen Williams for governor in 1950. The union regained CIO approval and its support for the miners' strikes in 1952 and 1955. Mine workers' locals, in turn, became vigorous supporters of CIO efforts to end racism.[20]

Failed hopes coupled with the anti-Communist legislation discouraged all but a core of remaining Communist Party activists. The stalwarts adjusted their tactics and went underground on the theory that they could not maintain the movement if members who were operating in the open were arrested. Wellman shifted his living quarters around from place to place so he could not be shadowed. In an attempt to increase efficiency and security, the size of party clubs was reduced to 6 to 8 members. Clubs were made of members living in the same general vicinity or according to language for those whose primary language was not English. Because the party operated more secretively, internal communication fell into disarray. Most delegates did not even know the site of the Communist state conference held on March 27, 1949—at the Jericho Temple in Detroit—until a few hours before it started. By then, the Communist Party had only 17 to 19 people on the payroll in Michigan. According to J. Edgar Hoover's figures, Michigan had 750 Communists known to the FBI in 1951 and ranked ninth in the country. Nationwide, the total of known Communists was put at 43,217, a decrease of more than 20 percent compared with just a year earlier.[21]

HUAC: A Mission in Michigan

Although the American Communist Party membership was withering away, fear mounted that "reputable" and "upstanding" Americans were Communist agents or sympathizers in disguise. This interpretation was part and parcel of the complicated explanations for the escalating hostilities between the West and the Soviet bloc. In 1949, the eleven-month Berlin airlift ended with that city and Germany still divided; the Soviet Union tested its first atomic bomb; the United States, Canada, and western European allies established the North American Treaty Organization (NATO);

the Communist forces of Mao Tse-tung won the Chinese civil war; and Chiang Kai-shek was driven into exile on Taiwan. Then in June 1950, Cold War gave way to armed combat when the Communist government of North Korea invaded South Korea. During the following three years, the United States provided most of the UN troops who fought in the Korean War. By the time a 1953 armistice restored the original boundary between North and South, 33,000 Americans had died in a war that many Americans saw as a victory. In Eisenhower imagery, the South Korea "domino" had not been toppled. Meanwhile, the struggle to contain Communism abroad was matched by the struggle to identify Communists at home.

The House Un-American Activities Committee had begun holding a series of hearings and, by 1948, caught public attention when it called prominent movie stars, writers, and producers to testify. Hollywood was a prime target for committee members' suspicions that Jews in the movie industry had socialist or Communist leanings and were using the screen to propagandize. When a few—soon called the Hollywood Ten—refused to answer the committee's questions, the public assumed they had something to hide and applauded their imprisonment for contempt of Congress. HUAC also uncovered the alleged Communist connections of Alger Hiss, a high-ranking state department official in the Roosevelt administration. Richard Nixon, a young congressman from California and a member of HUAC, doggedly pursued Hiss with the help of Whittaker Chambers, an editor from *Time* magazine who admitted that he too had been part of a chain that passed documents to the Soviets in the 1930s. A jury found Hiss guilty of perjury, and he went to prison for five years. Nixon had made a name for himself, and, in 1950, he won a seat in the Senate using the issue of Communism against his opponent who had been critical of the HUAC hearings. That same year, Governor Williams reestablished the Michigan State Police Red Squad, which he intended the public to regard as a "little FBI." Granted wide latitude, it was accountable only to the state police commissioner with no oversight from the attorney general. The Republican-controlled state legislature passed tough anti-Communist laws that also took effect in September 1950.

A politician's record on "Communists at home and abroad" was certain to come up in any campaign from the late 1940s onward. An obscure junior senator from Wisconsin demonstrated just how powerful the issue of Communism could be. In 1950, aiming to pave the way for his reelection that was coming up in two years, Senator Joseph McCarthy announced that he had a list of 205 "known" Communists who were in the State Department. He made the claim in an out-of-the-way speech before a West Virginia women's club, but within hours, the hunt for internal subversives was heading to new heights, and McCarthy's political fortunes skyrocketed along with it. Capitalizing on the atmosphere this undocumented announcement helped create, McCarthy began to use the Senate subcommittee he chaired to seek out the disloyal, harrying government officials in various agencies and harassing political enemies in his own Republican Party as well as in the Democratic Party. For the next four years he would stay in the headlines as he badgered witnesses using guilt by association, innuendo, and unsubstantiated charges—tactics that few in public office or the press had the courage to attack and tactics that most citizens, at the time, were willing to overlook. People were more concerned with the number of well-placed Americans who might be subversives rather than with the protection of suspects' constitutional rights. McCarthy not only had assured his own reelection but was in demand as a speaker and as a platform presence in election campaigns around the country.

Meanwhile, from 1950 through 1953, the dramatic case of Julius and Ethel Rosenberg was playing out in the press, in movie newsreels, and on television. The Jewish couple had been members of the Communist Party in New York before World War II. Arrested by the FBI, they were put on trial in 1951 on charges of conspiracy to help the Soviet Union develop the atom bomb by passing classified secrets from Los Alamos. After months of sensational revelations and bizarre pieces of evidence, they were found guilty and sentenced to death. Eisenhower, once in office, refused all appeals to spare their lives for the sake of their two young sons, and they became the first U.S. civilians executed for espionage.

Home to aggressive union champions and assertive civil rights activists, Michigan was deemed by those on the hunt for Communists and their sympathizers to be a likely breeding ground. When the House Un-American Activities came to Detroit to hold hearings in February and March 1952, the public was in a mood to pay attention. One of the members of HUAC was Michigan Republican Congressman Charles Potter from Cheboygan who intended to run for the Senate in November, and he promised "sensational disclosures" on Communist infiltration in the Detroit area. It was of obvious benefit to bring the traveling HUAC hearings to the state when allegations about the Communists and cover-ups in the Rouge Plant's Local 600 presented the justification. Two years before, the International UAW had put five men from Local 600 on trial for being Communist Party members or sympathizers. The trial was widely publicized and so was the guilty verdict. Then, the five appealed to the General Council of Local 600, which reversed the decision. All of this attention led HUAC to Detroit—a visit not entirely distasteful to the UAW International, which was trying to consolidate gains made over the leftist activists in the union. CIO-UAW leaders were not able to contain or restrict the committee's reach once it arrived in town, however.

In the process of securing his own position and worker solidarity for the union's bargaining efforts, Reuther and the UAW had become identified as champions of civil rights by the late 1940s. HUAC, McCarthy, and J. Edgar Hoover's FBI regarded their search for Communists in the unions as an entwined search for Communists within civil rights organizations. Linking the two groups was an easy leap for those who liked neither unions nor blacks. Detroit was a natural place to probe. When the hearings took place, Congressmen on the committee were preoccupied with calling witnesses who could help reinforce their suspicions. State police informants came forward to warn of a vast Communist conspiracy at work within Michigan factories and schools. Seventeen officers or former officers of UAW Local 600 were subpoenaed, and most were denounced by the committee. It had only praise for Walter Reuther's performance as a "friendly witness." Black activists refused to be intimidated. Among them was Coleman Young who would become Detroit's mayor 20 years later. Young and others won the admiration of the black community for speaking out on behalf of the right to free speech. By contrast, the white community proved almost uniformly in support of HUAC's aims and tactics. In all, 40 witnesses were called, most of whom took the Fifth Amendment, adding to the public's perception that these people must have something to hide. With the race riot of 1943 still a vivid memory, anyone looking for an easy explanation for that disturbance could lay the blame on Communist agitators, black and white.

So far as the press and public saw it, the most exciting revelations were offered by Bernice Baldwin, a Detroit grandmother who was a practical nurse. Now the truth was told. She had been a spy within the Michigan Communist Party for nine years. She named names. Just prior to the HUAC visit, Baldwin had testified in Washington before the Subversive Activities Control Board, describing the Communist "leadership" courses she took in 1947 and 1948 at the Michigan School of Social Sciences which offered a variety of classes with texts issued by the Communist Party, USA. As she and government lawyers described it, the purpose of the school was to educate "lesser leaders" like Baldwin so they could tell the rank and file how to translate worldwide Communist Party policy into action in De-troit. The Michigan effort was especially aimed at autoworkers, she said, to show them that Walter Reuther was part of the American industrialist for-eign policy and was sabotaging issues vital to workers such as wages, speedups, and Taft-Hartley restrictions.[22]

Ironically, her testimony demonstrated the failure to win over new members to the Communist Party in Michigan. Evidence Baldwin intro-duced into the record included recruitment quotas handed down in 1949 from the Communist Party, USA. Seemingly modest expectations aimed for 100 recruits from Dearborn, 75 from among the youth, 15 from Washt-enaw County, 50 from western Michigan, 25 from Flint, and 9 from the Upper Peninsula. Party directives targeted specific ethnic groups with the goal of 7 Russians and 5 Poles. They were not meeting those quotas, Bald-win assured the committee. The press and public did not stop to wonder why so much ado, then, about so few recruits. Mrs. Baldwin was "A Detroit Patriot," editorialized the *Detroit Free Press;* she was in a class with others like the much-publicized Herbert Philbrick, one of those who posed as "disciples of Moscow" while serving America as FBI agents.[23]

When state police commander Leonard testified, he stressed that no one had been arrested only because it was difficult to prove subversion since existing laws were too weak. Leonard pressed for a grand jury, but again the attorney general resisted. In the immediate aftermath of the HUAC visit, however, retribution more destructive than any grand jury hearings played out again and again. Dozens of alleged subversives were fired from their jobs or union offices, even evicted from their homes. Those accused of being Communist Party members were outcasts among their own—on factory shop floors where party members were beaten up, in the Detroit Federation of Teachers where an art teacher with twenty-three years' seniority was denied defense by vote of the membership, in the Musicians' Union that expelled a Detroit Symphony violinist. Diego Rivera's 1930s murals in the Detroit Institute of Arts were nearly slated to be destroyed for their unflattering portrayal of factory life, but the city art commission decided they held no trace of "ideology."[24]

Staying the Course

The threat of Communism at home and abroad was a prominent feature of the 1952 election season. Michigan Republicans were debilitated by infighting and were divided about whether moderate Dwight Eisenhower or conservative Robert Taft should be the party's standard-bearer. Before his death in 1951, the venerable Senator Vandenberg had chided fellow Republicans in Congress for having too eagerly followed Senator Joseph McCarthy in his use of Communism to discredit the Marshall Plan and other important bipartisan programs. Still, a number of Republicans insisted that any criticism of anti-Communist hard-liners was evidence that the critic was a traitor to his country.[25]

During the election campaign, Senator McCarthy came to speak in Michigan on behalf of his friends and fellow Republicans, congressmen Charles Potter and Alvin Bentley. Potter was running for the late Arthur Vandenberg's seat in the Senate and was one of the "patriots" recommended to voters by the right-wing *Chicago Tribune* publisher, Robert McCormick.[26] He was running against Blair Moody, appointed by Williams to the Senate a year earlier upon Vandenberg's death. Bentley was running for reelection to Congress. Potter's visibility was indeed boosted by the HUAC hearings, and his campaign emphasized his connection with its vigorous pursuit of Communism.[27] When the November ballots were tallied, Potter was elected to the Senate, and Bentley was reelected to his seat in Congress. With his promise of "Modern Republicanism" and a campaign pledge to do battle with "Korea, Communism, and Corruption," the personally popular Eisenhower won 55 percent of the votes in Michigan to Stevenson's 44 percent. G. Mennen Williams, the Democrat, was returned to the governor's office by a razor-thin margin. The meager vote for "radicals" was just one indication of the negligible support for the "left" in Michigan. Out of over 5,800,000 ballots cast for governor, 1,192 went to the Socialist Labor candidate and 628 to the Socialist Worker candidate. By comparison, the candidate running on the ever-present Prohibition Party ticket received 8,990 votes.[28]

The Korean War ended in 1953; the Cold War endured. Stockpiling of nuclear weapons by the United States and the Soviet Union had accomplished "mutually assured destruction," and both sides were more skilled at "brinkmanship" to avoid all-out nuclear war. By the mid-1950s, McCarthy was in disgrace, and the anti-Communist witch hunts were leveling off, significantly relieved by Cold War preparations and institutionalized precautions. In Michigan, Governor Williams and the state legislature had demonstrated their vigilance, and the union rank and file had conclusively chosen centrists over left-wing leaders. The state suffered from a sharp recession in 1954, but the auto industrialists and the people dependent upon it hoped that their industry, along with national security and free enterprise, was in good hands with cabinet members like secretary of defense Charles Wilson, former president of General Motors who reassuringly pronounced, "What's good for the country is good for General Motors, and vice versa." Nonetheless, worrying about future threats to personal and national security was a habit not to be neglected.

Michigan civic groups continued to welcome state police officers to their meetings to show films about Communist tactics and to speak about never-ending Communist intentions. Home and school bomb shelters emerged as one precaution. Arguments raged in communities torn over whether to put fluoride in their water—which some parents wanted for the sake of their children's teeth, but which others interpreted as a foreign-inspired plot to subtly poison Americans. Citizens heard unabated warnings from state legislators, congressmen, ministers, and priests about the insidious and subtle corruption of America's youth. At its peak, the number one television show was Archbishop Fulton J. Sheen's program "Life Is Worth Living," which aired weekly from 1952 to 1957 in prime time. His sermons on the evils of Communism seemed prophetic indeed when, in February 1953, he promised "Stalin must one day meet his judgment" and within a few days, the Soviet dictator was dead of a stroke.[29]

It was the Supreme Court decision in *Brown v. the Board of Education of Topeka*, read by Chief Justice Earl Warren on May 17, 1954, that set into motion the most serious of fears. Soon it became clear that court-ordered school integration would be applied not only in the South but in northern states including Michigan where it had been sidestepped by neighborhood segregation coupled with the historic custom of neighborhood schools. To its most strident opponents, the ruling signaled there were Communist influences at work within the Supreme Court aiming to destroy neighborhood schools and families.

For some years before the decision, the Communist Party in Michigan had been concentrating its efforts on racial justice, voting rights, police brutality, and fair employment practices. Hardly the stuff of violent revolution, these were issues that mainstream moderates and liberals supported too, if less stridently. Nonetheless, the party's emphasis on civil rights continued to link Communism and blacks in the mind of J. Edgar Hoover, just one of many Americans who saw a connection. This assessment was not without "evidence" because Communists were active participants in the mounting crusade to integrate schools and neighborhoods. The Communists in this cause were not automatically welcomed, however. Always, they were just a handful among the thoughtful citizens who, like the Court, regarded "separate but equal" to be inherently unequal.

Inevitably, the Red Scare had left a legacy to be tapped at will: No American was above suspicion. People who had followed the HUAC hearings, McCarthy's allegations, and the local revelations came away openly wondering how many other respectable Americans could be agents of the Communists or their tools. The Red Scare hunt had unearthed a new reality. Unlike the ragtag immigrant radicals earlier in the century, now subversives might be from among the native-born well-educated class, men in suits who parlayed Ivy League educations into influential appointments. It was not unthinkable that even the Supreme Court had been infiltrated. Here, some believed, was a clear and present danger.

Unwilling to be lulled into complacency, by the end of the decade a handful of the determinedly wary organized. They held meetings in city and suburban living rooms, basement recreation rooms, and small-town community halls where they talked and studied together. The men might arrive wearing suits and the women wearing pearls on matched sweater sets; they looked much like the "enemy within" they hoped to identify. A popular song by the Chad Mitchell Trio put words in their mouths. Socialism is the "ism dismalest of all," sang the three. They poked fun at the fearful who were on the look-out for Bolsheviks, socialists, and assorted dangerous types in towns large and small. Audiences cheered when the trio belted out the patriots' determination to use hands and hearts and, "if we must we'll use our heads."[30] Such mocking taunts did not daunt them. They were the members of the John Birch Society.

Few in number, Birch Society members and their fellow travelers would be a unified voice in the Michigan Republican Party cacophony. Their expressed determination to halt the progress of socialism and Communism in the nation gave them justification to speak with certainty on almost every issue under debate in the state—whether legislative reapportionment, property taxes, open housing, or water fluoridation. Many Birch members stood to gain some personal benefit or political advantage, but they spoke on behalf of all "patriotic Americans." They were confident that Michigan's record of promoting unions, civil rights, and social reform demonstrated the obvious. This state was just full of Bolsheviks.

8 · EXTREMISM IN DEFENSE OF INFLUENCE
The John Birch Society

The John Birch Society has more respectable community leaders and solid citizens than any extremist group in years.
—*Detroit Free Press* reporter after several months undercover in the Society

With a solid majority of Americans so obviously opposed to all that Communism represented, no vigilant minority needed to organize, or so it would seem. Robert Welch thought differently when he assembled 11 men from nine states for a two-day meeting in Indianapolis in December 1958. Before the meeting adjourned, the John Birch Society was on its way to a platform and structure that would soon make it the largest, most well-funded, best-organized, most-publicized anti-Communist group in the country.[1] Michigan had its first chapter within a few months, the twelfth in the nation.

Robert Welch, a prominent businessman living in Massachusetts, was a Baptist whose origins were in North Carolina. He had graduated from the University of North Carolina and attended law school at Harvard for two years. After early business failures, Welch joined his brother's candy manufacturing firm as the vice president of sales and advertising where his success established his reputation. He became a member of the board of directors of the National Association of Manufacturers and its regional vice president for a time. On business or pleasure trips, Welch arranged interviews with world leaders including Konrad Adenauer, Chiang Kai-shek, and Syngman Rhee; in England he looked for the "effects of the Socialist government" at first hand. Prominent in Massachusetts Republican politics, Welch was a supporter of Joe McCarthy, worked hard for presidential nomination of the conservative Robert Taft in 1952, and was bitterly disappointed that the convention nominated Dwight Eisenhower.

On the heels of the 1954 congressional elections, Welch had begun issuing a "private letter" titled *The Politician.* Eisenhower was the initial focus of his conviction that a deep-seated, far-reaching Communist penetration was under way in America. Eisenhower's failure to do more to help conservative candidates, he wrote, convinced him that the president was a "dedicated, conscious agent of the Communist conspiracy."[2] By 1956, he began editing and publishing a monthly magazine, *One Man's Opinion.* Welch had learned about John Birch in the process of reading through the reams of material turned up in the course of the McCarthy hearings. Birch was born in India while his parents were there serving as missionaries, but he grew up in Georgia. Like Welch, he was a Baptist and was serving as a missionary stationed in China when World War II started. Soon he joined the army air force and became a captain. Since he was able to speak Chinese, Birch was selected ten days after V-J Day to lead a special force of American, Chinese Nationalist, and Korean soldiers into China. The purpose of the mission remains unclear, but when he and his men encountered a group of Red Chinese, John Birch was shot and then bayoneted to death. The others were taken prisoner. Men along on the mission later reported that Birch tried to bluff his way out, insulted the Communist Chinese, and displayed such anger and arrogance that the Chinese leader shot him. But as Welch saw it and wrote in *The Life of John Birch,* this hero's death marked the first casualty of World War III, the war against the Communists.[3]

Most who came to the founding meeting in Indiana were older businessmen already familiar with Robert Welch through various contacts. They knew his views, whether or not they had much knowledge of John Birch. All but one of the eleven in attendance agreed to join the board of the new society named for Birch—whom they elevated to martyr status. Like Welch, the other board members believed the greatest danger to America came not from a possible military takeover by the Soviets or Chinese but from a conspiratorial cabal of Communists inside the country who were boring into its institutions. Like Welch too, they thought the situation had been worsening since the time when Woodrow Wilson put the country "in the same house" with European "collectivists" and that dangers escalated under Franklin Roosevelt who went even farther, putting the nation in the "same bed" with them while "lying in his teeth" about it.[4] With the Society agreed upon, the new board members went home to tap wealthy like-minded friends and political acquaintances for contributions. Welch went home to Belmont, Massachusetts, to direct the Society's hierarchical organization he headquartered there.

Within a few weeks, Robert Welch was traveling around to hospitable climates where he publicized the cause. A John Birch Society chapter in Grosse Pointe became the first in Michigan and the twelfth in the nation. Michigan's initial Birch Society chapter took root in Grosse Pointe not to "meet the devil" where he was strongest, but because Grosse Pointe was home to an activist base of well-organized, ardent conservatives with monied connections. Many of them already shared the same core convictions as Welch's Birch Society.

Home Base

Grosse Pointe, properly defined, was one of a cluster of five mostly wealthy separate suburbs all named Grosse Pointe, but each of the other four had a tag—Grosse Pointe Park, Grosse Pointe Farms, Grosse Pointe Woods, Grosse Pointe Shores. Outsiders, and residents too upon occasion, commonly referred to them collectively as Grosse Pointe, the Grosse Pointes, or, sometimes, just "the Pointes." Well before the advent of the Birch Society, the Grosse Pointes were viewed as a symbol of privilege. Even though there were social and economic layers among each of the five Pointes and their 31,000 residents, the median income was higher than in most Michigan communities at the time. A majority were Republicans, although it was home also to Governor G. Mennen Williams as well as other influential Democratic Party liberals.

The Grosse Pointes owed their distinctive character in part to the notorious "Pointe System," the means to scrutinize potential buyers in order to protect the community life that residents prized and to maintain the value of their property for which they paid a premium. A well-known secret for years, local realtors determined the eligibility of prospective buyers by surreptitiously assigning them a certain number of points based on race, religion, ethnic origin, and occupation. Black and Jewish families could never accumulate the required total score; Southeast European immigrants like Italians needed exceptional status such as the medical or legal professions if they were to make the grade.

By the late nineteen fifties, the Pointe System had come under sharp attack as illegal. Political party lines and alliances blurred in arguments about the importance of preserving real estate values and neighborhoods from those who, some insisted, would be "clannish" if they moved in.[5] On this issue plus controversies ranging from taxes for parks to the worth of fluoridating the water, editorials and letters in the local press revealed one preoccupation in common: how best to promote a good future for their children. People took seriously the need to be involved in schools, churches, and public affairs in order to foster the way of life they had chosen for their families. The Grosse Pointes were wealthier than many communities, to be sure, but residents' dreams and fears were not at all uncharacteristic of hundreds of other communities across Michigan.

A few men who were prominent on the boards of Grosse Pointe civic bodies like the park commission operated within the framework of citizens' concerns to press a quiet agenda of their own. They stood to profit from real estate investments and undeveloped parcels of community land such as Windmill Pointe if it were to be sold for private development rather than used for a park.[6] Maintaining political power and influence was important to their purposes. Profiteers along with aspiring politicians found it useful to bundle anti-Communism, antiunionism, anti-Jewish bias, and racism all together in a glossy package labeled "to safeguard the community."

The Grosse Pointes were tucked in one corner of Michigan's Fourteenth Congressional District, incidentally the same district singled out as a hotbed of Communist activists by FBI spy nurse Baldwin when she testified before HUAC in 1952. It was a far-flung, diverse district dominated by east-side sections of Detroit. The Detroit voters had repeatedly put it in the Democratic column since 1948 with the advent of the revitalized party under G. Mennen Williams. Republicans in the congressional district were so outnumbered that they had done little organizing among the grassroots. Then, in the late fifties, a conservative Republican faction led by Grosse Pointe investment counselor Richard Durant launched a successful offensive to take advantage of the situation.[7]

Opportunities on the Michigan political front beckoned just then. Governor Williams warned residents in early 1958 that the state government was running out of money to meet its bills; overall, the economy was facing trouble with a faltering auto industry, climbing unemployment, and sliding farm income. According to Williams, the combination of deficit financing by the previous legislative session and the national decline in business had put Michigan "in a grave crisis."[8] Wrangling between the two parties in the legislature that spring inspired Republicans to delay passing the budget bill in order to embarrass Williams, and for a few days, the state could not meet its payroll. Whether misunderstanding the situation or taking advantage of it, headlines all over the country announced, "Michigan Is Bankrupt!" The budget bill passed in time to avoid another "payless payday," yet the financial problems were real enough. Governor Williams was reelected in November, but his star was tarnished and his chances for a major post at the national level were diminished. Michigan Republicans appreciated that the Michigan Democrats were newly vulnerable.

People outside the factory shop floors, especially owner-industrialists and management, blamed the excessive power of unions and the "Reuther-Williams machine" for the "mess." Additional taxes in some form were looming. The questions were inevitable. Why not cut spending instead? Were new taxes really necessary? Who would pay the heaviest cost? Reapportionment was coming around again with the census of 1960. The likely result would be gains for urbanized regions at the expense of the rest of the state. Civil rights advocates were becoming ever more insistent about open housing, equal employment opportunities, curbing police abuse, and equitable political representation. These issues had explosive political implications. Conservatives calculated that they might have new leverage to use within their own Republican Party if liberals and moderates would understand they might seize the governor's office and win in other races by forging a united Republican front. Moreover, it seemed to conservatives that voters should now recognize that the reforms pushed through by liberals and moderates of both parties had proven to have dangerous consequences.

By the time the Birch Society came to town, a faction of Republican conservatives led by Richard Durant had been working block by block in Fourteenth District precincts and had gained control of the district's Republican Party apparatus. In the process, they passed district party planks that called for strong antiunion legislation, an end to farm subsidies, and a reduction of publicly financed foreign aid programs. Durant's Republican Voters Associated (RVA) had also been bold enough to publish a circular saying that moderate Republicanism as exemplified by Eisenhower had "done nothing but make Socialism respectable."[9] This was the theme Joseph McCarthy and anti-Communist conservatives like Robert Welch had been putting forward since the Eisenhower forces triumphed over Robert Taft in 1952. Durant and those around him were just the kind of Americans Welch hoped to enlist in his cause.

An impressed Robert Welch regarded the RVA as a network to reach potential Birch members with the message of anti-Communism. Durant and like-minded associates who already shared Birch Society convictions welcomed the affirmation and aid from Welch's organization. In common, they aimed for influence over the direction of the Michigan Republican Party and, beyond that, for influence over selection of the Republican presidential candidate and party platform.

Joining Up in Michigan

Over the next months other chapters were added until by 1962, Michigan would have perhaps 100 of them and 1,000 members.[10] These numbers were negligible compared with the state's Ku Klux Klan in the twenties and far below the subscribers to Coughlin's *Social Justice* newspaper, let alone the throngs in the priest's radio audience. Welch, however, was self-assured about the appeal of his cause once the word about it was out; when he launched the John Birch Society he anticipated it would quickly enlist 1,000,000 Americans. Never did it approach that level, and by 1961 he revised expectations to aim for 100,000. The Society probably enrolled closer to 60,000 members at its peak. Undaunted, Welch resolved that a committed hard core was preferable to a mass membership peopled by casual enthusiasts. The outnumbered but activist conservative minority in Michigan who were determined to fight Republican centrists well suited his philosophy.

Welch's *Blue Book* was at the ready to provide Birch Society members with a foundation. First published in 1958, the volume was a compendium of the author's anti–big government orthodoxy, anti-Communist rationale, and his organizational plans that mimicked Communists in order to beat the enemy at its own game. Always with a blue cover, the *Blue Book* eventually went through several editions, and it was required reading for all members. Critics cited it regularly to ridicule the Birch Society—its leaders, members, and positions—and thereby gave it publicity well beyond the circle Welch otherwise tapped. Certain Republicans, and Democrats too, piggybacked on *Blue Book* rhetoric if their political survival seemed otherwise at risk because of Birchers' influence.

Welch continually put his themes before the public in writing. His *One Man's Opinion* magazine became *American Opinion,* a measure of his intention to speak for the citizenry at large. About 27,000 copies came out monthly with over 15,000 going to subscribers and the rest to various news dealers. Issues ran around 80 pages and sold for 50 cents until 1964 when the magazine grew to 100 pages and its price doubled. American Opinion bookstores opened in one community after another, including near Detroit's Wayne State University, and magazine advertisements told how to order by mail. Central to his political philosophy was Welch's conviction that the American people for years had been taken steadily down the road to Communism by steps "supposedly designed and presented" as the ways to fight Communism. Welch tutored his audience to recognize one form of deceit after another. Money that was poured into foreign aid programs actually made it easier for Communists and socialist agents to take over those countries. The Soviet space missile Sputnik was also part of Soviet agents' devious plan to get the United States to expand government spending for missiles and defense, which, in turn, raised taxes and put the country billions of dollars in debt. *The Politician,* which Welch wrote before organizing the Society, went into a new edition so more people could know Eisenhower for what he was: "the most completely opportunistic and unprincipled politician America has ever raised to high office."[11]

From its headquarters in Massachusetts, Welch directed the hierarchical organization. By intentional design, Welch explained, he had structured the John Birch Society to fight the Communists with their own party tactics as a model.[12] At the bottom were the members, then the section leaders who were volunteers and supervised the activities of several chapters. Above the section leaders was an intermediary group of full-time paid employees who had statewide responsibilities determined by Robert Welch and the Council, a core group of advisers he appointed.[13] Local chapters—which he sometimes referred to as cells in borrowed Communist terminology—should be small, usually from 10 to 20 members with a chapter leader appointed by headquarters. Such a plan, he pointed out, built the organization from the ground up and also enabled headquarters to "keep strict and careful control of what every chapter is doing, and even every member of every chapter." If someone was not actively involved, said Welch, he would "get his money back."[14] In other words, he would be expelled from the Society.

Welch was primarily funded by wealthy contributors. These donors regarded free enterprise as a key to the battle against Communism, welcomed his shared sentiments, and appreciated that Welch operated the Birch Society like a well-oiled, top-down business. Dues set in 1958 were whatever the member wanted to make them, but for men the minimum was $24 and for women $12.[15] Neither Welch nor the *Blue Book* mentioned whether this halved fee for women reflected their status in the Society or in the family, or assumed they had less independent income. They became, in practice, the foot soldiers who trekked through their local precincts at election time and pressed Society literature on neighborhood schools and clubs year-around.

Michigan chapters followed the leader's dictates; as a chapter grew in size to become self-sustaining it split to give life to another "cell." Chapter 69, perhaps a typical group, met in the Detroit home of the chapter leader who was vice president of a paint and chemical operation. The immediate neighborhood was solidly white and middle class, with some homes dating from the 1920s and others built since the war. When an undercover *Detroit Free Press* reporter attended the first of her meetings in the spring of 1962, she was one of twelve people including three students from Wayne State University. During the five months of her role as a member, she was dispatched to other chapters when it was necessary to supplement certain small groups. From the experience, she concluded that the chapters had more "respectable community leaders and solid citizens than any extremist group in years." Members' common bond was "alarm," she assessed, and their "constant suspicion of conspiracy" set Birch members apart from the more mainstream conservatives.[16] Theirs was an informed alarm that stemmed from the conscientious but selective effort to educate themselves about conspiracy threats. They dutifully read *One Dozen Candles,* the Birch Society set of required books about government actions that helped the Communists. The U.S. failure to help the Freedom Fighters in the Hungarian revolution, Roosevelt's "betrayal" of Poland at the Potsdam conference, entering into the United Nations—these were just the tip of the iceberg of deliberate treachery.

Meetings were sometimes attended by state coordinator Edward A. Kelly, one of 38 such paid coordinators around the country charged with the responsibility to organize and steer chapter activities. Kelly lived in Roseville, a village in Macomb County that turned into a small Detroit suburb of modest single-family homes once the postwar boom allowed white families some upward housing mobility. Kelly's salary was only about $200 a month, not much compared to a union worker's wage or even a teacher. But he believed in the Birch Society cause, welcomed this salesman-type white-collar job that involved a lot of talking, and had the chance to travel. During visits to chapter meetings he instructed members on recruiting tactics, emphasized the reading assignments, and announced the 10 or 12 projects Welch outlined each month. Coordinator Kelly reminded members they were to select at least one to pursue.[17] Chapter members were needed to staff local reading rooms, write letters, support certain radio programs, provide lists of speakers, and work on political campaigns.

Part of Kelly's role was to broaden the base. He recommended that members might organize study groups of friends, explaining it as an anti-Communist education course. They might invite a conservative speaker to the neighborhood PTA meeting and watch the reaction of individuals in order to single out those who likely shared Birch Society convictions; after all, there were "good conservatives everywhere." But when recruiting, members should take care to "steer clear of nuts." Kelly promised that when a member had assembled an interested audience he would come to show a film. Favorites included *Communism on the Map, The Red Web,* and *Operation Abolition,* which dealt with the Communist influence in student riots in San Francisco when the House Un-American Activities Committee held hearings in the city.[18]

Copious Welch-dispatched literature drilled members about the value of "front groups," one of the Communist Party strategies that he mimicked.[19] Birch proponents were told they should organize or join people who were concentrating on certain crusades of their own. Such single-issue people were potential "crossovers" who were unaware they were really tackling one manifestation of the multitenacled Communist plot. Because Birch members were better trained, Welch reminded them, they could spread the word about the overarching crusade of anti-Communism once within such circles of concerned citizens. Yet, Birch leaders and followers were not indiscriminate in their search for potential allies; they distanced themselves from far right-winger George Rockwell with his American Nazi Party and Gerald L. K. Smith's Christian Nationalist Crusade. Solidly acceptable were the Daughters of the American Revolution, the Committee for Constitutional Government, and William Buckley's Young Americans for Freedom. A number of front groups took shape, including the Michigan Independent American Party formed in 1960, Education for American Freedom, which was promoted to the public as an "educational" force against Communism, the anti-Communist "Crusaders," and the antifluoridation movement, which was one of the major John Birch Society cover efforts in Michigan.

Chapter members were often at work in related Birch-approved movements out of genuine commitment to those causes. Many of the most militant activists on behalf of conservative issues were women, but they regarded themselves as defenders of the family and readily joined hands with anti–women's rights advocates. School busing opponents were other compatible allies. Birch member Wilma Oswolt was an organizer of the Northwest Parents Club to protest busing black children to three Detroit schools in her neighborhood. She worked vigorously against Fair Housing legislation and recruited for the broader anti-Communist cause in the course of her campaign. Wayne State University student Donald Lobsinger, a devoted Bircher early on, was an extremely conservative Catholic who urged others of the faithful to stand up against the archbishop's "diversion" of Catholic contributions to fund left-wing and Communist speakers on campus.

Demands on members were time-consuming and mind-absorbing. Birch supporters joined the assorted sign-carriers who picketed the Leningrad Ballet when it came to Detroit's Masonic Temple. They picketed a Tractors for Freedom meeting where the featured speaker was Eleanor Roosevelt, who was long regarded by many arch-conservatives as having "pink" sympathies. Throughout all such activities, Society members reached out to fringe people with pet causes who were looking for fellow travelers and might return the favor. When it came to identifying potential allies, Birch believers were resourceful.

Men and women who filtered into a growing number of small chapters throughout Michigan shared the orthodox perspective on national issues that Welch and Society ideology fashioned. Their communities were the battleground where they intended to defend the flag—from organized labor with "leftist" leaders who bullied free enterprise; from "un-American trouble-makers" using civil rights as a cover; from insidious propagandists who bored from within schools and universities. Welch generally succeeded in keeping rank-and-file membership lists private, but in short order, academics and poll takers pieced together data from a variety of sources to assess, describe, and categorize the people who joined. Studies probed their personalities and socioeconomic status. Birchers were "authoritarian" or paranoid, victims of declining status or status seekers, self-serving opportunists or naive. Estimated counts indicated that California had the largest concentration of Birch supporters; Texas, Phoenix, Wichita, and the north shore of Chicago were other significant bases.[20] As a state, Michigan was sometimes thought to have the third largest concentration, but only a handful of self-announced Birchers, including Grosse Pointe's Richard Durant, were conspicuous.

Whatever personality traits impelled them and however many there really were, matters closest to home propelled Michigan members. Birch meetings were supposed to stick to the Society's prescribed issues of the month—from condemnation of the National Council of Churches to recruiting petition signers to "Impeach Justice Earl Warren" and to "Get the U.S. Out of the U.N." Despite Welch's proscriptions, people at the meetings were usually the type who could not be gagged. Race, a forbidden topic, came up frequently. Civil rights advocates who were pushing for open housing and realtors who were showing black families around white neighborhoods energized many Michigan residents like no other issue. Informal discussion at Birch meetings regularly veered off to center around "changing neighborhoods." Typical was the member who would not stop talking about personal experiences that started, he claimed, when the NAACP targeted the northwest Detroit area around James Couzens and Six Mile where he lived. After being arrested for assault and given two years' probation for standing on his front porch and shouting "Nairobi" when the NAACP moved one family of Negroes into a house on his street, he had joined the John Birch Society. He had indeed found a sympathetic audience. Coordinator Kelly chimed in that a man could work 25 years to get equity in his home and then "these people come" and property becomes "X per cent less valuable."[21]

Here and there, black families had been venturing out of their segregated blocks since the days when Ossian Sweet's family made the jump in 1925. In the midst of World War II, the Sojourner Truth housing project for blacks opened in a white working-class section of Detroit after considerable strife. After the war, more black families could take advantage of union salaries and home loans to move into housing left behind by upwardly mobile white families. In 1948, the NAACP and lawyer Thurgood Marshall appealed a lower court ruling to the U.S. Supreme Court on behalf of Orsel McGhee, a black Detroit resident whose home purchase in a white neighborhood had been ordered revoked on the basis of the deed's restrictive covenant. The case of *McGhee v. Sipes*, together with the similar *Shelley v. Kraemer*, was decided in favor of the McGhees when the high court struck down discrimination in property rights.[22] Restrictive covenants, proliferating since the era of Ossian Sweet, were now illegal. Real estate and insurance ruses multiplied to minimize black options but the civil rights advocates had become louder and had more company by the late 1950s. It was a common perception among Birchers that Communists were behind any and all assertive behavior to locate blacks amid white neighborhoods.

Issues and Tactics in Michigan

Given the local climate, it was not at all surprising that so many people who went to chapter meetings, picketed anti-Communist speakers, and handed out Birch literature focused much of their attention on politics within their home state. They shared one immediate and overarching political goal: They wanted to wrest control of the Republican Party from the hands of moderates at the state level and in targeted legislative districts. Related to that goal was a key objective: to minimize the impact of redistricting, which would be based on population resulting in gains for Detroit at the expense of outlying and rural Michigan. They wanted to limit the influence of Detroit in order to hold off legislation and court decisions that would mandate integration of neighborhoods and schools. They wanted also to clamp down on labor unions and on voters who differed with them about taxes, voters who were inclined, for example, to support a personal or corporate income tax over higher sales taxes and who would preserve "costly" government programs rather than cut spending. Most of the energy behind Birchers' efforts spun off from these entwined political purposes, wrapped as they were in anti-Communist convictions.

Formation of Birch chapters in Michigan coincided with momentum on behalf of a convention to revise the state's constitution. Plans for a constitutional convention started by the summer of 1959 when Citizens for Michigan organized to spearhead the drive and to give it direction. Republican corporation leaders, including Ford Motor Company vice president Robert McNamara and American Motors president George Romney, were responsible for initiating the nonpartisan Citizens for Michigan. Romney became the chief spokesman.[23]

Written in 1908 and many times amended, basic provisions in the existing constitution had been ignored. Even before the politically prompted "payless payday" of 1958, realistic observers recognized that the need for a general overhaul of the state's political structure went well beyond tax reform. Citizens for Michigan formed chapters across the state and required only that members must be registered voters in the chapter's area. The group sponsored forums, wrote position papers, and reached out for allies. The League of Women Voters, the UAW, and other interest groups ran parallel campaigns to educate voters about changes they would like to see in a new constitution. Conservatives within the Michigan Republican Party were sharply at odds with Romney's proposed constitutional revisions and opposed calling a constitutional convention altogether. Most vehement were the John Birch Society chapters that, by now, had spread well beyond the first in Grosse Pointe and enrolled respectable conservative leaders, although sometimes Birch adherents were at odds with "regular" conservatives as well as with party moderates.

The most successful battleground in the fight against a new constitution was in the Fourteenth District Convention where Richard Durant's precinct workers were well organized. Durant's delegates dominated, and they passed a resolution that opposed calling a constitutional convention because the "excellent amendment process" in the existing constitution made a new one unnecessary.[24] Other resolutions were passed that demanded no increase in taxes and a reduction of existing taxes. If any additional tax proved necessary, it should be a 1 percent increase in sales taxes but no state income tax in any form, personal or corporate. The majority of Fourteenth District delegates voted for "drastic" curtailments in federal aid to education and "substantial increases" in tuition at state supported institutions to bring them in line with the fees private institutions charged. Several resolutions focused on waste in the state universities. Examples demonstrated the need to rein in "costly proliferation of courses" and to eliminate such frivolous classes as fly-casting. Many resolutions were antilabor in content, demanding stronger protection of employers' rights during labor disputes. The John Birch Society position on national defense also won a majority at the District Convention. Delegates wanted Congress to make "drastic" reductions in foreign aid, and they recorded opposition to further disarmament talks because any agreement would be "a fraud and a trap set for Communist benefit."[25] For Birchers as for everyone else on whatever side, at stake were taxes, government spending, civil rights, and apportionment of seats in the state legislature. Since legislators would have the biggest impact on taxes, spending, and civil rights legislation, the method of apportionment was the key.

According to the 1908 constitution, seats in the state legislature were to be reapportioned every ten years beginning in 1913, but despite some revisions in the formula, the legislature repeatedly distributed seats to limit the influence of Detroit and to overrepresent outstate counties. By the end of the decade, four counties in the Upper Peninsula with a total population of 55,806 had one representative, and so did Oakland County with a population of 690,583. "People, not pine stumps" should make the law in this country, insisted AFL-CIO's August Scholle, and he headed for the courts in 1959 to challenge Michigan's apportionment as a violation of the equal rights clause in the Fourteenth Amendment. That suit would drag on in a five year process.[26] The whole time, Birchers insisted the legal battle was a Communist-influenced effort.

A petition drive obtained enough signatures to put a proposal calling for a constitutional convention on the November 1960 election ballot. This divisive statewide proposal alongside an acrimonious presidential contest made the 1960 election season especially bitter. Conservative and moderate Republicans were already sharply at odds when the GOP state convention met in the summer, but conservatives were in a minority, and they lost on every issue. Republican delegates adopted a platform that called for a civil rights commission with authority to investigate discrimination in public housing, education, and public accommodations; this was the strongest civil rights plank the party had ever developed. The moderate majority overrode conservative opposition and endorsed the ballot proposal for a constitutional convention, as did the Michigan Democratic Party and its candidate for governor, John Swainson. Moderate Republicans trounced their conservative wing again when it came to support for Richard Nixon as the party's nominee. Leading moderate Republicans at the state convention were active in the Volunteers for Nixon, and a large majority of the 46 delegates Michigan Republicans sent to the national convention were pledged to him. Although Nixon had used the issue of anti-Communism to catapult him into Congress at the outset of his career, Birch adherents did not consider him an ally, and they were furious about a Richard Nixon and Henry Cabot Lodge presidential ticket.

Robert Welch regarded Nixon as an opportunist, not a leader but rather a manipulator who rode the waves of public support. Welch and those like-minded remained bitter about the rejection of Taft in favor of Eisenhower in 1952. They had not been placated by the alleged "deal" conservatives made to accept Eisenhower in return for placing Nixon on the ticket as vice president. Now, Birch Society members decried the deal they were sure Nixon and his supporters made with the "leftist" Nelson Rockefeller in 1960; this one put the liberal Henry Cabot Lodge on the ticket as vice president and let Rockefeller have control of the party platform.

Like Robert Welch, Durant and other Michigan Birch Society members backed the conservative Arizona senator Barry Goldwater who took a firm position on defending the nation against Communism. Robert Welch had favored Goldwater above other possibilities when he reviewed likely candidates because he believed Goldwater was the only one with the political and moral courage to stand by "Americanist principles."[27] Birchers thought Goldwater should not have agreed to support the Nixon-

Lodge ticket and instead should have moved over with a conservative coalition from both parties into a third "American Party" ticket. Election season 1960 marked the real beginning of an organized effort to present Goldwater and his idea of "a choice not an echo" to Michigan voters. They wanted choices of their liking to be offered also at every level of state and local government.

Ironically, despite the Birchers' claim that Eisenhower was a Communist, it was during Eisenhower's administration that Americans were put on high alert about possibilities of a Communist attack on American soil. People were a more receptive audience for Welch's dire warnings precisely because of their 1950s Cold War indoctrination. Being prepared had become a habit. Grade school children practiced drills, filing into basement bomb shelters marked by recognizable symbols. College ethics classes debated whether a family with a shelter was morally obligated to harbor neighbors. Civil defense officials used occasions like Farm Safety Week to urge farmers to plan for their safety from nuclear, biological, or chemical weapons because, in case of such an attack, America's victory would depend upon farmers' production of food. The Michigan Office of Civil Defense Mobilization provided newspapers with convenient photos to illustrate the articles they also provided. There was a barn improvised with bales of straw to shield cows against radiation. There was a fallout shelter built for $2,300 on a farm near Hickory Corners that served a dual purpose as a carport-patio; moreover the shelter had just provided refuge to the farmer's family of three plus eight neighbors when a tornado struck. What a bonus! As a do-it-yourself project, a shelter could cost as little as $150 and was the "most economical" way to save the most people.[28] News accounts emphasized, meanwhile, that Cuba presented an immediate reason for fear. In August 1960, Castro expropriated about a billion dollars of American business investments, and Khrushchev threatened to use force if the United States went in.[29]

In the November election, John F. Kennedy won Michigan. Williams had resigned, and his former lieutenant governor, John Swainson, captured the governor's office. Democrats again controlled the state legislature along with nearly every other statewide elective post. Voters approved the proposal to call a constitutional convention, but it won by a razor-thin margin and only because of support in the 4 heavily populated counties in southeast Michigan. In each of the other 79 counties, a majority went against a convention. Opponents of the constitution were odd bedfellows. A number of union activists had campaigned against the convention on the grounds that it underrepresented the urbanized metro area because the 144 delegates were to be elected on the basis of the 1950 rather than the 1960 census. The Michigan Farm Bureau was against it too, in their case because a new constitution would likely wind up taking greater account of population as a basis for apportionment and thereby diminish farmers' longtime influence. This issue of representation at the constitutional convention was more immediately divisive than the substance of a new constitution itself because it was the delegates, of course, who would shape that document.

In 1962 when the delegates convened, conservatives managed to block George Romney from chairing it, and instead he held the position as vice chair. This, in fact, worked to his benefit since inescapable criticism fell hardest on the chairman. The issue of an income tax was one of many compromises between moderates and conservatives in each party. Conservatives finally agreed to an income tax but insisted that it be set at a flat rate. Reapportionment was also hammered out in a compromise, only to be reversed two years later by the Supreme Court in the case of *Reynolds v. Sims*, which ruled that all state legislatures must draw their districts according to population. Reformers and moderates joined forces across party lines and did prevail in inserting a strong antidiscrimination section in the constitution. In its final form, the constitution offered a streamlined government headed by a governor who would have more centralized authority and would be elected for four years rather than the two-year term existing since Michigan became a state in 1837. The new constitution was ready to go before the voters in time for the 1962 elections, but legal maneuvering by the Swainson administration and the AFL-CIO delayed it until a special election could be held April 1, 1963.

George Romney had gained important political visibility while working to craft the constitution and helping to forge compromises that made the document a reality. Following the convention, he announced he would be a candidate for governor in the fall election. Romney was popularly known for having "saved" American Motors, and he wanted Michigan residents to know he would do his best to save the state. It was apparent he would have to reach voters beyond his own party since hard-line conservatives disliked him. He had antagonized that wing of his party by his advocacy of the constitution, and, in addition, he continued to emphasize that the influence of big business over the Republican Party was just as bad as the influence of big labor over the Democrats. Romney was a devout member of the Church of Latter-day Saints who prided himself on being a moral straight shooter, and he did not hesitate to blame "partisan Republicans" in the state legislature as much as Democrats for the "financial mess" in Michigan. With more determination than ever, conservatives set out to identify their voter base and add to it in time for the 1962 elections. As moderate Republican leaders urged the election of Romney and championed bipartisan efforts to address pressing social problems, the John Birch Society was an angry and occasionally vicious presence in the party's midst.

Commanding Presence, 1962

Enthusiasm for the Birch Society had been cooling off in Detroit, Birch headquarters noted. New recruits were down, and attendance at meetings lagged. However, headquarters was optimistic about the suburbs where continuing growth was anticipated. Chapters formed in Birmingham, Royal Oak, Redford Township, and Warren. Detroit and its suburbs now accounted for about 60 chapters. Sturdiest growth was outstate in Lansing, Grand Rapids, Flint, Saginaw, Benton Harbor, and smaller communities, in all adding up to 35 to 40 chapters. Several Birchers joined the Seventeenth Congressional District Conservative Club, but the Fourteenth District remained the stronghold with the most "virile element" in conservative Republican circles.[30]

Birch stalwarts could feel they were making inroads once Republican Party leaders decided to publicly repudiate them. When the Republican State Central Committee met in advance of the 1962 election, Birch adherents were there. A woman from Midland who identified herself as a member of the John Birch Society spoke out during the resolutions committee deliberations. Birchers had proof, she insisted, to back Robert Welch's claim that former president Eisenhower was a Communist. She was just one such determined voice trying to refocus the meeting in ways that would publicize Birch issues. By the end of their session, the Republican State Central Committee had adopted a statement denouncing the John Birch Society. Not only did the committee disassociate their party from Birchers, but in this single resolution, it demanded also that the Democratic Party "repudiate immediately and fully the Americans for Democratic Action and other organizations of the extreme Left."[31] On the part of the committee, it was a tactical move. With this righteous call, they effectively drew attention to potential trouble that the Left posed for the

Democrats. Democratic Party leaders did not seize the bait to denounce their allies, the ADA, but they were quick to repudiate the John Birch Society. To the delight of Democrats and the dismay of Republicans, the Birch camp presented a greater potential danger to Republican candidates than did their Democratic opponents.

Harboring Birchers had become intolerable to responsible conservatives and moderates in the Michigan Republican mainstream. The battle was on and in full public view by the time of the summer conventions. Durant's supporters gave up the idea of nominating him for governor, and Romney was unopposed for the Republican nomination. With the AFL-CIO and United Auto Workers leaders campaigning against him, Romney's victory over Swainson would depend on persuading a share of traditionally Democratic voters to cross over. Romney genuinely opposed Birch Society principles and the reactionary Republicans who had fought reform in the state legislature, but it was also politically important to distance himself from that wing within his own party.

Toward that end, a number of prominent Republicans organized a Republican Action Committee (RAC) to elect moderates as delegates to the state party convention to be held in August. Durant's Fourteenth District base was a key focus for their attention. Grassroots organizers for each side concentrated an unusual amount of time, energy, and money on the district delegate races. Durant's precinct canvassers made careful "RAC" notations by each opponent's name they identified on delegate lists. George Romney opted to use personal pressure and held a series of private meetings with Durant, asking him to resign as Fourteenth District vice chairman. The same demand had been made several months before by Robert Waldron, a Fourteenth District moderate Republican state legislator who was waging an uphill and ultimately unsuccessful race for a seat in Congress.[32] Unconcerned about the damage a "Birch taint" might mean for any Republican candidate, Durant refused to leave the post unless given a voice in choosing his successor. Romney was in no mood to compromise with him. In turn, Durant announced he was "proud" to be one of the four Michigan members of a John Birch Society national "committee of endorsers."[33]

Durant's role as an investment counselor had become an issue for many Republicans within the Grosse Pointes. Over the previous months, allegations had surfaced that he and some of his closest allies had been associated with quiet real estate ventures that, had they succeeded, would have profited them to the disadvantage of long-term community interests.

Men in the Durant cabal had purportedly used their positions or their friends on the Grosse Pointe Park Planning Commission to encourage the sale of Three Mile Park. A piece of land jutting into Lake St. Clair, the park had recently reverted back to the community from the federal government, and its future was under debate. If sold to developers as the planning commission proposed, the land would have meant a private bonanza. A group of residents managed to ferret out the plan, block the sale, and have the land designated as a park. The publicity demonstrated the extent of behind-the-scenes maneuvering going on. Durant's opponents in the community also charged that he and several friends who had significant real estate investments were encouraging rumors that would arouse racial fears designed to foster opposition to open housing.[34] The *Grosse Pointe News* characterized Durant's role as part of "picayune personal ambitions" that were the cause of most of the local district bickering. Personal ambitions were indeed the cause, but the amount at stake was not so picayune.

A few weeks before the district and state conventions, Romney came out swinging against Durant in an address to over 300 Republican candidates at a breakfast meeting held on the lawn of the Grosse Pointe War Memorial: "If delegates from this district reelect this man, you will have repudiated me." Audience supporters of both Romney and Durant shouted "No! No!" but Romney held firm. Durant was costing the GOP independent and "discerning Democratic" votes, Romney warned. Candidate Romney never mentioned political philosophy or ideology to the crowd. Rather, he stuck to matters of winning elections. Leaders should not be identified with "the viewpoint of a minority group" if they hoped to gain the breadth of support needed for success in any election. Durant, who followed Romney to the platform, perfunctorily endorsed him as the GOP gubernatorial candidate and made a brief plea for party unity. Moderates were not impressed by Durant's pronouncement that "the spectacle of Republicans quarreling among themselves distresses me."[35]

Romney supporters proceeded to wage war against Birch-backed candidates running for slots as party delegates. Political ads in the *Grosse Pointe News* called out in large headlines: SUPPORT ROMNEY—DEFEAT DURANT. Sample ballots listed the Romney-pledged delegates running in each precinct. A few days before the election, Durant officially resigned from the Birch Society, but it was a political statement designed to show that labels did not define the man; he had not surrendered his convictions. Durant lost in his bid to be precinct delegate, and of the 306 elected from the Fourteenth District, 125 were acknowledged Romney delegates while 50 others were pledged to Durant. Both sides courted the "uncommitted" although there was no doubt that Romney would be the ultimate choice at the State Party Convention. Durant was reelected vice-chair of the Fourteenth District Republican Party apparatus, and since the elderly, longtime chair was just a figurehead, Durant remained in control. Grosse Pointe had always provided only a small, determined nest of Birch members, and Durant's appeal in his own community was narrow. Thanks to his years of careful organizing, he pulled in his greatest support from Detroit wards where few other Republicans wasted time courting residents since it was a heavily Democratic area.[36] Some who did support Romney for governor nonetheless resented his intrusion into what they considered "a family squabble" in the district.

Unrelenting, Romney wrote a "Dear Dick" letter to Durant emphasizing that "the news of your resignation from the John Birch Society is very welcome." It was "a crucial first step" in what was Durant's "heavy responsibility" to demonstrate that others were welcome to participate in district affairs. Romney told his Fourteenth District supporters that he would be watching to see if Durant's resignation from the Birch Society was "complete in spirit as well as in letter." A woman in the district quickly contacted Romney, claiming Durant had visited her home 24 hours after he mailed his Birch Society resignation and gave her Birch literature in the process of campaigning.[37]

When the Republican state convention got under way in mid-August, there was little doubt that Durant and the Birch strategists intended to persevere. Field coordinator Edward A. Kelly booked a room adjacent to Romney's suite in the Statler Hotel and gleefully posted a sign announcing, "Headquarters John Birch Society." As planned, the sign was close beside Romney's door and could not be missed by all who arrived to visit the gubernatorial candidate. It soon prompted a confrontation in the hall when an older Romney staff member and Kelly had a heated exchange. Romney adviser Richard Van Dusen hurried to the defense of the staffer. Van Dusen, a member of one of Detroit's most prominent law firms, put his hands on Kelly's shoulders to stop the fight that seemed about to take place. It was a stroke of luck for Kelly who, within hours, filed suit against Van Dusen, charging assault and demanding $50,000 in damages. Durant also soon filed charges against the *Detroit News* and several Republicans including state senator John H. Stahlin, a Romney supporter. In *Durant v. Stahlin et al.*, the plaintiff claimed he had been libeled in the 1962 campaign by advertisements that referred to his "fascist" behavior, linked him with the American Nazi leader George Norman Rockwell, and charged he was a member of the Independent American Party.[38]

Since both the Durant and the Romney camps included skilled lawyers, these lawsuits dragged on. Court testimony became a prime forum for the Birchers—much like the political trials common in the Soviet Union. Cross-examination focused on Kelly's role as field coordinator of the John Birch Society and whether he shared the same ideas as Welch. Did he agree with Mr. Welch's description of Dwight Eisenhower as "the most completely opportunistic and unprincipled politician America has ever raised to high office"? Did he believe that chances are "very strong" that Milton Eisenhower is actually Dwight Eisenhower's superior and boss within the Communist Party? Van Dusen's attorney charged that Kelly was a racist and had disrupted a Congress of Racial Equality meeting at an area school by standing on top of a table with an American flag in his hand, singing "The Star-Spangled Banner."[39]

In his address at the party's state convention, Romney demanded legislation permitting political parties to disassociate themselves from "any so-called leader . . . whose actions have clearly labeled him unworthy or unfit to hold his office." A majority of delegates cheered wildly at this direct attack on Durant and "Welchism."[40] During the campaign, Romney won widespread praise from the Michigan press and notice in the national news for taking a public stand against the Birch fringe in his party. He seized every opportunity to emphasize that he was the "moderate" on the Michigan political scene by demanding that candidate Swainson disavow those among the Democratic Party who were dangerously on the left—always singling out the Americans for Democratic Action (ADA).

Romney defeated Swainson in November by a small majority of 78,497 votes out of 2,759,595 cast, with outstate votes providing his victory margin. The Democratic candidate was elected lieutenant governor, however, since that post was filled separately under the existing constitution. Southeast Michigan helped Democrats win all other state offices. Since redistricting had not yet given southeast Michigan voters their fair proportion of state legislative seats, Republicans maintained a majority in both houses. This was little comfort to the Republican moderates, however, since too many in their own party were conservative foes of Romney and reform.[41] The governor set about building a nonpartisan coalition that could help back the new constitution in the forthcoming April 1963 election and support his intent to shore up the state's economic health by initiating an income tax and other tax legislation. Enemies of the constitution—organized labor from one side and the outstate Republican strongholds from the other—campaigned vigorously. The constitution carried by less than 11,000 votes out of over 1,600,000 cast, but it would take effect.[42] Meanwhile, civil rights demonstrations came to Michigan.

The Heart of the Fear

Romney had pushed for the bipartisan Civil Rights Commission that was included in the new constitution. Five months after his inauguration as governor, he made his first appearance in a civil rights demonstration. On June 29, 1963, side by side with the president of the Detroit chapter of the NAACP, he joined a racially mixed group of about 1,000 in a march through the streets of Grosse Pointe to protest housing discrimination.[43] Just a few days earlier, Martin Luther King had led a huge march down Woodward Avenue in Detroit, and although Romney did not attend for religious reasons since that march was on a Sunday, he sent two representatives.[44] Birch members reacted with angry alarm. Following the reasoning of Robert Welch, they knew civil rights protests were the work of Communist agitators. Welch often talked about the days of harmonious relationships between black and white people when he was growing up on a North Carolina farm. In his recollections, mythical or idealized, it was a time with a "very, very tiny amount of injustice."[45] Communists were at the root of sowing unrest and dividing America today. According to Birchers, gullible politicians like Romney were playing into the hands of the nation's most treacherous Communist, Martin Luther King.

Birchers had potential allies on that issue. White Detroiters continued to leave the city that had already experienced a 23 percent drop in the white population during the 1950s. Homeowners groups had been using McCarthyite terms for some years, claiming there was a Communist or socialist conspiracy behind demands for public housing and neighborhood integration. Animosity grew after Jerome Cavanagh, a young "Kennedy Democrat," was elected Detroit mayor in 1961. He supported the Supreme Court's decision that struck down restrictive covenants and pressed the mayor's Interracial Committee to take bolder steps than had previous mayors. Under Cavanagh's leadership, Detroit would become a focus of "model cities" projects in Lyndon Johnson's Great Society. So far as many white families who could not afford to move saw it, the politicians, bishops, ministers, and union leaders who agitated for open housing were hypocrites. They would not have to live among their "black brothers" because they could afford exclusive neighborhoods.[46] People in upper-class neighborhoods also regarded the integrationists as hypocrites. They saw them as do-gooders trying to win office, gain favor in the union, or earn places in heaven at the expense of communities like the Grosse Pointes. A heckler along the route of the Grosse Pointe march taunted George Romney about his own exclusive suburban neighborhood: "Hey, Governor. Bloomfield Hills tomorrow."[47] Issues of race and class, complex in their combinations, were difficult to untangle. Laying the problem at the doorstep of "outside Communist agitators" made sense to some on one side; charging it up to "racist bigots" made sense from an opposite perspective. Too many residents were wary of one another and on edge. It was not an infrequent condition in twentieth-century Michigan.

Extremism in Defense of Liberty

Bitter feuds within the state's Republican Party raged on as the 1964 election year approached. Birch forces mobilized in the Fourteenth District in hopes of having a strong say in the state party convention. Durant was elected chair of the district convention in a contested process that was finally appealed to the Republican State Central Committee. That body left him in place and said "Behave." Of the ten committees in the Republican Fourteenth District Committee, six were chaired by people from Durant's Grosse Pointe base, a lopsided representation given their small proportion of the district's population.[48]

Romney and Barry Goldwater became the focus of attention as possible Republican presidential candidates when polls showed that Nelson Rockefeller's divorce and remarriage seriously hurt his chances for the party's nomination. Durant was outspoken in his opposition to a Romney candidacy and backed Goldwater again as he had four years before. Birch members were active participants in the Michigan Goldwater Committee from the time it was put in place in 1963.[49] Goldwater's supporters were unable to outmaneuver Romney, who had the 41 votes of the Michigan delegation at the convention and maintained his "favorite son" status throughout the week. He focused on contributing moderate planks for the Republican platform. One was an amendment that denounced extremism, although without naming the John Birch Society or any other specific

organization. Goldwater advisers rejected it. Instead, Goldwater repudiated the "character assassins, vigilantes, Communists, and any other group
such as the Ku Klux Klan, which seeks to impose its views through terror
or threat or violence." Birch Society members heartily agreed with his
choice of words. Goldwater had the number of delegates needed, and the
badly divided Republican convention ended with his nomination. Civil
rights and law enforcement topped the list of issues as Republicans tried
to muster unity for a campaign against Lyndon Johnson.

Romney advised Goldwater that a "difficult situation" in Michigan
confronted his presidential campaign. Polls showed Republicans now had
"thirty percent interested" among the state's Negro vote compared to 8 or
9 percent in 1962. The governor emphasized that, while Republicans did
not have a record of solving civil rights problems at the local and state
level, "We are doing it in Michigan." But, warned the governor, people in
this state were wondering if Goldwater might be waging "a racist campaign" given the support he was receiving in the South.[50] Goldwater could
and did point to his solid record for hiring blacks in his family department
store in Phoenix, for integrating the Phoenix schools and the Arizona National Guard, and for his positions as U.S. Senator. As a presidential candidate, however, he remained consistent in his long-standing conviction
favoring local responsibility and local action. Romney regarded Goldwater's civil rights stand as inadequate and did not endorse him in Michigan.

Ardent Michigan Goldwater supporters considered Romney's displea-
sure to be one more recommendation for the Arizona senator. Even
though he had attacked Robert Welch, Goldwater was one of the few
highly visible Republicans acceptable to Birch members. He convinced
their hearts and minds by his hard line against Communism and, further,
by his bold National Convention declaration, "Extremism in defense of
liberty is no vice."

Going into the November elections, the Fourteenth District had two
separate Republican headquarters. The Durant group referred to their
candidates as the "Official Group," yet their faction was never able to gain
control of the Wayne County Republican Party or offices in it. Michigan
voters contributed a hefty majority to Lyndon Johnson, giving him more
than two million votes to Goldwater's one million. In only 3 of the 83
counties did Goldwater receive a majority of votes cast.[51] Romney was one
of the few Republicans to survive the Johnson landslide, and moreover, he
increased his margin over 1962. Michigan elected both Democrats running for the U.S. Senate and 13 of the 19 Democratic congressmen. The

state legislature now had 23 Democrats and 15 Republicans and the state House of Representatives a very lopsided 72 Democrats to 38 Republicans.[52] It was a blow to Goldwater supporters in general.

Onward!

Undaunted, Birch Society members took up leader Welch's cry, "Had enough?" and literature titled "*Now* Will you Join The John Birch Society?" poured out. Recruitment efforts were redoubled and membership increased after the election but still did not reach 100,000 nationwide.[53] Birch literature flooded campuses. "Concerned citizens" signed letters to the editor and stood up at local PTA meetings to charge that parents and teachers were supporting Communists by allowing children to collect money at Halloween for UNICEF, the United Nation's fund for children. Testimonial dinners for Welch were held in several major cities to raise money, but none took place in Michigan. Welch decided the Society's most critical enterprise was to emphasize that Communists were behind the "civil rights fraud." The Birch Society pressed the point that there was nothing wrong with civil rights, but much was wrong with what was being done in the name of civil rights. Truth About Civil Turmoil (TACT) became a new front group. Membership overlapped; in Detroit, the chairman of the Committee for the Prevention of Civil Disorder associated with TACT was the same person with the same post office box number as the chairman of the Birch front, "Support Your Local Police Organization."[54]

Too many Birch Society theories seemed outlandish among those otherwise inclined to be sympathetic with the Society slogan: "Less government, more individual responsibility and a better world." A 1964 issue of *American Opinion* reported experiments "may have been" carried out in the mid-1930s in Asiatic Russia where researchers were trying to breed women with male apes in hope of developing a species better adapted to life under Socialism than human beings.[55] Established conservatives became publicly critical of the Society by 1965, following the lead of *National Review* editor William F. Buckley Jr. As a founder of the Young Americans for Freedom, Buckley also steered that group of mostly college-age Republicans away from the Birch Society. At the time, conservatives objected especially to the Birch Society position that the United States should get out of Vietnam unless the government in Washington could be replaced with leaders who were "Patriotic anti-Communists with a desire to win."

According to Welch, if the nation had such people in charge the war could be won in three months.[56]

Internal dissension began to hurt the John Birch Society. The council expanded to 24 in 1964, and with additional members came additional strong viewpoints. General A. C. Wedemeyer had been the wartime commander of the American forces in China at the end of World War II, and, unlike Welch, he had known John Birch personally. All along he warned Welch not to make a hero of the missionary-soldier, arguing that Birch was arrogant and had provoked the attack that killed him. Wedemeyer eventually withdrew from an advisory post at *American Opinion* magazine because of the hero worship of Birch. Another army man, a colonel who had been Douglas MacArthur's personal aide, disagreed with Welch's determination to impeach Earl Warren. The Court's problems, he maintained, should be handled by a set of appointment criteria to keep all inexperienced, unqualified men out of federal judgeships. Often more moderate and reflective than Welch, he resigned in disgust.

Council members disagreed over defining other Welch crusades as well. One member insisted they should speak of "galloping treason" not "creeping socialism."[57] Revilo P. Oliver, a University of Illinois classics professor on the Birch Society's National Council, insisted Kennedy was assassinated by Communists because he was about to "turn American."[58] He proved too outrageous for the Birch Society, and the council expelled him in 1966 because he had gained such notoriety about his beliefs—that whites were racially superior, that the Holocaust was a hoax, and that FDR was a "diseased creature." Welch offered a twisted rationale of his own about anti-Semitism: He would have no anti-Semites in the Society because Jewish Communists were really behind the creation of anti-Semitism so they could use it for their own purposes. Yet American Opinion bookstores routinely stocked anti-Semitic tracts.

Michigan congressman Gerald Ford, House Minority leader, joined other Republicans who issued statements opposing the Birch Society as it stepped up its efforts to oust Republicans in the upcoming congressional elections in 1966. In response, Welch included Ford among those GOP leaders who were part of the Communist conspiracy without always knowing it. Ford was singled out for attack, described as belonging to "one of the most highly active left-wing groups in the country." The charge referred to his attendance at meetings of the Bilderberger group sponsored by the Crown Prince of the Netherlands that assembled leaders from the Atlantic Community twice a year to discuss world problems.[59]

Prominent Michigan Republicans remained unrelenting in demands for the party to repudiate this Birch "cancer" in their midst. That characterization, which Romney first applied in the heat of his 1962 battle against Birchers, was part of Durant's complaint in his ongoing suit for libel. As the case proceeded, Durant's lawyers called a list of important Republicans including the chair of the Michigan GOP and Governor Romney. The suit dragged on to an appeal before the Michigan Supreme Court in 1965. The court rejected Durant's claim that there was a conspiracy to libel him, but as he intended, he had kept his charges before the public and had cost his opponents aggravation, time, and money too—since the lawyers politely submitted bills to their client-friends.[60]

Detroit was one of the places where membership in the John Birch Society reportedly expanded in the 1965 recruitment drive.[61] Gains were not enough to make a difference at the polls or within the state party, however. Buoyed by a strong economy, Michigan had gone from running a deficit to having a surplus. Romney had impressed reformers by promoting improved workmen's compensation and the new minimum wage law, and he had worked with Johnson and Mayor Cavanagh on behalf of Great Society programs for Detroit. In the race for governor in 1966, Romney was endorsed by the *Detroit Free Press,* which most regularly supported Democrats. He won with about 50 percent of the labor vote and more than 34 percent of the black vote. Such success was proof, so far as Birchers saw it, that he was in league with dangerous un-Americans. They were not gratified that his coattails had brought along the Republican candidate for Senate running against former governor Williams plus five new Republican members of the House and Republican majorities in both houses of the state legislature.

Birchers felt avenged, convinced that their dire warnings about civil insurrection had proven correct, when Detroit became the site of the worst race riot in the nation's history in the shocking, horrible summer of 1967. Beginning on the night of July 23 when police raided a blind pig on 12th Street, a predominantly black crowd answered force with violence. Within hours that stretched into days, a generation of pent-up rage and disappointment exploded in rebellion, spreading as fast as the flames that engulfed miles of city blocks. At the end, much of Detroit was in ruins, never to be the same again, and 43 people were dead.[62]

It took federal troops to finally restore order, but, against the odds, Governor Romney's efforts during the crisis won general praise. In no mood to compromise his moral principles, Romney did not hesitate to place blame—on economic inequities coupled with a decline in religious conviction, on failed moral character, on weakened family life. In addition, he blamed power blocs within organized labor that, he said, had frozen out too many of the younger generation from unionized workplaces. He called for consequences; he charged that Black Power activists like Stokely Carmichael should be treated as traitors.[63] In the aftermath, the governor expanded the state police special investigation unit (the Red Squad) from 12 to over 30, and 20 of the detectives were assigned specifically to monitor unrest and black militants in Detroit.[64] Birch members were not persuaded of any conversion on Romney's part. Rather, they regarded this as a political move.

Violence in urban American was playing out side by side with the escalating war in Vietnam. As the 1968 election season edged closer, Birchers stepped up their claim that Republicans like Romney continued to misunderstand the stakes in Vietnam. Romney, who had appeared sometimes to be a hawk on Vietnam and sometimes a dove, was finally doomed as a potential candidate by his candor in a Detroit television interview program in September 1967. When asked about his change of mind, he explained that during a visit to Vietnam in 1965, the generals and diplomatic corps provided him "the greatest brainwashing anybody can get" to win his support for the war. Once back home, he explained, he had made a thorough study of the history of the conflict and had concluded it was not necessary for the United States to get involved in South Vietnam to stop Communist aggression.[65] In time, other prominent politicians would describe this same experience, but immediately following the interview, Romney was "cut to pieces" by the media, as he put it. He was also ridiculed by prowar Democrats and Republicans, by Pentagon spokesmen, and by anti-Romney Republicans. To the average observer, he appeared weak rather than realistic or reflective. Birchers viewed his new stand against the war as evidence of his "brainwashing" by Communists.

Durant maintained a firm hold on the Fourteenth District party apparatus, and if he had renounced his membership in the Birch Society, he had not renounced its principles. California governor Ronald Reagan was the Birch Society's first choice for the Republican nomination as the presidential election approached. Looking toward the campaign and election, Durant gathered about 200 Michigan conservatives in Grand Rapids for a meeting in March 1968. They organized the United Republicans of Michigan, and Durant was unanimously elected chair. He had headed a smaller group with the same name that claimed about 450 members and anticipated the Grand Rapids action would lead to a doubling of its numbers.[66] The United Republicans aimed for influence within state party circles; intentionally or not, the group also fit with the tactics Welch advocated. Here was one more potential Birch front.

More important than anything else at the time were the millions of Americans throughout the land who were trying to get a grip on the incomprehensible, on what began to seem, indeed, like the "coming apart of America." By the time of the 1968 Republican National Convention, the urban race riots, the campus antiwar riots, and the chaos in the streets of Chicago during the Democratic convention helped tip the scales for delegates who saw a chance to win back the presidency in November. Badly divided, Democrats nominated Hubert Humphrey, who had been Johnson's vice president. Burdened by animosity toward Johnson and his own reputation as a civil rights champion, Humphrey ran on Great Society accomplishments, winding down the war, and the "politics of joy."[67] Richard Milhouse Nixon won out, pledging law and order in the streets at home and a secret plan to end the war. Out of more than 3,000,000 total votes cast, Humphrey carried Michigan, winning over Nixon by a margin of 222,414 votes. It was the Wallace tally that caught the attention of Republican strategists, however. The 331,968 votes that went to George Wallace on the American Independent ticket could have turned this into a Michigan victory for Nixon had he won over a majority of Wallace supporters, most of whom who were traditionally Democratic voters.[68]

So far as Birch members saw it, a Nixon presidency was no comfort; they continued to consider him deceitful and opportunistic. Moreover, the new president's choice for secretary of Housing and Urban Development was George Romney, the unpalatable symbol of all that was wrong with the Michigan Republican Party. Perhaps *now* voters would agree they had "had enough." And indeed, it seemed reasonable for Birch Society organizers to anticipate that their ranks would increase more significantly in Michigan than in most other states.

From the Birch perspective, examples of the internal Communist threat multiplied all around the state throughout the 1960s, with "leftists" unchecked. Students for a Democratic Society, spearheaded by University of Michigan students, organized in a meeting at Port Huron in 1962. Wayne State University had its own chapter of SANE in the early part of the decade, and its Center for Teaching about Peace and War was one of the first peace and conflict centers in the United States.[69] Every spring from 1969 to 1972, campuses in the state experienced antiwar demonstrations quieted only by local and state police troopers. Rock festivals were common, accompanied by drug raids. Michigan was an epicenter of racial unrest; by the late 1960s angry residents took to the streets not only Detroit but Flint, Kalamazoo, Jackson, Grand Rapids, Saginaw, Pontiac, Muskegon, Albion, Niles, Benton Harbor, Hamtramck, Battle Creek.[70] Militant farmers, angry over falling farm prices, organized chapters of the National Farm Organization soon after it was founded in 1958 with the goal of bargaining as a group with meatpackers to get better prices in exchange for a steady flow of livestock. Aided by Reuther and the UAW, in the 1960s NFO members in Michigan took direct action by pooling their commodities for sale and, in some cases, resorting to violence against truckers.[71] Michigan Democrats became increasingly divided by internal factions, with blue-collar and union voters contesting the pro–civil rights and antiwar positions of liberals and young activists.[72] Catholic leaders, including the archbishop in Detroit, caused fissures among the faithful by supporting open housing and integration.

If Birch proponents hoped Michigan voters would say they'd finally "had enough" and join the Society, they were disappointed. Despite all the events that might have persuaded more people to join, the John Birch Society failed to expand its ranks—even given its locally intertwined crusades against civil rights, Communists, and taxation. People who shared those concerns did not need to join Birch cells and read Welch literature on a schedule. Evidence from one community to another soon demonstrated that "fed up" folks flocked elsewhere. When they got involved in organizing, if they did, they went to local homeowners and neighborhood improvement association meetings. When they turned out to vote, they aimed to win rather than cast a ballot to make a statement. They were not a nucleus wedded to one party but, rather, gave their support to whatever candidates reflected their views. Political parties and candidates put their fingers to the wind and tailored their programs accordingly.

9 · OTHER OPTIONS, OTHER CAUSES

> The American middle class is being programmed for extinction. . . .
> If you are going to fight this stuff, you might as well be in the major
> leagues. The John Birch Society has a plan to sustain and build freedom
> here in our country.
> —JOHN MCMANUS, *The New American* publisher emeritus,
> Centerline, Michigan, speech, April 22, 2005

Apart from serving as a point of reference when commentators reported
on other anti-Communists, anti–United Nations advocates, or extreme
patriots, the Birch Society slipped out of the news. Society leaders insisted
this did not follow from a loss of supporters. Rather, they were positive
that once media corporate heads recognized that their barrage against the
John Birch Society had unwittingly contributed to the organization's
growth, they made a deliberate decision in the summer of 1965 that they
would no longer mention the Society at all. They simply "flipped a switch"
and shut off coverage, as one Birch Society coordinator saw it.[1] The Birch
Society had peaked well short of the 100,000 Welch once talked about, but
he reminded his followers that he never expected the numbers that would
make a mass movement; instead, he wanted a few stalwarts with the "dedication" of that small core of patriots who brought about the American
Revolution. A few stalwarts persisted, but the Birch Society could not
manage to reach beyond the base it had already tapped, and many of those
early joiners began to slip away.

The Communist threat dropped down the list of people's concerns,
falling behind the immediate and looming realities of court-ordered
school integration, open housing, spiraling unemployment, or the impending landgrabs that were uniquely significant to certain Michigan
communities. There was no time for meetings or study groups where the
preoccupation was still with the United Nations and Communist subversives. People had backyards to protect and fronts of their own to organize.

"Communism" was mostly just a familiar, convenient tag-on within the single-issue movements that rallied Michigan citizens to the street protests and into the voting booths during the 1970s and 1980s. Die-hard Birch Society advocates would struggle to keep their main issue of Communism alive by insisting that every social and economic issue troubling America's workers and middle class could be explained by the persistent, insidious influence of Communists or subversives within. They lent just one more voice to an atmosphere rife with rumors, suspicions, and righteous intolerance.

School Busing Opponents

If they even knew about the John Birch Society, it would have been of no interest to angry assortments of people who decided that the time was past for anything but direct action on behalf of their children. The catalyst was the segregated school system in Pontiac, an auto-factory suburb of 85,000 residents north of Detroit. Pontiac's black population had risen nearly 30 percent between 1960 and 1970, and black children now accounted for a third of the school population, yet housing patterns meant that most went to school separately from the white youth. In the late 1960s, black protesters had demanded that the district improve facilities and opportunities for their children. They finally forced the school board to agree that a new high school would be located near downtown instead of in the all-white neighborhood as originally planned, but this was not enough to address the extent of segregation that existed.[2] Civil rights leaders helped black parents in Pontiac press on in the courts.

In February 1970, District Judge Damon Keith handed down an order to force Pontiac to desegregate its schools by busing children. Keith stated that the Pontiac school board had intentionally supported school segregation. Opponents were outraged that the case had been assigned to Keith, who was the only black jurist in the Detroit federal district, and they pinned their hopes on an appeal. But, after months of apprehension on both sides, in May 1971 the U.S. Court of Appeals upheld Keith's order and insisted it must be implemented at once. According to the plan worked out, 10,000 of the 24,000 children in the district would be bused from their own neighborhood schools to others beginning that September.

Tensions escalated all summer over the looming implementation of court-ordered busing. Nonetheless, even busing opponents were stunned when bomb explosions destroyed ten Pontiac school buses about two weeks before the new school year was to begin. School opened as scheduled, but over half of the white parents supported a boycott and kept their children at home. In these first days of September, scuffles at a Pontiac junior high school injured eight white students and one black student, and seven men and two women were arrested at the school bus depot for trying to block buses and throw stink bombs into them.[3] Meanwhile, protesters armed with American flags stood in the street, demanded the schools be closed, and dared buses to run over the Stars and Stripes. Demonstrators sang "God Bless America." They recited the Pledge of Allegiance. They told anyone who listened: School busing was un-American.

Energized, a grassroots following rallied around Pontiac housewife Irene McCabe who had organized the National Action Group (NAG) to protest busing. The issue was of immediate personal concern to McCabe because one of her three children was scheduled to be transported. NAG, she told reporters, was nonviolent. To emphasize the righteousness of her cause, she withdrew her picketing group from the Pontiac schools following the melee. NAG, she said, was opposed to such violence; instead, she blamed trouble in the streets and fights at the schools on "radicals" who were pushing integration. The outspoken, plainspoken woman in her miniskirt was a reporter's dream, and McCabe was catapulted to fame on the nightly news. NAG soon claimed to have 71 chapters in Michigan.[4] As opposition spread nationwide, she began to travel the country speaking to other antibusing groups and led a 620 mile march from Pontiac to Washington in the spring of 1972 to publicize her demand for federal legislation outlawing busing. It was not about race, she insisted; rather, it was about keeping children in their neighborhood schools.[5] Sweatshirts proclaimed her group's message: "BUS JUDGES, NOT OUR CHILDREN!"

Fear Spreads: Cross-District Busing

The Pontiac busing hurricane slammed communities far and wide when, on September 27, 1971, federal judge Stephen Roth ruled that the Detroit public schools were segregated and gave the state board of education 120 days to come up with a plan to solve the problem. In Wayne, Oakland, and Macomb counties, there were about 208,000 black public school students; 184,000 were in the Detroit schools. Judge Roth believed it unlikely that segregated classrooms could be eliminated without creating a metropolitan area school district. Cross-district busing loomed.[6] Other cities like Flint, Lansing, Benton Harbor, and Grand Rapids that had segregated neighborhoods waited for disaster to strike them.

Panic and anger immediately swept through the white Detroit suburbs, whether exclusive enclaves or middle- and working-class areas. Judge Roth said that segregated housing patterns had created the current segregated schools. Suddenly, to many residents, integration in their neighborhoods became less unacceptable and less disruptive than transporting their children to distant classrooms where their physical safety and quality of education would be at risk. "It would be different if a colored person moved in and sent their children to our school," said a Roseville housewife." "If they take care of their property," added her neighbor.[7] Black parents did not want their children to face long bus rides out of their own neighborhoods to sit by unfamiliar and unfriendly classmates each day either, but it appeared their only route to a better education. The Detroit school board spent $675 per child compared to as much as $1,200 in the suburbs. To the smug satisfaction of conservatives, liberals parted company among themselves. Suburban liberals were not always enthusiastic about this new reality of cross-district busing that would affect their own children. The liberals who lived in Detroit saw it as a desirable solution to bring more whites to join their children's classrooms.

School busing captured politics in Michigan. Before Judge Roth's order, Democrats were in a solid position to carry the 1972 presidential and senatorial elections. Now their fortunes were in jeopardy. Republican senator Robert P. Griffin had been worried about reelection with his opponent likely to be the popular attorney general, Democrat Frank Kelley. Griffin, who generally bridged conservatives and moderates among Michigan Republicans, had backed a measure in 1967 to let local school officials determine whether they would use federal funds for busing. Now, however, he quickly introduced a constitutional amendment against busing. Griffin's friend and fellow Michigan Republican Gerald Ford, the House Republican Leader, signed on to the movement for a constitutional amendment to prohibit busing for integration. Like several leading Democrats, Attorney General Kelly signed a statement supporting busing for purposes of school integration but then backed away; he had not meant busing between cities and suburbs when he signed it, said Kelly. Congressmen James G. O'Hara and John Dingell were up for reelection and represented suburban voters; these two liberal Democrats announced their strong opposition to busing. Antibusing rallies became a common sight around school board meetings and political events.

A few protesters went beyond sign-carrying or marches; they joined the Michigan Realm of United Klans of America Inc., Knights of the Ku Klux Klan. Usually referred to as the "third" Klan, this new KKK version was populated by single-minded racists powered by violence, much in the mold of the Black Legion of the 1930s. Michigan's Klan was led by Grand Dragon Robert Miles, the minister of a white supremacist church a few miles outside Howell who had, for a time in his youth, been a member of the John Birch Society. Klansmen were looking for opportunities to make their determination clear, hoping also to intimidate integration support-ers. In April 1971, Miles and allies tarred and feathered R. Wiley Brownlee, a white principal of the Willow Run High School who had been advocat-ing peaceful integration and racial harmony in that district.[8] When the court ordered desegregation of district schools in Pontiac, Miles and his group laid their plans. It was he and several others who planted home-made bombs that destroyed the ten parked school buses the night of Au-gust 30, 1971. A plan to knock out a power station as a diversion had not happened. Nine days later, the FBI arrested six Klansmen 275 miles from Pontiac, not far from the Canadian border. An unpaid undercover agent had been involved with the Pontiac unit of the United Klans of America and had been providing regular reports to the Detroit office.[9] Miles ulti-mately spent six years in federal prison and went back then to pastor his flock near Howell. People who claimed Howell as home would be sen-tenced forever to a preconception: Since they were from there, maybe they were Klan supporters too.

When a U.S. district judge did order cross-district busing between Detroit and its suburban neighbors in 1972 in the case of *Bradley v. Mil-liken,* the exodus from the nearer suburbs accelerated. Cross-district bus-ing was thrown out two years later by the U.S. Supreme Court, but bus-ing opponents expected it was just a short-term victory. They knew that cases similar to Detroit's were pending in Grand Rapids, Kalamazoo, and Benton Harbor. And, too, both the Michigan Civil Rights Commission and state department of education were seeking ways to bring black and white children together in the classrooms. The fearful anticipated that a different Supreme Court might well come up with a different decision in the future and that cross-district busing would be upheld. Recognizing the potential power the government had to intervene into family life, people became more mistrustful than otherwise about issues that came up. Fear fed upon fear.

Fear of Federal Funding

At the same time as the busing controversy, the city council in the Detroit suburb of Warren applied for a HUD grant in 1971 to build a school building and a new low-income apartment complex. Warren was a World War II–created suburb, and decay was setting in on the southern border adjacent to Detroit. The council hoped for federal funding to help revitalize that section of town. Even though that area was home to low income white residents, when the council talked about a grant for "low income" housing, the phrase translated as "black" to people in the neighborhood. Just two years before, in 1969, a homemade bomb damaged a Warren family's garage when they put their house up for sale with an African-American real estate agent from Detroit, and while there were only 30 black families among the 190,000 Warren residents, people on the border feared they were in the path of an impending influx. Now a significant number of residents in Warren decided it would be better to reject much-needed federal funding rather than risk unwanted federal strings that might be attached.

The council itself had been divided about the request for a federal grant because certain members were convinced that HUD secretary Romney might attach conditions that would bring desegregation along with the funding. The *Detroit News* fueled this worry when it published a HUD memo that suggested Warren had been picked as a "prime target" to integrate all suburbs. Romney visited Warren to assure officials that it had not been picked as a "prime target" at all. But fears continued to spread among people who worried that the federal government was usurping local rights and would force integration.[10]

Polish Catholics, a significant portion of the Warren population, were urged by Church leaders to support the housing project and to reach out across racial barriers. Many of these families had started out a generation earlier across the border in Polish Detroit or in Hamtramck; when they moved, they packed along stories. Now they pulled out that box of memories and passed them around—about the Sojourner Truth Project the government forced into one Polish neighborhood during wartime; about the way their blocks and shopping areas "used to look" until black families began to move in; about being afraid for their children to play outside. In-

232 • RIGHT IN MICHIGAN'S GRASSROOTS

tegration revived old hostilities between Polish Catholics and their Irish or German bishops and showed, also, the class-based animosity among Catholics. Privileged clergy could afford to "reach out," sniped Warren Catholics; preaching "racial toleration" came easier with no children or property of their own at stake. On the other side, civil rights activists in the Church were quick to label fellow Catholic opponents as "ignorant" blue-collar "bigots" and "racists." Breakthrough, Donald Lobsinger's conservative Catholic organization, moved into the situation bearing leaflets and picket signs.

Lobsinger had been a regular at Birch Society cell meetings in the early sixties but drifted off to create Breakthrough and devote his time to alerting other Catholics about the "betrayal" the faithful suffered at the hands of Cardinal Dearden and the archdiocesan hierarchy. His organization was dedicated to the "defense of Christianity and our country against the anti-Christian and anti-American forces of militant Atheism, Communism, Zionism, and Socialism." Breakthrough issued a monthly publication, *Battle-Line,* that predictably headlined a central theme: "CARDINAL DEARDEN CONTINUES FINANCIAL AID TO BLACK REVOLUTIONARY AND OTHER RED FRONT GROUPS."[11] Lobsinger's Catholic organization fit the strategy of separate Birch front groups, but his out-of-control demonstrations, personal antics, and periodic arrests did not fit the local mold of conservative Republicans. At any rate, Lobsinger had moved beyond the Birch structure to concentrate on his own crusade, seeking out allies in places like Pontiac and Warren. Breakthrough members distributed thousands of anti-HUD leaflets and disrupted community meetings where Warren residents gathered to discuss the issue of federal funding.

When a referendum was held in the fall of 1971, 57 percent of the Warren voters rejected the urban renewal proposal, whereupon the council rescinded authority to proceed with the HUD programs. Just four years earlier when Romney was running for governor he had received half of Warren's votes, many from people who were Catholics, UAW members, and longtime Democrats who approved of his moderate to liberal reform agenda.[12] Now, their single-minded concern about integration trumped old allegiances and enthusiasm for reforms—especially among those who were living closest to Detroit. The Birch Society did not win members from among these working-class and union members in Warren; and while many of them were Catholic, they did not sign up as members of Breakthrough either. Instead, at election time they began to place a check

Protesters march in advance of HUD secretary Romney's appearance to speak about low-income housing in Warren, July 27, 1970. In Warren, a working-class suburb adjacent to Detroit, many of the residents were Polish, Catholic, union members, and Democrats. They had grown up in Detroit or Hamtramck where property values fell and neighborhoods changed along with integration. Now, the determination to keep their community white trumped any pleas from clergy or union leaders. In 1971, protesters mobilized, and voters rejected an urban renewal grant rather than risk any federal demands for open housing; for another ten years, Warren did not receive any federal housing funds. (Walter P. Reuther Library, Wayne State University.)

by the name of conservative politicians who were promising protection and then went home to cultivate their gardens—or to sell their homes and move on to a more distant suburb like Sterling Heights. Warren received no federal housing funds for the next ten years.

Government Bulldozers Are Coming!

Not many miles from Warren, eight suburban communities in south Oakland County were fighting to halt or change the planned route of the last link of I-696. The Walter P. Reuther Freeway had been tunneling toward them for a decade, with eminent domain swallowing up land to make way for it all the way. When completed, I-696 would stretch 28 miles across Detroit's northern suburbs from east to west. It originated with the Eisenhower administration, got under way in 1961, and then was halted in its tracks because of a few strong, organized, and angry communities in its path. Oak Park, Pleasant Ridge, and Huntington Woods were among the suburbs that put up a fight, arguing with the government and among themselves over how the route should be redrawn to spare one community in place of another. Freeway costs and tempers escalated in the delay. The 3,000 Pleasant Ridge residents agreed to a special head-tax so they could use the money to carry on their campaign. At one stage, then-governor Romney locked quarreling suburban officials in a community center overnight and said he would not let them out until they came to an agreement.

All manner of objections were raised. Oak Park, a community with nearly 10,000 Orthodox Jews in the path of the highway, protested on the ground that the freeway would split through their community. The Orthodox were unable to drive on the Sabbath, and since the freeway divided homes from synagogues, it would be impossible for many families to get to temple. Environmental rules were invoked by freeway opponents who previously cared little about environmental issues. Officials tried to block the course of the road because it bordered on the Detroit zoo. Detroit entered the fray because the route threatened to take a chunk of the city's golf course. Republicans along the planned path said it was deliberately run through their neighborhoods by Democratic politicians who wanted to punish them and had already insulted them, to boot, by naming I-696 after union leader Reuther. Democrats said it was bulldozing toward their neighborhoods by intentional design of Republican politicians who were punishing them. Federal and state highway bureaucrats consulted a rabbi; they looked into the impact of fumes and traffic noise on zoo animals. Compromises pleased no one. Certain of these communities had at least a sprinkling of Birch members who were pleased to say "I told you so" to their neighbors who might at last understand the threat the government posed.[13]

This Land Is My Land, It's Not Your Parkland

Over 250 miles to the north, meanwhile, the John Birch Society had another potentially receptive recruiting ground for its message that the federal government had become dangerously intrusive. Between 1959 and 1970, thousands of acres along Lake Michigan in Leelanau and Benzie counties were under consideration for the Sleeping Bear Dunes National Lakeshore Park. Unlike many other national parks carved mostly out of wilderness land, the larger areas proposed for the Sleeping Bear Dunes Park would take as many as 1,600 privately owned homes, summer cottages, farms, and businesses. In addition, it would impact all the other properties in the area.[14] Prolonged controversy led to ugly characterizations—of the residents as selfish and self-serving, backward-looking, and not only unsophisticated but bigoted; of park proponents as unethical abusers of power, arrogant liars, and un-American if not outright socialists or Communists. Castro was the Communist-of-choice for this side of the debate. The Saginaw newspaper editor viewed the Department of Interior's methods as differing "only in the degree of their application" from Cuba's Land Reform Institute, which controls all the once private lands seized by the Castro government.[15]

Birch Society literature had been circulating in these counties during the sixties but residents in this heavily Republican region needed little prompting to reach their own conclusions, even about the popular Romney. The governor ventured the cautious comment, "I feel that some type of an area should be developed up there." This remark led one Dunes area Republican to claim Romney stood "with the PINKS!"[16] Over the next two years Romney remained neutral on the issue.[17] Throughout four presidencies, bills kept coming back to the House and Senate. In an area with almost no black residents, it was his anti-Communist and anti–big government position that gave American Independent Party presidential candidate George Wallace a smattering of votes in Leelanau and Benzie counties in 1968. Then, in October 1970, President Nixon signed the last park bill into law. Park agents at once set about acquiring land from owners amid outraged complaints that the U.S. government aped socialist and Communist practices. Just as frequently, residents spoke of their belated recognition that they now knew "how the Indians felt when the white man took their land."[18]

Eminent Domain Takes "Poletown"

By the late 1970s and the early 1980s General Motors set its sights on a neighborhood straddling Hamtramck and Detroit. Residents made common cause with concerned citizens on both the right and the left to save Poletown, as it came to be known during the fight over its fate. This was a low-income, integrated neighborhood, home to an aging population of Polish and black residents living alongside newer arrivals from the Middle East, Yugoslavia, Albania, the Philippines, and an assortment of other areas. A busy, crowded, and factory-centered area in the first decades of the century, it had fallen on hard times once the shift to new factories and new homes in the suburbs accelerated after World War II. The Dodge Main Plant finally closed its doors in 1979. Once the area's beacon and anchor, the huge hulking factory joined others—idle, abandoned, and with no future in sight.

Desperate to keep jobs in the city, Mayor Coleman Young and the Detroit Common Council agreed with a plan put forward by General Motors that offered to build a sleek new assembly plant on the site if the city would seize it for "public use" under the right of eminent domain, clear it, and provide tax incentives to the corporation. General Motors promised this modern plant with its robotic technology would employ 6,000 people. The facility would stretch across into Hamtramck where, as in Detroit, politicians and many residents saw the advantage of a new factory in place of those that had become only a drain on city coffers. In all, the area to be cleared included 4,200 residents, 1,300 homes, 140 businesses, several churches, a school, and one hospital. Hard-pressed to support city parishes with their dwindling congregations, the Archdiocese of Detroit's Cardinal John F. Dearden agreed to deed the two Catholic churches in the path to the city so they could be demolished. Only Detroit councilman Kenneth Cockrel, a black civil rights activist and the one Marxist on the council, voted against clearing the area and handing it to the auto company.

Two rival neighborhood organizations took form. Desperate to keep jobs in the city, there were those who thought placating GM was worth sacrificing buildings, many in ill repair anyway. Some of the first residents who were approached signed up to take the buyouts offered for their homes. They were people who wanted to go and welcomed the chance to get the price that averaged $13,000-plus up to $15,000 to help toward the cost of a new home. Others were outraged that their neighborhood was to be cleared by bulldozers, and, too, they were facing an almost nightly wave of vandals who preyed on now-empty houses and set fires that threatened nearby homes and businesses. A number of homeowners reached for their guns and rifles, sat on their porches all night, or patrolled the streets themselves. As soon as the scope and certainty of the plan became known,

Father Joseph Karasiewicz rallied with his parishioners at the doomed Immaculate Conception parish to "Save Poletown!" They vowed to fight the archdiocese, fight the city, and fight General Motors to save their neighborhood and the church where many of them had been baptized and married, and from which they intended to be buried. Father Karasiewicz and his flock were joined by other residents at the headquarters in the church basement and launched a campaign to publicize their plight. Their letter-writing and publicity campaign brought in help from Ralph Nader and his staff, Maggie Kuhn and her Gray Panthers, and sympathetic journalists from the *New York Times,* the *Washington Post,* the *Los Angeles Times* plus CBS news cameras. Help came, too, from people outside the neighborhood whose family roots were there or who were angry over the "conspiracy" between corporations and politicians.

Quiet housewives, small proprietors and factory workers, young and old, black and white, joined together in demonstrations. They parked a GM car in front of the GM headquarters and, in turn, wielded a sledgehammer to smash it. They rented a bulldozer, loaded it on a truck, and paraded to the gated suburban home of General Motors chair Roger Smith on Mother's Day. Politely, they explained to the guard who turned them away that they were there to ask if Mrs. Smith would also want to save her home from a bulldozer. Devout Catholics joined their neighbors to picket outside Cardinal Dearden's office, many of them carrying signs that likened him to Communist leaders in the Soviet Union who had closed churches. A Native American Poletown resident marched with the protesters, saying to his neighbors, "Now you know what its like to be relocated. It is a trail of tears."[19]

Appeals to halt the condemnation went all the way to the Michigan Supreme Court. In a 5-2 decision, the court ruled in March 1981 that eminent domain could be used to clear the land for General Motors. Wrecking balls dismantled Immaculate Conception church three months later. The once mild-mannered, obedient, and unassuming Father Karasiewicz had angered the cardinal, his Polish bishop, and many in the Catholic hierarchy; he was not reassigned to another parish and died within a few months after the church fell. The new General Motors Poletown Plant opened on schedule, and it created jobs, if only 3,000 rather than the 6,000 workers that corporation heads originally promised to employ there. Apart from the Poletown assembly center and the greenbelt around it, the surrounding area became one more section of abandoned buildings and trash-filled lots to be overlooked and avoided even twenty-five years later when Detroit promoted itself as host of the Super Bowl. A few years after their relocation, a follow-up study by the University of Michigan showed that over 80 percent of former residents were happy with their new homes.[20] At the time, it was a different story. People from both the Right and the Left came away more alarmed about what they regarded as the unchecked abuse of eminent domain.[21]

"Send Them a Message!"

In the spring of 1972 Michigan held its first presidential primary in 44 years. It was successfully reestablished by the liberal wing of the state's Democratic Party and was set up as an "open" primary in which voters could choose either party's ballot but need not be registered in that party to vote among its candidates. Liberals and even conservative Democrats regretted that primary plan in its very first go-around. It created an embarrassment in their midst and a shocking public portrayal of Michigan attitudes. George Wallace was on the primary ballot this time as a Democrat, not the third-party candidate he was in 1968 when he won 10 percent of the Michigan vote. Alabama governor Wallace was an avowed segregationist, and he was against crime, civil rights, forced integration, and school busing as well as Communists and "establishment" politicians. Michigan was his target for winning a state in the North, and he campaigned hard with his slogan: "Send them a message." He well knew that the message from Michigan in 1972 was busing. One day before Michigan held its primary Wallace was shot in Maryland and would live permanently paralyzed. As he lay in the hospital on election day he may have gained some sympathy votes, but he certainly lost no support. Leaving his competitors George McGovern and Hubert Humphrey trailing far behind, George Wallace won 79 of the 83 counties. He collected 51 percent of the vote, with strongest support coming from the southeast corner of the state. Michigan voters chose, indeed, to "send them a message" that reverberated loud and long in Democratic and Republican ears nationwide.

In November, the presidential race was between Richard Nixon and George McGovern. Richard Nixon won 56 percent of the votes cast and Michigan's 21 electoral votes, a significant increase over the 41 percent he had received here four years earlier. John Schmitz, a little-known Californian, ran as the American Independent Party candidate. He was an ar-

Breakthrough protest. Breakthrough founder Donald Lobsinger and his followers were conservative Catholics who claimed they had been betrayed by Cardinal John Dearden and liberal clergy who used donations from the laity to fund black revolutionary and other "Red" front groups. Lobsinger had begun his anti-Communist career as a member of the John Birch Society. Liberal Catholics responded by labeling such conservative Catholics ignorant and bigoted. (Walter P. Reuther Library, Wayne State University.)

dent Birch Society member. Statewide, Schmitz won over 63,000 votes, picking up the hard-core antigovernment holdouts and some would-be Wallace supporters since Wallace was not on the ballot in the general election.[22] Many more of the Wallace Democrats had opted for Nixon's "law and order in the streets" and victory with honor in Vietnam over their party's stand on behalf of civil rights and peace in Vietnam. That worrisome year of 1972 when Michigan majorities opted for Nixon as their president, they elected Republican Robert Griffin as their senator, and in congressional and in local races, as always, voters made choices according to the candidate. Their known and approved positions, for example, sent Republican Gerald Ford and Democrat John Dingell back to Congress. Statewide voter turnout slipped below 60 percent for the first time since 1960.

Staying the Birch Course

If recent years had reinforced any Birch Society message, it was the potential the federal government had for interfering at the local level. It also remained clear that politicians with an acceptable message within the two-party system were the voters' perennial port in a storm when and if they set off to the voting booth. Michigan Birch supporters like Durant together with like-minded others persisted in their determination to shape the course of the state's Republican Party. Shrewd analysts understood the need for a multipronged approach. They planned to help tap broad-based public concerns with recommended solutions people could buy into; then voters would seek out candidates who agreed with those solutions. That, in turn, would force the party to put such suitable candidates forward. Strategists were at work.

As early as 1969, Durant announced he would issue "position papers" on "vital state issues." The first, on education, was a call to break the government's monopoly. Parents should be able to deduct private school tuition from their income tax to the amount the government would otherwise pay. The school board should be able to hire and fire at will. Boards should be able to expel and prosecute students who interfere with the right of others to receive an education. A position paper on welfare insisted it should not be considered a right and should not be tax-supported. Another would stop the "tax and spend policy" that Durant said had been going on in Michigan for ten years. He would cut the state income tax by as much as half or cut the sales tax in half or eliminate all other taxes except those two. The governor should veto waste; every department should be cut by 10 percent and most by 20 percent. Directly or indirectly, reductions in taxes and state spending were at the root of each position he championed.[23]

At least one avowed Birch Society member, Richard Friske, was elected to the state legislature. Friske, a Charlevoix apple farmer and a Republican from the 106th district, was a Birch Society organizer in northwestern Michigan and also an organizer of the Wallace for President campaigns in 1968 and 1972. He used every opportunity to insist there was a direct link between the Nixon administration, sex education, the growing welfare population, and excessive taxation. He attacked Nixon's population commission for presenting abortion as an "exercise of individual freedom" and for recommending sex education in schools. Friske believed sex education encouraged the poor to have sex, which resulted in children who had to be

supported by food stamps and welfare checks; moreover, the poor regarded having more children as the ticket to more federal money. "These
people think only of the dollars their babies will bring them, not of the
babies." The wrong people, the "drone population," were having too many
children, while the bright young people in college were being persuaded
that they shouldn't have more than two children because of the global
population explosion.[24] The *New York Times* that reported on Friske's
comments mentioned early in the article that Friske was a former member of the German Luftwaffe during World War II, as if to put his remarks
in their proper context, but once again missing the local context. Friske's
issues were the issues that churned in both Republican and Democratic
circles throughout the 14-year administration of Republican governor
William Milliken in the seventies and eighties.

Taxpayers Revolt

Milliken had been Romney's lieutenant governor before succeeding him
in 1969. The Republican conservative wing tried to keep him off the Romney ticket in 1964 and continued to object to his positions. Like Romney,
however, Milliken was popular with people in both parties for his evenhanded and enlightened government, but the economic slide continued.
In 1972, voters approved a state lottery with the assumption that revenue
from it would go to the state's school fund. A year later, the state legislature
approved an income tax credit that benefited most property owners
whose income was under $73,650. State and local taxes still increased faster
than personal income.[25] Finally, in 1978, the same spring Californians
passed Proposition 13 to reduce real estate taxes, Michigan residents proclaimed their own revolt.

Conservative businessman Richard Headlee organized and chaired
Taxpayers United for Tax Limitation. This group backed the Headlee
amendment to the constitution, while Robert Tisch gathered supporters
for his own separate Tisch amendment. Each plan would provide tax relief. Petition drives gathered a total of nearly 700,000 signatures that put
the two different proposals on the ballot. Voters approved the Headlee
plan that limited the amount of state income that could be used for government spending, provided that all millage increases must be submitted
to voters, and required a rollback of millage rates if property assessments
increased faster than the rate of inflation.

With tax relief accomplished, Democrats joined Republican voters to keep the moderate Milliken in office until he chose to leave at the end of his term in 1982. That year, Richard Headlee won the Republican nomination with the backing of party conservatives and fellow Mormon George Romney, but his reputation among voters rested primarily upon his drive to limit property taxes, now accomplished. Headlee was defeated by the Democrat, Congressman James Blanchard. Michigan majorities went to the Republican presidential candidates from 1972 onward, yet voters kept the Democratic Blanchard when he ran for a second term in 1986. Blanchard continued the middle-of-the-road policies of Democratic and Republican governors since the end of the 1940s. But the economy and unemployment rates staggered up and down, which revived the inevitable battle over taxes and government spending. When a temporary 38 percent tax increase was added in 1983, suburban voters recalled two of their Democratic legislators who had supported that Blanchard-pushed tax plan, elected Republicans in their place, and thereby the legislature had a Republican majority dominated by the state senate majority leader, the conservative John Engler. When Engler ran for governor in 1990, he defeated Blanchard in a very close election.

"Regular" Conservatives Triumph

John Engler's triumph marked a triumph for the philosophy of Michigan's Republican conservatives. In office until January 2003, Engler pressed a course of action very different from nearly all of his twentieth-century predecessors, Republican or Democrat. He sharply reduced government services, consolidated state departments, and supported a reduction in taxes for businesses and individuals. He was also determined that government should take a strong stand when it came to education. Republicans had regained a majority in the legislature, and Democrats understood the mood of their constituents. Yet a majority of Michigan voters backed the Democratic senatorial candidate in every election but 1994 and helped elect Clinton to the presidency in 1992 and 1996.

A top priority of Engler's administration was improving education, with a focus on high standards, equity, and accountability. The legislature joined with the governor to propose a significant change in school funding, historically reliant upon property taxes and as a result varying widely from rich to poor districts. Voters approved the plan that would decrease property taxes and offset the lost revenue by an increase in the sales tax from 4 to 6 percent. The state now took over nearly all public school funding, and Engler used the momentum to mandate statewide uniform testing at several grade levels with sanctions placed on districts that did not measure up to state-established standards. Most controversial, Engler implemented state support for privately operated charter schools. In crafting these reforms, the Engler administration drew upon individuals in groups such as the Mackinac Center for Public Policy. This think tank headquartered in Midland was funded by wealthy business and corporate heads who were advocates of lower taxes, less government, and schools held accountable for teaching American values on the foundation of "the 3 R's."

Critics took note that Engler's themes overlapped with points in Durant's position papers and Birch Society publications. If they dug through files or had long memories, they could see ideas harking back to the platform planks that Richard Durant and the Fourteenth District Convention tried to push on the whole party in 1962. Hostile analysts labeled Engler advisers as "Birchers." Some may indeed have been Society members or sympathizers. But the Republicans now in power in the state were more in the mold of the party's new generation of conservatives who were focused on economic issues such as removing barriers to free trade, providing business incentives, reducing government's role, privatizing services, and cutting government spending.

Although the governor and other Republicans often expressed outrage about Bill Clinton's presidency, across most of the decade the Michigan economy was buoyed by a boom in the national economy. By the time Engler left office, he had signed 32 tax cuts into law. Republicans pointed out that the state budget had gone from a deficit to a large surplus, that 800,000 new jobs had been created, and that unemployment rates were at a record low.[26] Still, the times were reminiscent of the 1920s. Some Michigan families exulted over their high-paying jobs, soaring ceilings, and manicured lawns, while a growing number of others went without health insurance, watched their roofs leak, and saw their hopes turn to dust.

A Widening Divide

In the 1990s, a complex economic and social environment in Michigan left the fortunate believing everyone could make a good living if they tried and the unfortunate believing the odds were stacked against them, maybe deliberately. Families were not all just moving up in place; rather, the gulf between the rich and poor was increasing, and many families were actually losing ground. People on the wrong side of the divide were correct when they invoked the old adage, "the rich get rich and the poor get poorer."[27]

The health of the state's economy could be correctly pronounced "sound" by a reading of some statistics, as strong by the mid-1990s as any time since the 1960s. The rust was off; chrome and titanium glistened in the modernized auto plants and high-tech industrial parks. Michigan's economy remained critically entwined with the ever-volatile auto industry. The state was still the nation's leading producer of motor vehicles, although its percentage continually slipped. Michigan never again reached the 37 percent of the national market it enjoyed in 1960, and by 1996 its share was only about 25 percent. The Big Three auto companies retained their edge by their new sleek robotics plants, by sophisticated research and development divisions, or by complicated multinational mergers. Manufacturing jobs created between 1991 and 1997 multiplied three times, with companies having 500 or fewer workers accounting for most of that expansion; these small factories amounted to over half of the manufacturing jobs in the state by 1999.[28] After another recession at the beginning of the decade, Michigan employment increased and unemployment rates dropped below the national average.[29] Union workers, with an average wage over $60,000 not including benefits, gave truth to the popular image of a Michigan working class with RVs and cottages "up north." An increasing number of families felt, however, that they were "up a creek without a paddle."

The North American Free Trade Agreement that went into effect in January 1994 added to controversies about the health of Michigan. NAFTA immediately eliminated most of the tariffs on goods traded between the United States, Canada, and Mexico, and it phased out remaining tariffs over the following 10 years. This trade agreement had a major impact on Michigan, but whether it was to help or hurt the economy and its workers was often in the eye of the beholder who either gained new business or lost a job. Major corporations and big business lobbied actively for its passage, none more determinedly than Michigan's Big Three auto firms and the National Association of Manufacturers. Governor Engler supported it too, and, within a few years after the act was implemented, the Mackinac Center for Public Policy provided him with statistical evidence from studies that demonstrated NAFTA was good for

Pontiac antibusing demonstration, September 1, 1971. Fears for the well-being of their children were often at the heart of grassroots protest movements. Here, a woman and two children sit on grass at an antibusing demonstration in Pontiac, Michigan. The mother's picket sign speaks to the familiar fear of government interference with families: "Is America free?" Her child's sign announces: "I won't be a bus baby." (Walter P. Reuther Library, Wayne State University.)

Michigan with an increase in exports to Mexico, Canada, and the world as a whole.[30] Other studies offered counterevidence, and the Department of Labor certified that over 3,000 workers in Michigan had lost their jobs due to NAFTA in the first three years after it was passed.

People who preferred to regard themselves as part of the great American middle class were coming to think that a new label suited them better: They were part of the "working poor." Union wages were good, give or take some concessions at the bargaining table, but union membership was dwindling along with auto manufacturing jobs. The growing companies with 500 or fewer employees typically were not unionized and generally paid less than the state's average wage in a given occupation.[31] Despite figures showing Michigan unemployment was lower than any time in the last 30 years, high-paying blue-collar jobs declined. Instead, many found work in the jobs that were growing most—as cashiers, janitors, retail sales clerks, waiters and waitresses. Twenty percent of the Michigan workforce, full and part time, earned less than $7.50 an hour by 1999.[32] A growing number of working adults, most of them employed full time, were in jobs that offered no health benefits, but they were usually ineligible for Medicaid benefits in contrast to those who were unemployed.[33]

The best-paying new positions were those in the research and development laboratories, engineering, information technology, health services, and specialized medical fields. Given trends in employment, education opened doors. But a majority of Michigan residents over the age of 25 lacked that important qualification. In 1990, Michigan ranked thirty-fifth among all states in terms of those 25 and older who had a bachelor's or professional degree. Over half had no education beyond high school.[34] For much of the twentieth century, higher education was not necessary to earn good factory wages. Parents routinely discouraged their children from going on to school, reminding them that their teachers did not make as much as someone working on the line. And so it was that the new high-paying jobs went to people recruited from out of state, or well-trained immigrants from Asian countries, or to young residents who got the message in time and went on to college or skilled training programs. Older people, finding it difficult to make up for lost years and opportunity, were passed by, left standing in line alongside younger folks—the dropouts or indifferent or disadvantaged students who belatedly realized their limited options.

While almost all of the regions in the state shared in the resurgence according to Michigan Employment Security Agency employment statistics, within any given region were clusters of working people working ever harder to hold on to the lifestyle or dreams they held a decade or two earlier. Several small communities in western and central Michigan and in the Upper Peninsula were hard-hit when their single industries took advantage of the new NAFTA opportunity and moved their plants to Mexico or Canada. In some entire regions, employment and income levels were below state averages, and any turnaround remained out of sight.

Detroit was the core of the most segregated metropolitan region in the nation, and the city received the most consistent attention in public policy and media circles when it came to exposing the state's glaring gaps in wealth and opportunity. Jobs continually flowed out; Detroit itself lost 100,000 workers in the decade of the 1980s, while the region's workforce grew by more than 180,000. Of the largest central cities in the nation's metropolitan areas, Detroit's loss of workers was most steep.[35] Three new casinos and two new sports stadiums led to hopeful predictions of a spectacular recovery for the once-proud city. Still, unemployment rates climbed toward double digits, and high school graduation rates slid on downward past the halfway point. Meanwhile, opposition to affirmative action programs gained ever more supporters among white residents across Michigan. More people began to talk of court challenges to rulings that, as they saw it, gave an unfair advantage to blacks and women

Farmers could reasonably conclude that their fortunes depended not only on the weather but on many more conditions beyond their control. Agriculture, including the food industry, was the state's second-largest employer in the mid-1990s. Michigan ranked sixth in the nation for agricultural exports. During the 1980s, farmers shared in the national farm crisis, and trouble persisted selectively throughout the decade of the 1990s. Farm costs had been climbing dramatically. As machinery, seed, and chemicals became more expensive, farmers sometimes expanded the size of their farms in the 1980s when land values dropped, hoping that because they could now grow more, a market turnaround would make the investment profitable. But, especially in areas of population growth and development, rising land values could push taxes up faster than profits. Governor Engler and the legislature worked to give tax relief to farmers, but the measures were generally too little and too late to help. By the early 1990s, only one-fifth of all Michigan farms reported a net income above $10,000; nearly 60 percent reported no profit at all. Farmers with small and medium-sized holdings were losing ground to the big farms averaging 775 acres.[36] The picture was much the same for livestock farmers. Large operations backed by investors expanded to specialize in hogs, beef, turkeys, or chickens, and volume helped them cut costs and maximize profits.[37] Over two-thirds of Michigan farmers held jobs off the farm in an effort to stay on it and, in their spare time, tried to cope with new Environmental Protection Agency regulations designed to protect against soil erosion and contamination from pesticides and fertilizers, to clean up streams, to preserve wetlands. The government offered some grants to help meet the new regulations, but it took time and savvy to fill out those applications, so the money went to the prosperous farmers and to agribusiness operations. Many families, tired of the struggle or without children to carry on, sold out to developers. Michigan acreage lost to farming between 1985 and 2000 totaled more than the size of the state of Rhode Island.[38]

Many urban and suburban residents no longer realized the place agriculture had in the economy, and fewer now had farm roots or experiences. Farmers were the people one met on occasional Saturday visits to their stalls at farmers' markets. They were a group admired from afar according to handed-down notions about their "rugged independence," envied because they were their own bosses. Farmers resembled that common image less and less over time, however, and from the 1970s onward, farmers were less and less a group in common. Across the state and within individual communities, too, the distance between groups of people widened.

Separation by the 1990s was not only along lines of race and income as in previous decades. Schools sorted children from prekindergarten onward, even within a single community. Nearly two-thirds of the children in Oakland County's affluent Bloomfield Hills attended private schools, while in the city of Detroit and the working-class suburbs, some parents chose one of the new charter schools or a school operated by their church. Catholic schools in the central cities and oldest suburbs closed, while new facilities went up in the exurbs. Congregations in churches of the same denomination might have little contact, even if they were just a few miles from each other. Long-established Protestant churches fought internally over gay rights and abortion, all the while failing to attract such attendance as the large new evangelical churches where families centered much of their time around church-sponsored activities. Patterns of family life in one community were alien to those in another, and an increase in the number of single parents or families in which both parents worked meant that patterns of family life were divergent even among middle-class neighbors.

"Had Enough?"

John Birch Society leaders updated their message to warn the public about the threats now facing them, threats represented by continued membership in the United Nations, passage of NAFTA, and escalating globalization. President Ronald Reagan had told Mr. Gorbachev to "tear down this wall," and mainstream conservatives—along with most all Americans— soon were no longer preoccupied with the Communist enemy of old. Not so with the persistent, consistent Birch Society. Forty years after it was established, the John Birch Society affirmed its constant resolve: to expose schemes that intentionally and systematically undermined American sovereignty beginning in the years following World War I and continuing to the North American Free Trade Agreement and beyond.

After Robert Welch died in 1989, the Birch Society moved its headquarters to Appleton, Wisconsin, perhaps coincidentally the home base of the late senator Joseph R. McCarthy. The Society continued to publish books as well as the monthly magazine, retitled from *American Opinion* to

The New American. Publications tracked the sellout of sovereignty by presidents of both parties. Authors warned of the "new world order" and tracked the unrelenting progress of Communism too: "Beijing is making large inroads ... in Latin America" and "dominoes are falling south of the border, but no one seems to be noticing."[39]

For a time, riding the wave of Reagan enthusiasms, the Birch Society gained members again until it approached an estimated 55,000.[40] Sheer numbers, however, were not a priority to headquarters since throughout its organizational life, the Society's money came from major donors rather than from members' dues.[41] Chapters and their members were important as the means to circulate the Birch Society message and educate the public; top-down directives with monthly agendas sent from the home office remained the pattern. Chapter leaders were to hold a planning meeting followed by an informative meeting. The Appleton office provided a speakers list, materials for discussion, and recommended videos such as "Who Is Bill Clinton?" and "Revolution By Treaty." As one speaker on the lecture circuit put it to a Michigan audience, "If you are going to fight this stuff, you might as well be in the major leagues. The John Birch Society has a plan to sustain and build freedom here in our country."[42]

Just as in 1958 when it started, the John Birch Society platform did indeed reflect concerns shared by a broad slice of the American population. Then it had been Communist subversives and loss of sovereignty that the United Nations represented. Polls indicated that approval for the United Nations had been dropping from at least the 1980s, and Birch spokesmen claimed this as evidence of their success.[43] By the 1990s, hostility toward NAFTA was on the rise as it began to appear more costly than beneficial to ordinary American workers; more Michigan residents were inclined to agree with a Birch message that shadowy, vaguely defined conspirators were subverting the American economy. Still, audiences at Birch meetings remained small, and people who did remember the John Birch Society of old were usually surprised if they learned it still existed. Grand Rapids maintained a John Birch bookstore, but the Society counted most now on its website where people could learn about its message and place orders for material.

For a time, the Birch Society's anti-Communist crusade had offered a coterie of professionals and businessmen within the Republican Party the opportunity to build a base of followers. For a time, Birch chapters in Michigan offered a home for perhaps as many as 1,000 rank-and-file members fearful about Communist penetration of American institutions.

It was superseded, however, by antibusing and anti–open housing groups, by library, curriculum, and school board watchdog committees, by taxpayers united against government spending, by church boards reining in social justice activists. The contribution of the John Birch Society in Michigan was not in its message that Communism abroad and Communists within were a threat to the American way of life. Rather, it contributed a persistent, insistent voice to a groundswell among those who were convinced that property taxes were too high, that "civil rights" were interpreted too broadly by recent courts, that schools had become too lax, that big government was a serious threat to traditional American freedoms, and, indeed, that there were those in our own government who were part of a plan to put an end to American sovereignty.

Harking back to the Second Amendment "right to bear arms," some alarmed citizens became convinced that gun control was unconstitutional, that such measures were part of a conspiracy intended so American citizens would not be able to defend the nation from a takeover. A small but determined cadre decided that staying informed was not enough; preparing for the worst was imperative. By the mid-1990s, they found a congenial home in a new movement—the Michigan Militia.

THE MICHIGAN MILITIA

10 · THE "DUTY OF DEFENSE"
Organizing the Michigan Militia

> The militia MUST pose a tremendous threat to tyrants and terrorists who hide within the government. They pose no threat whatsoever to the U.S. Government or the citizens since the militia is made up of the U.S. Government (We the People) and its citizens. . . . The citizen militia, then, becomes the threat to a bad government system that will not change. The Declaration of Independence mandates that the citizen militia rise up in arms against tyrants and despots.
> —NORM OLSON

In November 1994, a weekend military practice drill in the far northwestern corner of the Lower Peninsula merited one of the first of many accounts that would appear in the *New York Times*. According to the article, "some 100 members of a group calling itself the Michigan Militia" turned out in Brutus, preparing "to defend itself against the United States Government." People who assembled in the remote village that day included small business owners, executives, autoworkers, and nurses. Ninety of them were white men; among the women was the one black person in attendance, a nurse from Detroit. More startling, leaders claimed that the militia had 12,000 members in chapters or "brigades" throughout the state.[1] About the same time, Channel 7 in Detroit (WXYZ) aired "Secret Soldiers." This series of reports on the state's paramilitary movement subsequently won the prestigious duPont award, broadcast journalism's Pulitzer Prize equivalent.[2] Viewed from a distance—as well as up close—the specter of camouflage-clad gun-rights advocates in training, perhaps 12,000 of them statewide, connoted a newly dangerous opponent to the government and rule of law. What was this all about?

What the *Detroit Free Press* would come to describe as "this unseen army and its strange little war" was the self-proclaimed citizens' militia, a conglomeration of regional brigades commonly known by a generic label, the "Michigan Militia."[3] In an optimistic aim for unity, they came together in the mid-nineties to form the Michigan Militia Corps–Wolverines, a broad umbrella organization with "headquarters," websites, and sympathizers all eager to explain their existence. A concise website statement described their mission for all to see: The Militia was about citizens who said they no longer trusted government leaders and who believed an armed, trained populace might prove the last line of national defense in time of internal threat or external invasion.[4] Why now?

The Brady Bill had just gone into effect in February 1994. This law made it harder to purchase a handgun. Two of the most important men among the Michigan Militia organizers were gun shop owners; moreover, gun owners were commonplace in Michigan where about one in nine residents held a hunting license, and hunting was a tradition, a family affair.[5] Men and women attracted by the Militia's mission, however, were unlike most orange-clad hunters who took to the woods in the fall. Clustering in the Militia were people who actively feared their government's leaders—national, state, and local. So far as Militia members saw it, the Brady Bill was just the first step toward wiping out Second Amendment rights. Recent events at Ruby Ridge and Waco provided them with ominous evidence of a government bent on destroying basic rights and freedoms of the American people. They could wait no longer to ready a citizens' defense.

Epiphany

A sort of shorthand language would trigger visceral responses among them over the next years—Ruby Ridge, Waco, Oklahoma City, Y2K, 9/11. But when the Michigan Militia groups were first organizing, Ruby Ridge and Waco were their fire alarms in the night. On August 21, 1992, federal marshals and FBI agents gathered around Randy and Vicky Weaver's mountain retreat in Ruby Ridge, Idaho. They intended to arrest Randy Weaver for missing a court date on a minor weapons charge, but the Weavers' Christian Identity and white separatist-inspired lifestyle was at the root of all this attention. According to Weaver's subsequent account, he had rebuffed efforts of the Bureau of Alcohol, Tobacco, and Firearms (BATF) to recruit him as a "mole" within Christian Identity circles, and, in turn, he became a target. Government surveillance agents and local law officers regarded Weaver, his family, and his friends as dangerous.[6] A melee started when an agent-in-hiding shot the Weaver's barking family dog; their 14-year-old son Sam shot toward the marshals who then shot him in the back as he ran toward his father in the family cabin. The next day, as Weaver and a friend came back to the cabin from placing Sam's body in a nearby shed, an FBI sniper fired a shot that blew off the head of Vicky Weaver who was holding the door open for the men. She died holding their baby daughter. After a nine-day standoff, Weaver, his two remaining children, and his friend surrendered to authorities. By then, people across the country were watching on nightly news, hearing about it on shortwave broadcasts, reading about it in the papers. A year later, well-known attorney Gerry Spence won an acquittal for Randy Weaver. The jury agreed with his argument that Weaver's Christian Identity beliefs were irrelevant to the case, that the government had gone too far, that its agents were out of control. The government eventually settled with the Weaver family for $3.1 million. Within two months after the standoff in Ruby Ridge, leaders from various antigovernment groups reportedly gathered in Colorado to form a common front and to plan strategy for "a citizen's militia movement like none this country has ever known."[7] An even more horrifying episode soon made Ruby Ridge appear to be part of a dangerous pattern.

In April 1993, the Justice Department laid siege to the Branch Davidian community in Waco, Texas. At Waco, 81 died in flames when the BATF and the FBI ended a 51-day standoff by storming the religious community's compound with the expressed purpose of rescuing "hostage" children inside. Twenty-five who died in the fire were children. The fire's origin is still in dispute. Some angry observers likened the Branch Davidians to the mass suicide of Jews who would not surrender to Romans at Masada in AD 73.[8] Militia members would often speak of Waco in terms of a personal epiphany.

The wary and the fearful combed Internet sites and exchanged information from antigovernment publications; a lengthening roster of "government victims" began to circulate. The list often reached back to 1983 beginning with Gordon Kahl, a World War II veteran and farmer near Medina, North Dakota. Hard-hit by high interest rates and falling farm prices, Kahl had become convinced that the farmers' plight added up to a conspiracy engineered by Jewish bankers who extended loans knowing borrowers would have to default. According to Kahl, Jewish "enemies of Christ" intended to drive whites and Christians from the land. They had replaced the Constitution with their "Jewish Communist manifesto."[9] Kahl refused to pay his taxes and, in 1976, was sentenced to prison for tax evasion; after serving several months, he was released on parole. Once out, he was involved in assorted groups aiming to restore the "Christian Common Law" that they believed the founding fathers intended. One, the *Posse Comitatus* movement, argued that the only legitimate authority was the county sheriff. In February 1983, when four carloads of federal marshals came to arrest Kahl for parole violation, he engaged in a shoot-out. Two marshals died and several were wounded; Kahl's 23-year-old son was also wounded in the exchange of fire. Kahl escaped by stealing a marshal's car and went underground in Arkansas with help of Posse members. In absentia, he was convicted of two counts of second-degree murder and six counts of assault. Federal agents tracked him down and, with the local sheriff, went to the Arkansas farmhouse to get him on June 3, 1983. Again there was a shoot-out, and Kahl died. Accounts would vary from that day on. Possibly, agents threw a smoke grenade into the stove flue and set off several cases of ammunition in the house where he holed up.[10] As far as Michigan Militia adherents saw it, if Kahl went too far, the government went way too far and drove him over the edge. Many of them first heard about Kahl about ten years after the fact, however, once Ruby Ridge and Waco gave "government victims" significant attention among a widening circle of Americans.

Shouldering the Duty

By all accounts, Norman Olson and Ray Southwell initiated the statewide Michigan Militia Corps at a meeting they called in Olson's gun shop in Alanson in April 1994. Alanson was a town of fewer than 700 people located near Burt Lake in Emmet County. The 48-year-old Olson had settled there after spending ten years in the Air Force. In addition to operating his gun shop, Olson served as pastor of the Calvary Baptist Church in Brutus, about three miles up the road. Southwell, Olson's close friend and a deacon in Calvary Baptist Church, was a 43-year-old real estate agent and registered nurse. He had served in the navy in the early 1970s.[11] In the aftermath of Waco, Olson and Southwell organized and headed the Northern Michigan Regional Militia, a group local to two northwestern counties. After about a year—a year when the Brady Bill made its way through Congress, was signed into law by President Clinton, and then took effect—they decided the time had come to make common cause with other clusters of the like-minded. The Brady Act, although very limited in scope, required gun shop owners to do background checks on customers before selling them handguns. According to Olson and other conspiracy-oriented gun rights advocates, this was just the beginning of the government's sinister campaign to disarm the American citizenry.

Gathered at the April 1994 meeting were 28 men "who felt that they must share the duty of defense."[12] Seventy years earlier when a small group of men met on Stone Mountain in Georgia, they fashioned the Ku Klux Klan to protect the institutions of government from the undesirable residents—blacks, Jews, Catholics, immigrants, Prohibition violators, and assorted others—who threatened the country's white, Anglo-Saxon, Protestant foundations. Alarmed critics would liken the Michigan Militia to the KKK, regarding them too as a group of dangerous vigilantes. Such a comparison was an eager effort to find some historical precedent, but it was incorrect. Michigan's Militia organizers identified and shouldered a very different obligation than the Klan, which had attracted prominent leaders at every level of government. According to Militia assessments, the American people needed to be protected from their own leaders. They were convinced that people in high places no longer had the wisdom or will to preserve the individual liberties, personal freedoms, and cherished institutions that were the birthright of America's people.

Militia rhetoric did echo many of the points expressed by the eleven men who gathered with Robert Welch in 1958 to launch the John Birch Society. Militia file cabinets held well-read Birch pamphlets about internal subversion, magazine articles detailing foreign entanglements, and reports chronicling the progressive betrayal of the republic "our founding fathers" intended.[13] Periodically, in the name of the founding fathers, both Birch and Militia members would emphasize that "this is a republic, not a democracy." Yet, if Militia leaders shared the broad perceptions and fears of Welch and the Birch Society, Militia discourse focused on the government's abuse of power and on the extreme measures taken by the government against its own citizens. Moreover, the Militia's emphasis on readying an armed defense sent Birch Society leaders scrambling to disassociate themselves from any connection with "these types."[14] What the Michigan Militia most inherited from the past was the vague but powerful creed: True Americans must stand up and be counted.

In the organizing phase, those assuming leadership roles would assemble the details and evidence that documented the urgent need for a citizen militia. Over the following years when a succession of Michigan Militia websites explained who and what they were, the case would remain much the same even if the wording and tone might change. More doggedly than their mainstream allies, the Michigan Militia invoked history's weighty promises and constitutional guarantees to justify their opposition to gun control. Again and again they repeated the same refrain. The founding fathers' intentions were written into the Second Amendment: "A well regulated Militia, being necessary to the security of a free State, the right of the people to keep and bear Arms, shall not be infringed."[15] Militia members usually went farther than the NRA; Americans not only had the right to own guns, they *needed* to own guns. They recited details about FBI and Bureau of Alcohol, Tobacco, and Firearms agents' illegal behavior in Ruby Ridge and Waco. But they did not make heroes of Gordon Kahl, the Weaver family, or the Branch Davidians; the Militia had no counterpart to the martyred John Birch. Rather, so far as Militia advocates saw it, one need not like survivalist lifestyles and strange beliefs to recognize that Kahl and the rest were unfortunate victims of willful men habituated to force, cover-ups, and abuse of power. Which Americans might be next? As reassurance that they were on the right path, Militia champions could find historical figures who had fought their same fight—from Patrick Henry onward. On a xeroxed article titled "According to Father Coughlin," one member had written, "He Would Have Backed the Militia Today."[16]

Studious members cited specific sections from the Constitution, the federal code, UN resolutions, the Geneva Accords, and international treaty agreements to demonstrate that the nation's interests had been systematically betrayed dating from the presidency of Woodrow Wilson onward. The United Nations was, by now, seriously undermining national sovereignty. The North American Free Trade Agreement and the World Trade Organization were the most recent economic charades intended to draw the United States into the global economy and thereby sap the country's self-sufficiency. Flowing from this situation, as they saw it, the internal threat was as apparent as it was ominous. Certain economic and political leaders had maneuvered America into foreign entanglements and simultaneously weakened American military might. Naive people had been hoodwinked into supporting gun control legislation. Such gullible if well-intentioned citizens were playing into the hands of devious subversives who knew that once disarmed, the American citizenry would be unable to defend their traditional rights and freedoms. Takeover would be complete.

Founding Fathers of the Michigan Militia

A few individuals figured prominently in spearheading a unified, statewide Militia movement at the outset. They not only were named in outsiders' accounts but also were consistent participants in internal correspondence. Along with Norman Olson and Ray Southwell, Lynn Jon Van Huizen, Tom Wayne, Ken Adams, and Mark Koernke were most conspicuous in defining the rationale for a citizens' militia and most vocal about militia issues of policy, tactics, and organizing. An additional handful emerged within the first year, especially Rick Haynes, Joe Pilchak, and Ron Gaydosh. Yet these men were no inner circle or representative steering committee. Best described, they were activist-acquaintances mutually convinced of the need and devoted to the concept of a citizens' militia. What they said and did, however, shaped the actuality as well as the myth of the Michigan Militia.

In the early stages, organizers were men with similar backgrounds who often knew each other or had mutual acquaintances within circles such as the tight-knit gun shop network. Like Olson, Lynn Jon Van Huizen was in his mid-forties, and he, too, owned a small gun shop. Except for his time in Vietnam, Van Huizen had always lived on the west side of mid-Michigan in the area long dominated by other descendants of the Dutch immigrant pioneers. Although he could have had a farm deferment, he left the family farm near Allendale when drafted and served in Vietnam between 1967 and 1969. He earned a Purple Heart as a member of a quick response team that rescued pilots and crew from downed helicopters. After his discharge, Van Huizen farmed until 1978 when he developed a neuromuscular disease that confined him to a wheelchair and his gun shop business.[17] In 1994 when he learned about Norm Olson's regional militia, Lynn Jon Van Huizen was head of what he described as a "small group of politically-minded people" in Muskegon County. Welcomed by Olson, they formally organized as the Muskegon County Brigade, and Van Huizen was elected to be their commander. As part of the early leadership cadre, he reached out to help surrounding counties form militias, and he participated in organizational decisions that divided the state into divisions. At first there were four and then nine as membership grew.

Tom Wayne, a Vietnam veteran living in the small south-central Michigan town of Bronson, came to the expanded statewide militia as commander of the Southern Michigan Regional Militia. He had been in various businesses and held several patents, including one for electronic signs inside city buses. He was especially disturbed by what he regarded as the loss of American economic autonomy through globalization. It was the General Agreement on Tariffs and Trade (GATT) agreement, he told a television interviewer, that put him "over the edge" and motivated him to be in the militia movement. Wayne believed the country faced economic collapse, and the citizens needed to become active.[18] Educated at Catholic schools and a former altar boy, Wayne chafed under discipline in his youth, but he absorbed classroom lessons and homilies. Convinced that "in our lifetime we are here to make a difference," Wayne "saw something in the Michigan Militia I hadn't seen in other groups."[19]

Tom Wayne shared a concern commonly voiced by militia advocates. There was a "little-known" but "long-standing" agenda designed by certain highly placed Americans to move the nation toward "a socialist program for world government." A voracious Internet reader who followed congressional legislation, Wayne objected to the Sixteenth Amendment and the income tax it established on the grounds that it was neither properly worded nor properly ratified. Like his compatriots, he traced the decline of constitutional protections back to the administration of Woodrow Wilson but emphasized that the habitual pattern of illegal and excessive government action dates from the 1930s with Roosevelt's abuse of executive power. In Wayne's view, which mirrored a position taken by Robert Welch and Birch literature, the Spellman-Rockefeller Foundation at the University of Chicago has long been the place where "all [direction] emanates from." Wayne conscientiously monitored foundations, politicians, and statements by the Anti-Defamation League, and he tracked remarks by Southern Poverty Law Center's Morris Dees. He became involved with the Michigan Militia, Wayne sometimes claimed, "to be sure only that they didn't put out disinformation" in their literature.[20]

Controlling the statements sent out from the Militia or in its name became of critical importance to the men at the Alanson Armory "headquarters." Ray Southwell held the title of Information Officer, with the responsibility to manage the content put out in news releases and bulletins. His was not an easy task since the Militia's perspective was controversial at best; to its most severe critics, Militia statements and activities verged on sedition. Rumors flew, especially among people who got information from local radio stations, shortwave broadcasters, and Internet websites. Many who publicized the Militia championed a variety of antigovernment causes and regularly embellished their "evidence." Ken Adams, one of the initial five-man staff, was the Militia's voice in the northern Michigan region. As host of *Take America Back,* he hammered on the Militia's key concerns in his radio talk show transmitted from Harbor Springs, a lakeside town not far from Olson in Alanson.[21]

Mark Koernke, kept at arm's length by the others, was the most influential and controversial Militia publicist. Koernke was from Dexter, a small town just outside Ann Arbor. Known to audiences as "a.k.a. Mark from Michigan," he had been broadcasting nationally on a regular weekly shortwave radio program, *Intelligence Report,* before the Michigan Militia Corps–Wolverines took form. Koernke's broadcasts were phoned in to World Wide Christian Radio, WWCR, a shortwave station in Nashville with a large national following among people who mistrusted the "controlled" mainstream media. Airtime for *Intelligence Report* was underwritten by the owner of a precious metals company in Arizona who liked what Koernke had to say.[22] His radio messages pitched the need for a citizens' militia, and he also produced several videos about the pending threat of a world government.

Koernke, a building mechanic at the University of Michigan, was never an insider among the Michigan Militia leadership cadre. They recognized that "a.k.a. Mark from Michigan" was a maverick gadfly given to outlandish evidence "revealing" the New World Order menace in the nation's midst. He was less inclined than the others to any organizational burdens of office had a role been offered to him, although he did form his own small band of dedicated followers into the Michigan-Militia-At-Large.[23] The extent of Koernke's military background was unclear; he claimed to have served as an army intelligence analyst and brigade commander but the older military-trained men like Olson, Van Huizen, and Wayne regarded him warily. His army role seemed so unlikely that someone obtained his records through the Freedom of Information Act, which indicated that Koernke had served only in the U.S. Army Reserves, and at the time of his discharge his rank was Specialist Fifth Class. This, a militia member jotted on the report that circulated, was "comparable to someone in charge of KP [Kitchen Patrol]."[24]

Olson distanced himself from Koernke within a short time, especially after it came out that Koernke was linked to an alleged plot to bomb the National Guard's Camp Grayling in January 1995.[25] As a consciousness-raising publicist in the cause, however, Koernke was of inestimable value in bringing people to their first Militia brigade meetings. Rick Haynes was first alerted to the threat posed by the New World Order when he saw

Koernke's video, *America in Peril,* in 1991. Haynes, a recent migrant from the Lubbock, Texas, oil fields, had moved to Michigan with his keyboards to join a 12-piece band, and he worked gun shows for a living. Koernke's video persuaded him that he should concern himself with more than music, and from then on, he was engrossed in the cause. Once the Michigan Militia–Wolverines organized, the quiet, serious Haynes became the unofficial record keeper–historian of the movement as well as something of a broker between various factions and individuals.[26]

Recruiting: All Are Welcome

Apart from a handful of news-capturing spokespersons, brigades were headed by little-known men, and occasionally women, who were indistinguishable from the other members except for the time and effort they devoted. Generally, each brigade had a commander, but the command structure was not always the same from one locale to another. Members in at least one brigade agreed to subdivide into two battalions, and the battalion commanders would work together rather than electing a single brigade commander. This plan, they thought, would promote efficiency, membership, and unity.[27] Since meetings and planned activities were linked to the personal style of the leader at each level, members often gravitated to one brigade instead of another because they found it more congenial.

Brigades gathered participants friend by friend, coworker by coworker, much like a fraternal group. Generally, the active members were less secretive than mainstream established fraternal groups such as the International Order of Odd Fellows or the Masons. In sharp contrast to their image as shadowy and mystifying, Michigan Militia advocates were anxious to make their cause known and bring in newcomers. Unless they had reason to expect trouble with their employers, members were eager to discuss their militia affiliation, convinced more ordinary citizens needed to know about the group and its purposes.[28] Some enthusiasts seized opportunities to recruit wherever they went. A newspaper carrier worked to get out the word about Common Law Grand Juries as he traveled along his 150-mile route each day. Weekly he gave away 100 copies of *The Spotlight,* an extreme right-wing newspaper published by the Liberty Lobby, and he handed out countless xeroxed copies of information tuned to whatever Militia-related concerns were on the front page of the local papers.[29]

Shortwave radio and a few mainstream programs like the Mark Scott

Show on station WXYT in Detroit gave voice to the Michigan Militia, but the Internet and e-mail provided its lifeline. Previous generations of grassroots organizers relied on face-to-face encounters, local meetings, parades, and conventions, but the Militia adherents most frequently communicated through quick, economical cyberspace. If it promoted isolation and anonymity even among their own, conversely, electronic communication introduced the Militia to a vast audience who could take it, leave it, or eavesdrop. Early on, the Michigan Militia–Wolverines' site listed contact individuals for 32 of Michigan's 83 counties, often providing phone number, fax number, and e-mail address for each person. Other websites that began to appear represented a group in some specific area— the Macomb County Volunteer Militia, or a region—the Southeast Michigan Volunteer Militia. Sites were added, disappeared, or stalled out of date, but all of them generally grew more sophisticated in layout and content. One analysis of the militia presence on computer networks pointed out that the Michigan Militia described itself with words such as *defensive* and *peaceful* in contrast to the strong, ideological polemic characteristic of the Militia of Montana site.[30] Michigan Militia web contributors commonly provided explanations of the need for a citizens' militia, told of planned events, posted photos of members in the field training or socializing, and assured readers that "all are welcome."

Females were welcome too although those attracted to the movement were generally women who shared the same concerns as their husbands or male friends. One membership form asked if the newcomer's spouse would be interested in a women's auxiliary, but this idea apparently did not take root. Instead, women were active participants, even as commanders in some brigades.[31] Still, the Militia was disproportionately male, and at least one group saw no problem with promoting their $20 annual calendar featuring wives, sweethearts, or friends. Whether having a little fun or unconcerned about a little friendly stereotyping among themselves, the twelve gun-waving, scantily clad women were "Militia Babes."[32]

The hostile reaction of friends and acquaintances about their affiliation with the Militia could anger, hurt, or baffle the ordinary member. We have always come across to each other "as polite people" when we met in the community, at gun shows, at the supermarket, wrote one militia member to an area classic rock station host. Why then, on air, did he paint everyone in the Militia in such a false, unfavorable way?[33] Adherents were always grateful for kind words. On the way back from a statewide meeting, four uniformed members explained their patches to an inquiring waitress where they stopped to eat. To their delight, "one of the cooks, a young man around mid twenty's came out for information on us." They exchanged phone numbers and addresses. Soon after, the young restaurant manager came to their table to let them know "how much support" the Militia has "out there," thanked them for their efforts, and gave each a $5 gift certificate for the next visit. Such heartening encounters were worth passing on by memo to "all members and friends of the Michigan Militia—Corps Wolverines."[34]

Tactics and Strategies

If Michigan Militia organizers shared many of the same fears as the John Birch Society founders, they took a very different approach with plans for action. Although they generally regarded themselves as political independents, their strong political views represented the most conservative of Republican positions. Yet, unlike Birch Society tacticians, they did not mingle amid party conclaves to maneuver for power. Militia members held meetings of the like-minded, and they supported National Rifle Association initiatives since many were members of the NRA, but they did not spin off "front groups," embrace terminology like *cells,* or guard the identity of members. They read selectively from magazines and literature that reinforced their convictions, but they had no authoritative *Blue Book* for guidance or enthusiasm for study groups with required reading. Just as they read past and present events from their own perspective, they had their own answers for restoring America's historical promise. Militia members armed themselves with pagers or picked up their guns and headed for the drill ground, preparing to be the first line of defense when the government marched against its own citizens.

As the name indicated, its architects intended the Militia to be patterned after the military with a clear chain of command, complete with ranks and lines of authority. Yet Militia commanders never managed the top-down control Welch wielded within the Birch Society. Almost from the outset, all efforts to claim and enforce authority within the Michigan Militia proved futile at best and divisive at worst. Among the leaders, Olson would remain most dedicated to a fixed and top-down organizational description, but he could not manage strict army structure even in the first year because the growing membership included those with little or no real army training. The memos that Olson fired off reflected just some of his concerns. There must be a halt, he ordered, to "grade creep," the self-promotion by members who took a rank on their own before their offices and corresponding ranks were created.[35] The principle of "span of control" must be strictly observed, he warned. This required that a person be given a job not greater than he or she can manage. Specifically at point, brigades were to understand one person cannot command both a brigade and a division.[36]

The Information Officer in each brigade was second-in-command and record keeper. When Paul Reiber became information officer of the Fourth Division, 4th Brigade in the fall of 1994, his brigade commander provided a written "overview of duties and responsibilities." The position, he was instructed, carried with it the obligation to develop meeting agendas; keep minutes, Militia Manuals, and forms; and maintain records of all communications outside the Brigade. The Information Officer was to assume command duties when the Commander was unable to serve and he had the authority to assign or delegate work to members as needed.[37]

There were also chaplain positions. Douglas F. Hall, the new corps chaplain attached to headquarters, sent out a memo to the commanders and staff with a request rooted in historical precedent: "Because General Washington earnestly desired soldiers of his command attend Divine service," Hall asked for "input from all Cmdrs. concerning Rabbis, Roman Catholic Priests, and Protestant Clergy interested in serving militia units as chaplains." Prior military service, he said, "is not prerequisite."[38]

With so many fronts requiring attention, there were always opportunities to contribute. Some members were sought out for their special expertise whether in weaponry, website development, or proficiency with legal documents, court records, government records, and constitutional interpretations. One brigade's membership form, probably fairly standard, had space for indicating any preference among the areas of possible service. Giving one's name, mailing address, and home phone was optional, however. This single-page form asked, among other things, whether the prospective member owned a computer with a modem, could be a driver for a carpool, had a CB, and if it were "Fixed, Mobile, Both." There was also a query about the member's long-gun preference and caliber and military background and experience, if any. Another version asked the prospective member to circle the types of transportation he could operate—a list that included a bicycle as well as an airplane and helicopter—and whether he owned property where the militia could meet.[39] Joiners understood from the outset that as members of the Michigan Militia, whatever division and brigade, their core mission was not defined as just "eternal vigilance." They must be ready to take action on behalf of the nation when elected and appointed leaders failed.

New brigades emerged like cells splitting apart upon growth, and new members often became sudden brigade leaders. Joseph M. Pilchak was one. Pilchak lived in Capac, a small town in St. Clair County north of metropolitan Detroit. Given that Capac was more than 250 miles from Olson's hometown and about the same distance away from Van Huizen, the Michigan Militia–Wolverines network indeed had a statewide reach already within its first few months. Pilchak's swearing-in as a Militia member in August 1994 took place in neighboring Genesee County, which had a brigade. Within a month, he was cofounder and brigade commander of the St. Clair County Brigade, his home county. By April 1995, at the end of its first year, the Michigan Militia claimed to have brigades in 73 of the state's 83 counties, and the umbrella organization had taken the name Michigan Militia–Wolverines at Olson's insistence.[40]

The group was making headway toward one of Olson's original goals: By their conspicuous presence, they would publicize the Militia and thereby its issues. He regarded the first year (1994–95) as devoted to "Operation Visibility" and admitted to using the same methods that other popular front movements have used, "Extreme Rhetoric and Propaganda," to exploit the media as a means to carry the message of the Patriot Movement nationwide.[41] Unbidden, however, the Michigan Militia was suddenly headline news around the world when, on April 19, 1995, a horrified world learned that 168 men, women, and children were bomb casualties in Oklahoma City's federal building. Timothy McVeigh and Terry Nichols were soon arrested as the suspected bombers and almost as quickly were alleged to have connections to the Michigan Militia.

After Oklahoma City

Almost anyone who admitted Militia membership became part of the feverish scramble to sort out details and speculate about motives, to disclaim, claim, and assign blame. Information quickly circulated about faked evidence used to blame Oklahoma City on Timothy McVeigh and Terry Nichols. The highly visible Militia champions did not back away from the fray, but neither did they agree about what to think, say, or do. Independent men, each responded according to his own lexicon.

With little or no consultation inside the command staff, upon news of the bombing Olson and Southwell immediately released a joint press statement even before McVeigh and Nichols were arrested or the Militia implicated. They claimed to have reliable information from a California-based woman with CIA connections; she reported that the Japanese government was involved in the bombing in retaliation for the poison nerve gas released in the Tokyo subway on March 20, 1995. That theory circulated among Americans particularly hostile to current government leaders and, in its elaboration, rested on the notion that President Clinton and the CIA were behind the nerve gas attack because the United States had failed to win big trade concessions with Japan.[42] Others in the Militia, although uncertain about who might be involved in the bombing, were outraged that Olson and Southwell spoke as representatives of the Militia when they went public with their own interpretation. Ten days later, Olson and Southwell agreed to step aside temporarily from their command positions, but they continued to speak out. There was no shortage of "considered" opinions, attention-grabbers, and advice-givers among the Michigan Militia leaders or rank and file.

Upon the arrest of McVeigh and Nichols and the early bulletins linking them to the Michigan Militia, Tom Wayne began to carve out his own role. As he soon explained to the members, in his role as commander at Division 5 HQ, he contacted the FBI; by April 29, his weekly bulletin gave details of the "FBI CONVERSATION." The commander reported he learned in "speaking with a Michigan FBI agent" that at this time the FBI "IS NOT investigating the Michigan Militia Corps organization." And "we asked if there was any way we could help in the McVeigh and Nichols investigations." The commander elaborated, "He [the FBI agent] commented that they are seeking John Doe #2 and associates of McVeigh for questioning and if any of the members knew anything to have them contact the FBI or Division 5 HQ."[43] The newsletter emphasized the FBI agent's position that it must be "our responsibility to 'police' our own group and to dispel bad elements or to inform police of criminal activists." This mirrored Tom Wayne's routine position, and his compatriots did not openly dispute that "we can not harbor criminals."[44] Questions began to be raised among them, however, about Wayne's cooperation with the FBI. Mark Koernke, meanwhile, was interviewed by Ted Koppel on ABC's *Nightline* and by CBS, NBC, and CNN and was featured in *Time, Newsweek,* and the *New York Times.* He maintained the bombing was a plot of the federal government to discredit militias. As he saw it, Bill Clinton was the one who profited from the bombing.[45] Within Militia circles, a scramble for the high ground was just beginning.

President Clinton was the scheduled speaker at Michigan State University's May 5 commencement. The day before he was to arrive, Norm Olson and Ray Southwell faxed an urgent press release to the *Lansing State Journal* and probably to other papers in the state. Olson identified himself as former commander and Southwell as former Michigan Militia chief of staff in their signed statement headed "POSSIBLE AMBUSH BEING PREPARED TO TRAP MILITIA." It reported receiving information that morning from Militia counterintelligence sources that "30 CIA members were in our area." Ominously, they said, a few hours later "a call came in from a Lansing television station wanting to confirm that the Michigan Militia would be present to demonstrate against the President." This suggested to them the possibility that, for the CIA, "the President's visit may provide a 'setup.'" Olson and Southwell persisted in the conviction that their disclosure of the conspiracy involving the Japanese embassy and CIA in the bombing was correct. Accordingly, their press statement expressed their suspicion that the CIA might harm the president during the visit, blame and discredit the Militia, hasten the pace of antiterrorism legislation through Congress, and cover up the CIA involvement in Oklahoma City. Olson and Southwell were "asking the President to postpone his visit to Michigan" until the secretary of defense and newly appointed director of the CIA had a chance to investigate and discover the CIA conspiracy, but meanwhile, "we are urging all militia members to stay as far away from President Clinton as possible." The 400-word statement that also went to Militia members displayed a honed sensitivity to paper trails, concluding, "This news release is to be kept as a matter of record. Widest distribution is urged."[46] The press did indeed pick it up. The warning added more substance to the popular image that here were paranoids, "nuts in camouflage."

President Clinton followed through on his planned trip to address the Michigan State University graduates. Just days after the bombing the president told congressional leaders he would propose a broad range of new powers to let federal authorities investigate antigovernment groups.[47] In his commencement speech he directly addressed the Militia: "How dare you call yourselves patriots and heroes?" And he linked them with "all others . . . [who] say violence is an acceptable way to make change."[48]

The press and government agents soon acknowledged that McVeigh and Nichols were only tangentially connected to the Michigan Militia; Militia literature was reportedly found on the Nichols brothers' farm near

Decker, and McVeigh was seen at a Militia meeting in 1995.[49] Guilt by association flourished nonetheless. All of Michigan was implicated. Photographers, reporters, cameramen, and network anchors arrived in cars, vans, and trucks. They set up camp in Dexter to be near Mark Koernke's farm since McVeigh was said to have listened to Koernke's radio broadcasts; they collected in Harbor Springs near the Michigan Militia headquarters; they gathered in Milan where Nichols was held in prison.[50] Decker area residents were at the center of the scrutiny because they lived near the Nichols brothers' farm.

At James and Terry Nichols' farm, FBI agents swarmed through buildings for any trace of explosives that might be linked with the Oklahoma City blast. Ted Koppel's *Nightline* aired from the United Methodist Church in Decker before April was over. The 90 or so people in the town and their rural neighbors around it felt wrongly embroiled. "The media talked to half the people, and the FBI talked to the other half," said one farmer.[51] Townswomen put on a fundraiser for the beleaguered Nichols family at the Fire Hall and netted $1,500, some of it in $100 and $50 bills. Farm families drove muddy roads to eat the sloppy joes, green beans, and carrot cake familiar at all their fundraisers for neighbors hit by some tragedy. Probably they'd have held the supper anyway, even without this unwelcome link to the bombing, but now the community wanted to show the world their humanity. "We're not a county of kooks. We're a county of hard-working, rural people," a resident assured one reporter. Added another: "Somebody was talking about the Michigan Militia at the bank. . . . I said, 'I might be dumb, but what's the militia?' "[52]

The Michigan Militia Corps–Wolverines struggled to gain its balance. On June 11 a "summit" meeting in Winn brought together 39 brigade commanders with voting power, seven division commanders and representatives, approximately 50 other brigade representatives, plus several other staff members. They assembled to deal with problems since the Oklahoma City bombing, the need to unite the Corps, "to pull together and move forward." Olson was in attendance, but the members agreed he and others currently in the state command staff would step down immediately. Lynn Van Huizen was unanimously elected interim state commander, and members appointed an interim public relations officer with an election for permanent leaders to be held after 30 days. Again by unanimous decision, as former State Commander, Norm Olson would go to Washington along with other Wolverines to meet with Congress in the Senate subcommittee hearings scheduled on domestic terrorism.[53]

Despite their unanimous votes, members of the year-old Michigan Militia–Wolverines were not of one mind by the time of the Winn meeting. Some had begun to chafe at Olson's militaristic rigidity, which, they complained, was accompanied by a lack of organization. Disagreements over statements that Olson and Southwell released to the media brought several more internal issues to the fore, fundamental problems brewing months before Oklahoma City. How should the chain of command be structured? How were state commanders and staff to be elected and removed? What was the appropriate flow of information? How much emphasis should be placed on paramilitary training and readiness? Should members continue wearing military-style uniforms? After lengthy discussion, changes intended to initiate better communication and to clarify the chain of command went into the minutes. Within two days of becoming interim commander, Van Huizen sent a letter to all Wolverines that left no doubt about where he stood. "I like seeing the militia command structure run from the bottom up," he stressed. He also contended that the paramilitary training, "over-elaborated on by the media," is necessary for a prepared militia unit. But the organization should put its emphasis on communication, information, and "voicing opinions on local, State and Federal legislation that threatens our Constitutional rights."[54]

Alongside militia leaders from Montana and Ohio, Olson testified before the Congressional Subcommittee on Terrorism, Technology, and Government Information in June. Pennsylvania's Senator Arlen Specter who convened the hearings testily charged the militia representatives to get their theories and ideas "out in the open." He conjectured, "Much of what has been said today will fall of its own weight—but let's hear it out." The press made much of Olson's battle fatigues and his statement before the committee that "the federal government needs a good spanking to make it behave." Still, his dress for the occasion was as consistent as his position in front of the subcommittee: "You're trying to lay at the feet of the militia some culpability," he charged. "You're trying to make us something we are not, much as the press has done. We stand against corruption and the tyranny of government. We're coming to believe you all stand for that corruption." He persisted in the conviction that "foreign interests" were involved in the bombing.[55]

Militia critics persisted also. Michigan's Senator Carl Levin testified about "paranoid conspiracy theories" that showed up in the Militia group's publications, and he described harassing phone calls that Bureau of Alcohol, Tobacco, and Firearms agents in Detroit received from self-identified Militia members. Levin told about the group on "night maneuvers" who were stopped the previous September in Fowlerville, Michigan, with a car of loaded weapons including an AK-47 and gas masks. California's Senator Dianne Feinstein was concerned about stockpiling of weapons and found nothing in the Constitution providing "for these kinds of private armies."[56]

The hearings changed few opinions on any side among people in the room. But it was one more chance for the wire services and press corps to give shape to the Militia image. Here, testifying before a congressional committee was Olson in battle fatigues. There were, in Michigan, private armies on missions of their own answering to their own commanding officers—men in camouflage stockpiling weapons, out on night maneuvers in cars loaded down with weapons. It seemed difficult to reconcile Olson's appearance with disclaimers by Ken Adams and other Militia voices who insisted there is no time when people should "go against the laws of their government and take those laws into their own hands." Almost certainly, the Michigan Militia had no connection to the Oklahoma City bombing, but new federal antiterrorism legislation went forward, and two state legislators introduced bills to limit paramilitary organizations in Michigan.

As planned, Michigan Militia members gathered again in Winn on July 9 to elect a permanent state commander to serve a one-year term. Candidates standing for election submitted position statements, and Olson persevered in his view of proper organization, although his language was convoluted: The "natural process of authority going *upward* feeds pride which weakens rather than strengthens the Corps." Pride was a form of sin resulting from the fallen nature of humans. If reelected, he would "push power *downward* so that every member is equally powerful." To Olson's way of thinking, this was not the same as top-down authoritarian leadership. Members were not forced to think or act, he pointed out. Rather, every member was empowered to stay or leave, and should do so as conscience dictates.[57] Others were equally convinced that a proper civilian militia was organized from the bottom up, deriving power from its constituents.

Olson received nearly half the votes, but Van Huizen won the office, and Tom Wayne became executive officer, second in command. Within days, Olson announced he was pulling the Northern Michigan Regional Militia out of the statewide group "in order to get it back on course." He opposed what he saw as the "soft, compromising, and conciliatory" direction the Michigan Militia was taking. "The citizen militia is not political and should not become political." Its role, he insisted, is defense against governmental abuses of power. In the press release announcing that his group was declaring its independent status, Olson's position was steadfast: "A soldier may be personable and good-natured, but never should he deny his intent, show vulnerability, or compromise his convictions."[58]

More than most of his cohorts, Olson anticipated an inevitable armed conflict. This conviction undergirded his insistence on a top-down chain of command, an established hierarchy of officers who in a "real life situation" will "make sure the mission succeeds and that each and every soldier will survive." But "what about conscience's sake?" What about those who believed in following their own convictions or strategies? A year earlier in a broadside titled "Questions Often Raised," Commander Olson had addressed the matter of those who disagreed with the command staff and believed in following their own consciences: Get out, he told them. "The final act of liberty is left to the individual to leave the corps if he/she feels that orders cannot be obeyed. The door is always open to enter and to leave." For the member who chooses to stay, "obeying orders is not optional," and there were to be no discussions, arguments, or votes about it.[59] Now, out of the command position, Olson would not be able to set the agenda, and he believed the Militia's current direction compromised his principles. Since Olson and his Northern Michigan Regional Militia supporters were not interested in being part of a political action group, they chose to get out.

Ray Southwell turned to a war of his own against Southern Poverty Law Center director Morris Dees. The SPLC's December 1994 *Klanwatch Intelligence Report* published a photo of Southwell captioned, "Michigan militia leader, Ray Southwell, recently met with Aryan Nations regional director . . . in Tennessee." The same report gave Michigan as one of eight states where the militias had known racist ties. In the summer of 1995, Southwell lodged a libel suit charging that Dees destroyed his good name as part of the SPLC's effort to raise money to fight racism and hate in America. The suit would drag on through months of depositions and fact finding until in December 1996, the case was decided in favor of Dees.[60]

Mark Koernke was more in demand than ever as a speaker at gun shows and rallies around the country where audiences, even if not buying into all of his conspiracy notions, generally agreed that the government was covering up all the facts about Oklahoma City and scapegoating McVeigh. The radio station in Nashville that carried Mark Koernke's program pulled him off the air rather than have the station linked somehow to the terrorist extremists through him. His shortwave broadcasts continued, however, and he maintained an erratic presence at various Militia gatherings.

Olson departed, blaming the shift in emphasis on the new members who had come to the Militia since Oklahoma City. Chapters in the southern part of the state, he assessed, "filled up with professional people" who were "materially rich and have much to lose or think change can be had through the existing corrupt system." They "don't like the uniforms and guns."[61] Olson's critics countered, however, that Olson was a demagogue without ability or interest in organizational matters; that he was temperamentally given to issuing orders, making irresponsible statements, and grandstanding in television interviews. As Tom Wayne saw it, Olson "wasn't a team player."[62] As they struggled in the aftermath of the Oklahoma City bombing to distance their movement and also to define it, Olson's critics had some reason to regard his intransigence and egotism as responsible for discord. But there was more behind the lack of harmony in the Michigan Militia–Wolverines than disagreement over Olson's leadership style; discord did not end.

From its inception as a unified command structure in 1994, the central organization and its spokespersons had a weaker claim to members' loyalty than county brigades. Once the movement attempted to become a quasi-formal, statewide organization it was plagued much like other organizations that had fluid, self-selected constituencies—like the Populists of old, or not always so different from the Republican, Democratic, and Green parties. It was one thing to set forth a platform and another to maintain harmony when it came to carrying it out.[63] Those who took positions of leadership at the brigade level or in the remnants of the "command headquarters" were regularly at odds with one another. Personality clashes and ego-driven ambitions often at the root of dissension were masked as disagreements over tactics. Still, differences were significant— over the chain of command, over inclusiveness, over the emphasis to put on field training, over collaborating with government agents, over political involvement, over means justified by ends.

Shortly before he announced he was leaving the Corps, Olson and his insistent supporters had dropped *Regional* and added *Wolverines* to reflect their broadened organizational vision.[64] And so the name became the Michigan Militia Corps–Wolverines at the time when the enthusiasm for bringing regional brigades together under one set of officers was waning—after about only one year. The Michigan Militia Corps–Wolverines

would continue to hold periodic meetings over the next few years, bringing representatives of the brigades together for annual elections, to discuss
their common causes, and to air their disagreements.[65] The label *Michigan
Militia* would continue to best describe the constellation of separate
brigades if only because members had shared concerns and continued to
refer to themselves as being "in the militia."

Why Michigan?

For a time after Oklahoma City, outsiders' assessments had it that the
Militia could no longer "reach the plumber, the hardware dealer, people
they had been getting to before."[66] Some press accounts reported with relieved approval that the adverse publicity had decimated Militia ranks.
The movement was presumed all but dead, a victim of internal disarray
and disrepute. A *Washington Post* ABC News poll taken about three weeks
after the Oklahoma City bombing found that only 2 percent of the respondents said they strongly supported militia groups; another 11 percent
supported them "somewhat." Yet, the same survey found 36 percent who
said they feared the government as a threat to their "personal rights and
freedoms."[67] Despite predictions to the contrary, the public spotlight on
the Militia brought a flood of new members from among that slice of
Americans who were indeed concerned that the government had become
too powerful and too intrusive. Michigan's Militia constituted the largest
or second largest such group in the country by the end of the 1990s according to government agents, watchdog organizations, and the press. According to estimates by various Michigan Militia insiders, membership
climbed to 10,000 or 14,000 or even to 25,000 by 2000.[68]

Why was it in Michigan that this manifestation of antigovernment
sentiment emerged so visibly and continued to grow? The economic, de-
mographic, and political patterns added up: This state was no microcosm
of the United States. Michigan's industrial might had once been the envy
of other states and the salvation of a world at war. Now, that base was
shrinking away, a victim of outsourcing and globalization. Good-paying
factory jobs and many auto-related white-collar positions were lost in the
process; but when it came to the new jobs—from gas shop proprietors to
service to high tech—longtime residents were competing with recent immigrants from the Middle East, Asia, and Mexico. Metropolitan Detroit,
already the most segregated of the urban regions, was growing more seg-

regated. Old, once-proud suburbs were decaying, and exurbs with expensive homes were gobbling up farmland while the accompanying strip malls with big-box stores drove small-town shopkeepers out of business. Michigan, once a political powerhouse, was losing representation in Congress, and worse, from the vantage point of those in the Militia, local government officials too often abused or misused their power. At the approach of the twenty-first century, few states lent so well to a citizenry caught up in the contradictions of life in America and also convinced that the nation's people could make a difference if they lived up to their crucial duty as citizens.

Whatever else prompted them, the men and women attracted to the Militia spoke in common of the need to restore personal rights and freedoms promised by the founding fathers. Some aimed to do it by participating in military-style tactics, and they would limit membership to those willing to train. More wanted to gather, talk, and share their alarm. A few wanted to stockpile weapons, carry out surveillance, and take direct action against federal and state law enforcement agents. People who wanted to go the route of the Militia in order to make a difference could find what they wanted someplace within this fluid network of local brigades and regional commanders. After its first year, the gun-carrying Militia that continued to attract so much attention was, rather, an assortment of people who expected more from their country than they presently saw around them. Whether in battle fatigues, John Deere caps, or suits and ties, Militia enthusiasts found like-minded people with whom they could gather. They were not merely an unseen army in a strange little war.

11 · AN UNORGANIZED, ORGANIZED MILITIA

> Disclaimer—The SMVM is devoted to individual rights and the ideals
> that lie at the foundation of our society. We have no affiliation with, nor
> do we promote or encourage, any subversive or quasi-subversive entities
> or acts against the United States of America or against the American
> People, inside or outside of U.S. borders. Any and all instruction and
> training conducted by The SMVM is done in accordance with Federal,
> State, and Local Laws and regulations. The SMVM does not and will not
> train any foreign or domestic entity(ies) that could pose a threat to—or
> has denounced—the United States of America.
> —**Southeast Michigan Volunteer Militia website statement**

As the shock over the Oklahoma City bombing diminished, more people
began to wonder what the government might once again be covering up.
The plumber and the hardware dealer who returned to meetings brought
along friends sympathetic to the Militia's plain talk about a government
bureaucracy out of touch and perhaps out of control. Who *were* these
people? Neither a single portrait nor a group portrait within a single
frame provides a realistic snapshot of the Militia in Michigan. One after
another, the "insider," "scholar," and "undercover agent" offered characterizations anew. Militia members were the Chamber of Commerce with a
Doberman; they were grown-up men playing soldier; they were plotting
terrorists or at least accepted the company of people who embraced violence; they were anti-Semites and racists. In the wake of Oklahoma City
and, still, after the disasters of September 11, 2001, the Michigan Militia
was the elephant described by the nine blind men.

Racists, Anti-Semites, Religious Extremists

Watchdog groups and investigative journalists insistently described the
dark and dangerous side of this Militia elephant. Although brigade websites occasionally showed an African-American amid others in field-train-
ing exercises, black members were the exception, giving substance to
charges of racism. One brigade commander had a "Thank you for your in-

terest" form letter at the ready when inquiries came in and head-on, he addressed the ever-present accusation: "Unlike the media propaganda of us, we are not racists. All denominations are welcome and will not be turned away." Those who were interested were invited to just show up at his home any Monday at 7:00 p.m.[1] A website similarly welcomed everyone, "regardless of race, creed, color, tint, or hue; regardless of your religion (or lack thereof); regardless of your political affiliation (or lack thereof)."[2] Soon after he split off to go his own way, Norm Olson made a direct appeal to Detroit's black community to join his group, and for a time in the late 1990s, an African-American group existed under the name of the Detroit Constitutional Militia, but it was short-lived.[3] Given the generally negative publicity about the Militia and its redneck reputation, there was little reason for black citizens to join even if they shared some of the same concerns as the whites who found it a congenial home.

Christian Identity Movement followers who hitched their cause to the Militia's gave reason for the reputation of a Militia that was anti-Semitic and racist. This version of biblical-based theology dated from the late nineteenth century. The story played out with separate twists from one version to another, but all were rooted in biblical interpretations that regarded Anglo-Saxons and Germanic people as the lost tribes of Israel whose descendants included Jefferson, Washington, Adams, and others of the founding fathers. The Jews and the dark-skinned "mud people" were descended from Cain, who was the son of Eve and the Devil.

According to leaders of the Christian Identity Movement, some Jews scattered throughout Europe and became a "Hidden Hand," a clandestine group whose leaders took the name Order of the Illuminati on May 1, 1776. These descendants from the Devil infiltrated Masonic orders, gave birth to Karl Marx, and issued the Protocols of the Elders of Zion. Certain other elaborations maintained that Cain's descendants subverted the U.S. Constitution; they gave blacks and women the vote, instituted the income tax, and created the Federal Reserve Bank in the United States, all to ruin the country and bring on the final battle of Armageddon. To Christian Identity believers, this was foretold in the Bible. The present day, they said, is the time of Tribulation or Apocalypse with its series of calamities in the last years before the Second Coming. Strife, famine, pestilence, and war are the work of the Devil's children.[4]

Identity theology wrapped up a multitude of otherwise confounding problems in a single Satanic package. Such comprehensive simplicity attracted Americans' interest in the late nineteenth century and gained new life with the Cold War. The John Birch Society's Robert Welch referred to the Illuminati's role behind the scenes in many governments, and a specific list of those in the conspiracy began to circulate, naming John D. Rockefeller, David Rockefeller, and Alger Hiss among others.[5] From the 1950s onward, Christian Identity notions were appearing in fiction. *The Turner Diaries* was a particularly influential, virulently anti-Semitic and racist novel written by William S. Pierce under the pseudonym of Andrew Macdonald; it was first published by the neo-Nazis' Alliance Press in 1978. Pierce, a PhD in physics, had been a disciple of Robert Welch and a member of the John Birch Society. He resigned his faculty position at Oregon State University to join George Lincoln Rockwell and help found the neo-Nazi party.[6] *The Turner Diaries* introduced the U.S. government as ZOG—the Zionist Occupational Government. Powered by an international Jewish conspiracy theme, the futuristic novel is an account of the American people under siege from Jewish masterminds who promote racial intermarriages, flagrant pornography, and rampant homosexuality. ZOG outlaws guns so white men cannot protect their wives and families. Earl Turner, the hero, strikes back by attacking the FBI headquarters with a truckload of homemade explosives and dies a martyr in a suicide attack against the Pentagon. A search of Timothy McVeigh's possessions after the Oklahoma City bombing turned up a copy of *The Turner Diaries*.

Michigan-based Robert E. Miles was one of the nation's leading Identity preachers until his death in 1992. From the pulpit of his church near Howell, Pastor Miles warned that the New World Order was coming; that Satan had taken control of people in government. Miles did more than preach; he acted on his reading of the Bible. It was Miles, the notorious Grand Dragon of the Michigan Ku Klux Klan, who instigated the Pontiac school bus bombings in the 1970s and served time in prison for "seditious conspiracy" to overthrow the government. Prisons, he informed all listeners, were part of the ZOG conspiracy.[7]

Most if not all Militia members would have said they believed in God and were religious, whether they attended any church regularly or not; in this, they mirrored poll results about attitudes in the American public at large. And, like a majority of other Americans, Michigan Militia members came from Catholic or mainstream and nondenominational Protestant backgrounds. The Christian Identity believers among them were vocal and zealous, but they were a decided minority in the Michigan Militia and often were a factor in conflicts within and between brigades. More common were the followers of evangelist preachers like Pat Robertson, Jimmy Swaggart, and Jerry Falwell who proclaimed the Constitution to be divinely inspired and corrupted by recent generations. Militia website rhetoric sometimes echoed evangelists' millennial message: With the end time of Tribulations not far away, Christians must seize power in the nation.[8] Still, there were sufficient disagreements about the Bible's message that made it all the more difficult for any leaders who wanted the Militia to speak with "one voice."

The ordinary member could agree with a public position that "we do not side ourselves with any one particular religion; on the contrary, we welcome everyone's beliefs, as it tends to stimulate intellectual conversation." But there was disagreement about whether this welcome meant to include religious extremists. There were those who wanted no part of "individuals or groups that claim to be militias that say they are God's army fighting 'demonically controlled people who are being activated by Satan.'"[9] According to some Militia leaders, the most dangerous infiltrators in their midst were the hard-core survivalists who openly or covertly harbored white Christian supremacist goals of the Christian Identity Movement (CIM). Members were kicked out of at least some brigades for expressing Identity views, something Militia leaders hastened to point out when one such "former member" was involved in violence.[10] But others argued against excluding anyone for their words alone because "we believe in the First Amendment, not only the Second!" Brigades dominated by "moral militia" members who favored legislating against pornography, gay rights, and abortion were more willing to welcome those from the extreme religious Right, including Christian Identity adherents. The large Wayne County brigade tried to straddle the problem, promising, "Officially, we will 'suffer the fool.'" Anyone who came to their meetings could "say what you will, but don't be surprised to be ridiculed by our members."[11] Such arguments persisted.

"Disciplined Citizen Soldiers"

Whether or not brigades should hold mandatory drills and emphasize paramilitary training was one more issue causing internal discord. So far as some saw it, the Michigan Militia was a collection of brigades training to constitute a small army. Hard-liners, usually men who had served in the military, insisted that training together reminded members of their commitment as "disciplined citizen soldiers . . . liable for home service in a home defense role in emergencies."[12] According to Larry Thomson who helped conduct monthly training sessions for the St. Clair County militia, "An unarmed militia isn't a militia."[13] Militia colonel Bridges, a determined advocate of combat training, believed readiness was itself an effective tactic. "Under the leaders of the MMC Wolverines we have deterred any criminal Federal Waco's from happening in Michigan."[14]

At the outset, the Michigan Militia–Wolverines who were under Norm Olson's command trained seriously, 12 times a year.[15] Olson, Van Huizen, and Wayne were among those who persisted in the conviction that regular attendance at training sessions was requisite if they were to be a well-trained and disciplined force ready and able to carry out their defensive obligations. The version of the Michigan Militia Corps–Wolverines Manual revised after Olson's resignation continued to require at least one division training session every other month to maintain active member status with voting rights. Exceptions could be made for those who were unable to make it to training or were physically incapable.[16] A policy of the Southeast Michigan Volunteer Militia specified another exception; it prohibited anyone who could not legally own a firearm from handling a gun at a training session, an event, a meeting, or a function. This, they explained, was a preemptive, cover-our-tails policy to prevent any legal action against the group should anyone claim that felons were allowed to handle firearms.[17]

In certain brigades, however, participating in paramilitary training was not a requirement for membership. "Scared to death" of unknown dangers, the Eaton Rapids group armed themselves with pagers so they could send out a coded alert if any of them faced trouble. One member who did not drill believed "pagers are better." He and his compatriots were "not looking forward to any military action."[18] They did know who to call for armed backup if need be, but preferred to act as intermediaries between officials and citizens to calm dangerous situations. Indeed, on various occasions they resorted to the coded alert when a member was visited by the sheriff or police and, at least in Eaton County, the members had a sense that once they arrived on the scene, they were successful in deescalating disputes with law officers.[19]

Even if not mandatory, training sessions were frequent brigade events. They could be elaborate operations including search-and-rescue missions with an airplane providing overhead help for the soldiers who were required to come with battle-dress uniform, wet weather gear, a rifle and 30 rounds of ammunition, ear and eye protection, a compass, a notebook and pencils. Calls to training carefully stipulated, "All members are directed to transport all firearms in accordance with Michigan laws."[20] On scheduled weekends an army encampment came to life on Frank Stasa's farm, the regular training center between Lansing and Flint that drew members from various brigades in lower Michigan. The agenda included hikes, training exercises, and a sermon on Sunday morning.[21] These weekends were likely to be family affairs. Just as gun control advocates feared, children in Militia families learned how to care for and fire rifles. Boys and girls alike went along on outings but were taught their limits. Announcements of one serious training day specified "no children under 14 years of age will be allowed in training areas."[22] Although they were often mocked as "weekend warriors," Militia training could be as demanding as weekend National Guard sessions. In 1999, on the eve of anticipated Y2K troubles, a former Green Beret readied one group of county brigades associated with Van Huizen's camp. He advised members on equipment, taught them guerrilla warfare, how to set an ambush, the benefits of camouflage, and how to kill a man instantly in complete silence.[23]

Battle dress was required for field training, but uniforms were not required at meetings. More commonly, people showed up in jackets or hats with special Wolverine patches, minuteman patches, and flags stitched on. One woman advertised she did custom embroidery. Hats, her most expensive item, cost $8.50.[24] T-shirts with insignias or messages, along with camping gear, were available on certain websites, but Militia-related items and uniforms were not a built-in source of revenue for the brigades. Wearing them was a matter of pride. In response to a legislator's criticism that they were impersonating members of the armed forces, one member wrote to explain these were badges of rank, and similar to the police and fire departments as well as countless organizations, they were for purposes of internal structural organization "and no more."[25] Another jibed, "Will these legislators be asking the Salvation Army to remove their ranks and uniforms next?"[26] "Citizen soldiers" reinforced their group identity with uniforms and badges. Training sessions readied the Militia to shoulder their duty. At the same time, they remained photo opportunities for the local press and kept the specter of an armed body of renegades before the public.

"Bubba Clubs"

In the press and even on their own websites, gun-toting men and women in camouflage would continue to stereotype the membership. There were those who fit the picture. More the norm were the men and women in everyday work clothes meeting around tables in neighborhood restaurants or church halls, fortified by pots of coffee and armed with cups. Local militia meetings were usually small gatherings of people who were established friends or, now, new acquaintances. They turned out to see each other as much as to stay informed about the issues, sharing family stories and work problems as well as political concerns. "On the surface this militia may look like a bubba club," they joked among themselves. "We like the opposition to think this."[27]

Children came along to the meetings as a matter of course. Occasionally they offered help of their own. One grade-schooler prepared a hand-printed recruitment flyer decorated with stars and a flag in Uncle Sam poster fashion: "Sarah Wants You To Join the Militia!" All who were interested could call "Dad or Mom" or two other names and numbers provided.[28] Personal news was also a matter of course, sometimes communicated in keeping with their common cause. Said one handwritten xeroxed birth announcement:

IT'S A BOY!
THOMAS EDWARD SMITH BORN 6:30 AM
May 22, 1995
8 LBS. 2 OZ.
We don't do cigars . . .
so have a copy of our CONSTITUTION!
read it, and help assure "TOMMIE"
of a lifetime of
LIBERTY and JUSTICE.

Meetings routinely touched on the general threat facing America if not the particulars. Almost anyone who went to even a few meetings could gain a grasp of the broad picture—the intentions of the founding fathers had been subverted—whether or not they went home to study the Constitution and the Federalist Papers. World government also figured into most discussions: "Right now we can't even control our own government. You think we're going to be able to do any better with the World Government?" And gun control: "Once the citizens are disarmed, next the police; then only the federal government officials and military will have guns. Semiautomatic weapons are called that if police have them but they are 'assault weapons' when civilians own them."[29] Militia members trumpeted the issues about "shadow governments" and the looming "world order." These threats frightened them. Still, it was state and local abuse of their personal sovereignty that angered them, that gave passion to their determination to "do something" and reinforced their militancy even in the face of ridicule. Talk of the New World Order might initially engage a patriot's enthusiasm, but clear and present dangers in his own backyard brought him to meetings and dictated his staying power. Hers too.

Like meetings of the John Birch Society cells, people at Militia gatherings commonly veered off the Militia's emphasis about wrongs at the federal level to focus on matters close to home. The most animated talk centered around localized problems resulting from day-to-day experiences with agents of their state and local governments—wrongs committed against citizens by the public schools, unjust property taxes, excessive spending, unreasonable zoning ordinances, overregulation, arrogant cops and sheriffs and judges. They complained about the excessive proportion of Americans in prison—more than any other country per capita; Michigan was creating an industry out of imprisoning people who weren't a threat to anybody but themselves, and the taxpayers were footing the bill. Taxes kept coming up in one Militia gathering after another, always taxes; the tax burden aroused as many interpretations as there were participants in any discussion. According to one, "The government works by taxing the middle class." The rich, on their part, always have money left after taxes, he figured, because of their tax shelters. "Then, since the churches have given up on the job of helping the poor, the government gives the lower class the money it took from the middle class. Next, when the poor spend their money on drugs, alcohol, and the lottery, they pay tax on all of them but the illegal drugs. So the government gets back all the money it gave out! What a scheme!"[30]

Meetings took on a tenor of their own, depending upon the place and purposes of the people who showed up. On one snowy winter night, twelve people including four women plus four children sat in the pews at the unprepossessing wood-frame church where the Monroe area Militia congregated. The group, smaller than usual they noted, included a truck driver, a unionized construction worker, an Ameritech worker, and a printer. The commander in charge was Pastor Dan Hardin of the Gateway

Anabaptist Church; a mild soft-spoken man, he reported on the Indianapolis Baptist Temple with which his congregation was affiliated. The Indianapolis church had just been closed two months earlier by court order for failure to pay income taxes. It could not claim tax-exempt status, and the IRS had come in 1994 to assess the congregation over three million dollars for back taxes from 1987 through 1993. The plight of the congregation had become a cause among patriot movement radio personalities, and activists occupied the church after it was ordered closed. Pastor Hardin encouraged Monroe Militia members to accompany him in an upcoming trip to Indianapolis where they would join the protest. No one in this group raised the point that some churches had deliberately taken a different position than the Indianapolis Baptist Temple and had given up tax exemptions. Norm Olson's nondenominational Freedom Church was one that refused to register with the state as a nonprofit institution because it "means the state becomes head of our church instead of Jesus."[31]

The major topic of the night was the privacy of one's social security number. Members rose from the audience to explain a citizen's right not to disclose the number. Attentive listeners were assured it was illegal for federal, state, or local officials to deny a person any right, benefit, or privilege provided by law because he refused to disclose his social security number. Handouts were passed around, and various pamphlets dealing with income tax law and IRS codes were available in the back of the church. So, too, were reprints. One, published in the Winter 1995 *Kansas Journal of Law and Public Policy,* dealt with "The Racist Roots of Gun Control." Another, "Reclaim Your Right to Refuse Vaccines," was available along with a copy of the state of Michigan immunization waiver forms distributed for the purpose of copying them. Part of the two-hour meeting was spent hearing from individuals who had tips to share after encounters with the state and county highway patrol. They were pulled over "only" because cops disliked the way they looked, or needed to make a ticket quota, or just enjoyed hassling people. They were neither treated correctly nor given their rights. Various people rose to pass on warnings and identify particular stretches of area highways patrolled by especially nasty cops. The meeting ended in general agreement: Various local and state police are corrupt and "on the take"; judges are in on it too.[32] They planned to meet again the next month.

About 40 miles away, another brigade met regularly at a family restaurant in suburban Detroit. One evening, the 25 or so who gathered for supper talked about helping a member's family with a planned move. It was

Second Amendment rally, Michigan Capitol in Lansing, April 13, 2010. Militia members have held frequent rallies at the capitol since the early 1990s, most often to publicize the constitutional right to bear arms and their opposition to the United Nations. Here, they gather with other citizens who are concerned about any threats to the Second Amendment. (Courtesy of the Lenawee Militia.)

understood that everyone present could come in advance of the public garage sale. Over and over, just as at other Militia gatherings, people passed around stories about their own or friends' various personal experiences with overzealous, omnipresent agents of government at one level or another. More enthusiastic about armed readiness than some other brigades, these people were attentive to information about the next scheduled outdoor weekend training camp.

Although the weekend training exercises meant an initial outlay for gear, participants camped in tents, shared the expense of food, and took part in its preparation. As with so much else about the Michigan Militia groups, members' costs were kept to a minimum. Even dues were optional; more than one brigade was "broke all the time." The expenses of informational handouts, brochures, and announcements were usually covered by free will donations at the end of meetings plus out-of-pocket subsidies that came, one activist lamented, "from the usual few pockets" in each group.[33]

Along with their meetings and training get-togethers, some Militia brigades took on the role of good citizens within their communities. They searched for lost children, adopted highway stretches, and gathered for cleanup days. "PLEASE HELP THE MICHIGAN MILITIA HELP THEM OUT" read one flyer requesting donations of gloves, sweaters, coats, boots, or "any garment at all" to help the homeless men, women, and children.[34] Tom Wayne was one Militia leader who urged that they reach out to their mainstream neighbors and townspeople for tactical reasons. "Remember," he instructed, "the main stream is our stream. Without them we will all be relegated to running around in the woods."[35] In part, members reached out because they were indeed eager to counter their unfavorable image, but just as often, they offered help because so many of them for one reason or another could empathize with people in trouble.

In the Political Arena

They might sometimes be regarded as just a bunch of people running around in the woods, but for the most part, the Michigan Militia members were politically attuned activists. Norm Olson intended that "the citizen militia is not political and should not become political, it is a natural consequence of frightened people joining together for their common defense."[36] He insisted that the Militia should "intentionally separate our group militia activities from our individual political beliefs, because politics is controversial in nature and would only serve to damage the cohesive quality of our unit."[37] Separating activities from beliefs proved difficult, however, since people who joined the Militia were inclined to be true believers in their chosen causes and often held competing notions about what the Militia was or should be. Those possessed by strongly held moral concerns saw the Militia as one more forum to promote laws that would censor pornography, halt gay rights, and outlaw abortion. But legislating morality ran counter to the Militia's advocacy of minimal government—their opposition to gun controls and mandated quotas. Militia members could shake their heads in common over pornography, television violence and smut, foul-mouthed radio announcers, and the openness accorded homosexuality. They tried to minimize certain areas of disagreement; the few who were prochoice advocates assured prolife compatriots they would not personally choose an abortion, for example. But separation of church and state remained as troubling within Militia circles as within the broader public.

On the front of international politics, the Michigan Militia emphasized a single issue: unyielding, active opposition to U.S. participation in the United Nations. One member wrote another to appeal, "Let's get Christians and Godly ministers to brainstorm to come to some conclusion as to what 'God wants us to do—and when.'" There was no time to waste, "due to the fact that one world government is foretold in the scriptures, and due to the fact that the evidence continues to mount pointing to its soon being a full blown reality."[38] On the need to get the United States out of the United Nations, all factions could agree. When the mayor of Lansing raised the United Nations flag on United Nations Day in October 1994, Norm Olson was in the early days of his enthusiasm for a unified Michigan Militia. He sent out the call to rally in front of the Michigan state capitol and his troops answered. They listened to the speeches and they joined in chanting, "JUST SAY NO TO THE U.N.!" Olson, in battle dress, circulated through the crowd handing out flyers with the words to "America," "The Star-Spangled Banner," and "America the Beautiful."[39] The Militia was just then coming to the attention of a broader public and such outspoken opposition to the United Nations seemed one more sure sign of their extremist views. Ten years later when the annual call to rally in Lansing on United Nations Day went out over Militia websites, a wider public had come to question whether U.S. policy in Iraq should be tied to UN decisions and if other nations were doing their fair share of the fighting. Feeling vindicated, the Michigan Militia, like the John Birch Society, could say, "We told you so." And, "Had enough yet?"

The right to bear arms was their main cause on the domestic front, and the Michigan Militia's most important litmus test for any politician was that individual's position on protecting that right. Word passed quickly among Militia circles about Michigan Democratic congressmen and legislators who favored the Brady Bill and all other forms of gun control. Like the best legislator, conscientious Militia members kept the others informed about bills passed or pending: "HR3610 in about 1997 said you couldn't have a firearm within 1000 feet of a school. The proposed S2099 gives the IRS the power to register all hand guns."[40] Militia members were well schooled in battling gun control, often already shaped by involvement in the John Birch Society or the National Rifle Association, and on this issue, they were solidly in the Michigan mainstream. The state had nearly 200,000 National Rifle Association members at the end of the century, a disproportionate share of the nation's 4.1 million members. Moreover, about one in nine residents in Michigan held a hunting license.[41] When the state legislature voted in favor of allowing residents to more easily qualify for concealed weapons permits it was, said one legislator, because of what they were "hearing from their districts."[42]

Family oriented, Militia members occasionally phrased their right to bear arms in terms of protecting their children. One militia-linked website after another pilloried the women who participated in the Million Mom March on Washington in support of gun control legislation. They were abdicating parental responsibility, foolishly and arrogantly saying their children would be safe and protected in the hands of the state. "Did the mothers in Armenia think the same thing? Did the Jewish mothers across Europe reach the same conclusion? Rwandan mothers? Bosnian mothers? . . . Did gun control keep them all safe? . . . Is this the same 'safety' that you would impose upon my children? IS IT?"[43]

When it came to party identification, most would declare they were unaffiliated with any party, but nonetheless, when they expressed personal convictions they were in line with the most conservative Republican policies and politicians. Libertarian Party positions on taxes, gun ownership, social security, and government regulations or subsidies echoed Militia members' attitudes more faithfully than the Republicans, but Militia newsletters and private assessments complained that Libertarians failed to distinguish liberty from license. Militia members did not automatically support Republicans, however, and were often critical of any—including George H. W. Bush and then George W. Bush—who "sold out" to the United Nations. Still, if pressed, Militia supporters claimed to know no one in their midst who was a Democrat.

They reserved their unrelenting venom for President Bill Clinton for his betrayals of America—a list without end. They picked up items, especially from the Militia of Montana websites, that circulated names of Clinton acquaintances who had met untimely deaths, deaths "arranged" so they would not be able to reveal Clinton-related scandals.[44] More frequently, Michigan Militia members criticized the Monica Lewinsky affair and Clinton's support for NAFTA and gun control legislation. Even those who readily admitted to affairs themselves were disgusted by his abuse of the Oval Office. Their outrage on this topic was constant, but mainstream conservatives and even moderates shared these same sentiments.

In presidential elections during the last decade of the twentieth century, Militia members generally viewed Pat Buchanan as one of the rare candidates with few liabilities. After Buchanan won the February 1996 New Hampshire primary, the Wayne County brigade meeting rang with cheers, and members tussled over Buchanan bumper stickers. They regarded him as pro-American for his position on NAFTA and appreciated his support of Second Amendment rights. They were upset when Buchanan's campaign chairman, the director of Gun Owners of America, was linked to the Klan and other hate groups. He was unjustly "painted with the same broad brush that the militia was right after the Oklahoma bombing."[45] Buchanan's opposition to abortion was his biggest negative among those Militia supporters who were indeed prolife but maintained that efforts to outlaw abortion were like efforts to outlaw guns—unwarranted government interference in personal rights. On balance, they were willing to overlook Buchanan's prolife position, thinking that once they could get the right people in office, they could "then work on the rest of freedom."[46] It was a disappointment when Buchanan once again lost his presidential bid in 2000, that time running on the Reform Party ticket.

Attentive political observers spread the word about "good guys" on the congressional scene. House Majority Leader Dick Armey was "a rare congressional leader who is part of the solution."[47] Fax messages went to congressmen deemed potentially supportive of matters of significance to Militia members. The list of recommended contacts differed depending on the issue but was likely to include such men as Alan Simpson (R-Wyoming), Lamar Smith (R-Texas), Chris Cox (R-California), Henry Hyde (R-Illinois), and Spencer Abraham (R-Michigan). U.S. senators and representatives who lined up on the side of gun control laws were on another list.[48]

Politicians generally regarded as conservative or arch-conservative were not immune from the Militia's criticism. Michigan's Governor John Engler and various state legislators gave "much to be frightened of" because they discriminated against the Militia and would try to prevent citizens from defending themselves against governmental abuses of power.[49] State senator Jim Berryman, a Democrat from Adrian, and representative Jim McBryde, a Republican from Mount Pleasant, were targets for Militia opposition once they introduced a package of bills to restrict paramilitary organizations in Michigan in June 1995 following the Oklahoma City bombing. Engler and Republican legislators were also roundly condemned for championing NAFTA, thereby damaging job interests of Michigan's workers and further endangering national sovereignty.

Only a few avowed Militia members seized the tactic of running for public office. Joe and Clara Pilchak were unusual in their determination to put themselves forward as candidates. Pilchak, founder and leader of the St. Clair County Militia Brigade, came to the Militia experienced in political ideology and activism. In 1968 he had joined the John Birch Society and was briefly a chapter leader. From 1974 through 1977, he was manager of an American Opinion bookstore. By the time he was in the Militia, Pilchak had been an engineer in middle management for 20 years. More in keeping with his Birch compatriots than those in the Militia, Pilchak was active in elective politics. He had been a Republican precinct delegate for three terms and had participated in campaigns for numerous conservative office-seekers including tax reform advocate Robert Huber who ran for U.S. Senate on a tax reform platform and championed property tax caps in Michigan.

Clara Pilchak, his wife of more than 30 years, was similarly involved. Staunch Catholics, the Pilchaks had been speaking against sex education in public schools since 1969. By the mid-1990s, parents of eight children and several grandchildren, they were homeschooling their youngest children. Mrs. Pilchak, an X-ray technologist, was for a time a Republican state committee member in her district, and in the late 1990s, she ran in the Republican primary as a candidate for state representative. In the November 2000 election, Clara Pilchak was on the statewide ballot for the Michigan Board of Education. Her platform was consistent; her flyers asked, "How did we get to the point that we spend more on government than we do for food, clothing, housing, education, recreation and transportation combined?" She promised, "When it comes to spending taxpayers' money, I can and will say NO."[50] Her business card with its logo of a mother and baby identified her primary concern: "Mrs. 'Clara Cares' Pilchak, Defender of Traditional Family Values." Schools, she insisted, "must teach our children reading, writing, and arithmetic, not how to put on condoms or do drugs." Children "properly belong to their parents, not to the state" and need to learn "our traditional values and Godly heritage" rather than "how to bend to anti-American multi-culturalism."[51] In 2002 they ran as a team, Joe Pilchak for governor and Clara Pilchak for lieutenant governor, on the U.S. Taxpayers Party and received 12,411 votes for .39 percent of the total cast.[52]

Taking Aim

Appropriate tactics were sometimes a matter of internal discord. Members agreed with the patriotic message in its broadest outlines: The greatness of the United States is in its political system, designed by the founding fathers to be government of the people, by the people, and for the people; democracy is the will of the people in action; the price of liberty is eternal vigilance. Beyond a commitment to these elementary civics precepts, cherished issues and "uppermost" concerns depended upon the member's perspective. Preoccupations might range from particularized local examples of injustice to state ballot propositions to flawed national leaders or NAFTA or the United Nations. Given such individualized ends, Militia tactics in the public arena resembled scattershot fired from a blunderbuss. From the outside, it appeared that the Michigan Militia was popping up everywhere.

Militia members and fellow travelers began noticeably packing township meetings in the fall of 1995. An executive director of the Michigan Township Association affirmed that about ten townships in the state reported that members of paramilitary groups were showing up and demanding a right to vote on everything. Press accounts regarded such activities as a "shift of tactics" in the aftermath of the Oklahoma City publicity. From afar, the *London Guardian* dismissed their interest in local government as just part of the "infamous Michigan Militia" attack on "all forms of sinful government." The *New York Times* assessed that these Militiamen chose "to look homeward for sinister plots."[53] Such judgments, opting for sarcastic elitism, overlooked the appeal the Militia held for a significant segment of followers. They wanted to put *every* issue up for an open vote; they wanted to return government to the people.

William Ordiway, a "mountain of a man" at over 6 feet 7 inches tall and 340 pounds, was accompanied by about 50 followers who showed up at a Norman Township meeting in the tiny northwest Michigan town of Wellston. At issue were the Norman Township zoning laws. A majority of residents supported a 1993 law intended to clean up the countryside of dilapidated trailers, old cars, and junked implements. Ordiway was, the press

reported, "a leader in the Michigan Militia," and his remarks were a mix-
ture of ideas from the Constitution, the Bible, and the *Posse Comitatus.*
People should understand, he lectured the assembled crowd, that the
township is superior to state governments that, in turn, are superior to the
federal government. Ordiway maintained that township officials were trying to advance the cause of global government by failing to let voters know
they can post a notice for a meeting, get together, and pass what they want
enacted.[54]

In Cheboygan County, several Militia members in camouflage uniforms attended the trial of Judy Chall who was arrested after pulling a
gun on a county zoning officer investigating a tip that she and her husband were putting up a building on their 16-acre property without a permit. Chall said the zoning officer ignored no-trespassing signs, refused to
leave, and then began taking photographs to substantiate his tip. At the
trial, Chall testified that this officer did not have a uniform or a marked
car, nor did he identify himself properly. She claimed to have a patent to
the land that exempted it from zoning and building codes. The press
identified Chall's husband as a former training officer for the Michigan
Militia, said the couple met at a pro-gun rally in Lansing, and said that
both were Militia members who participated in military-style training in
Florida where they lived much of the year. She was convicted of four
charges including felonious assault but was given a month in jail rather
than seven years in prison when she withdrew her motions for a new trial
and her right to appeal.[55]

Downstate in the Detroit suburb of Warren, the *Detroit News* reported
that "even the Michigan Militia" showed up along with neighbors and
lovers of historic homes to support a 72-year-old homeowner battling to
save her home when the city council decided to bulldoze the 100-year-old
house it considered abandoned and uninhabitable.[56] The year before, the
Michigan Militia sent a representative to a small town near Springfield,
Illinois, to offer a show of support for a widow under siege for 16 days by
state troopers trying to take her to a court-ordered psychiatric evalua-
tion.[57] As Militia activists saw it, interference with private persons and
property in these situations was meddlesome, legally dubious, immoral,
and un-American. They would not take on all causes or people who
sought them out, however. One Militia leader rebuffed extreme prolife
representatives when they approached him looking for allies who would
help blow up abortion clinics, and subsequently he used it as an example
that the Militia was commonly mischaracterized. "They believed what

they'd heard about the Militia"—a group willing to use bombs as a tactic—but the Militia "is not into that."[58]

Presumed Dangerous

Seriousness of purpose and some legitimacy were important among a
group regularly as nervous about their own members as they were about
outsiders. Militia regulars were on the lookout for moles—"agents who
pretend to be trustworthy but who are mainly focused on obtaining information about militia members and their activities." Or, there could be
"dissipaters"—agents who pretend commitment but really try to divert
the group into ineffective activities such as "endless debate, socializing,
and divisive disputes." Worse, agent provocateurs might engage in acts intended to discredit the Michigan Militia.[59] Some brigades asked any
prospective member to sign a statement swearing or affirming, "I have
read the Militia Handbook and agree to follow the Code of Conduct of the
Militia Member. I have read the Constitution of the United States . . . and
I am a volunteer patriot and not a subversive agent, spy, or provocateur of
the opposition."[60] The ever-present tension between Militia members who
had served time in the military and those who had not could readily surface when it came to internal standards of conduct. A memo from one
commander to another referred to an undisciplined breakaway group as
filled with "civil disobedience types" who preferred to function as "democratic mobs" rather than "disciplined forces." Unlike "those of us who had
the courage to serve our country as soldiers in the army and marines and
other . . . regular military forces," the "nonmilitary types are whining complaining losers."[61]

State police and federal agents stepped up their surveillance in the late
1990s, anticipating serious trouble since the "militia types" persisted.
From the outset, the relationship between the state police and the Militia
was hostile. Unlike the Ku Klux Klan and citizen patriot groups that
joined with federal agents and state police to "protect" America and the
status quo, the Militia regarded the state police, the FBI, BATF, and FEMA
as repressive and un-American. These agencies were part of the problem
that prompted the Militia to organize. Norm Olson threw down the
gauntlet with a fax to Governor John Engler sent also to the Michigan
Sheriffs Association in November 1994, an early point in the Militia's development. Olson called upon the governor to make the state police sub-

ordinate to elected county sheriffs since "the State Police, who often violate civil and constitutional rights, and are training black-hooded SWAT teams, never have to answer to the people directly, but rather hide behind the 'skirt' of their civil service status." Olson minced no words: "Power without accountability terrifies peaceful citizens. Is it any wonder that your State Police are referred to as Gestapo?"[62]

In turn, the state police recognized their hand was strengthened by any extremist act connected with the Militia. They anticipated "significant public support" if they took repressive action against the Militia when such incidents arose. The state police post commander at Ithaca, a small rural detachment, had a quick lesson in public sentiment on the day of the Murrah Building bombing in Oklahoma City. As soon as television reports alleged involvement of Michigan Militia, the post commander began receiving "a flurry of phone calls from local citizens wanting to report someone whom they knew to be a militia member." The state police were also well aware that many local government and public safety officials in Michigan regarded the Militia as a serious threat that should be suppressed.[63]

It worked to the advantage of law agents that there were those inside the Militia who wanted respectability for the movement and would implicate renegades. Certain brigade leaders and members enjoyed a "contact as needed" relationship with selected federal marshals, state police officers, and FBI agents in their vicinity. Each side tapped into their contacts on occasion to check on rumors, offer help, or stem precipitous mobilization from any corner.[64] As spokesmen like Tom Wayne saw it, their collaboration was entirely appropriate. The Militia should properly serve as "the bridge between those other people out there that want to do something stupid and the people in the government who want to use the 'no knock' . . . and break into somebody's home without a warrant, or with hearsay evidence."[65]

Beyond the Fringe

The southwest corner of Michigan was of particular interest to government agents. The FBI, BATF, and state police occasionally infiltrated a variety of groups in the area. After months of surveillance Brendon Balsz of Kalamazoo was arrested in 1997 and subsequently sentenced to prison because he had made three pipe bombs, built a private arsenal, and allegedly spoke of blowing up an IRS building. Headlines labeled him an "EX-MILITIA MEMBER," and articles explained he was kicked out of the militia, but the link was made between the Militia and one more who "fit the profile of a potential domestic terrorist."[66]

Balsz was within the circle of a small group calling itself the North American Militia of Southwestern Michigan or the North American Patriots Association. Starting in 1996, a BATF informant kept the government aware of "plots hatched" by the regulars who held their meetings at Speed's Koffee Shop in Battle Creek. These were mostly bland gatherings that coupled discussion about the state of the nation with various speakers. According to a meeting announcement, in November 1997 the topic would be "Herbs and your Body"; in December, "Clara Cares" Pilchak would speak on children, public education, and home schooling. It is likely that few people were turning out since this same announcement was trying to counter rumors about the "demise" of the association's Thursday evening meetings.[67] At some point, however, a member in the group allegedly told the undercover BATF agent that he had been waiting for a conflict with the federal government for a decade and intended to create chaos for three or four days until the entire country would rise up against the government. The frightening import of his plans—bombing an interstate highway and federal buildings, killing federal agents, destroying power facilities, fuel depots, and gas stations, taking over and broadcasting from a Kalamazoo television station—ultimately brought in about 80 law enforcement officers from the BATF, FBI, IRS, and state and local police.[68]

Three men were arrested and brought up on illegal weapons charges and, in one case, on a charge of conspiring to manufacture marijuana and smoking it while possessing a firearm. A raid of one man's 40-acre farm turned up a cache of weapons including a .50 caliber machine gun for antiaircraft use. The charge became conspiracy and illegal weapons possession. In court, an FBI agent testified his agency was tipped off about the splinter group by leaders of the Michigan Militia who had kicked them out earlier because of their advocacy of violence.[69] Tom Wayne readily admitted, "We've worked with the ATF and the Anti-Defamation League to expose them." Wayne referred to them as the "goof troop" who "were threatening to do stupid stuff."[70] Norm Olson, by then commander of his separate Northern Michigan Regional Militia, was of a different opinion. He was alarmed that these people were "arrested for advocating their point of view." They had not blown up any buildings or assaulted anyone. "These aren't bad people. These aren't anarchists; they're soldiers," said Olson. "Soldiers sit around the campfire and talk. Are we going to arrest people because they talk?"[71]

According to the assistant prosecutor in the Grand Rapids district court, the three were "armed and dangerous men." They represented a "fringe group, a radical group." By focusing on the leadership, the prosecutor was confident "we dismantled the entire group."[72] Lawyers for the defendants argued that the Militia members who cooperated with the federal agents had ulterior motives, and the case deepened the rift within the Militia.

Efforts at policing their own prompted Lynn Van Huizen's command staff to convene court-martial hearings if at least two witnesses provided evidence that a member was guilty of acts that would discredit or put the corps at risk. After "counsel and prayer" a vote would be taken that could lead to permanent dismissal. At least one member was brought up on the charge that he "knowingly and willfully engaged in conduct prejudicial to the good order and discipline of the Michigan Militia Corps." The command reduced his rank from major to captain and relieved him of duties in his brigade for a minimum of 90 days.[73] Van Huizen estimated that by about 2000–2001, the militia had "booted out" a third of its membership. "Many of those were in jail or on their way to jail," he noted.[74]

One on his way to jail was the ever-controversial Mark Koernke. Time and again Koernke reinforced public perceptions of a violent—and wacko—Michigan Militia. In 1996, the body of Bill Gleason, Koernke's self-appointed bodyguard, turned up in rural Hillsdale County in an area said to have been used for paramilitary exercises by Koernke's United States Militia At Large.[75] Gleason's family blamed Koernke. They said Koernke and his strange coterie of obsessed associates wooed their 26-year-old Catholic-raised son with talk about the New World Order and the duty to wage a patriotic holy war against this satanic conspiracy.[76] Koernke fit the "paranoid personality" label favored by press accounts, social scientists' analyses, and government agents' reports. His shortwave broadcasts and broadsides were filled with bizarre evidence that the nation was at great peril—a statue of Satan hidden on the top floor of the UN headquarters; bar codes on money that allowed government agents to scan people's houses and count their money.[77] His farmhouse was surrounded by no-trespassing signs, and he was ever vigilant, anticipating foul play from authorities.

Despite felony charges and numerous court appearances, Koernke had stayed out of prison but, ironically, it was his fear of police coupled with their attitude about him that proved his undoing. In the spring of 2000, while waiting for his son in front of a bank in his hometown of Dexter, the bank was robbed. When local police responded to the bank's call, they saw

Koernke's car, immediately decided he was connected with the robbery, and gave chase for 50 miles when he fled. Perhaps he believed he was being set up or targeted; perhaps he had illegal weapons in his car and did not want to be searched. Nonetheless, he was back on the front pages, back in court with his lawyer who made the case that Koernke was a victim; ultimately he was sentenced to prison from three to seven and a half years for fleeing from officers and probation violation. He would serve the entire sentence. Militia leaders had always disagreed about whether even to allow Koernke a forum at their meetings. Some of them adamantly disavowed him and his ideas; others took Koernke "with a grain of salt" and shrugged off his most weird notions. During the trial, the Washtenaw County sheriff's office received calls from people as far away as California who were seeing a live broadcast of the trial and complained that Koernke was being railroaded. Tom Wayne who was pleased about the conviction expressed a different opinion: "I will not gloat over this, but find this is a very troubled man." In response, a member of the East Texas Constitutional Militia leveled a charge going around among some in Michigan who believed Wayne was a "Federal informant" and challenged him to come to the national meeting in Kentucky where "there will be people standing in line to show you . . . just how troubled you are."[78]

Kent County Brigade Commander Michael John Modena was one whose reading of the laws sent him to prison—and disillusioned many of his followers. Modena believed income tax policies were illegal, and he taught friends how to follow certain steps so the government could not force them to pay. The IRS thought otherwise. Charges were brought against Modena for helping five Grand Rapids area men evade hundreds of thousands of dollars in income taxes. He went into hiding for 14 months but was captured by a dozen officers at a Flap Jack Shack near Lansing, and in November 2000 he was sentenced to five years in prison.[79] Modena's meetings had attracted large crowds, and after his departure the numbers dwindled to around a dozen regulars, but the commander who replaced him thought it was just as well. "We consider ourselves nothing but good respectable citizens doing our duty."[80]

Y2K and 9/11

The impending new millennium caught the interest of the general public, but in Militia circles it gave rise to months of fearful planning and preparation. There were those who anticipated a cataclysm based on their reading of the Bible; others believed that it would give the government an opportunity to declare martial law and suspend the Constitution. According to one Michigan Militia brigade's *Weekly News* in March 1999, a FEMA "Guide for State and Local Emergency Managers" referred to plans for calling in the National Guard and local law enforcement. Local governments in Michigan hired consultants to help them prepare. One contributed to the apprehension when he said the government would place citizens in shelters and take control of private businesses during the emergency.[81] Some people claimed they had sighted black helicopters and offered that as evidence of a plotted takeover by the United Nations and the forces of the New World Order. Still others shared more commonplace fears—the nation's various systems had become dependent on computers and other technology that would not have the capability to make the necessary adjustments when the calendar rolled over to 2000.

Militia members held drills within their families and arranged a system of contacts within their brigades to implement a response plan in case of attack. They set up generators, bought gallons of bottled water, loaded up on canned food, and stockpiled ammunition. It was also one more chance to reach out and demonstrate the Militia's sense of civic responsibility. John Lynn Van Huizen contacted the state police and local law enforcement agents with offers of shelter, supplies, or help should they need it. When January 1, 2, 3 came and went without disaster, some felt foolish and began to drift away. Others were convinced that preparedness warned off the enemy.

By spring, Timothy McVeigh's trial focused the nation's attention once again on the Michigan Militia. The Militia continued to point out that McVeigh had no connection with the organization other than a shared fear of the government. Yet the matter of his innocence or guilt demonstrated the persistent divisiveness among them. Hard-core antigovernment types circulated information "proving" McVeigh was the victim of a conspiracy; the bombing had been carried out by forces within the government—whose reasons were various, depending on the account. Others regarded him with horror; he was a "cold-blooded murderer," said a woman in a Grand Rapids brigade. "Children die and he calls it collateral damage? I don't comprehend that. Someone like that is not safe to have in society."[82]

McVeigh's execution in 2001 took place without any Militia retaliation that alarmists had predicted. But, like the Militia, many Americans wondered what secrets he took to his grave and thought it unlikely that he had acted alone. Author and political liberal Gore Vidal who interviewed McVeigh in prison and wrote about the case maintained that McVeigh did bomb the federal building and indeed acted alone. But the conduct of the investigation also proved to Vidal's satisfaction that McVeigh was correct in believing that the FBI was corrupt and dangerous and that the cover-ups of the government's crimes at Ruby Ridge and Waco were just part of tangled conspiracies in a government run amok.[83]

Then came September 11, 2001. Militia groups in Michigan met at once to discuss their response to the attacks. They submitted a formal offer to the Justice Department to provide their expertise in training domestic an-titerrorist forces. The government did not respond, but brigades went forward with training on their own.[84] Michigan, with its large population of Middle Easterners, was under special watch, and there were more eyes to look at "right wing Militia types." Instead of seeing them as allies, government agencies regarded the Michigan Militia as part of the "homegrown" terrorists who posed an expanded threat to "homeland security" and one more justification for the Patriot Act. Texas radio personality Alex Jones, well known in militia circles for revealing government "conspiracies," maintained the government was doing "exactly what I said they would do. And I even predicted they would try to connect it to the Michigan militia, following the same pattern of Oklahoma City."[85]

No one was more fearful of the government now than Tony Liuzzo, a member of the Militia who lived in mid-Michigan. Liuzzo's mother Viola had been killed when she went from Detroit to Selma, Alabama, on a voting rights march in the spring of 1965. An FBI informant within the Ku Klux Klan took part in the murder to impress his Klan brothers and maintain his cover. All the while Tony grew up, he fought other children and neighbors who ridiculed his mother, and he watched his family disintegrate. Viola Liuzzo's five children sued the FBI, claiming it could have prevented their mother's death and charging that the agency had deliberately smeared their mother's reputation to protect their informant. The suit was finally thrown out in 1980, leaving Tony even more embittered. He joined the John Birch Society, but then he heard about the New World Order on his shortwave radio; tuned in to Mark Koernke, he learned of other threats including foreign troops training in Michigan. It was no stretch for Tony to see his mother as one more government victim and a victim also of racism turned against whites since Detroit mayor Coleman Young refused all his requests to name a street after Viola Liuzzo in honor of her role in the civil rights movement. He joined the Koernke faction of the

Michigan Militia in 1996, and when Koernke went to prison, Liuzzo took over his radio show. As he saw it, he had honored his mother by taking up her cause of fighting for individual rights. After 9/11 and the passage of the Patriot Act, Liuzzo went into hiding, fearful that he would become a target of the government.[86]

Norm Olson, with renewed vigor after 9/11, was determined that the Militia was more necessary than ever to protect the homeland. In 2002, he described how the Militia's training program was different from previous exercises: "We used to shoot at U.N. Flags, but now we shoot at Middle Eastern rag-head terrorists."[87] But by 2004, he had returned to his main, long-standing theme: "My friends we have far more to worry about with George Bush, John Ashcroft, Tom Ridge and others. . . .We have far more to worry about than Osama bin Laden and Al Quida." Olson agreed with the hard-liner John Trochman of the Militia of Montana that the government was up to something, "nothing less than the creation of a police state." It was Olson's "basic theory" that "this is a wonderful way to rebuild the CIA and the FBI and the military after it was decimated by our friend Bill Clinton."[88] But Olson was soon disgusted once again with his compatriots in the movement for their failure to take training seriously enough. He disbanded his group and announced plans to move to Alaska. Many other initially prominent leaders were gone by 2004–5—out of disgust, because of infighting, to prison, to new homes or jobs in other places, to more pressing private concerns.

Membership shifted in leadership, composition, and numbers. Wayne estimated the group may have peaked with some 14,000 members but was down to a "real hard core" of about 7,000 by the spring of 2001.[89] An accurate count remained impossible, in dispute as always. The Southern Poverty Law Center's *Intelligence Report* listed nine active Militia groups in Michigan in 2004, more than any other state, but the count represented website addresses rather than brigade activity.[90] In his 2002 movie *Bowling for Columbine,* filmmaker Michael Moore featured and mocked the Michigan Militia, all the while exaggerating their danger and their stockpile of weapons. Some studies described an ominous nationwide trend, with militia numbers down but militia members who were more committed to the cause, more "militant and dedicated," and more "aggressive in their embrace of destruction."[91] There was little evidence of such a development in Michigan, but the Militia remained much as the nine blind men described the elephant. As watchful government agents saw it, the Militia was a potential breeding ground for homegrown terrorists.

Training at Frank Stasa's farm continued with sufficient regularity that anyone wanting to join in, spy, or write yet another article about weekend warriors could find them. They appeared still to confirm the stereotype: "THE SERIOUS ARRIVED AT DAWN, painted their faces green, and began drilling . . . clad in camouflaged fatigues that they said were required by the Geneva Conventions. . . . Some hauled glow sticks and radios with attachable throat mics. Others carried flashlights with red lenses and parachute cord and zip ties, which, they explained, would be helpful in securing prisoners. Everyone carried loaded guns, two or three each."[92] These men in training were the most visible remnant of the Michigan Militia as it had been envisioned by the original organizers. But it was no more an organized, unified movement than before.

Certain brigade websites were the focal point for links to other brigades that, like the websites, continued to come and go or merge. A few of the new and younger citizen soldiers now talked of their Militia cause in personal blogs, on YouTube, and on MySpace where they reached different audiences than the brigade websites.[93] Conspiracy theories continued to circulate, most of them documenting problems with the government's official explanation of the bombings on September 11. Committed members believed that it was just a matter of time before more attacks would happen; websites and radio talk-show hosts fed fears that these attacks would be government orchestrated. Readiness to serve was critical. A MySpace contributor explained that the cost for personal gear and uniform was low ($179 for an entire uniform) and directed all who were interested to an army surplus store in Wayne. His "Militia's Blurbs" assured readers that there were opportunities based on the "mode of service" one was prepared to take on, from driving a Hummer to piloting a plane, and that "the main Militia compounds keep all hardware from tanks to helicopters on standby."[94] That there were indeed numerous arsenals well equipped with tanks and helicopters was surely as exaggerated as his claim that the state's militia was over 250,000 strong. Whatever their numbers, those who carried on in the Michigan Militia brigades believed their role as part of the citizens' militia had become more essential than ever. *Theirs* was the way to true homeland security. *They* were the patriots safeguarding America. A favored symbol on their websites, badges, and communications echoed previous generations who saw themselves as American patriots: "Don't Tread On Me!"

Ten years after they were first observed in 1994, the camouflage-clad soldiers in the field remained only part of the story. The Michigan Militia was always more than just a "strange little army." Men and women who joined or hovered around at Militia gatherings were worried—about their nation, about their own well-being—and they believed that not enough other Americans understood. Now, if there were fewer at Bubba Club coffee shop meetings or in church halls or actively training, it was in part because the mainstream had edged in their direction.

Some Company

Patriotism was in vogue across the land. U.S. flag pins were affixed to the lapels of politicians, pundits, and personalities; anyone without the pin could expect questions if not criticism. Public discontent grew about the role of our UN allies in the Iraq war, and there was more support for independent action. Politicians were taking notice of constituents' escalating anger about the North American Free Trade Agreement and the outsourcing of jobs. Respected scholars and the mainstream media took up the cause of defending constitutional guarantees when they stepped up to challenge the Patriot Act and denounce the government's claims of "national security" as cause for denying citizens' rights.

The Militia's fight for the right to bear arms had been won—if quietly. The Brady Bill was amended and rendered nearly meaningless. School shootings led to demands for better security on campus, not to demands that handguns or rifles be outlawed. Michael Moore's *Bowling for Columbine* presented a heavily armed Michigan Militia brigade that was understandable in the context of the times. Vice president Cheney and his friend Supreme Court justice Antonin Scalia smiled for the cameras on one of their hunting trips; when running for president in 2004, liberal Massachusetts senator John Kerry was pictured with rifle and duck in hand. Support for the right to bear arms was coming from strange bedfellows all the way around. Gay gun owners who called themselves the Pink Pistols said they were vulnerable and needed to defend themselves. So, along with Jews for the Preservation of Firearms Ownership, women wanting to arm for self-defense, and disabled veterans, the Pink Pistols were among the 65 groups that filed friend of the court briefs in a case before the U.S. Supreme Court that would strike down strict handgun bans in place in the District of Columbia since 1976.[95] In the spring of 2008, by a five to four decision, the Court ruled that the handgun ban violated the Second Amendment that, said Justice Scalia, "surely elevates above all

other interests the right of law-abiding, responsible citizens to use arms in defense of hearth and home."[96]

In Michigan too, the urgency to "be prepared" was less imperative on some fronts. A more widespread animosity toward NAFTA offered some consolation, and state and local leaders scrambled—if not yet successfully—to bring jobs and provide training that would prepare residents for the high-tech and health service positions that soon should be coming Michigan's way. Charter schools proliferated, giving more choice to parents who had been unhappy or downright angry about their local schools, and homeschoolers received more approving recognition. The excessive percentage of Michigan residents who were in jail or prison had caught the attention of the state's major newspapers, news channels, and reform advocates, who decried the human and financial cost. The public mood swung in the direction of Militia opinion, too, with a successful ballot initiative in 2006 that ended preferences for women and minorities in public university admissions and government hiring. Dependable allies remained determined. When Michigan's Department of Natural Resources wanted to raise fees for hunting and fishing licenses, the NRA not only blocked the effort but used the issue to strengthen the base of a new political action group, Michigan Coalition for Responsible Gun Owners.[97]

Brigade events fell off, and membership dwindled. But once-active members would not be lulled into false optimism just because more citizens were raising the Militia's same issues and asking their same questions. Convictions held firm. There were people in positions of power not to be trusted, and basic American freedoms were at risk. These citizens would stick to their guns.

EPILOGUE

There Is Just Something About Michigan!
—SARAH PALIN, Grand Rapids, November 2009

FBI agents swept into Lenawee and Hillsdale counties in southern Michigan as winter was fading in 2010. They arrested eight men and one woman and, acting perhaps on a tip from an inside informant, charged them with plotting to kill local police officers with the intent to spark an uprising that would lead to overthrow of the government. The nine, four from the same family, were members of the Hutaree Militia. They were "warriors for Christ," Hutaree, a little-known Christian militia group that organized in 2008 to defend themselves from the coming of the Antichrist. Almost before marshals unloaded their prisoners from the van, reporters, television news anchors, bloggers, and talk-show hosts of every persuasion were clamoring for a story: Who *are* these people and what is going on in that state *now?* Michigan's "long tradition of spawning anti-government groups" was back in the national news.[1]

Watchdog fact-finders were ready with their most recent tallies. The Midwest had become a "hotbed" of militia activity since Obama's election in 2008. With 47 "patriot groups," Michigan topped the list. Nationwide, it was second only to Texas.[2] Spokesmen within Michigan militia groups quickly stepped forward to denounce the Hutaree. Determined to disassociate themselves from any fanatic fringe, they insisted that this small band was no more representative of the rank-and-file militia member than was Timothy McVeigh. Headlines persisted for over a month. Were these really domestic terrorists with weapons of mass destruction who hoped to overthrow the government? Were they demented loners guilty only of vicious ravings and hate speech?[3] Claims and counterclaims from the government and defense lawyers turned into distant court dates; months later, five were still in jail awaiting trial, four were out on tethers. Interest in this little group waned. Another type of protest was proving more newsworthy.

Citizens who identified themselves as Tea Partiers began to attract notice around the state within weeks of Barack Obama's inauguration as president in 2009. Part of an emergent movement sprouting up across the country, the Tea Party members claim to be in the tradition of colonists who dumped tea into the Boston harbor. The nation, they insist, has strayed from its historic moorings; elected leaders are violating the principles in the Declaration of Independence and the Bill of Rights. These protesters aim to sound the alarm, rally their fellow citizens, and restore government to the people.

The Tea Party is a new phenomenon but with familiar concerns, reminiscent of other volatile periods when people cast about for answers. Once again times are especially hard in Michigan. The economy was deep in trouble even before the stock market took its sharp dip in the last months of 2008; the unemployment rate had climbed into double digits by the time of the election.[4] With an unpredictable electorate, Michigan was a battleground state, so it was a significant victory when Barack Obama won the state by an impressive margin.[5] The optimistic were hopeful; perhaps Michigan residents were putting aside their divisions based on class, race, community, and region. But on closer analysis, it became clear that the victory relied significantly on independents, a bloc that generally accounted for about one-third of the otherwise evenly divided Michigan electorate. Fears about the economy had helped push swing voters toward the Democrats this time around. Just as after Roosevelt's victory in 1932, voters hoped for change—a dramatic change. But, just as in those earlier hard times, the downhill slide did not come to a sudden halt. Citizens were now accustomed to "breaking news"; they expected a faster turnaround. Some voters who had supported Republican John McCain were quick to jibe, "Had enough yet?"

The Tea Party immediately attracted people who had opposed Obama's candidacy all along. They soon found more reason in the stimulus programs, the bank bailouts, and the health-care reform proposals. At every opportunity, the Tea Party denounced big government and taxes, anticipating that the public's growing uncertainty about spending programs could win converts from among others who distrusted the government—and demanded that the government remedy their economic problems. Enjoying the support of spirited champions like Glenn Beck and Sarah Palin, the movement was buoyed by almost constant publicity from the start. To top off issues of substance, "evidence" was constantly on parade to "confirm" rumors. The president was not born in America. He was not a Christian. He was a socialist. Like the Model Ts that carried Klansmen to rallies and the radio that captured Coughlin's audience, technology propels this grassroots generation. Members stay informed through 24-hour cable news and radio talk shows. They are linked together with the speed of e-mail, blogs, tweets, and websites. Aided by the tactical skills, connections, and resources of conservative advocacy groups, the Tea Party is not such a spontaneous, bottom-up phenomenon as some grassroots members believe. Nonetheless, their determination to speak up for themselves is inbred and homegrown.

Supporters turned out in 33 Michigan communities when national Tea Party organizers planned their first big public demonstration for Tax Day—April 15, 2009.[6] They waved flags, carried children who carried flags, and hoisted signs to announce their message. One Lansing protester's hand-lettered placard summed up the rest: "America: in *DISTRESS* from the Leftist, Socialist, Crazy Tax & Spend Policies! Throw the Liberal Bums Out!"[7] In the months that followed, true believers reached out to establish a presence around the state. By the time the 2010 primary elections approached, the Tea Party Patriot website listed over 70 different groups throughout Michigan. These groups fit the decentralized image partisans advertise and at the same time suggest their own internal disputes.[8] Some communities had two or more patriot groups with different members—the Ann Arbor Tea Party and the Ann Arbor Tea Party Patriots; the Traverse City Patriots and the Traverse City Patriots!!!—the three exclamation points apparently chosen by the latter to signify their separate identity. Only two Tea Party websites claimed to have reached 25 members in the summer of 2010; most had fewer than a dozen, often just one or two people who were also the organizers. The appeal of grassroots causes cannot be gauged, however, by a list of the actively committed.

Accurate polls and serious studies of the Tea Party movement are still in the making, but local television coverage and website photos of Tea Party events in Michigan show crowds that are nearly all white. They include a mix of the young with their children in tow, the middle-aged, and the gray-haired. Their website comments are in a vocabulary familiar among Christians whose religious concerns, like their political agenda, are reminiscent of the John Birch Society. They fear nonbelievers will tread on

Christmas. Whenever they describe themselves, Tea Party partisans consistently maintain that they represent ordinary Americans. "We are the common folks, . . . a Truck Driver, a Farmer, a stay-at-home Mom, a small business Owner, a Waitress, a Barber, . . . working people just like you!"[9] They are counting on thousands of ordinary Americans to identify with them come election day.

Like all of the other Michigan grassroots movements before them, Tea Party partisans are men and women bent on making a difference within the existing political system. They have set their sights on influencing the Michigan Republican Party, and most dismiss any talk of a Tea Party ticket, local or national, that would run candidates in opposition to the Democratic and Republican parties.[10] Tea Party websites announce broad, sweeping goals—"Fiscal Responsibility, Constitutionally Limited Government, and Free Markets." Free enterprise advocacy groups are at the ready with specifics. Tax policies top the list of necessary changes; Michigan should lower individual and corporate income taxes, sales taxes, and inheritance taxes. Business unfettered by government is the key to an improved economy—right-to-work laws, market-based health care, more privatized services, more chartered schools.[11] Armed with such litmus tests, concerned voters will be able to identify candidates who are right for the job.[12]

Given the experience of earlier Michigan grassroots movements, Tea Partiers' success in this troubled time depends, again, on the extent of discontent shared by a broader voting public. Michigan's jobless rate continues to pace the nation. It was over 14 percent at the beginning of 2010, significantly higher in places like Detroit and Flint.[13] People accustomed to considering themselves part of the middle class now face a reordering of familiar jobs and opportunity. Housing values have plummeted, and the state ranks near the top in home foreclosures.[14] Tax revenues continue to dwindle, but the need for services continues to escalate. Too many school districts fall below national averages on a range of measures, and the state continues to lag in the proportion of residents who are college-educated. Metropolitan Detroit remains the most segregated region in the country. Economic anxiety, an uncertain future, patriotic fervor, and a general sense of disenfranchisement are once again a potential political force. It was not by chance that Sarah Palin chose Grand Rapids, Michigan, as the place to launch her book tour for *Going Rogue.*[15]

Tea Partiers recognize the challenges they face. They are too often factious, inexperienced, and hampered by the local control they prize. Opponents charge they are extremists or mock them as "wing-nuts." In previous grassroots movements, members became worn out from the effort or quit when their own leaders proved disappointing or dishonest. Always in the past, marginal sympathizers deserted when bad times got better. At this point in 2010, recovery remains slow, but here and there, people are again reassuring each other, "Michigan always comes back." Meanwhile, it seems to be the right time and the right place for an organized, determined, and visible grassroots movement to take a stand. Even if Tea Party candidates fail to win despite the fevered efforts of flag-waving supporters sometimes wearing Revolutionary War hats, Tea Party issues like lower taxes and less government have a chance of making it into mainstream respectability. Sober-suited men and women sitting in corporate boardrooms and think tanks understand lessons of the past. A vocal grassroots movement can make a difference once again.

Although the Ku Klux Klan was denounced in its own time, by the end of the 1920s, both the Democratic and Republican parties in Michigan had given their nod to immigration quotas, state supervision of parochial schools, and more funding for the state police. Restrictive covenants were written into house deeds, keeping African-Americans and Jews out of many neighborhoods for at least another generation. Coughlin may be best remembered as an anti-Semite, but in the 1930s, his army of letter-writers persuaded legislators against joining the World Court, and citizen unrest prompted government involvement in far-reaching social programs. HUAC brought anti-Communist "witch hunts" to the state according to its critics, but in the 1950s Michigan citizens welcomed those hearings, turned on suspicious neighbors, and applauded setbacks to the labor and civil rights leaders who were branded "Communist agitators." John Birch Society members were few in number, but the Republican Party developed a permanent core dedicated to the free enterprise system, lower taxes, and an end to government interference. Protests halted cross-district busing before it began and kept low-income housing out of suburbs. When Michigan Militia groups sounded their alarm in the 1990s, they were called "kooks with guns," but others, too, began to wonder whether sinister forces might be responsible for trade agreements like NAFTA and whether the Second Amendment was in danger. Indeed, when the Hutaree and their cache of weaponry came to light, Michigan politicians did not blink; there would be no repeal of the citizens' right to bear arms.

Democracy is difficult to get right in America, this proud nation where we hold a list of valuable truths to be self-evident. Long-standing precepts underpinning the nation are the substance of our collective memories, our habits of the heart. Because the phrases we all embrace are indeed revolutionary, it has been harder by far to come up with the wit and the will to preserve our "more perfect Union." Democracy in America is awash in contradictory choices—how to unify competing beliefs in a nation that professes to prize pluralism, how to provide more reliable protection for the vulnerable in a nation that preaches free enterprise, how to make up for past injustices without creating new ones. The grand promises of American democracy trickle down slowly, unevenly, unfairly—too often deliberately so. Still the words echo all the while—those high-minded phrases, in this, our "government of the people, by the people, and for the people."

Michigan, time and again, saw ordinary men and women give witness to their faith. Foot soldiers in the grassroots, they aimed to set America right their way. These were people who did not shrink from self-defined duty to God, country, and family. They were men and women who saw cause to anticipate dangers not of their own making—threats to their religion from Catholics or Jews or Communists, damage to their country by the wrong people in power or duped voters, trouble in their own backyards from newcomers or from government interference. They were nearly all white and Christians and American-bred patriots; they denied allegations of racism, resented accusations that their actions were un-Christian, and denounced all charges that they were un-American. By the heat of their words and the visibility of their presence, they fueled racist attacks, pressed their version of morality into law when they could, and thrust simplistic slogans into public discourse: "America for Americans." "Better Dead than Red." "America: Love It or Leave It." "Don't Tread On Me!" A few in each era were cynical manipulators out for personal gain; a few were dangerous threats. Most were just alarmed, men and women who regarded themselves as concerned citizens and believed they were right about their concerns. If they often made a mockery of the American values they touted, they were forthright in their convictions.

The grassroots' hero Teddy Roosevelt shouted for Americans to join his Progressive Party on behalf of their country in 1912; together they would "stand at Armageddon and battle for the Lord." The men and women who rose up out of the Michigan grassroots were ready to do battle, one generation after another. Who were these people? They were Americans who believed for a while that they could make a difference and resolved to try. Empowered by enthusiasms that mixed fear with hope, they went on the march in the company of those like-minded. Wanting to be seen, they accomplished that aim. We have not seen the last of them.

Notes

Introduction

1. Roosevelt's speech at the Progressive Party (Bull Moose) Convention in Chicago, August 1912.

Chapter 1

Epigraph: Louis F. Post, *The Deportation Delirium of Nineteen-Twenty* (Honolulu, Hawaii: University Press of the Pacific, 2003, reprinted from the 1923 edition published in Chicago by Charles H. Kerr and Company), 143.

1. *Fremont Times-Indicator,* December 13, 1917; this incident was highlighted in Ted R. Mitchell, "White Sheets Over West Michigan: The Ku Klux Klan in Newaygo County, Michigan in the 1920s," Senior Honors Thesis, University of Michigan (2000), 30, Bentley Historical Library, University of Michigan (hereafter BHL).

2. The Highland Park Plant had 40,000 workers in 1920 and an average of 62,000 in 1923; Olivier Zunz, *The Changing Face of Inequality* (Chicago: University of Chicago Press, 1982), 293.

3. U.S. Bureau of the Census, *Fourteenth Census of the United States, 1920,* vol. 2, *Population* (Washington, D.C.: Government Printing Office, 1922), 961.

4. Jonathan L. Marwill, *A History of Ann Arbor* (Ann Arbor: Ann Arbor Observer Co., 1987), 94.

5. Willis F. Dunbar and George S. May, *Michigan: A History of the Wolverine State* (Grand Rapids: Eerdmans Publishing Company, 1995), 461–65.

6. *U.S. Census,* 1920, 2:47–48; Zunz, *Changing Face of Inequality,* 287–88.

7. Zunz, *Changing Face of Inequality,* 311.

8. Americanization Committee papers, BHL, as cited in Zunz, *Changing Face of Inequality,* 313.

9. Zaragosa Vargas, *Proletarians of the North: A History of Mexican Industrial Workers in Detroit and the Midwest, 1917–1933* (Berkeley: University of California Press, 1993), 74–75.

10. David Allan Levine, *Internal Combustion, The Races in Detroit, 1915–1926* (Westport, Conn.: Greenwood Press, 1976), 116–17.

11. Detroit Urban League Papers, Executive Secretary's General File, speech by Forrester Washington in New York, Jan. 1918, BHL, as cited in Zunz, *Changing Face of Inequality,* 322.

12. Ibid., 323.

13. U.S. Espionage Act, June 15, 1917, http://www.firstworldwar.com/source/espionageact.htm.

14. Stephen Meyer III, *The Five Dollar Day: Labor Management and Social Control in the Ford Motor Company, 1908–1921* (Albany: State University of New York Press, 1981), 173; William A. Link and Arthur S. Link, *American Epoch: A History of the United States Since 1900* (New York: McGraw-Hill, 1993), 1:159–62.

15. Carlotta R. Anderson, *All-American Anarchist: Joseph A. Labadie and the Labor Movement* (Detroit: Wayne State University Press, 1998), 219.

16. Richard G. Powers, *The Life of J. Edgar Hoover* (New York: Free Press, 1987), 46–48.

17. Minutes, March 19, 1917, Americanization Committee Papers, BHL, and *Detroit Saturday Night,* December 22, 1917, as cited in Zunz, *Changing Face of Inequality,* 318.

18. *Fremont Times-Indicator,* December 13, 1917, as discussed in Mitchell, "White Sheets," 30, BHL.

19. Dunbar and May, *Michigan,* 460; the authors give no source for this particular rumor, however.

20. Marwill, *Ann Arbor,* 95–97.

21. This is a point well made in Meyer, *Five Dollar Day.*

22. An excellent archival collection of letters, clippings, and other records on the Polar Bear regiment can be accessed at the Bentley Historical Collection, UM.

23. Richard Whitney, *Reds in America* (New York: Beckwith Press, 1924), 197. Whitney was a journalist who, in the process of detailing the Bridgman raid, also "reveals" the efforts the Communists were making to use the schools and colleges to subvert youth, to inflame the "Negro masses," to use women's organizations, the stage and movies, and even men in the armed services for their own purposes. This book was reprinted in 1970 by the publishing company connected with the John Birch Society in Belmont, Massachusetts.

24. Steve Babson, Ron Alpern, Dave Elsila, and John Revitte, *Working Detroit: The Making of a Union Town* (Detroit: Wayne State University Press, 1986), 40.

25. Babson, *Working Detroit,* 41.

26. Powers, *J. Edgar Hoover,* 59–60.

27. Powers, *J. Edgar Hoover,* chaps. 3, 4, passim.

28. *Detroit News,* Jan. 3, 1920; for one examination of this episode see Christopher H. Johnson, *Maurice Sugar: Law, Labor, and the Left in Detroit, 1912–1950* (Detroit: Wayne State University Press, 1988).

29. Wilma Henrickson, ed., *Detroit Perspectives: Crossroads and Turning Points* (Detroit: Wayne State University Press, 1991), and quoting Senate Judiciary Committee, Hearings on Charges of Illegal Practices of Department of Justice, 66th Congress, 1 March 1921, U.S. Cong. Hearings, 41st–73d Cong., 1869–1934, 169: 709–23; see also

Post, *Deportation Delirium*. Post was Woodrow Wilson's undersecretary of labor at the time of these raids.

30. Henrickson, *Detroit Perspectives*, 314.

31. *Detroit News*, Jan. 3, 1920; see also Post, *Deportation Delirium*, 144.

32. Post, *Deportation Delirium*, 145–47.

33. Post, *Deportation Delirium*, 143.

34. See Whitney, *Reds in America*.

35. Sidney Fine, *Sit-down: The General Motors Strike of 1936–1937* (Ann Arbor: University of Michigan Press, 1979), 101–3; Arthur Thurner, *Strangers and Sojourners: A History of Michigan's Keweenaw Peninsula* (Detroit: Wayne State University Press, 1994), 236–39; *Census of Religious Bodies: 1926*, 1:421; *Michigan Official Directory and Legislative Manual, 1917 and 1918* (Lansing: Michigan Department of State); Levine, *Internal Combustion*, 134–35; *Detroit News*, Nov. 8, 1916.

36. Lisa M. Fine, *The Story of REO JOE: Work, Kind, and Community in Autotown, U.S.A.* (Philadelphia: Temple University Press, 2004), 29, 52.

37. Philip P. Mason, *Rumrunning and the Roaring Twenties: Prohibition on the Michigan-Ontario Waterway* (Detroit: Wayne State University Press, 1995).

38. Nora Faires, "Social and Political Development in Michigan," in Richard J. Hathaway, ed., *Michigan: Visions of Our Past* (East Lansing: Michigan State University Press, 1989), 205.

39. Zunz, *Changing Face of Inequality*, 324; Vargas, *Proletarians of the North*, 81–82.

40. Thurner, *Strangers and Sojourners*, 224–27.

41. Vargas, *Proletarians of the North*, 84.

42. Frank B. Woodford, *Alex J. Groesbeck* (Detroit: Wayne State University Press, 1962), 234, 283.

43. James Hamilton, *The Michigan Public School Amendment* (Detroit: Public School Defense League, n.d. [ca. 1922]), a pamphlet of 132 pages in "Anti-Parochial School Amendment Collection," Archives of the Sisters Servants of the Immaculate Heart of Mary, Monroe, Michigan (hereafter SSIHM).

44. Hamilton, *Michigan Public School Amendment*, Anti-Parochial School Amendment Collection, SSIHM; and talk by Hamilton, *Detroit Free Press*, Oct. 27, 1924. Discussed in detail in JoEllen McNergney Vinyard, *For Faith and Fortune: The Education of Catholic Immigrants in Detroit* (Urbana: University of Illinois Press, 1998), chap. 8.

45. "Published Miscellanea" file, box I, Lutheran Church—Missouri Synod, Michigan District, Lutheran Schools Committee Collection, BHL; and James Hamilton, *Michigan Public School Amendment* (SSIHM).

46. I would like to thank Dan Crots, one of my graduate students, and his friend Bonnie Berry for sharing their knowledge and research about this episode in Monroe County. Mr. Crots made trips to the Notre Dame archives, tracked down sources, and copied them for me; Ms. Berry provided a copy of her manuscript "The 1920 Monroe County Church Riot," written for a class at Monroe Community College. It includes extensive research from the Monroe and Toledo newspapers.

47. *The New Menace*, June 26, 1920. This weekly was published in Branson, Missouri, beginning April 10, 1920, and continuing probably to 1931 according to records with the microform holdings in the Notre Dame University Library.

48. Hamilton, *The Michigan Public School Amendment*, Anti-Parochial School Amendment Collection, SSIHM.

49. John C. Baur, executive secretary of Missouri Synod, Michigan District, to Dr.

C. W. Brayman of Cedar Springs, March 17, 1922, in "File B" box I, Lutheran Church—Missouri Synod, Michigan District, Lutheran Schools Committee Collection, BHL.

50. Sister M. Rosalita [Kelly], *No Greater Service: The History of the Congregation of the Sisters, Servants of the Immaculate Heart of Mary, Monroe, Michigan, 1845–1945* (Detroit: Congregation of the Sisters, Servants of the Immaculate Heart of Mary, 1948), 554; "Pamphlets" file, Anti-Parochial School Amendment Collection, SSIHM.

51. Groesbeck and Leland in Educational Liberty League advertisement, *Detroit Free Press,* Oct. 21, 1920.

52. *Free Schools Bulletin* (Feb.–March 1924): I, in "Press Articles" file, Anti-Parochial School Amendment Collection, SSIHM.

53. *Fremont Times-Indicator,* Nov. 11, 1920.

Chapter 2

Epigraph: Kreed indicates it is the Original Creed Revised, in file "Materials Relating to Women of the Ku Klux Klan," Acc. Box 14k, Record Group 67-102-A, B14 F2, State of Michigan Archives, Lansing.

1. Jackson, *Ku Klux Klan in the City,* 120; Calvin Enders, "White Sheets in Mecosta: The Anatomy of a Michigan Klan," *Michigan Historical Review* 14 (Fall 1988): 61, citing Norman F. Weaver, "The Ku Klux Klan in Wisconsin, Michigan, Indiana, and Ohio" (PhD diss., University of Wisconsin, 1954), 268.

2. Enders, "White Sheets in Mecosta," 61.

3. Jackson, *Ku Klux Klan in the City,* 273, citing Klan official in 1924; Norman F. Weaver diss.; *Detroit News,* Aug. 21, 1924; *Detroit Evening Times,* Dec. 5, 1939; Winfield Jones, *Knights of the Ku Klux Klan* (Hollywood, Calif.: Sons of Liberty, 1969, reprint of 1941 edition); *Henry C. Warner v. Arthur S. Nichols, et al.,* Wayne Co. Circuit Court, case number 132314 (1928).

4. In 1920 the U.S. census recorded that Michigan had a total of 467,192 American-born white males over the age of 21 whose parents had also been born in the country. *U.S. Census,* 1920, 2:1344.

5. Population figures are based on *U.S. Census,* 1920, 2:1344; http://fisher.lib.vir ginia.edu/cgi-local/censusbin/census/cen.pl; U.S. Bureau of the Census; *Census of Religious Bodies: 1926* (Washington, D.C.: Government Printing Office, 1929), 1:626, 627. Nancy MacLean, *Behind the Mask of Chivalry* (New York: Oxford University Press, 1994), 9, says that the Clarke County, Georgia, chapter drew in approximately one in ten of the native-born Protestant white men who were eligible.

6. *New York Times,* Oct. 13, 1921; Sept. 23, 1921.

7. *Lansing State Journal,* July 17, 1922, cited in Fine, *Story of REO JOE,* 65.

8. *Detroit Free Press,* June 2, 1923.

9. *Journal of the House of Representatives of the State of Michigan, 1923* (Lansing: Fort Wayne Printing Co., 1923), 1:439; 2:692, 879–80; and *Journal of the Senate of the State of Michigan, 1923* (Lansing: Fort Wayne Printing Co., 1923), 2:911.

10. *Detroit Free Press,* June 14, 1923.

11. *Detroit Free Press,* June 14, 1923.

12. Jackson, *Ku Klux Klan in the City,* 129–30.

13. *Detroit News,* Sept. 18, 1923.

14. *Newaygo Republican,* Sept. 27, 1923, Ku Klux Klan Collection, Clarke Historical

Library, Central Michigan University (hereafter KKK Collection, Clarke, CMU). This item and other information in chapters 2 and 3 are based upon research by the late Professor Calvin Enders of the History Department at Central Michigan University. His careful notes, the many newspaper clippings and logs he assembled, and the wide-ranging Klan records he managed to unearth were donated to the Clarke Library by Mrs. Enders. The Capen papers at the Clarke Library span the years from 1916 to 1974, mostly 1920 to 1939, and include organizational correspondence, membership cards, publications, forms, and photographs. This is a remarkable, invaluable collection; I owe a great debt to the dedicated, meticulous scholarship of Professor Enders.

15. *Traverse City Record Eagle,* Sept. 17, 1923.

16. *Saugatuck Commercial Record,* Sept. 28, 1923, KKK Collection, Clarke, CMU.

17. *Berrien County Journal,* Sept. 20, 1923, KKK Collection, Clarke, CMU.

18. *Niles Daily Star-Sun,* Oct. 6, 1923, KKK Collection, Clarke, CMU.

19. *Berrien County Journal,* Sept. 20, 1923, KKK Collection, Clarke, CMU.

20. *Jackson Citizen Patriot,* Sept. 27, 1923; *Newaygo Republican,* Sept. 27, 1923; *Royal Oak Tribune,* Sept. 28, 1923, Sept. 24, 1923; *Niles Daily Star-Sun,* Oct. 6, 1923, all articles are from clipping files in the KKK Collection, Clarke, CMU.

21. Ibid.

22. *Mt. Pleasant Times,* Sept. 27, 1923, KKK Collection, Clarke, CMU.

23. Ibid.

24. *Niles Daily Star,* Sun. Oct. 6, 1923, KKK Collection, Clarke, CMU.

25. Maureen DesRoches, talking about her father Bernard DesRoches and this experience he so often described, interview with the author on July 3, 2005.

26. Jackson, *Ku Klux Klan in the City,* 12–13; David Bennett, *The Party of Fear: From Nativist Movements to the New Right in American History* (Chapel Hill: University of North Carolina Press, 1988), 212.

27. Bennett, *Party of Fear,* 213–14.

28. *Dowagiac Daily News,* Aug. 8, 1923; *Grand Haven Press,* Oct. 2, 1923, KKK Collection, Clarke, CMU.

29. Enders, "Under Grand Haven's White Sheets," *Michigan Historical Review* 19 (Spring 1993): 55–61, describes the membership lists of the Grand Haven Klan and mentions the Klan units he studied in Mecosta and Newaygo counties; Enders also discusses the membership lists for the Mecosta Klan (60 n. 6).

30. The population of Newaygo County in 1920 was 17,378, with 4,292 white native-born males over the age of 21; in Mecosta County, the total population was 17,765 with 4,371 white native-born males over 21; Ottawa County, with 47,660 residents, was more than double the size of the other two; 6,075 were native-born, white, and over 21. *U.S., 14th Census, 1920,* 2:1345; figures are also based on 1920 census data recorded by the Inter-University Consortium for Political and Social Research (ICPSR) available at http://fisher.lib.virginia.edu/cgi-local/censusbin/census.

31. *U.S. Census, 1920,* 2:1345; *Michigan Manual,* 1921–22, 320–21. The religious census taken in 1926 showed that in Newaygo County, of 3,799 people who were listed as members of organized religious sects, 3,000 were Protestants and 344 were Catholics; 455 said they were "other." In Mecosta County where a total of 4,249 declared some religious affiliation, 1,238 were Catholics according to table 32 in *Census of Religious Bodies: 1926* (Washington, D.C.: Government Printing Office, 1929), 628–30.

32. Enders, "White Sheets in Mecosta," 63, citing *Evart Review,* Oct. 5, 1923, bylined *Big Rapids Star.*

33. Enders, "White Sheets in Mecosta," 63.

34. *U.S. Census, 1920*, 2:1345.

35. *Fremont Times-Indicator,* Nov. 11, 1920, KKK Collection, Clarke, CMU; *Michigan Manual*, 1921–22, 412.

36. Letter dated July 13, 1925, Ward S. Powers to "Dear Brother," Klan Collection, cited by Enders, "White Sheets in Mecosta," 73.

37. *Michigan Fiery Cross,* Feb. 29, 1924, KKK Collection, Clarke, CMU.

38. From in or around Remus, 47 quickly enrolled. Morley, a village of only 336 people, was the address on 52 klansmen's cards. Big Rapids, with a population of 4,558, added 72 more men to the Klan. Tabulated from names on microfilmed Newaygo County Ku Klux Klan membership cards, 1923–26, BHL.

39. Born in Michigan: 78 percent of those in the Mecosta Klan (n = 742 born in Michigan; 188 born nearby), 70 percent in Newaygo, and 76 percent in Grand Haven. Calculated from Mecosta County manuscript card list, Clarke Library, CMU, and Enders, "White Sheets in Mecosta," 77.

40. Of the 255 men on the list in Mecosta's Klan, 34 were father and son combinations, at least 16 were father-in-law and son-in-law combinations, another 28 were brothers, and 34 were brothers-in-law. The pattern was much the same in the Newaygo Klan, based on tabulations from the Newaygo manuscript membership cards, BHL, and Enders, "White Sheets in Mecosta," 75.

41. Newaygo County membership cards, BHL.

42. Bulletin No. 128 in Mecosta Co. "Organizational Correspondence" file, Jan.–June 1927, KKK Collection, Clarke, CMU.

43. Ibid.

44. Mitchell, "White Sheets," 72, BHL, citing *Fremont Times-Indicator,* Feb. 21 and Feb. 28, 1924, which was from a sermon he delivered probably on Feb. 14.

45. Mecosta Co. "Organizational Correspondence" file, Jan.–June 1927, KKK Collection, Clarke, CMU.

46. Mecosta Co. "Organizational Correspondence" file, Jan.–June 1927, KKK Collection, Clarke, CMU.

47. Mecosta Co. "Organizational Correspondence" file, Jan.–June 1927, letter dated March 24, 1927, Capen to Carr, KKK Collection, Clarke, CMU.

48. *Detroit Free Press,* June 4, 1923.

49. Mitchell, "White Sheets," 62–63, BHL; refers also to Enders paper dated March 11, 1996, Box 1 "KKK in the North," KKK Collection, Clarke, CMU.

50. In Newaygo County Klan No. 29, skilled workmen accounted for 105 members and another 48 were in semiskilled or service jobs such as cook or delivery man, tabulated from Newaygo manuscript membership cards, BHL.

51. Questions are stated on the membership forms included in the Newaygo and Mecosta lists.

52. Of the four foreign-born members in the Mecosta Klan, three came from Canada and one from Holland. In Newaygo, three were from Germany, two each from Scotland, England, and Finland, and one each from Sweden and France. Six had been born in Canada. Calculated from membership cards.

53. Calculated from Newaygo manuscript membership cards; 15 of the 18 foreign-born men gave their ages.

54. In Ottawa County voters had rejected the 1920 anti–parochial school amend-

ment by a margin of more than two to one: 3,806 for and 8,753 against. *Michigan Manual, 1921–22,* 412.

55. The county had a total of 47,600 residents, and over 28,000 were either foreign-born or had at least one foreign-born parent. *U.S. Census 1920,* 2:1345.

56. In addition to these over 30,000 Protestant churchgoers, there were 2,813 Catholic and 40 Jewish residents. *Census of Religious Bodies, 1926,* 1:626–28.

57. Enders is the source for the data on the Grand Haven Klan; Enders, "Grand Haven's White Sheets," *Michigan Historical Review* 19 (Spring 1993): 55–57, 60; grand total here of 1,519.

58. Of the 142 for whom parents' birthplaces are known, 46 had two parents from abroad, and 30 had one. Of those foreign-born parents, 51 of them were from the Netherlands, and 38 were from Germany. Calculations by Enders, "Grand Haven's White Sheets," *Michigan Historical Review* 19 (Spring 1993). Enders marshals data from the membership lists to challenge several contemporary accounts and historians' analyses, including David M. Chalmers, Norman Weaver's doctoral dissertation, and Bruce A. Rubenstein and Lawrence D. Ziewacz, who all accept contemporary press assessments that the Dutch in and around Grand Haven were eager joiners.

59. The membership lists for the Grand Haven Klan include 32 factory workers, 16 laborers, and 10 who either worked on the railroad or were sailors; 21 members were businessmen or merchants.

60. Mecosta Co. "Organizational Correspondence" file, Jan.–June 1927, KKK Collection, Clarke, CMU.

61. Jackson, *Ku Klux Klan in the City,* 14; *St. Joseph Herald-Press,* July 28, 1923, KKK Collection, Clarke, CMU.

62. Kathleen M. Blee, *Women of the Klan: Racism and Gender in the 1920s* (Berkeley: University of California Press, 1991), 28.

63. "Women of The Ku Klux Klan Kreed" (Kreed indicates it is the Original Creed Revised), in file "Materials Relating to Women of the Ku Klux Klan," Acc. Box 14k, Record Group 67-102-A, B14 F2, State of Michigan Archives, Lansing.

64. *Fiery Cross,* Dec. 21, 1923, KKK Collection, Clarke, CMU.

65. *Fiery Cross* (Indiana edition), March 7, 1924, KKK Collection, CMU.

66. *Fiery Cross* (Michigan edition), December 4, 1923, KKK Collection, CMU.

67. Blee, *Women of the Klan,* 30.

68. Blee, *Women of the Klan,* 4.

69. Among the membership, 196 came from Fremont or nearby; another 94 were from or around the town of Newaygo, 70 were from White Cloud, and 35 were from Hesperia.

70. Mitchell, "White Sheets," says the median age was 37 years, or the same as the KKK. Much like the pattern common among the men, of the 331 women for whom birthplace is known, 298 were from the Midwest, 210 of them from Michigan.

71. Calculations based on Newaygo membership cards indicate that 83.6 percent were married ($n = 320$) and 11.7 percent ($n = 45$) were single; 3.4 percent ($n = 14$) were widowed; and 4 were unknown.

72. Information from the Newaygo membership cards.

73. *Fiery Cross,* Nov. 30, 1923, KKK Collection, Clarke, CMU.

74. Blee, *Women of the Klan,* 158, 161.

75. *Fiery Cross,* Nov. 23, 1923, KKK Collection, Clarke, CMU.

76. Jackson, *Ku Klux Klan in the City*, 133.

77. *Fiery Cross* (Indiana edition), March 7, 1924, KKK Collection, CMU.

78. *Fiery Cross,* Jan. 11, 1924, KKK Collection, Clarke, CMU.

79. Bulletin No. 123, Mecosta Co. "Organizational Correspondence" file, Jan.–June 1927, KKK Collection, Clarke, CMU.

Chapter 3

Epigraph: Letter from Grand Dragon G. E. Carr to Lewis D. Capen, dated June 17, 1927, Mecosta Co. "Organizational Correspondence" file, Jan.–June 1927, KKK Collection, Clarke, CMU.

1. *Traverse City Record Eagle,* Aug. 13, 1924.

2. *The Hartford Day Spring,* Aug. 1, 1923, KKK Collection, CMU.

3. Mitchell, "White Sheets," 74, referring to the *Fremont Times Indicator,* Nov. 3, 1921.

4. *Detroit Free Press,* Feb. 16, 1924; March 1, 1924.

5. *Detroit News,* Sept. 14, 1923; Sept. 18, 1923; Oct. 12, 1923; Jackson, *Ku Klux Klan in the City,* 132.

6. *Detroit Free Press,* Aug. 18, 1923.

7. *Ironwood Daily Globe,* Sept. 26, 1923, KKK Collection, Clarke, CMU.

8. Jackson, *Ku Klux Klan in the City,* 131; *Detroit News,* Aug. 31, 1923.

9. *Detroit Free Press,* Dec. 25, 1923.

10. Letter from Grand Dragon Carr to Lewis D. Capen, dated May 9, 1927, Mecosta Co. "Organizational Correspondence" file, Jan.–June 1927, KKK Collection, Clarke, CMU.

11. Incident as described in "Movers and Shakers: Michigan Immigrants and Migrants" special exhibit, Michigan State Historical Museum, Lansing, 2005.

12. *Berrien Co. Journal,* Sept. 27, 1923, KKK Collection, Clarke, CMU.

13. Jackson, *Ku Klux Klan in the City,* 131.

14. *Herald Times and Ogemaw Republican,* Oct. 4, 1923, KKK Collection, Clarke, CMU.

15. *Newberry News,* Sept. 21, 1923, KKK Collection, Clarke, CMU.

16. *Newaygo Republican,* Sept. 27, 1923, KKK Collection, Clarke, CMU.

17. *Saugatuck Commercial Record,* Sept. 28, 1923, KKK Collection, Clarke, CMU.

18. *Adrian Daily Telegram,* Jan. 29, 1924, cited in Joel Carpenter, "Michigan's Klan in a Small Town: The Ku Klux Klan in Adrian, Michigan, 1923–25," unpublished paper (1974) by student at Calvin College, BHL.

19. *Traverse City Record Eagle,* Sept. 18, 1923.

20. *Michigan Fiery Cross,* Dec. 21, 1923, KKK Collection, Clarke, CMU.

21. *Traverse City Record Eagle,* Sept. 13, 1924.

22. *Fiery Cross* (Michigan edition), Sept. 24, 1923, KKK Collection, Clarke, CMU.

23. *Detroit Free Press,* March 12, 1924.

24. *Detroit Free Press,* Jan. 15, 1924.

25. *Lansing Capital News,* March 31, 1924, KKK Collection, Clarke, CMU.

26. *Fiery Cross,* Dec. 28, 1923, KKK Collection, Clarke, CMU.

27. Carpenter, "Michigan's Klan in a Small Town," citing Homer R. Powell, "History of Plymouth Church" (unpublished paper, 1946, Adrian College), BHL.

28. *Jackson Citizen Patriot,* Sept. 26, 1923, cited in Timothy Weber, "Crime Pays:

The Role of Prohibition and Rum Running along US112 in the Transformation of the Michigan State Police," Senior Honors Thesis, Eastern Michigan University, 2005, paper in possession of the author.

29. *Detroit Free Press,* Jan. 15, 1924; Jan. 21, 1924.

30. *Pontiac Press,* Sept. 22, 1923, KKK Collection, Clarke, CMU.

31. *Kalamazoo Gazette,* Sept. 28, 1923, KKK Collection, Clarke, CMU.

32. *Detroit Free Press,* Sept. 28, 1923.

33. Jackson, *Ku Klux Klan in the City,* 142.

34. *Traverse City Record Eagle,* Aug. 11, 1924; Aug. 12, 1924; Aug. 23, 1924; Jan. 8, 1925.

35. *Traverse City Record Eagle,* Aug. 12, 1924; Aug. 7, 1924.

36. *Detroit Free Press,* Oct. 3, 1923; *Detroit News,* Aug. 29, 1923.

37. *New York Times,* July 13, 1924, reported that it was especially a "mystery" because Van Loon had an undated letter in his pocket that he had written to someone named "Ed" he was planning to meet in Chicago for some business venture, perhaps connected with a traveling ministry.

38. *Royal Oak Tribune,* Aug. 3, 1923, KKK Collection, Clarke, CMU.

39. Michigan reformers succeeded in pushing this primary law through the state legislature in 1909 over the opposition of conservatives. Primaries were used in some counties as early as 1903.

40. *Jackson Citizen Patriot,* July 4, 1924, KKK Collection, Clarke, CMU. See Fine, *Story of REO JOE,* especially chapter 3, for a perceptive account of the Klan activities in Lansing.

41. *Benzie Banner,* Sept. 4, 1924.

42. *Detroit Free Press,* March 4, 1924.

43. *Michigan Catholic,* Oct. 23, 1924.

44. *Detroit Free Press,* Sept. 18, 1924.

45. William H. Chafe, "Flint and the Great Depression," *Michigan History Magazine* 53, no. 3: 246.

46. Ronald Edsforth, *Class Conflict and Cultural Consensus* (New Brunswick: Rutgers University Press, 1987), 79–83.

47. Edsforth, *Class Conflict,* 48, 79, 91–95, and citing Paul Douglas, *Wages and the Family* (Chicago: University of Chicago Press, 1925).

48. *Detroit News,* Sept. 20, 1923.

49. *New York Times,* July 17, 1924; Edsforth, *Class Conflict,* 108.

50. *Flint Daily Journal,* Sept. 16, 1924.

51. Edsforth, *Class Conflict,* 106–8.

52. *New York Times,* Nov. 7, 1923.

53. *New York Times,* Sept. 12, 1924.

54. *Detroit News,* Oct. 30, 1924; Melvin Holli, *Biographical Dictionary of American Mayors* (Westport, Conn.: Greenwood Press, 1981), 246–47, 334. Vinyard, *For Faith and Fortune,* 240–43.

55. *New York Times,* Oct. 22, 1924.

56. Frank B. Woodford, *Alex J. Groesbeck: Portrait of a Public Man* (Detroit: Wayne State University, 1962), 119; Sidney Fine, *Frank Murphy: The Detroit Years* (Ann Arbor: University of Michigan Press, 1975), 187, citing Frank Murphy Papers and Hester Everad Papers at BHL.

57. Vinyard, *For Faith and Fortune,* 242; see also chap. 8 for analysis and discussion of this issue.

58. *New York Times,* Nov. 5, 1925.

59. Edsforth, *Class Conflict,* 112–13.

60. Kevin Boyle, *Arc of Justice: A Saga of Race, Civil Rights, and Murder in the Jazz Age* (New York: Henry Holt, 2004), 142.

61. *New York Times,* Nov. 3, 1925.

62. Jackson, *Ku Klux Klan in the City,* 142.

63. *New York Times,* Nov. 4, 1925.

64. Jackson, *Ku Klux Klan in the City,* 142.

65. Jackson, *Ku Klux Klan in the City,* 273, fn. 8 describes a Circuit Court suit involving the Symwa Club and a creditor that has depositions illustrating the attitude of Symwa members about their Klan membership.

66. For the definitive study of this case, see Boyle, *Arc of Justice.* The discussion here owes a significant debt to Boyle's carefully researched study.

67. See Boyle, *Arc of Justice;* also see John F. Wukovits, "This Case Is Close to My Heart," *American History* (December 1998): 26–32, 66–68.

68. Jackson, *Ku Klux Klan in the City,* 142. Jackson says the Detroit Klan had ceased to exist by 1924 but kept trying to come back at various meetings in the 1930s without luck.

69. Letter is appended at end of the microfilmed manuscript Newaygo County list of members. BHL.

70. Letter dated Oct. 4, 1926, to Lucy Beardslee from La Vola M. Rice, in file "Materials Relating to Women of the Ku Klux Klan," Acc. Box 14k, Record Group 67-102-A, B-14 F2, State of Michigan Archives, Lansing.

71. Enders, "White Sheets in Mecosta," 62–64.

72. KKK files, Mecosta Co. "Organizational Correspondence" file, Jan.–June 1927, KKK Collection, Clarke, CMU.

73. Ibid.

74. Ibid.

75. Mecosta Co. "Organizational Correspondence" file, Jan.–June 1927; Undated bulletin from Carr (probably late May 1927), KKK Collection, Clarke, CMU.

76. Mecosta Co. "Organizational Correspondence" file, Jan.–June 1927; misc. correspondence, KKK Collection, Clarke, CMU.

77. Enders, "White Sheets in Mecosta," 69, 84.

78. Philip Korth, "Boom, Bust, and Bombs: The Michigan Economy, 1917–1945," in Richard J. Hathaway, ed., *Michigan: Visions of Our Past* (East Lansing: Michigan State University Press, 1989), 223.

79. Ibid.

80. Enders, "White Sheets in Mecosta," 66–68.

81. *Detroit Free Press,* Jan. 16, 1924; May 27, 1924.

82. Compiled from *Congressional Quarterly's Guide to U.S. Elections,* ed. John L. Moore, Washington, D.C.: Congressional Quarterly, 1994, in Jennifer Wolak, "Communists in Michigan During the Depression Years," Honors Thesis, 1998, Eastern Michigan University; paper in possession of the author.

83. Compiled from *Michigan Official Directory and Legislative Manual* (State of Michigan, 1929).

84. Farmington, Michigan, deed, a typical example, in possession of the author.

85. Henrickson, *Detroit Perspectives,* 367; Norman McRae, from unpublished manuscript in possession of the author.

86. Mecosta County file from Box 1 of 2 boxes, Lewis D. Capen, Biographical Materials, 1954; commemorative booklet or program for reception honoring Lewis D. Capen, Grand Master, Independent Order of Odd Fellows of Michigan, Saturday, Oct. 30, 1954, held in Armory, Big Rapids, including typed update through 1960s; Mecosta Co. "Organizational Correspondence" file, Jan.–June 1927, KKK Collection, Clarke, CMU.

Chapter 4

Epigraph: *Michigan Catholic,* March 24, 1932; Murphy speaking before 1,500 men at a Detroit district rally of the Holy Name Society, and Fine, *Frank Murphy: The Detroit Years,* 450–51.

1. Louis B. Ward, Coughlin's official biographer, writes that on August 15, 1926, Coughlin told several men in his new small parish that he planned to broadcast services from the Shrine although he reportedly first met his WJR mentor in September; Louis B. Ward, *Father Charles E. Coughlin: An Authorized Biography* (Detroit: Tower Publications, Inc., and Cambridge, Mass: Cosmos Press, 1933), 24.

2. This date is given on the "Shrine of the Little Flower Historical Timeline" and was provided to the author by archivist Jack Hoolehan. Jack Hoolehan has served as the archivist at the Shrine of the Little Flower Parish for many years.

3. *Official Directory and Legislative Manual for the State of Michigan* (also known as *Michigan Manual*), 1917–1918 (Lansing: Secretary of State, 1919), 483; *Census of Religious Bodies: 1926,* table 32, 626.

4. *Detroit News,* Aug. 28, 1923; Peter A. Soderbergh, "The Rise of Father Coughlin, 1892–1930," *Social Science* 42, no. 1 (Jan. 1967).

5. *Shrine of the Little Flower* (anniversary book) (Royal Oak: Radio League of the Little Flower, 1936), xix–xx; Donald I. Warren, *Radio Priest: Charles Coughlin, The Father of Hate Radio* (New York: Free Press, 1996), 17, citing the *Royal Oak Tribune,* Nov. 15, 1926. Some critics would later charge that this cross-burning was fabricated by Coughlin as an excuse.

6. *Michigan Catholic,* Dec. 9, 1926; Feb. 24, 1927.

7. *Michigan Catholic,* Dec. 16, 1926; April 29, 1926. The Catholic population in 1926 was 532,364; the total number of priests was 530.

8. Leslie Tentler, *Seasons of Grace: A History of the Archdiocese of Detroit* (Detroit: Wayne State University Press, 1990), emphasizes the economic necessity as Coughlin's reason for turning to broadcasting. Again, note that Ward, Coughlin's official biographer, writes that Coughlin told several men in his new small parish on August 15, 1926, that he planned to broadcast services from the Shrine; Ward, *Father Coughlin,* 24.

9. *Shrine* (anniversary book), 1936, 1; Ward, *Father Coughlin,* 27; Warren, *Radio Priest,* 21–24. Warren says the first broadcast was Oct. 17, 1926, at 2:00 p.m. Ward says it was at 3:00 p.m.—so controversy remains even over the time. But on matters of facts such as this one, Ward will be used because he was there and kept a record.

10. Typescript copy of biography of George Arthur "Dick" Richards, March 18, 1889, to May 27, 1961, BHL.

11. Jack Hoolehan's "Historical Timeline" and photo of "the Babe" in the Shrine Parish archives; article by Mary Ward, a parishioner who worked in the rectory office for Fr. Coughlin for 14 years, in the *Shrine Herald* at www.shrinechurch.com (accessed Nov. 3, 2002).

12. Ward, *Father Coughlin,* 30.

13. "Shower of Roses," vol. 1, no. 1; in Shrine Archives.

14. The Black Legion had been founded in Ohio. But when it reached its peak of 40,000 members by 1936, the largest contingent lived near or around Detroit according to Bennett, *Party of Fear,* 247.

15. PBS Video, *A Job at Ford's.*

16. Reynold M. Wik, *Henry Ford and Grass-roots America* (Ann Arbor: University of Michigan Press, 1972), 186–88; PBS Video, *A Job at Ford's.*

17. Thurner, *Strangers and Sojourners,* 230–35.

18. Thurner, *Strangers and Sojourners,* 237–39.

19. Willis F. Dunbar, *Kalamazoo and How It Grew* (Kalamazoo: Western Michigan University, 1959), 183–91.

20. Jonathan L. Marwill, *Ann Arbor,* 117–21.

21. Edsforth, *New Deal,* 128, citing Alfred P. Sloan, *My Years with General Motors* (Garden City, 1964), 446–47.

22. Edsforth, *New Deal,* 138–39.

23. Sidney Glazer, *Detroit: A Study in Urban Development* (New York: Bookman Associates, Inc., 1965), 98–99.

24. Norman McRae, "Detroit in Black and White," in Henrickson, *Detroit Perspectives,* 362; Glazer, *Detroit,* 99–100.

25. Cyril Arthur Player, "Gangsters and Politicians in Detroit: The Buckley Murder," an article reprinted from the *New Republic* (August 13, 1930), 361–63, in Henrickson, *Detroit Perspectives,* 340–44.

26. The 1922 figures are from www.wjr.net/listeningsentry.asp?ID=21190&PT=Station+Information (accessed Dec. 31, 2002). Leo Fitzpatrick Papers, 1926–1930 folder, BHL, typescript taken from *Detroit Times,* Oct. 17, 1930.

27. Miscellaneous materials in the Shrine Archives show these two broadcasts going on at least from 1929 through 1931.

28. *Father Coughlin's Radio Sermons* [sometimes, *Radio Discourses*] *Complete* (Royal Oak: Radio League of the Little Flower, ca. 1930/31–1931/32), 1930–31, 4; "Fr. Coughlin" file containing pamphlets of sermons dating from 1929, Shrine Archives.

29. *Father Coughlin's Radio Sermons Complete, 1930–1931* (Baltimore: Knox and O'Leary, 1931), 160.

30. Sermon dated Dec. 19, 1929, "Fr. Coughlin" file, Shrine Archives.

31. Sermon dated Dec. 29, 1929, "Fr. Coughlin" file, Shrine Archives; Ward, *Father Coughlin,* 38.

32. Sermon dated Jan. 12, 1930, pamphlet file, Shrine Archives; Robert S. Gallagher, "The Radio Priest," *American Heritage,* Oct. 1972, 41; Ward, *Father Coughlin,* 58; Prologue to *Father Coughlin's Radio Sermons Complete* (1930–31).

33. Radio Sermon, Dec. 15, 1929, "Fr. Coughlin" pamphlet file, Shrine Archives.

34. *New York Times,* July 26, 1930.

35. *New York Times,* July 26, 1930.

36. *New York Times,* July 26, 1930.

37. Sermon for Armistice Day, 1930, *Father Coughlin's Radio Sermons Complete, 1930–31,* 61–63.

38. Charles J. Tull, *Father Coughlin and the New Deal* (Syracuse: Syracuse University Press, 1965), 11.

39. Warren, *Radio Priest*, 96. Ward, however, does not address such a concern on the part of CBS.

40. Gallagher, "The Radio Priest," *American Heritage*, Oct. 1972, 40.

41. Bennett, *Party of Fear*, 255.

42. C. David Tompkins, *Senator Arthur H. Vandenberg: Evolution of a Modern Republican, 1884–1945* (East Lansing: Michigan State University Press, 1970), 66–67.

43. *Michigan Catholic*, Dec. 31, 1931.

44. *Father Coughlin's Radio Sermons Complete, 1930–31*, 160.

45. Fine, *Frank Murphy: The Detroit Years*, 254–55; Sidney Fine, *Frank Murphy: The New Deal Years* (Ann Arbor: University of Michigan Press, 1975), 1–2.

46. *Michigan Catholic*, March 24, 1932; Murphy speaking before 1,500 men at a Detroit district rally of the Holy Name Society; and Fine, *Frank Murphy: The Detroit Years*, 450–51.

47. *Michigan Catholic*, Feb. 18, 1932.

48. *Michigan Catholic*, Nov. 5, 1931.

49. McRae in Henrickson, *Detroit Perspectives*, 362–63; Harry Barnard, *Independent Man: The Life of Senator James Couzens* (Detroit: Wayne State University Press, 2002; originally published by Charles Scribner's Sons, 1958), 197; Vargas, *Proletarians of the North*, 172, says 250,000 were unemployed in 1931.

50. Barnard, *Independent Man*, 203, citing a letter to him from Couzens.

51. Benjamin Gitlow, *The Whole of Their Lives: Communism in America; A Personal History and Intimate Portrayal of Its Leaders* (Freeport, N.Y.: Books for Libraries Press, 1948), 278.

52. Daniel Leab, "United We Eat: The Creation and Organization of the Unemployed Councils in 1930," *Labor History* 8 (1967): 300–317.

53. PBS Video, *A Job at Ford's*; Vargas, *Proletarians of the North*, 169–200, passim.

54. Vargas, *Proletarians of the North*, 174, citing press release, March 7, 1932, in Governor Wilbur M. Brucker Papers, Box 13, BHL.

55. Vargas, *Proletarians of the North*, 181, citing correspondence between Zubrick and the U.S. Commissioner General of Immigration.

56. *Detroit Free Press*, Feb. 29, 1932.

57. *Michigan Catholic*, Feb. 25, 1932; March 10, 1932.

Chapter 5

1. *Detroit Free Press*, March 8, 1932; March 9, 1932.

2. Downriver "beer baron" Joe Tocco was one of the first to rush to the hospital bedside of the injured Harry Bennett. In the chaos of it all, no one reported on the irony that Tocco, prominent among the area's rumrunners, was a best friend of Harry Bennett whose boss and other best friend, Henry Ford, insisted that Prohibition must be continued and violators were a major threat.

3. Dead were Coleman Leny, 25 years old, of Belleville; Joseph York, home unknown; Joe DeBlasio of Detroit; and George Bussell, a 16-year-old Detroit newsboy whom the National Communist Party had selected to go to the Soviet Union in the spring to study.

4. *Detroit Free Press*, March 8, 1932; March 12, 1932.

5. "An Appeal to The Kidnapers," *Father Coughlin's Radio Sermons*, 1931–32, 224–26.

6. "Ballots—Not Bullets!" *Father Coughlin's Radio Sermons*, 1931–32, 227–39.

7. Ibid.

8. *Detroit Free Press*, May 26, 1932.

9. Tentler, *Seasons of Grace*, 319–20.

10. Keith Sward, *The Legend of Henry Ford* (New York: Rinehart, 1948), 240.

11. *Detroit Free Press*, March 5, 1932.

12. Tompkins, *Senator Arthur H. Vandenberg*, 71–73.

13. *Detroit Free Press*, June 27, 1932.

14. "Sermon for Armistice Day, 1930," *Father Coughlin's Radio Sermons*, 1930–31, 63.

15. "Christianized Democracy," *Father Coughlin's Radio Sermons*, 1930–31, 173.

16. *Father Coughlin's Radio Sermons*, 1931–32, 157–58.

17. Tull, *Coughlin and the New Deal*, 14.

18. According to Tull, he had an audience of 30,000,000.

19. The most perceptive analysis of this development is Walter Karp, *Indispensable Enemies: The Politics of Misrule in America* (New York: Saturday Review Press, 1973).

20. Tull, *Coughlin and the New Deal*, 16.

21. *Detroit Free Press*, July 2, 1932.

22. Gallagher, "Radio Priest," *American Heritage*, Oct. 1972, 100–101.

23. *Michigan Catholic*, June 30, 1932.

24. *Michigan Catholic*, July 7, 1932.

25. *Michigan Catholic*, Nov. 3, 1932.

26. *Michigan Catholic*, Sept. 29, 1932; Oct. 6, 1932.

27. *Michigan Catholic*, Oct. 6, 1932.

28. *Father Coughlin's Radio Sermons*, Oct. 30, 1932; "Radio Sermon," Nov. 13, 1932, pamphlet, Shrine Archives.

29. *Father Coughlin's Radio Sermons*, Oct. 16, 1932.

30. *Detroit Free Press*, Nov. 8, 1932; Nov. 10, 1932.

31. Compiled from *Michigan Official Directory and Legislative Manual* (State of Michigan) and *Congressional Quarterly's Guide to U.S. Elections*, ed. John L. Moore (Washington, D.C.: Congressional Quarterly, 1994).

32. Sermon, "The Human Standard—Old and New," Nov. 20, 1932, pamphlet, Shrine Archives.

33. *Michigan Catholic*, Sept. 22, 1932.

34. Letter dated April 1932 on Shrine letterhead, tucked in the back of one book recently found in a used book store, is just one example; in author's possession.

35. *Michigan Catholic*, Feb. 9, 1933.

36. *Michigan Catholic*, Feb. 23, 1933; March 2, 1933.

37. *Detroit Free Press*, March 5, 1933.

38. Russell D. Buhite and David W. Levy, eds., *FDR's Fireside Chats* (New York: Penguin Books, 1993). Note: the fireside chats as quoted here and below are from this edition; it includes the 31 speeches as the American people actually heard them over the radio, annotating changes the president made when he spoke; thus, they are slightly different versions than the official version in speeches printed in *The Public Papers and Addresses*.

39. *Detroit Free Press*, March 25, 1933.

40. *Detroit Free Press,* March 27, 29, 1933.
41. Barnard, *Independent Man,* 236–39.
42. *Detroit Free Press,* March 30, 1933.
43. *Detroit Free Press,* March 31, 1933.
44. *Detroit News,* April 1, 1933.
45. Tompkins, *Arthur S. Vandenberg,* 100.
46. Tompkins, *Arthur S. Vandenberg,* 98.
47. Farmer Labor Party Papers (Michigan), 1934–35 folder, Bentley: 851163 Bt; typescript originals, BHL.
48. *Michigan Catholic,* Nov. 8, 1934.
49. Gallagher, "Radio Priest," *American Heritage,* Oct. 1972, 102.

Chapter 6

Epigraph: Author's interview with 94-year-old Abe Rosenkranz, September 12, 2004.
1. *Detroit Free Press,* Nov. 12, 1934, quoting Coughlin's broadcast.
2. Gallagher, "Radio Priest," *American Heritage,* Oct. 1972, 102.
3. *Michigan Catholic,* Nov. 15, 1934.
4. *Michigan Catholic,* Feb. 7, 1935, citing his Sunday broadcast.
5. Farm Labor Party papers, typescript of platform of Michigan F-L Party as printed in the *Intransigent* (the party organ), Aug. 1, 1934, BHL.
6. *Michigan Catholic,* Nov. 29, 1934; Dec. 6, 1934.
7. *Michigan Catholic,* Feb. 7, 1935.
8. *Michigan Catholic,* Feb. 7, 1935.
9. *Michigan Catholic,* Dec. 20, 1934.
10. *Michigan Catholic,* Dec. 20, 1934.
11. Warren, *Radio Priest,* 63.
12. Fine, *Frank Murphy: The New Deal Years,* 220–21.
13. Ibid., 220–21, citing considerable correspondence with people within the Roosevelt administration.
14. *Detroit Free Press,* April 25, 1935.
15. Ibid.
16. *Detroit Free Press,* April 26, 1935.
17. Buhite and Levy, *FDR's Fireside Chats,* broadcast of April 28, 1935, 63–72.
18. *Detroit Free Press,* April 25, 27, 1935.
19. Sheldon Marcus, *Father Coughlin: The Tumultuous Life of the Priest of the Little Flower* (Boston: Little Brown, 1973), 95–97
20. *Time Magazine,* April 29, 1935, accessed at http://www.time.com/time/magazine/article/0,9171,754620,00.html?promoid=googlep.
21. Ibid.
22. Fine, *Frank Murphy: The New Deal Years,* 228.
23. Marcus, *Father Coughlin,* 87, citing his interview with the priest in 1970.
24. Gallagher, "Radio Priest," *American Heritage,* Oct. 1972, 103; Marcus, *Father Coughlin,* 100.
25. Broadcast on November 17, 1935, pamphlet in Shrine Archives; *Detroit Free Press,* Nov. 18, 1935.
26. *Social Justice,* April 3, 1936; all issues cited here are in the BHL.

27. *Social Justice,* March 13, 1936.

28. Miscellaneous materials, 1931, Shrine Archives.

29. Interview with Terrance Rhoades, Edgar Rhoades's great-nephew, on Aug. 9, 2007, Dexter, Michigan.

30. David H. Bennett, *Demagogues in the Depression: American Radicals and the Union Party, 1932–1936* (New Brunswick: Rutgers University Press, 1969), 96–100; *Social Justice,* May 22, 1936.

31. *Social Justice,* May 22, 1936.

32. Marcus, *Father Coughlin,* 141–42.

33. *Social Justice,* May 8, 1936.

34. *Social Justice,* May 15, 1936.

35. Edward C. Blackorby, "William Lemke: Agrarian Radical and Union Party Presidential Candidate," *Mississippi Valley Historical Review* 49, no. 1 (June 1962): 67–84.

36. *Social Justice,* June 29, 1936, states these points.

37. Gallagher, "Radio Priest," *American Heritage,* Oct. 1972, 105; Bennett, *Demagogues,* 10–13.

38. Edwin Amenta and Yvonne Zylan, "It Happened Here: Political Opportunity, the New Institutionalism, and the Townsend Movement," *American Sociological Review* 56, no. 2 (April 1991): 254, citing U.S. Congress House of Representatives 1936.

39. Warren, *Radio Priest,* 90–91.

40. Fine, *Frank Murphy: The New Deal Years,* 225–26.

41. *Social Justice,* June 29, 1936; Oct. 12, 1936.

42. Gallagher, "Radio Priest," *American Heritage,* Oct. 1972, 105.

43. *Social Justice,* Nov. 2, 1936.

44. *Social Justice.,* Oct. 12, 1936.

45. Bennett, *Demagogues,* 244–45; Tull, *Coughlin and the New Deal,* 160–63.

46. Bennett, *Demagogues,* 248–59.

47. *Michigan Catholic,* March 21, 1935.

48. *New York Times,* July 20, 1936.

49. Tentler, *Seasons of Grace,* 328.

50. Gallagher, "Radio Priest," *American Heritage,* Oct. 1972, 105.

51. Memo from Deufay B. Hovey Sr., Chair 5th District Committee, Farmer Labor Party papers, July 1936–Feb. 1937 folder, BHL.

52. Wayne County Resolution on Unity, adopted at their Nominating Convention, Aug. 8, 1936; in Farmer Labor Party papers, July 1936–Feb. 1937 folder, BHL.

53. Elmo Roper, *You and Your Leaders: Their Actions and Your Reactions, 1936–1956* (New York: William Morrow, 1957), 28.

54. Vargas, *Proletarians of the North,* 178–81.

55. *Social Justice,* Oct. 5, 1936.

56. Nelson Lichtenstein, *The Most Dangerous Man in Detroit: Walter Reuther and the Fate of American Labor* (New York: Basic Books, 1995), 61.

57. Lichtenstein, *Most Dangerous Man,* 62.

58. *Michigan Official Directory and Legislative Manual,* 1937–38, 248.

59. Samuel Lubell, *The Future of American Politics,* 2nd ed. (Garden City, N.Y.: Doubleday, 1956), 50.

60. Lichtenstein, *Most Dangerous Man,* 62; Warren, *Radio Priest,* 85.

61. Text of radio address, *New York Times*, Nov. 8, 1936.

62. Bennett, *Demagogues*, 309.

63. Correspondence cited in James P. Shenton, "The Coughlin Movement and the New Deal," *Political Science Quarterly* 73, no. 3 (Sept. 1958): 352–73.

64. Abe Rosenkranz, conversation with the author on March 12, 2004; he was then 94.

65. *Social Justice*, Dec. 21, 1936; Jan. 18, 1937.

66. Broadcast of Jan. 24, 1937, reprinted in *Social Justice*, Feb. 1, 1937.

67. *Social Justice*, May 10, 1937.

68. *Social Justice*, Jan. 18, 1937; April 5, 1937; May 3, 1937.

69. *Social Justice*, Sept. 13, 1937.

70. Tentler, *Seasons of Grace*, 333–34.

71. Marcus, *Father Coughlin*, 144–45, 154.

72. *New York Times*, April 1, 1938; Tull, *Coughlin and the New Deal*, 187.

73. *Social Justice*, July 11, 1938.

74. *Social Justice*, May 24, 1937.

75. *Social Justice*, June 28, 1937; June 21 1937; July 5, 1937.

76. Tentler, *Seasons of Grace*, 334–36.

77. Marcus, *Father Coughlin*, 148–59; Tull, *Coughlin and the New Deal*, 195–96; Gallagher, "Radio Priest," *American Heritage*, Oct. 1972, 107.

78. Deed, Farmington, Michigan, in author's possession.

79. Warren, *Radio Priest*, 151–65.

80. *Social Justice*, March 26, 1939.

81. *Congressional Record* 86:11142, cited in Philip A. Grant Jr., "The Michigan Congressional Delegation and the Burke-Wadsworth Act of 1940," *Michigan Historical Review* 18 (Spring 1992): 78–79.

82. Christopher H. Johnson, *Maurice Sugar: Law, Labor, and the Left in Detroit, 1912–1950* (Detroit: Wayne State University Press), 260.

83. Philip D. Schertzing, "Against All Enemies and Opponents Whatever, The Michigan State Police Crusade Against the 'Un-Americans,' 1917–1977" (PhD diss., Michigan State University, 1999), 280–83, citing Luren D. Dickinson to Philip Slomovitz, June 20, 1940, Reel 49, Alien Registration Files, Executive Office Records, Gov. Luren Dickinson, State Archives, Lansing. Schertzing was a Michigan State Police command officer and FBI National Academy graduate. He enlisted in 1977 and, by the time he was writing this dissertation, had unusual access to published and personal sources.

84. Schertzing, "Against All Enemies," 281; citing Combat 5th Column, *Detroit Times*, May 31, 1940.

85. *Detroit News*, Sept. 4, 1940, cited in Schertzing, "Against All Enemies," 281; also citing *Detroit News*, Feb. 7, 1941.

86. Maurice Sugar, *The Ford Hunger March* (Berkeley: Meiklejohn Civil Liberties Institute, ca. 1980), 261.

87. *Social Justice*, Sept. 23, 1939; Marcus, *Father Coughlin*, 176–77.

88. Tentler, *Seasons of Grace*, 338–40.

89. Author's interview with Maureen DesRoches, April 12, 2008. Bernard DesRoches also never forgot his grade-school field trip to see *Birth of a Nation* when the movie first played in the Upper Peninsula.

Chapter 7

1. These words came out of the mouth of wartime's beloved "Rosie the Riveter," her hair tied up in a red bandanna and sleeve rolled up to show her muscle. The poster "Rosie" was based on a sketch drawn from memory by the artist who saw her working on the line in a Michigan defense factory.

2. Johnson, *Maurice Sugar,* 264.

3. Edward C. Pintzuk, *Reds, Racial Justice, and Civil Liberties: Michigan Communists during the Cold War* (Minneapolis: MEP Publications, 1997), 72. Pintzuk, a long-time activist in Detroit left-wing circles, bases this book on research included in his PhD dissertation in history at Wayne State University. He has been able to draw upon extensive private papers, oral histories, and documents not otherwise available in archived collections.

4. Pintzuk, *Reds,* 38.

5. Schertzing, "Against All Enemies," 281–87.

6. Tentler, *Seasons of Grace,* 341.

7. Richard Grudens, "Henry Ford: Helped Lead American World War II Production Efforts," accessed at www.historynet.com.

8. Gerald L. K. Smith Papers, Box 1, Subseries: Radio Speeches; these speeches offer clear evidence of his themes, attitudes, and his approach to the election. Also in Box 1, see memos, drafts, and materials for the *Cross and the Flag.* BHL.

9. Jonathan Cutler, *Labor's Time* (Philadelphia: Temple University Press, 2004), 34, citing *New York Times,* Feb. 6, 1948, and article in the *Militant,* Feb. 16, 1948. Also, Box 1, File 24, Michigan Struggle for Trade Union Unity, Ganley-Wellman Collection, Archives of Labor and Urban Affairs, Walter P. Reuther Library, Wayne State University, Detroit, Michigan (hereafter ALUA). In the *Worker* of July 7, 1949, Nat Ganley charges that Reuther has "a long trail of broken promises." And the "Reuther record shows company-unionism at work covered with a light coating of 'liberal' phrases."

10. Harold L. Hitchens, "Influences on the Congressional Decision to Pass the Marshall Plan," *Western Political Quarterly* 21 (March 1968): 51–54; *New York Times,* April 4, 1948, accessed at www.mtholyoke.edu.

11. Pintzuk, *Reds,* 15.

12. Schertzing, "Against All Enemies," 290. This is a central point in Schertzing's study.

13. Pintzuk, *Reds,* 38; Schertzing, "Against All Enemies," 303–5.

14. Pintzuk, *Reds,* 22; Alan D. Harper, *The Politics of Loyalty: The White House and the Communist Issue, 1946–1952* (Westport, Conn.: Greenwood Press, 1969), 149.

15. Johnson, *Maurice Sugar,* 264.

16. Lichtenstein, *Most Dangerous Man,* 187–89.

17. Pintzuk, *Reds,* 32–33; Lichtenstein, *Most Dangerous Man,* 248.

18. Sidney Fine, *Expanding the Frontiers of Civil Rights* (Detroit: Wayne State University Press, 2002), 24–25; Doris B. McLaughlin, "Michigan Labor in Politics," in Alan S. Brown, John T. Houdek, and John H. Yzenbaard, *Michigan Perspectives: People, Events, and Issues* (Dubuque, Iowa: Kendall/Hunt, 1974), 261–64.

19. See Cutler, *Labor's Time,* chap. 1, for a perceptive discussion of Reuther's explanation about his revised position on the workweek; also see Pintzuk, *Reds,* 13, 29–32, 166.

20. Thurner, *Strangers and Sojourners,* 274–80.

21. Ganley-Wellman Collection, Box 1, File 5, "Communist Party: Appearances/

correspondence with government and other organizations"; Box 1, File 15, "Michigan Activities, 1945–59, with posters, cards, fliers pertaining to the Party meetings"; Box 19, "Michigan in post-WWII years, 1950–53," ALUA; Pintzuk, *Reds,* 22–25; *Detroit Free Press,* Feb. 14, 1952.

22. Ganley-Wellman Collection, Box 3, File 14, "Michigan School of Social Science; bulletins, 1948–50," ALUA; Pintzuk, *Reds,* 22–25; *Detroit Free Press,* Feb. 14, 1952. At the rate of $2 a class, the school did indeed teach Marxism-Leninism and one class in the "History of the American Labor Movement."

23. *Detroit Free Press,* Feb. 12, 13, 14, 15, 1952.

24. Schertzing, "Against All Enemies," 303–6; Lichtenstein, *Most Dangerous Man,* 317.

25. Albert Fried, *FDR and His Enemies* (New York: St. Martin's Press, 1999; all citations here and elsewhere are to the 2001 edition), 68–69; *Detroit Free Press,* Feb. 15, 1952, columnist Malcom Bingay reporting on a telephone complaint he had received from a Michigan old guard stalwart.

26. *New York Times,* Nov. 6, 1952, at http://proquest.umi.com.

27. Fried, *FDR and His Enemies,* 241, 245; *Detroit Free Press,* Oct. 1, 3, 8, 20, 26, 27; Nov. 1, 2, 6, 1952.

28. *State of Michigan, Official Directory and Legislative Manual 1953–1954.*

29. "Milton Berle Took Back Seat to Bishop Sheen," reprinted from the *Peoria (Ill.) Journal Star,* Sept. 18, 1989, www.elpaso.net.

30. www.metrolyrics.com/lyrics/98448/Chad_Mitchell_Trio/.

Chapter 8

1. Stephen Earl Bennett, "Modes of Resolution of a 'Belief Dilemma' in the Ideology of the John Birch Society," *Journal of Politics* 33, no. 3 (Aug. 1971): 735–72.

2. J. Alan Broyles, *The John Birch Society: Anatomy of a Protest* (Boston: Beacon Press, 1964), 8, citing Robert Welch, *The Politician* (Belmont: Robert Welch, 1963), 276–77.

3. Broyles, *John Birch Society;* Robert Welch, *The Life of John Birch* (Chicago: Regnery, 1954); *Detroit Free Press,* Aug. 12, 1962.

4. Robert Welch, *Blue Book* (Belmont, Mass.: Robert Welch, Dec. 9, 1959), 44.

5. *Grosse Pointe News,* April 14, 1960.

6. Author's interview with 1960s Grosse Pointe community activist Helen Graves, March 11, 2005.

7. Papers of the 14th Congressional District Republican Committee, 1958, Box 3, file, "Conventions, District, Miscellaneous," BHL.

8. Steve Meyer, "An Economic 'Frankenstein': UAW Workers' Responses to Automation at the Ford Brook Plant in the 1950s," *Michigan Historical Review* 28, no. 1 (Spring 2002): 69; G. Mennen Williams, weekly newsletter of Jan. 22, 1958, printed in the *Grosse Pointe News,* Jan. 23, 1958.

9. Papers of the 14th Congressional District Republican Committee, 1958, Box 3, file, "Conventions, District, Miscellaneous," BHL.

10. *Detroit Free Press,* Aug. 12, 1962.

11. Richard C. Van Dusen Papers, Box 7, file 1, "Political Lawsuits, Kelly *v.* Van Dusen (1962)," BHL; *Detroit Free Press,* Aug. 16, 1962; Broyles, *John Birch Society,* 2.

12. *Blue Book,* 1959 ed., 22–23.

13. Barbara S. Stone, "The John Birch Society: A Profile," *Journal of Politics* 36, no. 1 (Feb. 1974): 184–97.

14. Van Dusen Papers, Box 7, clippings file, Holliday article in Detroit Free Press, Aug. 15, 1962, BHL.

15. *Blue Book,* 1958 ed., 44.

16. Van Dusen Papers, Box 7, clippings file, Holliday article in *Detroit Free Press,* Aug. 12, 1962, BHL.

17. Van Dusen Papers, Box 7, clippings file, Holliday article in *Detroit Free Press,* Aug.13, 1962, BHL.

18. Van Dusen Papers, Box 7, clippings file, Holliday article in *Detroit Free Press,* Aug. 15, 1962, BHL.

19. *Blue Book,* 1961 ed., 16.

20. Although Welch generally succeeded in keeping rank-and-file membership lists private, social scientists pieced together data from a variety of sources including the 1964 American National Election Study in an effort to assess, describe, and categorize the people who joined. See Clyde Wilcox, "Sources of Support for the Old Right: A Comparison of the John Birch Society and the Christian Anti-Communist Crusade," *Social Science History* 12, no. 4 (Winter 1988). Theodore Adorno's influential study identified an "authoritarian personality" and argued that this personality "disorder" explained a person's fascist ideology rather than his class status. Following on Adorno's lead, some analyzed Birch members as rigid people who were psychologically fearful and in need of asserting control over others. Daniel Bell's *End of Ideology* (1960) argued they belonged among others on the right who were most threatened by changes in American social structures over the previous 30 years; they suffered "status anxieties" of an "unusual intensity." See Kendrick Oliver, "'Post-Industrial Society' and the Psychology of the American Right, 1950–74," *Journal of Contemporary History* 34, no. 4 (Oct. 1999). Birchers were variously characterized as undereducated, lower-status, or status seekers. It was said that the membership did not overlap with the Christian Anti-Communist Crusade and that Birchers were both more active in politics and felt more efficacious than other whites. One political scientist gained Birch Society cooperation to select a 50-person California sample that was, as she described it, "at least haphazard if not random." From this data she argued that a majority were not conservative according to the measures used by Herbert McClosky and other scholars who had maintained conservatism and radicalism are two distinct phenomena, not just on a spectrum and sliding into each other. Rather, they agreed with positions that must be categorized as liberal. See Barbara S. Stone, "The John Birch Society: A Profile," *Journal of Politics* 36 (Feb. 1974). From a separate Birch-selected sample of national membership in 1965 that resulted in 650 completed questionnaires, political scientist Fred W. Grupp concluded that nearly two-thirds of the members joined for ideological reason, far more than the number who joined to associate with like-minded people or to become better informed. Fred W. Grupp Jr., "Personal Satisfaction Derived from Membership in the John Birch Society," *Western Political Quarterly* 24 (March 1971).

21. Van Dusen Papers, Box 7, clippings file, Holliday article in *Detroit Free Press,* Aug. 12, 1962, BHL.

22. Cited in caselaw.lp.findlaw.com/getcase; *Shelley v. Kraemer,* 334 U.S. 1 (1948), *McGhee v. Sipes,* Nos. 72, 87.

23. Clark R. Mollenhoff, *George Romney: Mormon in Politics* (New York: Meredith

Press, 1968), 164–66; T. George Harris, *Romney's Way* (Englewood Cliffs, N.J.: Prentice-Hall, 1967), 214–15; George Romney Papers, Box 9E, "June 1960–January 1961"; Box 10E, "February–September, 1961"; Box 14E, "Citizens for Michigan," BHL.

24. Papers, 14th Congressional District Republican Party, Box 3, file, "1960 Convention, District, April," typescript document entitled "Platform Resolutions, Fourteenth Congressional District of Michigan . . . April 20, 1960," BHL.

25. Ibid.

26. Doris B. McLaughlin, "Michigan Labor in Politics," in Alan S. Brown, John T. Houdek, and John H. Yzenbaard, *Michigan Perspectives: People, Events, and Issues* (Dubuque, Iowa: Kendall/Hunt, 1974), 269.

27. Broyles, *John Birch Society,* 39, citing *Blue Book,* 119 (probably 2nd ed.).

28. *Grosse Pointe News,* July 28, 1960.

29. *Grosse Pointe News,* Aug. 11, 1960.

30. Van Dusen Papers, Box 7, clippings file, Holliday article in *Detroit Free Press,* Aug. 16, 1962. BHL.

31. *New York Times,* Jan. 28, 1962.

32. *New York Times,* Feb. 14, 1962.

33. *Grosse Pointe News,* Aug. 2, 1962.

34. Author's interview with Helen Graves, March 11, 2005.

35. *Grosse Pointe News,* Aug. 2, 1962.

36. *Grosse Pointe News,* Aug 2, 16, 23, 1962.

37. *Grosse Pointe News,* Aug. 23, 1962.

38. Van Dusen Papers, Box 7, "Political Lawsuits file, Kelly *v.* Van Dusen (1962)," BHL; *New York Times,* Dec. 30, 1966.

39. Van Dusen Papers, Richard Campbell Collection, Box 7, "Political Lawsuits file, Kelly *v.* Van Dusen (1962)," BHL.

40. *Grosse Pointe News,* Aug. 30, 1962.

41. Mollenhoff, *George Romney,* 185–87.

42. Ibid., 193–95; *New York Times,* April 3, 1963.

43. Ibid., 203; *New York Times,* June 30, 1963.

44. *New York Times,* June 24, 1963.

45. Benjamin R. Epstein and Arnold Forster, *Report on the John Birch Society* (New York: Random House, 1966), 24, citing a Welch television interview. Epstein and Forster were two of the ADL's top executives who did this report upon the ADL decision that the situation of the radical Right had become serious enough to "warrant full exposure."

46. Thomas J. Sugrue, "Crabgrass-Roots Politics: Race, Rights, and the Reaction against Liberalism in the Urban North, 1940–1964," *Journal of American History* 82, no. 2 (Sept. 1995): 572–76, citing various letters and sources.

47. Mollenhoff, *George Romney,* 204.

48. Papers, 14th Congressional District Republican Committee, Box 4, file, "Chronological District, Delegates, Miscellaneous," BHL.

49. Mollenhoff, *George Romney,* 206.

50. Ibid., 219.

51. *Michigan Manual,* 1965–66, 450–51. Goldwater won in Ottawa, Sanilac, and Missaukee counties.

52. Richard Scammon, ed., *America Votes: A Handbook of Contemporary Election Statistics,* vol. 6 (Washington, D.C.: Congressional Quarterly, 1966), 192.

53. Epstein and Forster, *Report,* 69.

54. Ibid., 49, 66, 9.

55. Ibid., 18.

56. Ibid., 22–23; Stephen Earl Bennett, "Modes of Resolution of a 'Belief Dilemma' in the Ideology of the John Birch Society," *Journal of Politics* 33, no. 3 (Aug. 1971): 763–64, citing *Bulletin of the John Birch Society,* June 1966, 24.

57. Van Dusen Papers, Box 7, clippings file, Holliday article in *Detroit Free Press,* Aug. 12, 1962, BHL; Broyles, *John Birch Society,* 48–55.

58. Epstein and Forster, *Report,* 21.

59. Ibid., 72, 73.

60. Van Dusen Papers, Box 7, "Political Lawsuits" file, *Durant v. Stahlin et al.,* 1962. BHL.

61. Epstein and Forster, *Report,* 84.

62. The most comprehensive, well-documented accounts of racial tension in the years from World War II leading up to 1967 and of that civil disturbance itself are Thomas J. Sugrue, *The Origins of the Urban Crisis: Race and Inequality in Postwar Detroit* (Princeton: Princeton University Press, 1996); and Sidney Fine, *Violence in the Model City: The Cavanagh Administration, Race Relations, and the Detroit Riot of 1967* (Ann Arbor: University of Michigan Press, 1989).

63. Mollenhoff, *George Romney,* 286.

64. Schertzing, "Against All Enemies," 330.

65. Mollenhoff, *George Romney,* 292–93.

66. *New York Times,* March 10, 1968.

67. Given the timing, this was a much discussed phrase after Humphrey used it in his speech declaring his candidacy for the presidential nomination, April 27, 1968. In context: "And here we are . . . the way politics ought to be in America, the politics of happiness, politics of purpose, politics of joy; and that's the way it's going to be, all the way, too, from here on out." www.4president.org/speeches/hhh1968announcement.htm (accessed Aug. 15, 2005).

68. http://uselectionatlas.org (accessed July 16, 2005).

69. Melvin Small, "Otto Feinstein, the McCarthy Campaign in Michigan, and Campus Activism during the Cold War," in Charles W. Calhoun, ed., *The Human Tradition in America: 1965 to the Present* (Wilmington, Del.: Scholarly Resources Press, 2003).

70. Schertzing, "Against All Enemies," 338; also see Sidney Fine, *Violence in the Model City.*

71. Jon Lauck, "The National Farmers Organization," *Michigan Historical Review* 24, no. 2 (Fall 1998): 97, 124.

72. McLaughlin, "Michigan Labor in Politics," in Brown and Houdek et al., *Michigan Perspectives,* 264–71.

Chapter 9

1. Author's phone interview with Michigan-Ohio Birch Society coordinator, April 1, 2005; name withheld by his request.

2. "Irene McCabe and Her Battle Against Busing," *Detroit News* Rearview site, http://info.detnews.com/history/story/index.cfm?id=161&category=people (accessed Sept. 7, 2007).

3. *New York Times,* May 29, Sept. 9, 10, 1971.

4. "Irene McCabe and Her Battle Against Busing," *Detroit News* Rearview site, http://info.detnews.com/history/story/index.cfm?id=161&category=people (accessed Sept. 7, 2007).

5. *New York Times*, Sept. 10, 1971; *Detroit Free Press*, Nov. 5, 2004.

6. *New York Times*, Oct. 18, 1971.

7. *New York Times*, Oct. 18, 1971.

8. *New York Times*, April 3, 1971.

9. *New York Times*, Sept. 11, 1971.

10. David Riddle, "HUD and the Open Housing Controversy of 1970 in Warren, Michigan," *Michigan Historical Review* 24, no. 2 (Fall 1998): 21–29.

11. Papers of the 14th Congressional District Republican Committee, Box 6, file, "Miscellaneous Material," BHL.

12. Riddle, "HUD and Open Housing," 31.

13. Author's experiences as a Pleasant Ridge resident in those years; *New York Times*, Dec. 15, 1989.

14. *Detroit Free Press*, April 8, 1963; *Saginaw News*, Feb. 18, 1963, in Genevieve Gillette Collection, Box 9, file, "Clippings," BHL.

15. *Saginaw News*, Feb. 18, 1962, in Gillette Collection, Box 9, file, "Clippings," BHL.

16. Brian C. Kalt, *The Fight over Establishment of a Sleeping Bear Dunes National Park, 1961–1970* (East Lansing: Michigan State University Press, 2001), 38–39, citing Romney Papers, Box 46, 1963, BHL.

17. *Washington Post*, Feb. 23, 1965.

18. Author's interviews and talks with residents of Leelanau County, 1999–2005, when the last of the 25-year leases were ending and people were forced to move from the national park, and ongoing interviews over the years with Carolyn Bumgardner, the last resident finally forced to leave in November 2007.

19. http://www.freepress.org/departments/display/20/2006/1844 (accessed Jan. 18, 2008).

20. See Jeanie Wylie, *Poletown Betrayed* (Urbana: University of Illinois Press, 1989), for a carefully detailed, well researched, if sympathetic, study. Several brief summaries are available including http://info.detnews.com/history/story/index.cfm?id=18&category=business.

21. This use of eminent domain was confirmed in *Kelo v. City of New London* (Conn.) in 2005.

22. *Michigan Manual, 1973–1974*, 121; Dave Leip's *Atlas of U.S. Presidential Elections*, accessed at www.uselectionatlas.org.

23. Papers of the 14th Congressional District Republican Committee, Box 6, file, "Position Papers," BHL.

24. *New York Times*, May 7, 1972.

25. *New York Times*, July 11, 1978.

26. Accessed at http://www.manufacturingcentral.org/s_nam/doc1.asp?CID=202103&DID=232083; after serving for a time in the Bush administration, Engler became president of the National Association of Manufacturers.

27. The top fifth of Michigan families accounted for 44 percent of the total income by 1995, while families from the middle to bottom ranks experienced an actual dollar loss in income. The gulf was increasing faster in Michigan than in all but ten states. See www.michiganbrief.org/text/appendix; calculated by Public Sector Consultants, Inc. (accessed Jan. 10, 2001).

28. Bureau of National Affairs 2000 Union Membership and Earnings Data Book; www.state.mi./us/medc/databook, Jan. 10, 2001; *Detroit Free Press* (accessed March 6, 2001).

29. Employment increased 12.5 percent from 1992 to 1997, according to the Michigan Dept. of Career Development; www.state.mi.us/medc/databook (accessed Jan. 10, 2001).

30. "Trade Liberalization: The North American Free Trade Agreement's Economic Impact on Michigan," Part IV, posted Dec. 20, 1999, at www.mackinac.org/ (accessed Jan. 8, 2001); also *Detroit News,* Dec. 19, 1999.

31. Between 70 and 80 percent; www.citizen.org/pctrade/nafta/reports/MIF.htm (accessed Dec. 17, 2000).

32. Michigan Department of Career Development, www.state.mi.us/medc/data book (accessed Jan. 10, 2001).

33. By the early 1990s 15 percent of working adults were without health benefits; in addition, in 1997, 20 percent, twice as many as ten years before, said they could not afford to contribute to their employer's health plan. *Detroit Free Press,* March 7, 2001.

34. U.S. Census Bureau; http://comnet.org/local/orgs.

35. *Detroit Free Press,* Aug. 17. 1992; figures calculated from 1990 census data.

36. www.michiganinbrief.org/text/issues (accessed Jan. 10, 2001).

37. www.michiganfarmbureau.com/publications/farmnews/mfn101598/live (accessed Jan. 10, 2001).

38. www.michiganinbrief.org/text/issues (accessed Jan. 10, 2001); *Leelanau Enterprise,* March 1, 2001.

39. *New American,* Jan. 24, 2005, 1, 44.

40. Center for Media and Democracy, accessed at www.prwatch.org.

41. Author's phone interview with Birch Society coordinator, April 1, 2005.

42. John McManus, address in Centerline, Michigan, April 11, 2005; from author's notes on that talk.

43. Author's phone interview with Birch Society coordinator, April 1, 2005.

Chapter 10

Epigraph: Norm Olson in e-mail to JoEllen Vinyard, March 28, 2000.

1. *New York Times,* Nov. 14, 1994.

2. *Detroit News,* Jan. 31, 1996.

3. The "unseen army" quote comes from the *Detroit Free Press,* Feb. 19, 1997.

4. "Frequently Asked Questions of the Michigan Militia Corps—Wolverines, Version 1.0" at http://militia.gen.mi.us/faq3.html (accessed Dec. 9, 1998) (site no longer operating). The original author was probably Norm Olson, but the "FAQ" appeared in several versions, depending on the brigade and leadership.

5. The *Los Angeles Times,* Oct. 22, 2000, reported that one million people in Michigan hold hunting licenses.

6. Telephone interview with Rick Haynes, March 26, 2008. This account of the background and the BATF's role is covered in Randy Weaver's book, *The Federal Siege at Ruby Ridge.*

7. Morris Dees of the Southern Poverty Law Center dates the modern antigovernment movement from Ruby Ridge because the tragedy brought 160 leaders from

various causes on the right together in October 22, 1992, at the Rocky Mountain Rendezvous. There, he maintains, they laid plans for a common front. Discussed in Joel Dyer, *Harvest of Rage* (Boulder, Colo.: Westview Press, 1998), 81–82; 83, citing *Boulder Weekly* 3, no. 31 (April 4, 1996): 12.

8. *New York Times*, April 17, 1994.

9. From a statement purportedly written by Kahl, probably on February 14, 1983, when he went into hiding after a shoot-out with police; given in its entirety at http://www.outpostof freedom.com (accessed Nov. 25, 2005); site not available but others have same accounts—for example, www.constitution.org; Catherine McNichol, *Stock, Rural Radicals: Righteous Rage in the American Grain* (Ithaca: Cornell University Press, 1996), 156–57.

10. James Coates, *Armed and Dangerous: The Rise of the Survivalist Right* (New York: Hill and Wang, 1987), 108–9; Neil Hamilton, *Militias in America: A Reference Handbook* (Santa Barbara, Calif.: ABC-CLIO, 1996), 24.

11. *New York Times*, Nov. 14, 1994; and "Dubious Charges Raise Questions About Klanwatch Credibility," in *New American*, Feb. 6, 1995. Southwell was identified as the information officer in the *New York Times* article.

12. E-mail from Norman Olson to the author, March 28, 2000.

13. The personal files of Joseph Pilchak and Rick Haynes have Birch literature. Joe Pilchak made a number of tapes, records, and files available to my graduate student, John Mayernik, and offered valuable insight in their taped interviews. This material, now in possession of the author, is cited hereafter as Pilchak Papers.

14. Author's phone interview with Birch coordinator, Ohio-Michigan District, April 1, 2005.

15. This is from "In Defense of Liberty II"; in some version, it is on almost every website and link and in the manuals.

16. Miscellaneous materials; xerox is from an unnamed magazine dated July/August 1999. Other articles in the magazine were "On Family Farm Foreclosures," "On the Lindbergh Kidnapping," and "On War." These are from Rick Haynes's personal archive in his house. Haynes was regarded as the historian or archivist by his compatriots. The many papers, faxes, minutes, letters, and other miscellaneous papers about the Michigan Militia that were so generously provided to the author by Rick Haynes are cited hereafter as Haynes Papers; most are also now in the possession of the author.

17. Van Huizen website at http://militia.gen.mi.us/commander.html (accessed Nov. 23, 1998). Site no longer available.

18. Transcript of Jim Lehrer's program "Hanging Tough," aired April 3, 1997; www.pbs.org/newshour/bb/law/april97/militia (accessed Dec. 29, 2000).

19. Author's interview with Tom Wayne at his home in Bronson, Michigan, Jan. 21, 1999.

20. Ibid.

21. *Detroit News*, April 15, 1996.

22. Desiree Cooper, "Who Is Mark of Michigan?" *Metro Times*, April 26, 1995, http://www.metrotimes.com/archives/militia/003.html (accessed Jan. 23, 2008).

23. Formed in the early 1990s, this group remained always on the fringe of the more organized, umbrella efforts.

24. Source unclear but may be from Van Huizen and/or Steve Bridges; fax dated April [?] 10, 1998; Haynes Papers.

25. Hamilton, *Militias in America*, 35.

26. Author's interview with Rick Haynes at his home in Leslie, Michigan, May 14, 2008.

27. Fax dated Jan. 19, 1998; Haynes Papers.

28. Author's interview with anonymous source at home of Rick Haynes in Holt, Michigan, March 21, 2000.

29. Letter from Paul Stephen Reiber dated July 5, 1994, sent to 41 organizations asking them to send back issues or information he could distribute; Haynes Papers.

30. See Matthew Zook, "The Unorganized Militia Network," *Berkeley Planning Journal*, vol. 11, 1996.

31. Mrs. Steve Davidson was identified as a Wolverine brigade commander in March 1998 in Haynes Papers, Memo to All Division and Brigade Commanders and Militia Members from Joe Pilchak, March 19, 1998. Joy Gerow was (in Jan. 1998) a colonel and Seventh Division Commander according to Memo from Joy Gerow to Michigan Militia Corps–Wolverines, dated Jan. 31, 1998; Haynes Papers.

32. www.michiganmilitia.com/SMVM (accessed Dec. 6, 2005; Feb. 4, 2006).

33. Letter from Rick Haynes to Tim Baron, Classic Rock 94.9, Lansing; no date; probably late July 1995; Haynes Papers.

34. Memo headed "To all members and friends of the Michigan Militia Corps—Wolverines," date: 17 March 1998, from: Joe and Clara Pilchak; Pilchak Papers.

35. Memo, TO: All Militia, FROM: Michigan Militia Corps HQ/CC, Alanson Armory & Mi Militia HQ, fax dated Dec. 6, 1994, 10:29 am; Haynes Papers.

36. Memo, TO: All militia; From: Michigan Militia Corps HQ/CC, fax dated Dec. 9, 1994, 1:03 PM; Haynes Papers.

37. Memo to Captain Paul S. Reiber from Major Steven S. Tyner, Commander, Sept. 28, 1994; Haynes Papers.

38. Memo dated 30SEP94/1400HRS from HDQSMICMICOR. Haynes Papers.

39. Fax dated Jan. 19, 1998; Haynes Papers.

40. *New York Times*, April 24, 1995.

41. E-mail from Norman Olson to the author, March 28, 2000.

42. Mark S. Hamm, *Apocalypse in Oklahoma* (Boston: Northeastern University Press, 1997), 221–22.

43. This division commander is not identified by name in the memo but other materials indicate that Tom Wayne was in that position at the time.

44. Fax dated April 29, 1995, 15:12 from CMRM WEST COMMAND HQ; Haynes Papers.

45. Hamm, *Apocalypse in Oklahoma*, 218–19.

46. Copy of the Olson-Southwell press release in the form of a fax to Paul Reiber from Faith Johnson of the *Lansing State Journal* on 5/4/95; Haynes Papers. Note, apparently the *Lansing State Journal* reporter was faxing material to Reiber and maybe to others in the Militia as well.

47. *New York Times*, April 27, 1995.

48. *New York Times*, May 6, 1995, reprinting the president's speech of May 5.

49. Michael Barkun, *Religion and the Racist Right* (Chapel Hill: University of North Carolina Press, 1997), 256; see also chap. 8; Rick Haynes made this same point when talking with the author.

50. *Monroe Evening News*, April 26, 1995.

51. *Detroit News*, Dec. 14, 1997.

52. *New York Times*, May 1, 1995.

53. Official Minutes, Michigan Militia Corps Meeting, June 11, 1995, Winn, Michigan, faxed from CMRM West Command HQ, June 13, 1995; Haynes Papers.

54. Official Minutes, Michigan Militia Corps Meeting, June 11, 1995, Winn, Michigan, faxed from CMRM West Command HQ June 13, 1995; Memo dated 13 June 1995, To: All Wolverines, signed by Lynn Jon Van Huizen; Haynes Papers.

55. "The Militia Movement in the United States," Senate Hearing 104-804, June 15, 1995, *104th Congress. U.S. Senate Judiciary Committee on Terrorism, Technology and Government Information* (Washington, D.C.: Government Printing Office, 1997); *Monroe Evening News,* June 15, 1995.

56. "The Militia Movement in the United States," Senate Hearing 104-804, June 15, 1995, *104th Congress. U.S. Senate Judiciary Committee on Terrorism, Technology and Government Information* (Washington, D.C.: Government Printing Office, 1997); *Monroe Evening News,* June 15, 1995.

57. Fax dated July 5, 1998, From: Norman Olson, To: Lynn Van Huizen, Interim State Commander. Haynes Papers.

58. News Release from Norm Olson, July 19,1995; faxed copy of July 19, 1995, release sent from CMRM West Command HQ; Haynes Papers.

59. Faxed message from "Alanson Armory & MI Militia HQ," Dec. 6, 1994. Haynes Papers.

60. *New American,* Feb. 6, 1995 and http://www.deeswatch.com/childish.htm (accessed Oct. 19, 2000). Also see http://mifindacase.com (accessed Dec. 15, 2010).

61. *Monroe Evening News,* July 10, 1995, probably citing *Traverse City Record Eagle.*

62. Article by Jeremy Steele, *State News,* reprinted in the Calvin College *Chimes,* May 5, 2001, http://clubs.calvin.edu/chimes/2001.05.04/community/story02.shtml (accessed Jan. 4, 2008).

63. Memo from Thomas R. Wayne to All Brigades, dated November 9, 1995, fax from Wolverine Command HQ dated Nov. 9, 1995; Haynes Papers.

64. News release from Norm Olson, dated July 19, 1995; Haynes Papers.

65. See "A Cause by Any Other Name," an account of the early years of development written by one member and posted on the Lawful Path website at http://www.lawfulpath.com/ref/causnam.shtml (accessed March 13, 2008).

66. *Detroit Free Press,* March 26, 1997.

67. Barkun, *Religion and the Racist Right,* 276, citing *Washington Post,* May 15, 1995; May 18, 1995; and *USA Today,* May 16, 1995.

68. Tom Wayne gives the number of members and sympathizers as probably 10,000 on a Channel 3 news interview, reported April 20, 2000; Clint Dare and Rick Haynes give the total as 14,000 to 25,000. Insiders were probably exaggerating the numbers, but federal and state agents as well as watchdog organizations seemed to offer confirmation by their preoccupation with what they regarded as a growing threat.

Chapter 11

Epigraph: http://www.michiganmilitia.com/SMVM/smvm.htm (accessed March 13, 2008); the Southeast Michigan Volunteer Militia, formerly under the name of the Wayne County Militia, remains one of the most long-lasting and consistent of the groups and website.

1. Michigan Militia Corps Wolverines, Commander 8th Division letterhead, signed by Rick Haynes; Haynes Papers.

2. www.michiganmilitia.com; posted sometime in November 2005 and accessed Dec. 6, 2005.

3. Author's interview with Tom Wayne at his home in Bronson, Michigan, Jan. 21, 1999.

4. James William Gibson, *Warrior Dreams: Paramilitary Culture in Post-Vietnam America* (New York: Hill and Wang, 1994); James Coates, *Armed and Dangerous: The Rise of the Survivalist Right* (New York: Hill and Wang, 1987), passim.

5. Coates, *Armed and Dangerous,* 82–85; 236–39.

6. Coates, *Armed and Dangerous,* 48–49.

7. See previous discussion of Miles in chap. 9.

8. Barkun, *Religion and the Racist Right,* 256; Coates, *Armed and Dangerous,* 250–58.

9. "In Defense of Liberty II."

10. *Detroit News,* July 14, 2003; http://infoweb.newsbank.com.ezproxy.emich.edu/iw-search/we/InfoWeb?p_product=NewsBank (accessed Feb. 28, 2008).

11. "In Defense of Liberty II." The many points (33 by 2007) in this statement of Militia intent and purpose are generally consistent through its several versions from the time of Norm Olson onward. This particular position remained on the Michigan Militia.com website at http://www.michiganmilitia.com/literature/in_defense_of_lib erty.htm (accessed June 7, 2008).

12. Port Huron, Michigan, *Times Herald,* March 30, 1997.

13. Port Huron, Michigan, *Times Herald,* March 30, 1997.

14. Memo to: MMC Wolverine State Command, from: Colonel Stephen M. Bridges, Commanding 8th Division, date: probably Jan. 31, 1998; Pilchak Papers.

15. National Confederation of Citizen Militias News Release, June 5, 1995; Haynes Papers.

16. Michigan Militia Corps "Wolverines" Manual 1-1 (revised manual after Olson's resignation, based on Winn meeting June 11, 1995; accessed Dec. 23, 2000, at ysi wyg://96/http://www.mmcw.homestead.com/MMCWManual.htm; and MMC Manual 1-1; accessed at http://militia.gen.mi.us/faq3.html.

17. www.michiganmilitia.com/SMVM (accessed Dec. 6, 2005).

18. Author's interview with Rick Haynes at his home in Holt, March 21, 2000.

19. Author's interview with Rick Haynes at his home in Holt, March 21,2000.

20. Memo from Mark Price, Acting Commander, to 1st and 2nd Brigade, 9/30/94, re: the assembly scheduled for Oct. 8 in Wolverine; Haynes Papers.

21. "Militia News," July 1999, from the 8th Division, Michigan Militia Corps Wolverines; Haynes Papers.

22. Memo from Mark Price, Acting Commander, to 1st Brigade and 2nd Brigade, dated 9/30/94; Haynes Papers.

23. *Sunday Times* (London): Foreign News, www.sunday-times.co.u . . . ages/sti/99/08/15 (accessed Dec. 23, 2000); the Green Beret was D. J. Breton.

24. Miscellaneous handwritten order form; Haynes Papers.

25. Memo to State Representative Jim McBryde from Rick Haynes, 5/2/96; Haynes Papers.

26. News Release from NCCM Harbor Springs Headquarters, June 5, 1995; Haynes Papers.

27. Michigan Militia Corps Wolverines, 4th Brigade, 8th Division, Weekly News, March 8, 1999; Haynes Papers.

28. Flyer and birth announcement below are from the Haynes Papers; author has taken the liberty to change the children's identifying information.

29. Comments made at various gatherings and meetings attended by the author.

30. Author's interview with Rick Haynes, Clint Dare, and an anonymous source at Haynes's home in Holt, Michigan, March 21, 2000.

31. Faxed copy dated 03/01/98; also see clipping from the *Daily Telegram*, Adrian, Michigan, n.d. but probably 3/02/1998; Haynes Papers.

32. Notes from meeting author attended on Jan. 30, 2001, at Freedom School, Pastor Dan Hardin, Gateway Anabaptist Church, Monroe.

33. Letter to Rick Haynes from Gibbs, Oct. 8, 1997; Haynes Papers.

34. Haynes Papers, n.d.

35. Memo: To All Brigades, From Thomas R. Wayne, Col. State Command XO, dated Nov. 9, 1995; Haynes Papers.

36. News Release, from Norm Olson, dated 7/19/95; Haynes Papers.

37. "In Defense of Liberty II." This position continues to appear on the Michigan Militia.com website at http://www.michiganmilitia.com/literature/in_defense_of_lib erty.htm (accessed June 7, 2008).

38. Miscellaneous correspondence; Haynes Papers.

39. Flyer with handwritten note indicating that this was handed out by Gen. Norm Olson at UN Flag Raising protest, Oct. 94; also news release from Michigan Militia State Headquarters, dated Oct. 19, 1995, fax dated Oct. 20, 1995; Haynes Papers.

40. Author's interview with Rick Haynes, Clint Dare, and an anonymous source at Haynes's home in Holt, Michigan, March 21, 2000.

41. The figure of 200,000 NRA members was again reported in the *Detroit Free Press*, Nov. 15, 2007. The *Los Angeles Times*, Oct. 22, 2000, reported that one million people in Michigan hold hunting licenses.

42. *Detroit News*, May 20, 1999.

43. www.michiganmilitia.com/MillionCowMarch.htm (accessed Sept. 20, 2000).

44. Barkun, *Religion and the Racist Right,* 264; Hamm, *Apocalypse in Oklahoma,* 1–6.

45. *Detroit News*, Feb. 22, 1996.

46. *Detroit News*, Feb. 22, 1996.

47. "Militia News," July 1999, 8th Division, Militia Militia Wolverine Corps; Haynes Papers.

48. *Detroit Free Press*, April 15, 1996.

49. News release from Norm Olson, 7/19/95; fax dated July 19, 1995; Haynes Papers.

50. Committee to Elect Pilchak flyer; Pilchak Papers.

51. Pilchak Papers.

52. http://uselectionatlas.org/RESULTS/ (accessed Feb. 8, 2008).

53. *Guardian* (London), November 14, 1995, http://web.lexis-nexis.com/uni verse/docu (accessed Sept. 24, 2000); *New York Times*, Nov. 12, 1995, http://web.lexis-nexis.com/universe/docu (accessed Sept. 24, 2000).

54. *New York Times*, Nov. 12, 1995, http://web.lexis-nexis.com/universe/docu (accessed Sept. 24, 2000); *Guardian* (London), Nov. 14, 1995, http://web.lexis-nexis.com/universe/docu (accessed Sept. 24, 2000).

55. Faxed copy dated 03/02/98; 7:06, from *The Daily Telegram*, Adrian, Michigan, n.d. but probably 3/02/1998, Haynes Papers; *Detroit News*, April 2, 1998.

56. *Detroit News*, Aug. 10, 1998.

57. *London Daily Telegraph,* Oct. 8, 1997, http://web.lexis-nexis.com (accessed Sept. 24, 2000).

58. Author's interview with Tom Wayne at his home in Bronson, Michigan, Jan. 21, 1999.

59. Team Leader Guide, on http://www.michiganmilitia.com (accessed Sept. 20, 2000).

60. Oath is among miscellaneous materials, Haynes Papers.

61. Memo to Rick Haines [*sic*] from Steve Bridges, fax dated Jan. 10, 1999, 15:30 A.M.; Haynes Papers.

62. Schertzing, "Against All Enemies," 400–401.

63. Schertzing, "Against All Enemies," 401.

64. Memo detailing possible siege on Kelly Russell, by the FBI, IRS, April 21, 1999; Haynes Papers.

65. Transcript of Jim Lehrer's program, "Hanging Tough," aired April 3, 1997; www.pbs.org/newshour/bb/law/april97/militia (accessed Dec. 29, 2000).

66. *Detroit Free Press,* March 29, 1997; *Detroit Free Press,* Aug. 27, 1999.

67. Meeting Call for the North American Patriots at Speeds, dated 11/1/97; Haynes Papers.

68. *Daily Telegram,* Adrian, Michigan, March 19, 1998; *Detroit Free Press,* March 20, 1998.

69. *Detroit Free Press,* March 25, 1998.

70. Author's interview with Tom Wayne at his home in Bronson, Michigan, on Jan. 21, 1999.

71. *Detroit Free Press,* March 20, 1998; March 25, 1998.

72. *Detroit Free Press,* March 19, 1998; March 20, 1998; November 17, 1998; July 6, 2000. The three men were Brad Metcalf, Ken Carter, and Randy Graham. Graham was sentenced to 55 years and Metcalf to 40 years, and Carter who cooperated with the government got 5 years in prison.

73. Memo from Lynn Van Huizen to Rick Haynes, 3/20/96; Haynes Papers.

74. *Grand Rapids Press,* May 13, 2001; http://infoweb.newsbank.com.ezproxy .emich.edu/iw-search/we/InfoWeb (accessed Feb. 28, 2009).

75. Associated Press wire report filed Aug. 25, 2000; *Detroit News,* June 27, 2000.

76. The government put together a case against two of Gleason's compatriots who had shared his ideology and joined in armed night maneuvers, and it sentenced them to brief prison terms. Associated Press wire report, Aug. 24, 2000.

77. *Detroit Free Press,* Feb. 19, 1997.

78. *Ann Arbor News,* March 30, 2001.

79. Ted Roelofs, "Militias Fade, but Not Away," *Grand Rapids Press,* May 13, 2001; http://infoweb.newsbank.com.ezproxy.emich.edu/iw-search (accessed Feb. 20, 2008).

80. Ibid., *Grand Rapids Press,* May 13, 2001.

81. Michigan Militia Corps. Wolverines 4th Brigade, 8th Division Weekly News, March 8, 1999; Haynes Papers.

82. Ted Roelofs, "Militias Fade, but Not Away," *Grand Rapids Press,* May 13, 2001; http://infoweb.newsbank.com.ezproxy.emich.edu/iw-search (accessed Feb. 20, 2008).

83. Gore Vidal, "The Meaning of Timothy McVeigh," *Vanity Fair,* September 2001; http://www.geocities.com/gorevidal3000/tim.htm (accessed Feb. 29, 2008); Gore Vidal, *Perpetual War for Perpetual Peace: How We Got To Be So Hated* (New York: Thunder's Mouth Press, 2002).

84. http://www.rickross.com/reference/militia/militia74.html (accessed Feb. 7, 2008).

85. Alex Jones radio show broadcast, Nov. 8, 2002, partial transcript at http://www.infowars.com/transcripts/1108RANT.htm (accessed Feb. 7, 2008).

86. *Detroit Free Press,* Jan. 22, 2004; http://www.udel.edu/PR/UDaily/2004/mar/may051805.html (accessed Jan. 25, 2007); the murder was investigated for a book by Mary Stanton, *From Selma to Sorrow: The Life and Death of Viola Liuzzo* (Athens: University of Georgia Press 1998), and this book is the basis of the documentary film *Home of the Brave;* a more recent study is by Gary May, *The Informant: The FBI, the Ku Klux Klan, and the Murder of Viola Liuzzo* (New Haven: Yale University Press, 2008).

87. Dan Laidman, "A Kinder, Gentler Militia?" in *Salon,* Sept. 13, 2002; also at http:// www.rickross.com/reference/militia/militia74.html (accessed Feb. 7, 2008).

88. Laidman, "A Kinder, Gentler Militia?" *Salon,* Sept. 13, 2002.

89. *Grand Rapids Press,* May 13, 2001.

90. Southern Poverty Law Center *Intelligence Report* 117, Spring 2005.

91. Jeffrey Gagnon citing Daniel Levitas, author of "The Terrorist Next Door," in his article "The Enemy Among Us," *Legal Affairs,* Nov./Dec. 2005, http://www.legalaffairs.org/issues/November-December-2005/feature_gagnon_novdec05.msp. (accessed March 1, 2008). The same article discusses concerns of an FBI member. An undercover agent for the FBI who believed the threat from militias was growing charged that he was frozen out by the Bureau after a 16-year career because he pressed the issue of domestic terror. He maintained that the FBI had gone soft on homegrown extremists, that investigations and warnings get bogged down in paperwork.

92. Jeffrey Gagnon, "The Enemy Among Us," *Legal Affairs,* Nov.–Dec. 2005, http://www.legalaffairs.org/issues/November-December-2005/feature_gagnon_novdec05.msp. (accessed March 1, 2008).

93. For example, see http://youtube.com/user/militia48186 (accessed Jan. 10, 2008).

94. See http://profile.MySpace.com/index.cfm?fuseaction+user.viewprofile&friendID+302411949, (accessed Jan. 10, 2008).

95. *Detroit Free Press,* Feb. 28, 2008.

96. *Washington Post,* June 27, 2008.

97. *Detroit Free Press,* Nov. 15, 2007.

Epilogue

1. ABC World News, March 29, 2010, http://abcnews.go.com/WN/TheLaw/michigan-christian-militia-hutaree-targeted-law-enforcement/story?id=10228716 (accessed Aug. 1, 2010); *Christian Science Monitor,* March 30, 2010, http://www.csmonitor.com/USA/Justice/2010/0330 (accessed Aug. 1, 2010).

2. *Christian Science Monitor,* March 30, 2010, http://www.csmonitor.com/USA/Justice/2010/0330 (accessed Aug. 1, 2010).

3. *Detroit News,* July 9, 2010, http://detnews.com/article/20100709/METRO/7090436/Hillsdale-man-charged-in-Obama-threat-claimed-Hutaree-link—FBI-filing-says (accessed Aug. 3, 2010).

4. Unemployment in Michigan was 3.4 percent in January 2000 and reached 11.3 percent by the time George Bush left office.

5. http://www-personal.umich.edu/~mejn/election/2008/ (accessed Aug. 25, 2010). Obama received 2,872,579 votes out of a total of 5,001,766.

6. http://www.surgeusa.org/actions/taxday.htm#MI (accessed Aug. 20, 2010).

7. http://blogshevik.com/2009/04/16/lansing-michigan-tea-party-april-15-2009-photos-of-violent-right-wing-extremists/ (accessed Aug. 20, 2010).

8. http://www.teapartypatriots.org/state/Michigan (accessed Aug. 20, 2010).

9. So said the nine members in the Traverse City Tea Party Patriots!!!

10. http://www.teapartyofwmi.org/ (accessed Aug. 4, 2010); and http://www.teapartypatriots.org/state/Michigan (accessed Aug. 5, 2010); *Detroit Free Press,* Aug. 26, 2010; *Detroit Free Press,* Sept. 9, 2010.

11. http://www.americansforprosperity.org/michigan/about (accessed Sept. 1, 2010).

12. http://www.teapartyofwmi.org/ (accessed Aug. 20, 2010).

13. Michigan unemployment, from U.S. Bureau of Labor Statistics: http://www.bls.gov/eag/eag.mi.htm (accessed Sept. 6, 2010).

14. http://detnews.com/article/20090416/BIZ01/904160369/t, *Detroit News,* April 16, 2009 (accessed Aug. 10, 2010). One out of every 136 housing units received a foreclosure filing notice in the first three months of 2009.

15. http://www.washingtonpost.com/wp-dyn/content/article/2009/11/18/AR2009111803918.html (accessed Aug. 5, 2010). No one in the press covering the Palin appearance recalled that a huge crowd gathered all along Woodward Avenue when Herbert Hoover visited Detroit in the fall of 1932. Out of work, many had nothing better to do that day.

Index

Page numbers in italics refer to illustrations.

Madison Square Garden, 147
Maine, 162
Markwell, Lulu, 62
Marquette County, MI, 86
Marshall, George, 180
Marshall, Thurgood, 206
Marshall Plan, 175, 180, 187, 193
Martin, Joseph A., 84, 85
Marx, Karl, 28, 236, 277, 329n22
Masada, 255
Mason, Stevens, T., 7, 8
Masonic Temple, 205
Masons, 58, 65, 84, 262, 277
Massachusetts, 147, 154, 157, 166, 196, 197, 202, 302, 312; House of Representatives, 147. *See also* Belmont, MA; Salem, MA
May Day, *107*
McBryde, Jim, 289
McCabe, Irene, 228
McCain, John, 306
McCarthy, Joseph, 189, 190, 191, 193, 195, 196, 197, 200, 248
McClorey, John A., 118, 130
McClosky, Herbert, 330n20
McFadden, Louis T., 116
McGhee, Orsel, 206
McGovern, George, 238
McKinley, Noble, 69
McNamara, Robert, 207
McVeigh, Timothy, 266, 267, 268, 269, 272, 278, 298, 299, 305
Mecosta County, MI, 315n30, 315n31, 316n39, 316n51; economy, 92; Klan, 50–57, 59, 60, 61, 62, 90–95, 315n29, 316n40, 316n52; Klan dues, 91, 92; Klan No. 28, 50. *See also* Remus, MI
Medina, ND, 255
Melvindale, MI, 120
Methodist, 39, 55, 73, 74, 76, 94, 269; Lansing, 75; Monroe County, 38; politician, 131; school, 75. *See also* Plymouth Methodist Church; United Methodist Church
Methodist Episcopal Church: Conference of Methodist Episcopal Churches, 76; Newaygo, 55

Methodist Protestant Church (Lansing, MI), 74
Mexicans, 23, 35, 36, 161; Detroit, 120; migrants, 176; Traverse City migrant, 76
Mexico, 27, 36, 120, 148, 244, 245, 246, 274
Michigan: Board of Education, 290; Branch of the National League of Postmasters, 95; Civil Rights Commission, 230; Coalition for Responsible Gun Owners, 303; Department of Agriculture, 108; Employment Security Agency, 246; Farmer-Labor Party, 159; Fourteenth District, 200, 208, 212, 213, 215, 218, 219, 223, 243; House of Representatives, 220; Independent American Party, 204, 216; Klan dues, 49, 54; Seventeenth District, 169; State Fair Grounds, *45;* Supreme Court, 222, 237. *See also* Jensen Law; *and specific city or area*
Michigan, Lake, 7, 8, 27, 32, 51, 54, 60, 61, 235
Michigan Catholic, 80, 126, 130, 131, 134, 139, 319, 321, 323, 324, 325, 326
Michigan Farm Bureau, 211
Michigan Militia, 1, 2, 5, 250, 251, 253–75, 285, 286, 287, 291–92, 295–302, 305, 309, 335n16; criticisms, 288; dues, 285; FBI, 267, 293, 294; intent, 338n11; and Oklahoma City bombing, 294
Michigan-Militia-At-Large, 261
Michigan Militia–Wolverines, 280, 336n31
Michigan State Police, 68, 169, 327n83; Fifth Column squad, 169
Michigan State University, 108, 268
Michigan Territory, 7
Middle East, 274, 299, 300
Miles, Robert, 3, 230, 278
Militia, 3, 4, 254, 257; activists, 292; Manuals, 265. *See also under specific geographic location*
Millbrook, MI, 56, 94
Million Mom March, 288
Minnesota, 133, 153
Missouri, 179. *See also* Branson, MO
Missouri Synod Lutheran Church, 39, 53
Model T, 2, 34, 307